THE WORD CARRYING GIANT

The Growth of the American Bible Society (1816-1966)

Creighton Lacy

William Carey Library

533 HERMOSA STREET • SOUTH PASADENA, CALIF. 91030

Library of Congress Cataloging in Publication Data

Lacy, Creighton.
 The word-carrying giant.

 Includes index.
 1. American Bible Society. I. Title.
BV2370.A7L33   266'.009   77-22655
ISBN 0-87808-425-8

       7902096

220.06

L119

In accord with some of the most recent thinking in the academic press, the William Carey Library is pleased to present
this scholarly book which has been prepared from an author-
edited camera-ready manuscript.

Published by William Carey Library
533 Hermosa Street
South Pasadena, California 91030
Telephone (213) 798-0819

PRINTED IN THE UNITED STATES
OF AMERICA

Contents

Foreword

In the Christian enterprise of seeking to make known to all the
world Jesus Christ as Savior and Lord the Bible Societies have a
distinctive part--distinctive because they confine their mission
to the effective translation, publication, and distribution of
the Bible and its parts. Their motto is: "Scriptures for everyone in his or her language at a price within reach or less."
Such Societies began at the start of the nineteenth century and
have multiplied into many lands.

Dr. Creighton Lacy, out of voluminous sources, has set down
compactly the history of the first hundred and fifty years of
the American Bible Society and of its work in the United States
and abroad. His interest is reinforced by the fact that his
father, the late Bishop Carleton Lacy, directed the work of this
Society in China for several years.

The complexity of the work, the vicissitudes of the times,
the persistence of the cause, and the devotion of its servants
will be illuminating to many a reader.

Eric M. North
General Secretary Emeritus
American Bible Society

1

The Founding Fathers

The morning of Wednesday, May 8th [1816], was, according
to available reports, a fine mid-spring morning.....James
Madison was President [soon to be followed by James Monroe],
The Capitol was being rebuilt after it had been burned by
a British force two years earlier. There were fifteen
states along the Atlantic seaboard with a population of
about 7,000,000, and west of them four states, four territories, and a great undeveloped area with about 1,500,000
population. In New York the streets were still dirt roads,
some with brick foot-crossings. Horse-drawn carriages,
stage-coaches and drays clogged the traffic; sailing ships
crowded the wharves. Gentlemen generally wore knee
breeches and waistcoats. Most of the 100,000 inhabitants
lived south of Bleecker Street.(1)

The fifty-six delegates who made their way toward the South
Reformed Dutch Church on Garden Street (now Exchange Place) had
converged on New York from many directions by many forms of conveyance. Some may have travelled by steamboat from Albany or New
Haven, others probably on horseback, most by stagecoach or private
carriage. Even from Philadelphia the journey took a long day or
a day and a half, with anywhere from thirty minutes to three hours
by ferry from Elizabethtown (Elizabeth and Jersey City), since
there were no bridges across the Hudson to lower Manhattan. Only
one delegate came from west of the Appalachians (Kentucky), but
one Bible Society in North Carolina, five in Virginia, eight in
upstate New York, and five in New England were represented. With
no public transportation in the city except for "hackney coaches"
most visitors found lodging within walking distance of the Garden

Street Church. Even so, road hazards in the New York of that day
included roving pigs as well as mud and garbage.

According to a letter written that evening to Elias Boudinot,
ailing President of the New Jersey Bible Society, it was a
"respectable" company. Respectable indeed, and extremely diverse,
bound together by a common Christian concern. Valentine Mott was
a young surgeon noted for ambidextrous speed and skill in days
before anesthesia; Eliphalet Nott as president of Union College
raised money for the school through a state-approved lottery, and
later preached a widely-renowned sermon on duelling. James
Fenimore Cooper, at twenty-seven, had not yet published any of
his famous novels of Indian life. Lyman Beecher (1775-1865),
already a popular preacher and later to become president of Lane
Theological Seminary, had left a large family in Litchfield,
Connecticut, including Harriet and Henry Ward, aged five and three

Gardiner Spring, future president of Princeton Theological
Seminary and longest survivor among the founders, represented the
New York Bible Society; his father, Samuel Spring, from the
Merrimack Bible Society in Massachusetts, was among the oldest
delegates, once described by John Quincy Adams in these words:
"His sentiments are extremely contracted and illiberal, and he
maintains them with the zeal and enthusiasm of a bigot, but his
delivery is very agreeable and I believe his devotion sincere."(2)
General Joseph G. Swift, one of the first two graduates of West
Point Academy, had already at the age of thirty-three become
chief engineer of the U.S. Army, and had been rewarded (for
setting up the defenses of New York in the War of 1812) by a
silver service, silver drawing instruments, and a portrait in
City Hall. Of General John Lincklaen, a former officer in the
Dutch Navy, born in Amsterdam but educated in Switzerland, Dr.
Nott once remarked that he knew of no foreigner who used "our
language" so correctly. Others were equally distinguished,
equally versatile.

Vocationally, the delegates included seven lawyers, four
editors, several judges, one inventor, one surgeon, eleven
bankers or businessmen (including one brewer), and numerous
ministers. Denominationally, their affiliations--though not
officially representative--were as follows: twenty-six Presbyterians, eight Congregationalists, five Dutch Reformed, five
Associate Reformed, five Episcopalians, four Quakers, two
Baptists, and one Methodist. What they did represent officially
--with the exception of the four from the Society of Friends--
were thirty-five state, county, local, or auxiliary Bible
Societies. Participants ranged in age from twenty-three to
seventy-two; ten were under thirty years of age and only three
over seventy. With diverse backgrounds of travel and experience,

eleven were graduates of Yale, eight each from Princeton and
Columbia, but no more than one or two from any other one college.

* * * * *

Although many individuals had contributed substantial effort
and earnest prayer to preparations for the actual organization
of a "general society," five men played a conspicuous and probably
decisive role: Jedidiah Morse, Samuel J. Mills, Elias Boudinot,
John E. Caldwell, and William Jay.

As editor of *The Panoplist*, a journal which he founded in 1805
to uphold evangelical Christianity against encroaching Unitarian-
ism, Morse (1761-1826) provided the first, fullest, and most
enthusiastic reports of the newly organized British and Foreign
Bible Society. His own academic career embraced both theology
and geography, his textbook in the latter field becoming a
classic through twenty-five editions. His pastoral career
stretched from Massachusetts to Georgia, but centered for thirty
years in the First Congregational Church of Charlestown (Massachusetts). He was active in the American Board of Commissioners
for Foreign Missions, in the New England Tract Society, in the
Society for Propagating the Gospel among the Indians and Others
in North America, and in the first (1811) colonization scheme
for the Christianization of Africa by freed Negro slaves. His
son, Samuel F. B. Morse, is generally credited with the invention
of the telegraph.

On his numerous travels Jedidiah Morse helped to establish
Bible societies as far apart as Massachusetts; Savannah, Georgia;
and Beaufort and Charleston in South Carolina. As early as 1809,
on a journey to the South for his health, he proposed to Robert
Ralston, Treasurer of the Philadelphia Bible Society, not only
the desirability of a national organization for the distribution
of Scriptures, but the outline of a plan which he thought appropriate: "that of conducting the business in a similar manner to
the National Bank and its branches." The Philadelphia group,
already urged in the same direction by the British and Foreign
Bible Society, consistently dismissed such a proposal as inex-
pedient--but did consider Morse's plan "a very good one."(3) In
addition to reports and correspondence from London, plus eloquent
descriptions and appeals from William Carey's pioneer mission in
India, *The Panoplist* published in extensive detail accounts of
Samuel J. Mills' travels to the South and West, as well as that
young missionary's urgent appeal for a national Bible society.

During his student days at Williams College, Mills (1783-1818)
had helped to organize a secret society of "Brethren" "to effect
in the persons of its members a mission or missions to the
heathen." Later at Andover Seminary, which Jedidiah Morse had

founded, Mills and some fellow students encouraged the formation
in 1810 of the American Board of Commissioners for Foreign
Missions, the first agency of its kind established in the United
States. While Adoniram Judson and others of the group volunteered
for service abroad, Mills took the assignment of education and
recruitment for mission. In 1812 he set out to survey the
religious situation and needs west of the Appalachians and along
the Mississippi Valley. On the first page of his Journal Mills
listed nine subjects of inquiry to keep steadily in view. The
first four were as follows: "Are the people supplied with Bibles
and Tracts? How many Bibles are wanted in a county or a town?
Have supplies of Bibles and Tracts been received in part? From
what Societies may supplies be expected?"(4)

Shocked by moral laxity and the scarcity of Scriptures on the
frontier, Mills wondered whether Bible societies might accomplish
the spiritual transformation of the West more effectively and
rapidly than churches. "South of New Connecticut," he noted,
"few Bibles or religious tracts have been received for distribution among the inhabitants." In Louisiana, where three-quarters
of the white population was assumed to be Roman Catholic, the
newly-arrived bishop offered not only permission and encouragement for the circulation of Scriptures, but a financial contribution for that cause. Letters, appeals, and a report from Mills
to the Philadelphia Bible Society produced a few hundred books--
but only six copies of the Bible in French, whereas Mills hoped
for four or five thousand "as a partial supply for the 40 or
50,000 French Catholics who are destitute," not to mention
Spanish Scriptures for residents of "New Spain."

Apparently realizing that the men in Philadelphia were not
disposed towards a "general society," Mills made a more direct
proposal in a letter which Morse published in *The Panoplist*
(October, 1813):

The American Churches are, at the present time, called
upon to favor the destitute, in a certain section of our
country, with the Bible. Although these people are called
Christians, they have not the Bible in their possession;
and of course are not acquainted with its contents.....

To the writer it appears a perfectly plain case, that as
a Christian nation we are not likely to labor at all
according to our ability, (I would charitably hope we
shall not want a disposition,) for the relief of the
needy in our country and abroad, until we have some general bond of union; and can, upon an emergency, as
circumstances may direct, bring some portion of the
resources of our several Bible Societies to one point.....

I would propose the formation of a *General Bible Society*,
open for the admission of all persons, of whatever
religious denomination, in the United States, who are
disposed to take an active part in this good work.....

Specifically, Mills suggested a meeting in Philadelphia in May
"at or near the time of the sitting of the General Assembly of
the Presbyterian Church." Although the new organization "should
not interfere with any Bible Societies already established," it
was hoped that such local and state groups might subsequently
contribute donations and annual delegates. But the formation
should be undertaken, according to Mills' plan, by representatives from the several religious denominations, rather than by
existing Bible Societies. In conclusion, the young writer
listed four advantages in such a united effort: more widespread
information about "destitute portions of our own country," more
effective solicitation for funds, more economical purchase and
distribution of Scriptures, more readily available resources for
supplying Bibles in other languages, at home or abroad.

Again in 1814-1815 Samuel J. Mills journeyed to the Mississippi
to distribute Bibles--and to send back urgent pleas for more books
and more missionaries. In the last years of his brief life Mills
devoted his energies to improving conditions for Negroes (through
a school in New Jersey to train black teachers and preachers)
and in stimulating evangelistic work in Hawaii and Latin America.
His final mission was a voyage to Africa, where he helped to
select Liberia as a resettlement colony for freed slaves. Mills
died on the return journey.

The most dedicated and persistent advocate of a general Bible
society was Elias Boudinot (1740-1821), chairman of the Board of
Managers of the New Jersey Bible Society. He was also one of
the most respected elder statesmen, a leader during the Revolution and the subsequent embryonic government. A devout and
devoted Presbyterian who had hoped to study for the ministry,
Boudinot had been baptized by the famous preacher, George
Whitefield. Becoming a lawyer instead, Boudinot was appointed
by George Washington as Commissary-General of Prisoners of War
in 1777. As a delegate to the Continental Congress, he served
occasionally as its chairman and as Secretary for Foreign
Affairs. One of his presidential acts was a proclamation
recommending the second Thursday in December, 1783, as a day of
public thanksgiving. In the House of Representatives from 1789
to 1795, he chaired the committee to welcome General Washington
to New York for his inauguration. For ten years before his
retirement from government service, Boudinot had been Director
of the Mint.

Presiding over one of the earliest and most active Bible societies, Boudinot had demonstrated his commitment to the cause of disseminating Scriptures. He was convinced that "the greatest union of christians, of every profession, in so desirable a cause, promises most success to the undertaking." Although not a member of the Presbyterian General Assembly when, in May of 1814, it indefinitely postponed Samual Mills' plea for a general Bible society, Boudinot may well have agreed that such a significant enterprise should be a cooperative effort rather than a denominational project.

A resolution adopted by the New Jersey Bible Society on August 30, 1814, presumably came from the pen of the distinguished president, Elias Boudinot. It called on the several Bible societies, by an annual or biennial meeting of delegates, "to conduct the common interests of the whole, where they respect the distribution of the sacred scriptures beyond the limits of particular states, or where a society in a state cannot furnish so many copies as are wanted." This proposal was circulated to Bible societies in each state, with the request that they designate at least two representatives to attend a meeting in May, 1815, at Philadelphia, "with full powers to digest and form a plan for a well organized and constituted body or society, to be called the 'General Association of the Bible Societies in the United States'...."

Boudinot's first "Call" to consider such an association fell on deaf ears. The "Objections" from the Philadelphia Bible Society and caustic criticisms from other quarters will be discussed in the next chapter. Even some of those who later participated enthusiastically in the new society were initially dubious. One of these was John E. Caldwell (1767-1819), Corresponding Secretary of the New York Bible Society, ultimately to serve as the first General Agent of the American Bible Society. Orphaned during the Revolution, Caldwell and his eight brothers and sisters had been raised under the care of Boudinot. The boy had been sent to France with the Marquis de Lafayette for six years of study. There he became a Roman Catholic, but on his return to America Caldwell joined the Presbyterian Church and devoted himself as a layman to many religious causes in New York.

As an officer of the New York Bible Society, Caldwell reacted negatively to his benefactor's 1814 appeal. A year later, however, moved by accounts from Samuel J. Mills and others of "the deplorable wants of these famishing fellow men!" he wrote: "I am apprehensive, however, that some of our very respectable members will not give this institution their decided support, until actual experiment shall have demonstrated the fact of its utility. The sooner the experiment can be made with propriety, in my humble opinion, the better." Thus, when Elias Boudinot issued a

second "Circular" on January 17, 1816, "To the Several Bible
Societies in the Unites States of America," John Caldwell pub-
lished it in the first number of his new magazine, *The Christian
Herald* (Vol. I, No. 1, March 31, 1816)—a month after Jedidiah
Morse had included it in *The Panoplist* (Vol. XII, February, 1816).

The most eloquent and comprehensive response to Boudinot came
from a lawyer barely one-third his age. William Jay (1789-1858),
younger son of John Jay, the first Chief Justice of the United
States, had studied law but was prevented by poor eyesight from
undertaking an active legal career. Among many civic and religious
interests, he served as Recording Secretary of the Westchester
(New York) Auxiliary Bible Society, of which his illustrious father
was president. The 16-page "Memoir" which William Jay submitted
to Boudinot in late March, 1816, was so comprehensive and well-
reasoned (see next chapter) that the elder statesman had it printed
for immediate circulation before the scheduled meeting, and
Caldwell reprinted it in *The Christian Herald*, although Jay
insisted on anonymity.

On May 8, 1816, Elias Boudinot lay abed in Burlington, New
Jersey, too weak from gout to make the journey to New York.
Samuel J. Mills, with characteristic modesty, sat in the balcony
as a guest to observe the proceedings which he had done so much
to stimulate. Gardiner Spring in his subsequent *Memoirs* of Mills
recalled how the young man's face lighted up with joy when the
decisive votes were taken. John Caldwell, busy as host in his
position as Secretary of the New York Bible Society, officially
represented the Female Bible Societies of Burlington (New Jersey)
and Kingston (New York) at their request.

Jedidiah Morse and William Jay, though not formally commissioned as delegates, were recognized on the opening morning, "from
satisfactory evidence to be substantial representatives of their
respective societies, or of a number of members thereof, for all
the purposes contemplated by this Convention." Actually the
Westchester Bible Society had called no special meeting to
authorize delegates for this founding session, but President
John Jay and three other officers designated his son William "to
attend the said Convention and to engage in the business thereof,
as far as the Convention shall think proper to admit him."

*   *   *   *   *

The gathering convened at 11 a.m. in the Consistory Room of
the Dutch Reformed Church and devoted its morning session to a
determination of "who are properly delegates." Joshua M. Wallace,
Elias Boudinot's alternate from the New Jersey Bible Society, was
elected president of the Convention, with Lyman Beecher from
Connecticut and J. B. Romeyn of New York as secretaries. An

effort to admit "every one who was even a *member* of a bible
Society and friendly to a general Bible institution" was defeated,
thus "preserving our character as a representative body," as
Samuel Bayard, prominent lawyer and delegate from the New Jersey
Bible Society, wrote to Boudinot the next day.

The company met that afternoon in "one [of] the most commodious
rooms in the City Hall." After the reading of "letters and communications" (presumably of encouragement and good wishes) there
were "some animated addresses" (though neither Bayard nor the
official minutes give any clue as to the speakers)--"for there
was no difference of sentiment here." Then the convention
"Resolved unanimously that it is expedient to establish, without
delay a general Bible Institution, for the circulation of the
Holy Scriptures without note or comment." The unanimous agreement was significant but not surprising, not only because of the
contagious enthusiasm generated among the delegates themselves,
but also because those groups which had been persuaded by the
Philadelphia Bible Society that such an undertaking was "unseason-
able" had not gone to the expense of sending representatives.
What was more heart-warming to active supporters, from old Elias
Boudinot to young William Jay, was the decision "without delay."
John Caldwell had written to Boudinot as late as April 25:

> I am persuaded that a majority of the Delegates will be in
> favor of the establishment of a General Society; and I am
> inclined to believe that this city will be generally pre-
> ferred for its location. It is doubtful, however, whether
> there will be a majority for organizing a Society at this
> meeting, or even determining on the details of a plan for
> such an institution.....

Contrary to that prediction, the convention elected a committee
at once to draft a constitution and an address to the public,
having previously voted to invite "*counsel & advice*" from "*all*
persons friendly to such an institution." Bayard in his report
to Boudinot referred to a committee of thirteen, but the official
minutes (apparently compiled some time after the event) list only
the following: Eliphalet Nott, John M. Mason, Samuel Bayard,
Simon Wilmer, Jr., Lyman Beecher, Charles Wright, John H. Rice,
David S. Jones, Jedidiah Morse, William Jay, and James Blythe.
The other delegates then adjourned until Friday morning, May 10,
to allow the constitutional committee time for its labors.

That group drew largely on the Constitution of the British
and Foreign Bible Society, so universal was the admiration for
that "clear, precise & comprehensive" document, which had been
"tested by experience" and effectiveness. "Yet to avoid *servile*
imitation," Bayard explained, "we have in several particulars so
far departed from the terms of that instrument as to give *our*

constitution an air of peculiarity suited to our national views
& circumstances." In his influential "Memoir" William Jay had
included a proposed Constitution, and Elias Boudinot had previously "prepared a very rough draught of one which greatly
coincides...in all the leading points..."

The issue on which the two men differed most sharply was that
of clerical influence. Although Jay had specified that "Every
clergyman who is a member of the society shall be entitled to
attend and vote at all meetings of the committee," he had
initially proposed that ministers should be excluded from the
Board of Managers.

> The greatest number of the members of the committee ought
> to be *Laymen*; because laymen are generally more conversant
> with the details of business, and better qualified to super-
> intend the concerns of an extensive establishment--to con-
> clude contracts--to make shipments, &c. than clergymen.
> Laymen are also possessed of greater leisure, and of more
> extensive influence than clergymen, while their religious
> tenets are less generally known: by the appointment of a
> sufficient number of laymen therefore, the society would
> acquire greater weight of influence, and would be less
> exposed to the effects of sectarian jealousy, than by the
> appointment of clergymen to perform the secular business.

Without contesting any of the young lawyer's assumptions, Boudinot
did warn against any provisions which would give foes of a
national society "a great weapon of opposition." "Especially
would I leave out," he wrote, "the Clause excluding the Clergy--
they would raise the Body as a formidable phalanx agt us. We
had better conciliate as much as possible." "Leave out the
clause" Boudinot did when he printed Jay's "Memoir" for circulation, only to have the Founding Fathers adopt just such an
article restricting the Board of Managers to laymen. In actual
practice through the years, laymen have comprised the Board membership, but staff officers of the Society have been largely
ordained clergymen.

The committee met from 9 until 2 on Thursday, May 9, to agree
on general guidelines, and then appointed two sub-committees:
Nott, Blythe, and Jay "to arrange the details, & language;" Mason,
Beecher, and Bayard to compose the Address. The first group "had
set up till 3 oclock in the morning on the Constitution," according to Elisha Boudinot's report to his brother; the second presented its document to the full committee between 6 and 8 Friday
morning.

When the delegates reconvened a few minutes after 11 on May 10,
1816, at City Hall, "a very large concourse of citizens had

assembled to hear the report." At this point not only were the
four Quaker representatives officially seated without objection,
but "a deputation was sent to request the Roman Catholics to join
us, which was done."

Article I of the Constitution, which was adopted unanimously,
contained the two central pillars of policy incorporated from the
parent organization in London:

> This Society shall be known by the name of the AMERICAN
> BIBLE SOCIETY, of which the sole object shall be, to
> encourage a wider circulation of the Holy Scripture
> without note or comment. The only copies in the English
> language to be circulated by the Society, shall be of
> the version now in common use.

William Jay's original document used the name of "The American
and Foreign Bible Society." Whether or not this appeared to be
"servile imitation," convention delegates considered the foreign
designation unnecessary, although the very next article testified
to their worldwide concern. The phrases "without note or comment"
and "the version now in common use" were to be challenged and
interpreted in various ways over succeeding years, but the intention of the founders has always been strictly observed.

Article II pledged the Society to "add its endeavours to those
employed by other societies," not to usurp their functions or to
compete with them. It went further to offer to "furnish them
with stereotype plates, or such other assistance as circumstances
may require." It resolved also that the Society, "according to
its ability, [would] extend its influence to other countries,
whether Christian, Mahometan, or Pagan."

Article III offered to *all* Bible societies the privilege of
purchasing Scriptures at cost for distribution within their own
districts, in return for which they would be expected to place
their "surplus revenue" at the disposal of the American Bible
Society. Members of these societies would be entitled to vote
in national meetings, and their officers would be *ex officio*
directors of the ABS. (In 1827 this section was revised to permit only officers, not members, of Auxiliaries to vote as members
--no longer directors--of the national society.)

The next five articles spelled out categories of membership
and subscription: three dollars for annual membership, thirty
dollars for life membership, fifteen dollars annually to become
a Director, one hundred and fifty dollars (in not more than two
installments) to become a Director for life (Directors being
entitled to attend and vote at all meetings of the Board of

Managers). (Annual subscription rates were changed in 1917 to
five dollars for members and fifty dollars for life members.)

Article IX specified that the Board of Managers, empowered "to
conduct the business of the Society," should consist of thirty-six
laymen (forty-eight since 1922), two thirds of whom should live in
or near New York, one fourth of whom should go out of office each
year but be eligible for re-election. To make sure that ministers
were not excluded, yet perhaps assured by Boudinot's earlier lette
to Jay that "very few [clergymen] can ever attend, and will not
willingly expose themselves to the Labour that may be required,"
the delegates included a provision that "Every Minister of the
Gospel, who is a member of the Society, shall be entitled to meet
and vote with the Board of Managers, and be possessed of the same
powers as a Manager himself." (As the Society--and the popula-
tion--grew, this invitation had to be rescinded in 1827, and the
ministerial vote restricted to those who were life members. In
1950 this privilege was further circumscribed by limiting it to
clergymen who held life membership *and* served on some committee
of the Board without remuneration.)

Article X enabled any member of the Society to purchase Bibles
and Testaments at the Society's prices, "which shall be as low as
possible." In a gesture of conciliation toward the Philadelphia
Bible Society, the oldest society in America and one which had
repeatedly opposed the formation of a national organization,
annual meetings of the ABS might be held in either New York or
Philadelphia. The Managers (to include the officers of the
Society *ex officio*, "for the time being") were to meet "on the
first Wednesday of each month, or oftener, if necessary." "No
alteration shall be made to this Constitution, except by the
Society at an annual meeting, on the recommendation of the Board
of Managers." The eighteen articles, extremely brief and simple,
reflected the single-minded purpose and the open-minded flexibility of these Founding Fathers.

When the vote was taken without dissent, Joshua Wallace
exclaimed from the chair, "Thank God! Thank God!" Elisha
Boudinot reported to his ailing brother that "all opposition is
done away and there appears nothing but good humour and harmony,
and all were regretting that you could not be there." Samuel
Bayard wrote to the New Jersey President in greater detail:

There is a fine spirit excited in this place on this
interesting subject. It will electrify every part of the
U States. It is the work of the Lord, & marvellous in
our eyes. Having seen this mighty tree which is to gather
millions of our sinful race beneath its healing shade
planted and taking root in so kindly & rich soil & fore-
seeing the immeasurable good it promises to produce in

future ages, you may now My Dr Sir say with good old Simeon,
'Now Lord lettest thou thy servant depart in peace for *mine
eyes* have *seen* thy *salvation*.'

It remained for the convention itself only to select the first
Board of Managers, "all of whom except 3 or 4," according to
Bayard, "are from the most respectable merchants & Gentlemen of
this place." Four of those initially selected declined to serve,
and five others were replaced before the annual meeting of 1817.
Because most of these men were mature, experienced businessmen,
the average age ran higher than that of convention delegates:
one third in their fifties, one fourth over sixty, only one sixth
under forth. As to occupation, at least seven were in shipping,
eleven in general business, two in the stock exchange, three
lawyers, two physicians, a printer, an engineer, an editor, an
architect, and an educator. Only five were themselves members of
the convention: Samuel Bayard, Thomas Eddy, John Murray, Jr.,
Joshua Sands, and Charles Wright. There was a smaller proportion
of college graduates than among the founders: three from Columbia
two from Edinburgh, one each from Yale, Princeton, Harvard, West
Point, and Aberdeen. Ironically--in view of vehement opposition
from Bishop John Henry Hobart of the Protestant Episcopal diocese
of New York--at least seven of the original Managers were Episcopalians, five Presbyterians, two Reformed Presbyterians, two
Dutch Reformed, two Baptists, four Quakers, one each Methodist,
Associate Reformed, and Congregationalist. The most famous public
figure on the Board was DeWitt Clinton (1763-1822), at various
times Mayor of New York, Governor of that state, United States
Senator, sponsor of the Erie Canal, and unsuccessful candidate
for President in 1812.

The first action of the Board of Managers was the election of
officers for the Society. Although the name of John Jay had been
prominently mentioned, the presidency was offered to Elias
Boudinot without dissent. Joshua Wallace reported to his wife
that, when the decision was announced to the delegates, "the
approbation of the Choice, by the Convention, was joyfully
unanimous." In transmitting to the new President the first
printed copy of the Constitution, "without waiting to have it
stitched," William Jay wrote: "The part you have taken in
bringing about this blessed consummation will be long remembered
with gratitude by the Christians of America & it will be registered in Heaven." Official notification was not sent by the
Secretary, John Romeyn, until June 1. To this Boudinot replied
on June 5:

...I am not ashamed to confess, that I accept this appointment of President of the American Bible Society, as the
greatest honour that could have been conferred on me this
side of the grave....So apparent is the hand of God in thus

disposing the hearts of so many men, so diversified in
their sentiments as to religious matters of minor importance, and uniting them as a band of brothers in this
grand object; that even Infidels are compelled to say,
it is the work of the Lord, and it is wonderful in our
eyes!--In vain is the opposition of man: as well might
he attempt to arrest 'the arm of Omnipotence, or fix a
barrier around the throne of God.' Having this confidence, let us go on and we shall prosper. I can say no
more: my feeble frame and exhausted spirit scarcely
suffer me, lying in my bed, to dictate language sufficiently efficient to represent my deep sense of the
polite attention of your honourable body. All I can
add is, that should it please a Sovereign God to suffer
me to meet my faithful fellow-labourers in the gospel
vineyard, I will most cordially endeavour to make up,
in unwearied attention and industry, what may be defi-
cient in the mind and understanding.

If business acumen seemed to have been a major criterion for
the selection of Managers, prestige and public influence loomed
large in the choice of Vice-Presidents. This is not to deny a
zeal for the distribution of Scriptures, which so obviously
motivated the original delegates to the convention--although the
number of refusals from both Managers and Vice-Presidents may
suggest the peril of naming public figures without prior consent.
Only fourteen of the 23 men initially elected as Vice-Presidents
accepted the office, with four more added during the following
year. But among these 18, four were state governors and two
others had previously served in that capacity. At least five
were presidents of their local Bible societies. After Boudinot's
death, John Jay, as First Vice-President, served as President
from 1821 to 1829, although never able to attend a meeting of the
Society. Other illustrious names included were those of Bushrod
Washington of Virginia, nephew of the first President of the
United States; Charles C. Pinckney of South Carolina, member of
the U.S. Constitutional Convention and unsuccessful candidate for
the presidency; Thomas Worthington, twice Governor of Ohio, who
expressed himself, on his election by the Bible Society, as
"thankful if I can be at all useful in an object so pleasing to
my feelings." Francis Scott Key, author of "The Star-Spangled
Banner," served as a Vice-President from 1818 to 1843 and, in an
eloquent address at the twelfth Annual Meeting, "anticipated the
day when pagan converts would begin to visit our shores, attend
our anniversaries, and in broken accents express in person their
gratitude to those who had sent them the word of life."

John Mitchell Mason (1770-1829) was named Secretary for
Foreign Correspondence, without salary. This noted clergyman
helped to establish the institution which later became Union

Theological Seminary, served as provost of Columbia University
and later as president of Dickinson College. In his recollec-
tions of the ABS Founding Convention Lyman Beecher wrote many
years later:

> There was one moment in our proceedings when things seemed
> to tangle and some feeling began to rise. At that moment
> Dr. Mason rose hastily and said: 'Mr. President, the Lord
> Jesus never built a church but what the devil built a
> chapel close to it; and he is here now, this moment, in
> this room, with his finger in the ink-horn not to write
> your constitution but to blot it out.' The laughter
> caused by this sally dispelled the storm, and the clear
> sun appeared again.(5)

John B. Romeyn, one of the most popular preachers in New York
City, served as a secretary of the convention and then became ABS
Secretary for Domestic Correspondence--until in 1819 the business
grew too large for a full-time pastor to handle. Richard Varick,
Mayor of New York from 1790 to 1801, acted as unpaid Treasurer
for the Society for three years, and later succeeded John Jay as
President (1828-1831). John Pintard, merchant, historian, state
legislator, a founder of General Theological Seminary, received
$600 a year as Recording Secretary and Accountant. The confi-
dence placed in Pintard by his associates loomed more significant
since, for eight years, he had been "exiled" from New York because
of a bankruptcy suit. As a Vice-President from 1832 to 1844, he
is reported to have attended practically every Annual Meeting of
the Society and most monthly meetings of the Board until he was
eighty years old.

"The Address to the Public"--substantially the product of John
Mason worked over by Bayard and Beecher and the larger drafting
committee--was hailed as an inspiring oration when it was adopted
by the convention and subsequently read in open meeting. Directed
"To the People of the United States," it declared, in part:

> ...The times are pregnant with great events.....An excite-
> ment, as extraordinary as it is powerful, has roused the
> nations to the importance of spreading the knowledge of
> the one living and true God, as revealed in his Son.....
> We would fly to the aid of all that is holy, against all
> that is profane; of the purest interest of the community,
> the family, and the individual, against the conspiracy of
> darkness, disaster, and death--to help on the mighty work
> of Christian charity--to claim our place in the age of
> Bibles.....
>
> The impulse which [the British and Foreign Bible Society],
> ten thousand times more glorious than all the exploits of

the sword, has given to the conscience of Europe, and to
the slumbering hope of millions in the region and shadow
of death, demonstrates to Christians of every country what
they cannot do by insulated zeal and what they can do by
cooperation. In the United States we want nothing but
concert to perform achievements astonishing to ourselves,
dismaying to the adversaries of truth and piety; and most
encouraging to every evangelical effort, on the surface of
the globe.

The "Address" went on to affirm the delegates' preference for
a national society supported by local groups and individuals,
rather than "independent associations in friendly understanding
and correspondence." It acknowledged that the vast size of
America, the population growth, the dangers of "reverting to a
species of heathenism, which shall have all the address and
profligacy of civilized society, without any religious control"--
all represented an enormous challenge to the purposes of the new
Society. Yet it rejected any notion of "geographical or political limits" in "raying out, by means of the Bible..the light of
life and immortality, to such parts of the world, as are destitute of the blessing."

Have you ever been invited to an enterprize of such grandeur
and glory? Do you not value the Holy Scriptures...as containing your sweetest hope, your most thrilling joy?.....

Be it impressed on your souls, that a contribution, saved
from even a cheap indulgence, may send a Bible to a desolate family; may become a radiatory point of 'grace and
truth' to a neighbourhood of errour and vice; and that a
number of such contributions made at really no expense,
may illumine a large tract of country, and successive
generations of immortals, in that celestial knowledge,
which shall secure their present and their future felicity.....We shall satisfy our conviction of duty--we
shall have the praise of high endeavours for the highest
ends--we shall minister to the blessedness of thousands,
and tens of thousands of whom we may never see the faces,
nor hear the names. We shall set forward a system of
happiness which will go on with accelerated motion and
augmented vigour, after we shall have finished our
career; and confer upon our children, and our children's
children, the delight of seeing the wilderness turned
into a fruitful field, by the blessing of God upon that
seed which their fathers sowed, and themselves watered....

On Friday, May 10, 1816, the Constitution of the American
Bible Society was adopted. On Saturday morning officers were
elected and initial subscriptions received.

Immediately after the convention adjourned, "a large meeting of ladies" resolved to organize the New York Female Auxiliary Bible Society and appointed a committee to draft their Constitution. The following Tuesday "a crowded assembly of ladies, consisting of every Christian sect in the city," heard the "Address," adopted their own Constitution, elected officers from the various religious denominations, and subscribed about seven hundred dollars.

"A meeting of as many of the Citizens of NYork as will attend" had been scheduled for Monday, May 13, at five o'clock in the City Hall. On Sunday notices of this rally were read in some-- but not all--of the city churches. The Chief Justice of the New York Supreme Court, Smith Thompson, opened the meeting, and the Mayor was invited to preside. After the reading of the new Constitution and the "Address to the People of the United States" two major resolutions were adopted unanimously: "That this meeting cordially approve of the Constitution of the American Bible Society" and "That this meeting will cheerfully contribute to the support of this great National Institution." In moving and seconding these proposals, the speakers employed such eloquence that their addresses were subsequently printed by the Society, and excerpts incorporated in "The Christian Orator...for the use of colleges, academies" (1818).

One of these orators was Peter Jay, elder brother of William and himself a noted lawyer, who had carried the precious Louisiana Purchase Treaty from Paris to Washington in 1802-- and in 1811 had unsuccessfully defended those charged with causing a riot at the Commencement exercises of Columbia College. In his speech Peter Jay highlighted several principal tenets of the new Society: its commitment to the unannotated Bible, its faith in the missionary power of the Gospel, its hope that the common task might reduce sectarian divisions:

Our object is to distribute the Holy Scriptures without note or comment. At this, no politician can be alarmed, no sectary can be reasonably jealous. We shall distribute no other book, we shall teach no disputed doctrine. Laying aside for this purpose the banners of our respective corps, we assemble under the sole standard of the great Captain of our salvation. We endeavor to extend his reign, and in his name alone we contend.....

The Bible is the best of missionaries. It will reach where no preacher can penetrate; it will preach where he cannot be heard; it will reprove, alarm, advise, console in solitude, when no passion interferes to drown its voice. Of these missionaries thousands may be sent abroad, and where the seed is abundantly sown, we may reasonably hope for an abundant harvest.

Though the diffusion of the scriptures is the great end of
our Institution, yet another blessing will also spring
from it. Too long have Christians been divided. Sect
has been opposed to sect; angry controversies have agitated
the Church; misrepresentations have been made, and believed;
and good men, who ought to have loved each other, have been
kept asunder by prejudices, which were the offspring of
ignorance.

In this Society, the most discordant sects will meet
together, engaged in a common cause, prejudices will abate;
asperities will be softened; and when it is found, as
undoubtedly it will be found, that the same love of God
and of man animates all real Christians, whatever may be
their outward rites, or forms of ecclesiastical discipline,
that most of them agree in fundamental doctrines, and that
their differences principally relate to points of little
practical importance, there must be an increase of
brotherly love, and of a truly catholic spirit....

Letters and resolutions of commendation, support, and auxiliary affiliation poured in to the New York headquarters and to
Elias Boudinot's home in Burlington, New Jersey. The Committee
of the British and Foreign Bible Society, through their secretary,
John Owen, sent "warmest congratulations on...an event which they
consider as truly auspicious, & pregnant with consequences most
advantageous to the promotion of that great work in which their
American Brethren & themselves are mutually engaged. To these
congratulations our Committee have added a Grant of five hundred
pounds....." Prince Galitzin, President of the Russian Bible
Society, acknowledged that the news "was certainly of a nature
to produce the most joyful feelings in the breasts of all who
take a sincere part in this great and salutary cause," and
pledged "to communicate mutually with your Society about our
proceedings and successes."

Within a year, before the members of the American Bible
Society met again in 1817, 41 societies already established had
become auxiliaries to the national organization and an equal
number were newly formed as auxiliaries. Some 930 subscribers
and donors had contributed to the Society, thirty-five of them
as Directors for life with payments of $150 or more.

The "Address" to the American people affirmed the faith of
these Founding Fathers that God had indeed chosen an instrument
"which contributes, in all latitudes and climes, to make Christians feel their unity, to rebuke the spirit of strife, and to
open upon them the day of brotherly concord--the Bible! the
Bible!--through Bible Societies!"

Despite the T'aiping Rebellion in China, the Crimean War in Europe, and the American Civil War, which marked and marred the middle of the nineteenth century, some historians would point to 1816 as the opening of an era of unprecedented world peace. That year, during a few brief days in May, a new organization came into being, committed exclusively to "the dissemination of the Scriptures in the received versions where they exist, and in the most faithful where they may be required." For all their great expectations and ornate language, the handful of dedicated Christians who met that week in New York--and others who upheld them in prayer--could not have foreseen the outreach of their labors around the world. As the "Address" attested:

> In such a work whatever is dignified, kind, venerable, true, has ample scope: while sectarian littleness and rivalries can find no avenue of admission.....Come then, fellow-citizens, fellow-Christians, let us join in the sacred covenant. Let no heart be cold, no hand be idle, no purse reluctant! Come, while room is left for us in the ranks whose toil is goodness, and whose recompense is victory. Come cheerfully, eagerly, generally.....

NOTES

1. Unpublished paper by Eric M. North, May 11, 1966.

2. Allen Johnson, ed., *Dictionary of American Biography* (New York: Charles Scribner's Sons, 1928), XVII: 481.

3. Cf. William B. Sprague, *The Life of Jedidiah Morse*, D.D. (New York, 1874) and Sydney E. Morse, *Memorabilia in the Life of Jedidiah Morse, D.D.....*(Boston, 1867).

4. See Gardiner Spring, *Memoirs of the Rev. Samuel J. Mills* (New York, 1820) and Thomas C. Richards, *Samuel J. Mills, Missionary Pathfinder, Pioneer, and Promoter* (Boston, 1906).

5. Henry Otis Dwight, *Centennial History of the American Bible Society* (New York, 1916), p. 24.

2

The Background

Behind these gratifying events lay months of earnest effort and prayer, years of local organization and activity, centuries of struggle to place the Scriptures in the hands of Christian people.

Few conjunctions in history have been more important for man-kind—and especially for Christianity—than the Protestant Reformation and the invention of printing. The Old and New Testaments (generally accompanied by the Apocrypha) had been accepted as the authoritative Word of God by most branches of Christendom for a thousand years. But two factors had restricted the circulation of Scriptures even among the few who could read: the laborious task of copying manuscripts by hand, and the conviction that Biblical interpretation should be confined to the clergy. Johannes Gutenberg (1400?-1468?) abolished the former; Martin Luther (1483-1546) challenged the latter.

Before the development of wood-block printing (xylographica) in the fourteenth century, written copies of Scripture were extremely scarce, limited almost exclusively to Hebrew, Greek, and Latin. Even parts of the Bible had been translated and pro-duced in only eighty other languages. Within the next fifty years the entire Bible was printed in five languages and portions of it in fourteen more. Gutenberg's movable type, invented between 1440 and 1450, prepared the way for a still more rapid expansion in available books. Yet the process was expensive, and the rights to such printing were often restricted to holders of special patents or royal privileges.

Gradually, however, various agencies assumed responsibility along with private printers for the publication of Scriptures. When the Geneva Bible of John Calvin was banned in England about 1616, other editions of the Scriptures were imported from Holland, and in 1629 the University Press at Cambridge printed the King James Version of 1611. By the end of that century new missionary societies in Great Britain included as one of their primary purposes the distribution of the Bible.

One of these agencies, the Society for the Propagation of the Gospel among the Indians in New England, supported the missionary work of a brilliant young Cambridge scholar, John Eliot, and of the Thomas Mayhews, father and son, on Martha's Vineyard. When the corporation's charter, granted by Parliament in 1649, was ordered to be read in every church in England and Wales, it inspired gifts of ₤2,333. The Massachusetts Indian Bible, translated by John Eliot and published in 1660-1661, was the first whole Bible printed in the Western hemisphere and the first whole Bible translated and printed in a previously unwritten language.

Until the American Revolution most books, religious and secular, were shipped from Europe. References have been found to some New Testaments (1749) and entire Bibles (1752) printed in the colonies with imported type on imported paper with "borrowed" imprints, but librarians and historians discount these reports, since the publication of English language Scriptures was limited in all British colonies to Oxford and Cambridge University presses.(1) Several German Bibles and Testaments found markets among Continental immigrants, and the second Bible published in America was a German edition of 1743. At the outbreak of the Revolution in 1775 perhaps fifty presses existed in British territories in North America, principally in the port cities of Boston, New York, and Philadelphia. Not for another half century would steam power replace horse power and hand-operated printing presses.

The War of Independence abruptly cut off or drastically reduced all kinds of shipments from the mother country to the American territories. In 1777 a chaplain petitioned the Continental Congress to finance the printing of an American edition of the Bible. Consultation with local printers disclosed that suitable type and paper would have to be imported, at considerable expense and delay. On a substitute proposal to import twenty thousand bound copies from Holland, Scotland, or elsewhere, seven states (New Hampshire, Massachusetts, Rhode Island, Connecticut, New Jersey, Pennsylvania, and Georgia) voted affirmatively, and six (New York, Delaware, Maryland, Virginia, and North and South Carolina) negatively. Apparently the very narrow approval was never implemented.

To meet the demand, the printer to Congress, Robert Aitken, began publishing Testaments in Philadelphia in 1777, and in 1782 issued the first whole Bible printed in English in America. After examination by two Congressional chaplains, this edition of ten thousand copies was approved by the representatives assembled in the Continental Congress and recommended "to the inhabitants of the United States." With the end of the war Bibles flooded in from Europe once more, cheaper than Aitken could sell his copies. Even a decision by the Philadelphia Synod of the Presbyterian Church to purchase only Aitken's Bible for distribution to the poor (anticipating later policies of auxiliary societies) did not enable him to continue publication of Scriptures.

Other printers, however, stepped in to supply the American market. Although most of these new editions followed the King James Version, the dedicatory epistle to the monarch was replaced by a "more suitable" introduction. The first Bible actually printed in New York in 1792 ("John Brown's Self-Interpreting Bible") carried a list of Subscribers, headed by President George Washington, Alexander Hamilton (Secretary of the Treasury), Aaron Burr (Senator from New York), Henry Knox (Secretary of War), John Jay (Chief Justice), and including many others identified as baker, stonemason, hairdresser, school madam, boatbuilder, cartman, distiller, etc. The three decades from 1780 to 1810 saw the publication in the United States of eighty-six editions of the Bible and ninety-five editions of the New Testament, roughly estimated at a quarter of a million Bibles for a population (in the latter year) of 7,239,881. Up until this time most books had been printed by individual type-set, which was broken up as soon as the edition was completed. A few bold, progressive publishers, however, began to import standing type, sometimes tied together in page form, from Scotland or England, and to make plans for the purchase of newly developed stereotype plates. As at the end of the fifteenth century, primitive technology was preparing the way for a vast expansion of Bible distribution.

Other events also provided favorable conditions for a fresh movement of the Holy Spirit. Political revolutions in America and in France at the end of the eighteenth century introduced new concepts of democracy and human freedom. The industrial revolution just getting under way offered prospects of greater material welfare for large portions of mankind. The rationalism and scepticism of the Enlightenment, still strong in Europe and America, created a counter-balance in the Pietist movement of seventeenth-century Germany. Although spasmodic efforts had been made to put the Scriptures into the hands of lay Christians ever since the Protestant Reformation, a famous German Pietist, Philip Jacob Spener, declared in 1675 "that one should be concerned to provide a more abundant supply of the Word of God for our people." In response to this challenge the Canstein Bible

Institute was formed in 1710. During the next century it issued
nearly three million Bibles and Testaments, priced extremely low
for the sake of the poor, and including Polish and Bohemian and
Greek editions as well as German. But it stimulated no similar
movements in other lands.

A French Bible Society lasted from 1792 until 1803, only to
be stifled by political and intellectual currents in the wake of
the French Revolution. "The Bible Society" organized in London
later changed its name to the Naval and Military Bible Society
in acknowledgement of its limited objectives.

A new era in the circulation of Scriptures may rightfully be
dated from the establishment of the British and Foreign Bible
Society in 1804. As early as 1787 a pastor in North Wales had
appealed for Bibles and Testaments, but a delayed response from
the Society for Promoting Christian Knowledge supplied only a
quarter of the needs. Moved afresh by a young girl's barefoot
journey of twenty-eight miles to ask for a Bible, the minister
addressed another plea to the Religious Tract Society. "Surely,"
remarked a Baptist pastor, "a Society might be formed for the
purpose, and if for Wales, why not for the Kingdom; why not for
the whole world?" Despite a threatened invasion of the British
Isles by Napoleon, a widespread campaign was launched to solicit
support for the formation of such a society.

Nearly three hundred people gathered in the London Tavern on
March 7, 1804, described by one participant as "a multitude of
Christians whose doctrinal and ritual differences had for ages
kept them asunder, and who had been taught to regard each other
with a sort of pious estrangement, or rather a consecrated
hostility."(2) Yet so united were they in common commitment to
the cause of Bible distribution as a means of evangelization
that a society was founded on the spot. John Lord Teignmouth
was selected as President, and the Vice-Presidents included
William Wilberforce, Charles Grant, and the Bishops of London,
Durham, and Exeter.

Local groups organized to support the movement were soon
formed into auxiliaries, which by 1816 numbered 175 in England
and 236 in the British Isles as a whole. By the same date
forty Bible societies had been established on the European
continent and four in British North America. From the outset
the "foreign" dimension received major emphasis. Scriptures
were sent to Africa, the Near East, New South Wales, China and
India; in thirteen years of operation the BFBS aided in the
production and circulation of Christian Scriptures in sixty-six
languages around the globe. With no sense of estrangement following the American Revolution, it contributed generously to at
least seventeen societies in the United States.

During the War of 1812 a New York privateer hijacked a ship-
load of Bibles en route to Nova Scotia. When the Massachusetts
Bible Society learned that the books, which were sold and resold
in the Portland area, had a list price of ₤157/2/9, it remitted
that sum to the BFBS in repayment. On a similar occasion, when
a vessel bound for the Cape of Good Hope was taken into harbor
at Bath, Maine, the Massachusetts Society purchased the cargo of
Bibles at a low rate and reshipped them to their destination by
a safer route.

Neither purchase from Europe nor capture of shipments destined
elsewhere could adequately supply the need for Scriptures in the
United States. Contrary to the usual assumption—inherited, no
doubt, from Pilgrim days—the inhabitants of the new United States
were not all devout and pious Christians. In fact, in 1790 only
five per cent of the American population belonged to any church.
By 1810 that figure had risen to nearly seven per cent, due
partly to movements of Evangelical Awakening which had swept the
Eastern seaboard.

In its first issue (January, 1805) the *Evangelical Intelligenc-
er*, a Presbyterian mission magazine published in Philadelphia,
announced the organization of the British and Foreign Bible
Society, rejoicing that the new body was "catholic in its principles" and not "liable to the objections of sectarian zeal." A
few months later *The Panoplist* reprinted the BFBS Constitution.
Subsequent issues of Jedidiah Morse's paper contained reports
from London of the Society's work and words of encouragement
for similar efforts in America. One such letter from England,
dated June 24, 1808, read in part:

> What time is so auspicious as the present! When uncer-
> tainty and disappointment are particularly stamped on
> worldly undertakings, when commerce in every channel is
> interrupted and when the kingdoms of this world are
> tottering to their foundation, surely christians are
> loudly called upon to look around and consider the part
> which they have to act in such circumstances; and can
> there be a question that it is to promote, with increas-
> ing zeal the interests of that spiritual kingdom which
> is righteousness, joy and peace in the Holy Ghost.
>
> The spread of the holy scriptures is undoubtedly the
> means best adapted to promote this valuable end, the
> means which has already been greatly blessed, and on
> which a divine blessing may still be confidently ex-
> pected. But in such an undertaking great difficulties
> may be looked for; on such occasions the great adversary
> of souls is never inactive, being always alive to his
> interest amongst men, and perhaps never more so than

when any good work is contemplated on an extensive scale.
Yet I trust it is the Lord's work, and he will not suffer
it to fail, but grant a spirit of union amongst christians of all denominations, and crown it with an abundant
blessing.....

The letter, published anonymously, concluded with a personal
offer of twenty dollars if such a Bible society should be formed
in America, together with the opinion that one hundred pounds
would be contributed by the British and Foreign Bible Society.

After some preliminary discussions and invitations, twenty-
five men met in Philadelphia on December 12, 1808, at the home
of Robert Ralston, a merchant in the China trade. Ralston
(1761-1836), one of the first organizers of a Sunday School in
the United States, had already demonstrated his profound concern
for orphans, Negroes, missions abroad. The most distinguished
member of the group was Dr. Benjamin Rush (1745-1813), signer
of the Declaration of Independence, Treasurer of the United
States Mint, a widely known physician, and an active leader in
the early abolition movement. The original company included
eleven ministers and fourteen laymen, but among the Board of
Managers and officers subsequently elected twelve were clergymen
and eleven laymen, belonging to at least the following denominations: Presbyterian, Episcopal, Lutheran, Quaker, Reformed,
Baptist, and Methodist.

The Constitution of "The Bible Society" (to which "Philadelphia" was added later), specified that "the Bible selected for
publication shall be without notes" and that "copies of it in
all the languages in which it is calculated to be useful, shall
be distributed when necessary by the Society." The "Address...
to the Public" issued early in 1809 revealed that two plans had
been considered: a large association of members "from all the
states in the American union" or a smaller society for work in
Pennsylvania and adjacent areas of New Jersey and Delaware. The
former was deemed impossible of success, and the latter was
chosen with "the confident hope that similar institutions would
be established in a number of other places in the United States..
which would contribute essentially both to the glory and the
safety of the American confederacy."

Through this Address from the President, Bishop William
White, the Philadelphia Society pledged itself to the following
guiding principles: Bibles published would contain only the
text and chapter contents (in order to unite all denominations);
they would be distributed "in the native speech of all who are
disposed to read it" (specifically English, Welsh, German, and
French); they would be offered "without money and without price"
to the poor chiefly, to those in prisons, in poorhouses and in

hospitals, to soldiers and sailors--but books would be sold to
families able to pay. Scriptures should also be made available,
the Address continued, for "the civilizing and christianizing of
the Indians...the poor Africans not only of Pennsylvania but of
some other states...[and] the vast number of persons and families
in our country absolutely destitute of the Bible, and likely long
to remain so, unless supplied in the manner contemplated..."

During the following year, 1809, at least seven societies--in
New York, Connecticut, Massachusetts, Maine, and New Jersey--came
into existence, at least temporarily, with similar aims.

The founders of the Connecticut Bible Society voiced "the
liveliest gratitude to God...that the bible is more universally
circulated here, than in any other country." Rejoicing that "by
public authority, the select-men of the respective towns are
required to be certain, that, in every family, there be at least
one bible," they regretted that there was no financial provision
to make this law effective, "no charitable fund, from which they
[the indigent] may hope to be helped by public bounty, to the
enjoyment of God's word." The Constitution adopted in Hartford
on May 11, 1809, specified: "The circulation of the Holy Scriptures shall be its only object. The common version of the bible,
and impressions that combine cheapness with plainness, without
note, or comment, shall be selected."

The Massachusetts Bible Society had the "unusual privilege"
of being organized in the state Representatives' Chamber, upon
petition of William Ellery Channing, one of several prominent
Unitarian participants. Taking a proposal from the Massachusetts
Society for Propagating the Gospel among the Indians and Others
in North America, the founders affirmed their desire "to secure
[man's] eternal felicity...to promote an *infinite good*...and to
promote the order, tranquillity, and happiness of the *present*..."
through the distribution of Scriptures. The Massachusetts
Address to the Public, published in *The Panoplist* (June, 1809),
emphasized further, with unintended condescension:

It becomes Christians to consider, that their master was
very mindful of the poor, and represented his gospel as
peculiarly designed for that class of society. Its great
truths are level to their capacities; and its precepts and
promises are peculiarly suited to impart that support and
consolation, and to form that patience, resignation,
uprightness, and freedom from envy, which are so necessary
in a state of poverty.

Such an undertaking, the Address continued, could hardly be
questioned. "We circulate not an imperfect production of man,
but the book of God; not a work of controversy, but the gospel

of peace." "A small annual subscription from Christians in
moderate circumstances," the organizers pointed out, "united with
the donations of the opulent, will be sufficient to distribute
the Bible wherever it is wanted." In concrete terms the Massachusetts Society pointed to needs in various parts of Rhode
Island, Vermont, New Hampshire, "and the District of Maine." To
"many unhappy individuals" in prison and in poverty the Holy Book
would be "a most acceptable present," and often "where the Bible
is found it is so much worn, and so wretchedly printed, that its
usefulness is very much diminished." Membership was granted to
all clergymen "who request it in writing." Among original signer
were such familiar names as John Quincy Adams, future President
of the United States, who enrolled as a Life Member at the start;
Charles Lowell, father of James Russell Lowell; Francis Parkman,
the historian, later to serve as Corresponding Secretary and then
Vice-President of the Society; Theophilus Parsons, Chief Justice
of the Commonwealth; Alden Bradford, descendent of two Pilgrim
families; and the enthusiastic Jedidiah Morse.

In the "province of Maine" eleven years prior to statehood
"the cry in 1809 was 'How to get a Bible.'" Trustees of the
newly organized Bible Society of Maine affirmed their concern not
only for the poor, but also for persons in jails, poorhouses,
hospitals, for soldiers and sailors, "as well as Africans and
the aborigines of our country."

At the end of the same year of 1809 President Elias Boudinot
of the recently organized New Jersey Bible Society looked forward
to the day when present and future bands of Christians might
"attempt to carry the word of God into *all nations*, and in a
language that they can understand."

In New York a series of interlocking or independent Bible
societies (Young Men's, Female Auxiliary, etc.) formed and
reformed--and were firmly advised by the British and Foreign
Bible Society to get together. Also in New York a group of
Protestant Episcopalians, fearful that readers could not always
understand the Bible without instructive notes, went "a step
further...to make known the Church of God" by establishing the
New York Bible and Common Prayer Book Society. Although they
were not indisposed to assist with the publication of unannotated Scriptures, they rebuked the BFBS for not distributing also
the Book of Common Prayer, and subsequently declined to participate in the founding of the American Bible Society, which
emphasized the policy of "without note or comment."

By early 1816 some 130 Bible societies had sprung up in
twenty-four states or territories, including fifteen "female"
societies, three in colleges, others for young men or children.
To many of these the British and Foreign Bible Society

contributed generously, not only in books and money, but in
advice and encouragement. Most of these societies dispensed
less than five hundred copies of the Scriptures per year. A few,
on the other hand, extended their outreach far beyond state or
regional boundaries. Books were transported from the East Coast
to the Illinois Territory, to Louisiana, and to the Columbia
River frontier; the Connecticut Bible Society in one year sent
shipments to eight other societies and small towns. But both of
these factors--relative ineffectiveness and competitive over-
lapping--demonstrated the need for central organization.

Most of these societies paid special attention to Indians,
soldiers and sailors, prisoners of war (in 1812-1814), and
"children of Ethiopia." Scriptures were printed, or purchased
for resale, in French, Gaelic, Welsh, and some in Dutch and
Spanish, for these were the principal immigrant groups at that
time. Although no regular provision had yet been established
for distribution abroad, Bibles were often entrusted to ship
captains or missionaries; for example, one hundred volumes to
Captain Benjamin Wicker bound for Canton, China, for the use of
English-reading sailors and for Robert Morrison, the first
Protestant missionary to China.

As the number of societies multiplied, so did the number of
voices calling for some national association. In March, 1814,
Jedidiah Morse published in *The Panoplist* a six-page communication signed by a still-unidentified "N". This powerful appeal
reviewed the efficacy of Bible distribution and the development
of numerous societies to date, but strongly endorsed the proposal
for "a Bible Society of the United States...not only as a means
of giving to the heathen a knowledge of the truth; but also of
arresting the progress of infidelity among ourselves; of
alleviating the various evils which we suffer; of saving us from
the destruction of those, who shall be found among the enemies
of God and of the Lamb."

Elias Boudinot's first "Call" for a national convention
appeared less than six months later. Soon afterwards, Joshua
Wallace, Vice-President of the New Jersey Society, communicated
directly with the "senior" society in Philadelphia, whose
influence might well be--and very nearly was--decisive. There
a committee was appointed to inquire further into the "Reasons"
and "Arguments" which the New Jersey Society "deemed of force
in favor of the Measure." Members in Philadelphia expressed,
from the outset, grave reservations. As B. B. Hopkins, Recording
Secretary of the Philadelphia Society, explained in a letter of
September 21, 1814, to Joshua Wallace;

> [They were] fearful that such an Institution would have a
> tendency to discourage the formation of Auxiliary Societies

--induce existing Bible Societies to relax in their zealous Efforts to circulate the Scriptures, and perhaps end in the dissolution of some of them--that too much dependence would be placed on the Gen. Society, while the Luke-warm would rejoice that they had an Excuse for their Indifference and a motive to continue inactive.

After further correspondence and a visit from Mr. Wallace to the President, Bishop William White, the Philadelphia Society sought a legal opinion and was advised that constitutionally "there can be no delegation of the power of this Board to control or dispose of the funds of this Society." On this basis, but with many other reservations, the Managers sent a negative reply to Dr. Boudinot and then to other societies across the country.

Although no copy of the Philadelphia resolution has been found, its tone and general content can be inferred from the fourteen-page pamphlet published by Boudinot in January, 1815: "An Answer to the Objections of the Managers of the Philadelphia Bible-Society, against a Meeting of Delegates from the Bible Societies in the Union, to agree on some plan to disseminate the Bible in parts [within and?] without the United States." As one of the pivotal documents in the history of the American Bible Society, it deserves quotation at some length.

After reviewing the previous correspondence between the New Jersey and Philadelphia Societies, and agreeing with Bishop White that "any difference that exists between our Societies relates only to the means most proper for adoption," Boudinot expressed regret that the "Objections" seemed to be addressed more to the New Jersey initiative than to the proposal itself. Then he took up specific points:

> *1st.* They say, *It is unseasonable*, this charge when closely considered will appear not to be well founded.....
> The British and Foreign Bible Society was formed and established in the midst of a long, perplexing and most expensive War, with the combined powers of Europe, that threatened the very existence of great Britain. Their zeal, activity, expenditures, and Success, arose almost to a miracle. Her praise is in every Christians mouth, and thousands, nay millions of prayers, ascend before the Throne of the Eternal for blessings on their Heads. To Her under God we owe the present Existence and Prosperity of our Societies, and in particular, no one more than that of Philadelphia....

Boudinot then went on to point out that Bible societies were springing up all over Europe, in lands where tyranny and war had devastated cities and economies. Surely, he implied, minor

disruptions following the War of 1812 should not justify the
excuse of inopportune timing.

> *2nd. You think this measure unsanctioned by Example.....*
> Your own Society was established in your own State,
> wholly unsanctioned by example in this Country, equally
> if not much more so, than the one we aim at. Again let
> me ask, if the British and Foreign Bible Society was not
> wholly unsanctioned by example, and would you expect or
> desire to make out better than they have done? They had
> tenfold the opposition that we have, or are likely to
> have. And the very learned and able opponents they had,
> urged tenfold stronger and more plausible arguments
> against the measure, than can be argued against us. All
> the Societies, except two, from whom I have yet heard,
> express themselves as delighted with the proposal, and
> consider it as suggested from heaven....

Boudinot deplored very frankly the suspicion that some of the
opposition to his plan might be due to "the Jealousies of
Rivalry." To allay this particular fear, he offered that, if
the Philadelphia Society would expand its operations "to the
whole family of the human race," members of the New Jersey
Society would take no further action in the direction of a
national body except "to aid the funds of so extensive a plan."
He warned, however:

> If your Managers 'cannot discover any real and important
> advantages likely to result' [from a central organiza-
> tion]...they ought not to endeavour to cast obstacles in
> the way of their Brethren who think they do see great
> and essential advantages, under the influence and direc-
> tion of the holy Spirit, likely to arise to the Church
> of Christ from some plan of more universal Extent...which
> may be produced by the united wisdom of the different
> Societies.

As this feeble old man warmed to his task of refutation, his
indignation, impatience, and sarcasm rose:

> The 3rd Objection is, that the proposition strikes you
> as USELESS. This is the first time, that among Friends
> of Bible Societies, an association for sending the glad
> tidings of Salvation to those who are deprived of the
> Good News, *without the limits of the United States*,
> could be thought USELESS. Surely the Soul of a man on
> the missouri, is as precious to him, as it is to a
> Citizen of any of the States.....

Since part of the objection seemed to assume that a sufficient
number of societies were already at work, Boudinot quoted

extensively from reports of the Philadelphia Society itself
regarding the deficiency of Bibles even in the city of Philadelphia, and the regrettable necessity of limiting operations within
Pennsylvania. He reminded his critics also that, though they
might be legalistic about constitutional freedom to delegate any
of their funds to broader activities, they had shown no hesitation about appealing to "Sister Societies" to share their funds
with the larger "parent organization."

As to the *4th Objection*, 'May not the *contemplated meeting*,
prove, *Injurious*.'.....May not the next meeting of the
General Assembly of the Presbyterian Church or of the Con-
vention of the Episcopal Church, prove Injurious to the
Interests of Religion? Surely they may. It is possible
.....But is it likely, or presumable within the Bounds of
Christian Charity, that a public meeting of respectable
and pious Brethren of all denominations of the Church of
Christ, meeting together, in a solemn and serious manner,
for the express purpose of forming a plan to promote the
glory of God, by sending his gospel to the Ends of the
Earth, and thus publishing the benefits of redeeming Love,
to those who sit in darkness and the shadow of death, should
prove Injurious,--injurious to whom? Certainly not to the
great Cause of gospel light and knowledge.....[Had] the
British and Foreign Bible Society attended to objections of
this complection, and indeed of much more formidable ones,
when they were invited--urged--terrified--and warned to
consider their dangerous Conduct; thousands, if not
millions, who are at this day sounding forth the praises
of the glorious Redeemer, would still have continued
under the Shadow of death.....

Of all places, Boudinot retorted sharply, Philadelphia should
have least complaint about the distance and cost of travel to a
national meeting--a complaint which might come more legitimately
from distant societies and which would apply with equal weight--
or unimportance--to denominational assemblies.

Further response from the Philadelphia Bible Society to
Boudinot's "Circular" repeated the same arguments: that it would
be inexpedient to impose a "national association" to supplement
the work of existing societies; that it was "a very unseasonable
time...to touch the wheel that moves well, even though our benevolent intention be to accelerate its motion;" that "publick
charity must...give way...to domestick necessity" (in direct
contradiction to the preceding point); and that acting on the
agreement of twenty out of nearly seventy societies would
advertise that "Bible societies, were at last, divided!"
Regretfully, however, Boudinot reported to Alexander Proudfit,
President of the Washington County (New York) Bible Society in

June, 1815, that "I have accidentally discovered that all this [opposition] has been occasioned by a Jealousy of certain persons lest their influence should suffer, if such a measure should take place."

There were other reservations and criticisms regarding Elias Boudinot's proposal. Some Anglicans hesitated at cooperation with "non-conformists" and insisted that any such publication project should include the Book of Common Prayer. Bishop John Henry Hobart of the New York diocese "viewed with alarm the avowed purpose of many of the Bible Societies to unite all Protestants in a common cause as an ignoring of essential difference of doctrine and polity." Believing that the spread of "Church principles" would be "greatly nullified by this so-called spirit of charity and fraternal comity," the Bishop warned in a pastoral letter of April 3, 1815: "In all associations of men professing different principles the most numerous will silently, gradually, but effectually bear sway and perhaps eventually absorb the smaller divisions."(3)

Not all Episcopalians agreed with Bishop Hobart. One rector who refused to participate actively in the Flushing (New York) Bible Society remarked that he would "only give my mite as an individual" on condition that there would be no religious exercises in connection with the society except Scripture reading. He added the ulterior observation that wider Bible distribution would release more Episcopal funds for the Prayer Book: "Viewing it in this light, Presbyterians, Quakers, &c, will aid our Bible and Prayer Book Society, although they may not be aware of it:--we shall put a greater number of Prayer Books into circulation." But the President of the Philadelphia Bible Society, already active on an interdenominational basis, was another Episcopalian, Bishop William White. General Matthew Clarkson, one of the original members of the Prayer Book Society, became a Vice-President of the American Bible Society, as did John Jay, future ABS President, both Episcopalians.

The first reaction of several local societies reflected the negative view of Philadelphia toward Boudinot's proposal:

"It is inexpedient at this time." (Jefferson County, Virginia)

"It might excite jealousies, which, if once roused, would operate injuriously to the common cause." (Albany, New York)

"[Our society deems] the appropriation of so much money as would be necessary to defray the expenses incurred by the delegate, unauthorized by the state of our funds, and unsanctioned by our constitution." (Fredericksburg, Virginia)

"[We are] not able to discover any advantages likely to result
from the contemplated institution, which could not be compassed
by a more simple, expeditious, and less expensive process; namely
by correspondence, [and we are] strongly impressed with the
weight and sufficiency of the objections suggested by the Philadelphia Bible Society." (New York City)

Positive influences continued at work, however, and some
early opponents later changed their minds. From his second
journey to the West Samuel J. Mills wrote of distributing seven
hundred Bibles, five thousand French New Testaments, thousands
of religious tracts and pamphlets, besides preaching countless
sermons. Even more convincing was his estimate, based on eleven
months of travel covering six thousand miles, that at least
76,000 families were without Bibles. This overwhelming need for
Scriptures only confirmed Mills' previous conviction that a
national society should be formed at once, or that an appeal of
unprecedented magnitude should be made to the British and Foreign
Bible Society for help.

The New York Bible Society, initially critical, reversed its
stand, perhaps under the persuasion of John E. Caldwell, and
declared (on November 20, 1815) its support for the New Jersey
resolution:

> That it is highly desirable to obtain, upon as large a
> scale as possible, a co-operation of the efforts of the
> Christian community throughout the United States, for
> the efficient distribution of the Holy Scriptures.....

> That as a mean for the attainment of this end, it will
> be expedient to have a convention of Delegates from such
> Bible societies, as shall be disposed to concur in this
> measure,....for the purpose of considering whether such
> a co-operation may be effected in a better manner than
> by the correspondence of the different societies as now
> established; and if so, that they prepare the draft of
> a plan for such co-operation, to be submitted to the
> different societies for their decision.....

Thus encouraged, Elias Boudinot drafted a second "Circular"
on January 17, 1816. In it, "after mature deliberation, and
consulting with judicious friends on this important subject,"
he called for a meeting to be held in New York on the second
Wednesday of May. The venerable, ailing President of the New
Jersey Society pledged all in his power toward the establishment
of such a national organization, which "will in time, in point
of usefulness, be second only to the parent institution (the
British and foreign Bible Society)--[and] shed an unfading
lustre on our Christian community, and prove a blessing to our

country and the world." A month later Jedidiah Morse published
Boudinot's "Call" in *The Panoplist*, together with accounts of
the founding of four national societies in Europe. In adding
his personal comments, Morse noted:

> It has always been a matter of surprise to us, that there
> should be different opinions, as to the expediency of such
> an institution. The embarrassments which must attend the
> operations of a hundred independent small Bible Societies,
> without any common centre of action, are numberless and
> inevitable.....Though such delegates [of existing Bible
> Societies] ought to be received with marked respect [at
> such a convention], we apprehend the notice should have
> been given to all friends of the Bible in the United States.
> In that case, many gentlemen from various and distant parts
> of the country, could have a voice in the deliberations.

In late March, barely six weeks before the proposed convention
date, Elias Boudinot received from William Jay the "Memoir"
referred to in the preceding chapter. Its first two pages
illustrated the desperate scarcity of Scriptures abroad, refer-
ring to 550 millions of souls who had never heard of Christ,
compared with a population of 213 million in nominally Christian
lands. Even in the latter territories, Jay pointed out, only
one out of five persons in Denmark owned a Bible, one in a
thousand in Ireland. No Bibles were available in their native
language for 350,000 Christians in Ceylon or 200,000 in Persia.

"At home" the writer referred to unmet needs for the Scriptures even in Connecticut, "a state that has long been distinguished for the religious habits of its citizens...the State
better supplied with Bibles, than probably any other district
of the same population in the world." Surely, Jay quoted,
"darkness has covered the earth, and gross darkness the people,"
among thousands of destitute families in Mississippi, Indiana,
Illinois, Louisiana, Tennessee, and Kentucky. Then, claiming
108 "Independent Local Bible Societies" in existence in the
United States by 1816, Jay emphasized how inadequate their
activities had proved to be. By contrast, the British and
Foreign Bible Society had, in eleven years, distributed nearly
1,300,000 volumes in fifty-five languages, in comparison to
150,000 circulated in the United States over a period of seven
years. The difference Jay saw as one of organization, wherein
British auxiliaries were literally that, directing their funds
and their requests to the "Parent Society," which coordinated
reports and appeals, publication and circulation.

Furthermore, the young writer warned, "some of the American
societies are already departing from that simplicity of design
which is...their surest pledge of success. I mean the distribution of the Scriptures without note or comment." Instead, at

the risk of offending various denominational groups, some local
societies were introducing religious exercises at their meetings,
or linking Bible distribution to sectarian Sunday schools. Everywhere but in the United States, this ardent crusader affirmed,
Christians had already recognized the greater efficacy of a
general or national organization: in Russia, Finland, Hungary,
the Netherlands, Prussia, Sweden, etc.

William Jay included in his memorandum a proposed Constitution
for such a general society, based on that of the British and
Foreign Bible Society. This draft Boudinot apologetically
"ventured to correct in one or two Instances," but it was
followed closely in the document adopted on May 10, 1816.   In
summation, Jay declared:

We have found that the light which we have dispersed,
consists of a few faint and scattered rays, streaking
our own horizon, but not penetrating the gloom beyond
it. At the same time we have found England, and other
nations who have adopted her system, kindling a flame
whose light is seen, and whose warmth is felt in the
darkest and remotest regions of the earth, and we have
ascertained that the same instrument by which this holy
fire has been lighted in Europe may be successfully
employed for the same purpose in our own country.

This eloquent document, with few minor amendments, was printed
and circulated immediately to the societies which had been
invited to send delegates to New York. No wonder that Elias
Boudinot, pitifully feeble in body but eager in mind and spirit,
began to write only two hours after receiving the Jay "Memoir":
"My Heart indeed was cheered & my Spirits revived if not renewed,
and I could not help giving Glory to God for the great encouragement afforded me to press on in this glorious Cause when I thus
beheld his special Mercy in raising up so powerful a Support in
this joyous Work & labour of Love."

NOTES

1. Margaret T. Hills, *The English Bible in America* (New York);
    see also *Christianity Today*, Nov. 20, 1970.

2. John Owen, *History of the British and Foreign Bible Society*,
    I, p. 44.

3. Arthur Lowndes, *A Century of Achievement, A History of the
    New York Bible and Common Prayer Book Society* (New York, 1909)
    pp. 51, 59-61.

3

Auxiliaries and Agents

In the first few years of the American Bible Society, its conscientious Board of Managers met much more frequently than the
required once a month. Enthusiastically committed to the
enormous task of supplying Scriptures for the expanding population of America, these laymen laid immediate plans for finance,
manufacture, and distribution. By January, 1817, they recognized the necessity for a Standing Committee of five, who would
handle the business of the Society--except for funds in the hands
of the Treasurer--during "the recess of the Board of Managers."
As chairman of this committee, John E. Caldwell became in effect
the first General Agent of the Society, although a "messenger"
to deliver notices of meetings, to run errands, and to act as
doorkeeper, had been the first paid employee (at $58 per year).

At one of its earliest meetings (July 3, 1816) the Board
authorized two actions which inaugurated two complementary long-
range policies. One was to seek the addresses of all clergymen
in the United States, so that each might receive a printed
circular letter enclosing the new Constitution and requesting
that it be read from the pulpit and a collection taken for the
Society. By November 6 the Secretary reported that this had
been done. The second action was to send to the president of
every Bible society in the country copies of the Constitution
and the Address to the Public, both offering and requesting
cooperation between local groups and the national organization.
These two approaches to the problem of fund-raising were intended
to supplement each other, but in actual practice they occasionally overlapped or even competed; that is, direct solicitation

from churches on one hand, cultivation through Auxiliaries on
the other.

Direct cultivation of funds from individuals and congregations
might have expanded far more rapidly in those early years if
postage had not been so expensive--or if the Bible Society's
efforts at "lobbying" had proved more successful. Postal rates,
when the Society began in 1816, were based on a graduated scale:
six cents under thirty miles, up to twenty-five cents for over
four hundred miles. In January, 1817, the Board of Managers
applied to Congress for three special dispensations. The first
was exemption from all postal charges, on letters and parcels,
addressed *to* the Bible Society as well as those sent *from* New
York headquarters. The second requested a lifting of the thirty
per cent duty imposed on paper imported from France or Italy.
Stereotype plates, the other essential for printing Bibles in the
United States, were admitted free for the Philadelphia Bible
Society in 1813 and for others after 1816. The third petition
was for tax exemption on gifts to the American Bible Society, a
forerunner of present deductions for charitable contributions.

The memorial to Congress based its arguments on the claim that
"the objects of the Society are of National Importance" and on
"the influence it will have in promoting morality and in increasing the happiness of Mankind." It also pointed out that similar
privileges had been granted recently to Bible societies in
Russia, Prussia, and Wurtemberg. The committees of Congress
handled even such mundane matters with despatch. Members of the
House of Representatives from New York and New Hampshire, who
were asked to present the memorial, reported very promptly that
"we have no hope at present of succeeding," especially as the
Committee of Ways and Means opposed the revenue aspects of the
petition. The Congressmen also suggested politely that, since
the Society was still in its "infant state," it might be able to
muster more public support and more experience to demonstrate
the advantages of such privileges before the next session of
Congress.

Meanwhile the most sweeping proposal of the three was referred
to the Committee on the Post-Office and Post-Roads. Less than
four weeks after the filing of the petition, that body responded
with a formal report which concluded "that the prayer of the
petitioners ought not to be granted." The reasons listed were
cogent and clear. Recognizing that there were many worthy
associations--"religious, benevolent, and literary"--the
committee voiced its conviction that such charitable institutions
would fare better "when unaided by public patronage, and consequently uninfluenced by political connexions." Secondly, the
report pointed out that such exemption from public payment would,
in effect, constitute the equivalent of appropriations from the

national treasury and thus represent "a precedent for similar or
more extensive grants to every institution that may happen to be
the favourite of the day." Finally, the committee indicated
that a waiver of postal fees would reduce the revenues ordinarily
applied to developing new roads and place an undue burden on the
mail carriers.

Three members of the Board of Managers (Samuel Boyd, Thomas
Eddy, and Samuel Bayard) were authorized to renew this memorial,
which they pressed at least until 1820. Eventually import duties
were lifted on bound Scriptures from abroad, and tax deductions
were allowed for contributions to the Bible Society. The petition for free postage, later limited to domestic mail only, was
never granted, despite the use of eloquent quotations from George
Washington about morality and religion, despite such precedents
as chaplains and divine services for the armed forces. One
significant benefit did accrue, however. On his first trip to
Washington to plead the Bible Society's case, Samuel Bayard, an
active participant in the founding convention, called on President James Monroe and the heads of the executive departments
of government, enrolling *all* of them as Life Members of the
American Bible Society.

Because so many local societies were already in existence,
and because greater enthusiasm and initiative seemed to be generated in a close-knit community, primary emphasis was placed on
Auxiliaries, both for income and for distribution. Within the
first year of national operation, over eighty such groups applied
for affiliation with the "Parent Society" (a term in common use
although many auxiliaries were older than the ABS). In the
second year another seventy-three societies joined the family.

The original conditions were simple: those who indicated
their intention to become Auxiliaries for the American Bible
Society might remit their surplus funds—if any—to New York,
or conversely might request assistance in grants of money or
books, the latter at a five per cent reduction from the cost
price. These Auxiliaries were to have no other object than the
circulation of Scriptures without note or comment (that is,
tract societies were not eligible) and were expected to submit
reports to the national organization by March 1 of each year.

One problem which became quickly apparent was that of defini-
tion and function. So many local associations were "formed for
Counties, Cities, or lesser districts," often auxiliary to
Auxiliaries, sometimes of uncertain financial credit, potentially
competitive or overlapping, that the ABS had to "draw a line."
In November, 1816, only six months after the inauguration, the
Managers rejected as unconstitutional the extension of privi-
leges, including *ex officio* membership in the "Parent Society,"

to these minor associations. But the line to be drawn was still
a vague, ill-defined one. Although the proposed resolution
referred to state societies as having special privileges, it
was obvious that many of the "charter Auxiliaries," some of them
antedating the ABS itself, were organized on county, city, or
regional lines and could not be forced into a strictly state
system.

Furthermore, before and after 1816, a number of special
societies arose, requiring special relationships. Fifteen
Female Bible Societies existed prior to the ABS; twelve more
were formed during its first year. Five Young Men's Societies
and at least four Children's Societies came into being. Washington College in Virginia and Jefferson College in Pennsylvania
joined Nassau Hall and Union College in establishing student
groups, some of whom used their vacation periods to distribute
Bibles. When an African Bible Society was organized in 1817,
in addition to two earlier Negro groups, it requested a hundred
Bibles from the ABS, offering to pay $25 on account. (This
appeal was not only met, on those unusual terms, but supplemented
by an outright donation of fifty additional Bibles.) In Charleston, South Carolina, in New York, and perhaps elsewhere, Marine
Bible Societies sprang up as local auxiliaries "whose attention
is exclusively directed to the spiritual wants of seafaring men."
In the harbor at Charleston some twelve hundred Bibles were distributed "with care and judgment" in a single year. And at the
New York Navy Yard, fifty members of the crew of the "sloop of
war, Hornet" subscribed about two hundred dollars for a two-year
period, ranging from six cents to a dollar per month.

In addition to cultivating these irregular associations, the
ABS sought to establish better relations with the Philadelphia
Bible Society and others which were reluctant to surrender their
autonomy. To this end an amendment was voted to the Constitution
in 1820, admitting to auxiliary privileges any society which had
printed and published Scriptures *prior* to the establishment of
the American Bible Society, with such "relaxation of the terms
of admission heretofore prescribed, as the said Board may think
proper." Even beyond this the Society stood ready to sell or
donate Scriptures to other worthy organizations, without any
auxiliary relationship. These included Bible and Tract Societies,
Benevolent and Prayer Book Societies, even Charitable and Debating
Societies.

Although the American Bible Society often reaffirmed its
policy of "gratuitous distribution" to destitute families, it
recognized both financial and psychological values in charging
nominal prices. With this in mind the Board of Managers in late
1819 accepted "the expediency of recommending to our Auxiliary
Societies...the more general adoption of the practice of selling

Bibles and Testaments at cost or reduced rates in cases where
there exists a willingness or ability to purchase." The
Managers pointed out that such reasonable sales would not only
extend the scope and efficiency of general circulation--and thus
of Christian stewardship--but would also enhance the pride and
appreciation with which recipients viewed the Scriptures. Even
for the poor, it was suggested, the payment of a shilling, or
sixpence, or a penny a week, until the price had been met, often
proved highly advantageous, and "comparatively few, of those who
commenced as *subscribers for Bibles*, have, after receiving them,
discontinued their subscriptions."

With the proliferation of smaller societies and auxiliaries,
the ABS found it necessary to propose certain guidelines, but
not uniform procedures. For example, it was suggested that local
groups ahould follow the practice of the "parent Board" in opening their meetings with Scripture reading "and no other religious
exercises." But a formal recommendation to this effect was
rejected lest it be regarded as undue interference in local
affairs. When it was found that some groups were reinvesting
surplus funds instead of remitting them to New York, and that
others were selling Scriptures beyond their own territorial
bounds, the Board of Managers issued gentle warnings. By 1829
Auxiliaries had accumulated a total of $36,000 of accounts due
to the "Parent Society," and the Standing Committee recommended
a six per cent charge on unpaid balances, but again the Board
was loath to adopt any such rigid rule.

On the other hand, the Auxiliary Committee did issue several
detailed exhortations to the local, state and regional groups.
It also provided for them various forms and instructions in the
hope of securing more uniform records and reports: a Visitors'
Book for Branch and Village Associations; a Secretary's Book,
containing Constitutions, By-Laws, Price Lists, Specimens and
Hints "with 32 blank pages;" a Treasurer's Book with Instructions; a Depositary's Book with instructions as to duties and
prices; a half-sheet for boards of managers and executive
committees; an abstract of ABS operations; and a Brief Analysis
of the structure, method, and auxiliary system of the ABS.

As one Manager expressed it in 1829: "Not more surely is the
cistern exhausted, if the rains of heaven cease to descend, than
is our Treasury, if the Auxiliaries withhold their supplies."
To encourage this continual flow, members and officers and
friends of the Society were urged to make "a visit and an animated address" at the annual meetings of the Auxiliaries, and
New York clergymen--presumably in closer touch with activities
of the "Parent Society"--were invited to attend such local
meetings in "the period of their usual summer excursion...or
early fall when the dirt roads were most passable."

As the invention of movable type had vastly accelerated the printing process, so now at the beginning of the nineteenth century the replacement of hand-set blocks by stereotype plates produced a revolution of economy and convenience. In its first year of operation the British and Foreign Bible Society had recognized the long-run advantages of using stereotype. Having no stock of Scriptures on hand and no prior printing commitments, the American Bible Society determined to devote its initial investments to the purchase of plates which could be utilized in various parts of the country, thus reducing shipment costs. As early as July 15, 1816, the Managers directed that this policy be announced "in all the newspapers of the United States" and that Bible societies and individuals "throughout the Union" be requested to aid "in the prosecution of this arduous undertaking by pecuniary contributions."

The usual agreement was that plates should remain the property of the American Bible Society, which had authority to move them if necessary. The Auxiliary would pay transportation charges, could print any number of books for distribution within its own district *but not outside*, and must report regularly to New York the number of copies printed and their cost. In turn, the "Parent Society" at its own expense could request any number of books to be printed from the plates so located.

Within a few weeks of his return home from the founding convention in New York, James Blythe, President of the Kentucky Bible Society, requested a set of stereotype plates to be located at Lexington. The Kentucky application was granted, and at least three editions of two thousand copies each were printed. After considerable negotiation, however, the New York headquarters rejected a request to supply Bibles from Kentucky to other societies in "the West." Meanwhile an investigating committee reported that the Lexington edition was "badly executed," poor printing on poor paper with poor binding. Nevertheless one of the Society's Agents recorded in his journal (December, 1822) the opinion that "the wisdom of the Parent Society in locating plates in this place is still evident, and the more zealous and prudent this Auxiliary becomes, that wisdom will also appear more clearly."

The Board of Managers remained unimpressed, apparently concluding that the reputation as well as the efficiency of the Society depended on closer supervision of the printing process. Requests for stereotype plates for Cincinnati and Miami (Ohio), Utica (New York), and Boston (Massachusetts) seem not to have been met, and applications from Maryland and Pennsylvania were denied in 1823 and 1824.

Despite certain practical difficulties and failures, and with due allowance for the pious rhetoric of the period, the impact of the American Bible Society and its multiplying auxiliaries cannot be overestimated. From out-of-the-way places, by often tortuous communication, came reports to the New York headquarters telling of plaintive need or thrilling conversion. From the Bible Society of St. Charles, Missouri Territory, July 30, 1819:

We assure you that the Bible is received by many as a Messenger from Heaven, bearing to them the words of Eternal Life; and that many, notwithstanding a number have been distributed, are still destitute of that invaluable treasure. We therefore present ourselves before you, and ask, in the name of the needy and destitute, to send us the Bible. And we trust that your enlarged munificence will not withhold from your brethren of the West this sacred volume.....

At almost the same moment, only a short distance from the Society's offices in Manhattan, a missionary wrote from Babylon, Long Island:

...I am confident no region will be found in a Christian land where Bibles are more needed. There are here multitudes of people but just able to live, and who live and die almost as ignorant of the gospel as the Heathen. Many who observe no Sabbaths, enjoy no religious ordinances, and have no religion, and they value them not, for they have no Bibles.....the remains of three tribes of Indians...[m]any of these able to read, but destitute of a Bible.....also a considerable white population, whose situation is but little, if any, better than that of the Indians.....

From Pittsburgh, the Rev. Joseph Patterson, distributing hundreds of Bibles and Testaments to emigrant families headed down the Ohio to "the western country," reported the testimony of one "man of genteel appearance" in gratitude for Bible Societies:

'I was an ignorant wicked sailor, who sailed from New York; once after an arrival, I heard of a Bible Society for which money was collecting. I, and some of my companions, in a kind of thoughtless frolic, gave two dollars each. I don't recollect ever thinking of it, until, on a Sabbath near the Banks of Newfoundland, on a voyage to Europe, I took up a book in the steerage, and on the cover read "New York Bible Society." I felt my heart sink in a kind of involuntary horror; I took it to my birth [sic] and read, and saw plainly,

and felt deeply, that I was a lost sinner, very near
eternal destruction. Every place I turned to confirmed
the dreadful tidings. My distress was very great, I
prayed and searched the Scriptures, and through infinite mercy, before we reached land, I found the way of
salvation, and, I humbly trust, obtained grace to
embrace it. This is some years ago. I have quit the
sea, and I am now on my way with my family to the new
settlements.'

As the establishment of Auxiliaries throughout the country
flourished with the institution of a central American Bible
Society, so did its system of Agents--although the interrelation-
ship of these two programs was not always clearly formulated.
At its second meeting (May 21, 1816) the Board of Managers authorized the employment of "as many individuals to collect subscriptions throughout the city at such allowance for their services
as they [the Committee] may deem necessary." This procedure was
extended to other areas at the August meeting. Here was a recognition that individual and personal solicitation would be
necessary to supplement mail and public communication. Yet it
was not immediately obvious that such a policy might well trespass on territory covered by Auxiliaries.

Before long the Agents' duties were enlarged to include the
organization of local Auxiliaries. Samuel J. Mills, contemplat-
ing a third journey to the western and southern frontier,
offered in July (1816) to collect subscriptions for the Society.
His offer was gladly accepted, and when that autumn he was
engaged to travel for six months in the southern states, his
assignment was to secure subscriptions *and* to assist in forming
Auxiliary Societies. To what extent these two purposes might
represent conflicting methods, financially and organizationally,
for accomplishing the same end was apparently not discussed.

By the fall of 1818 the Board of Managers was ready to
recommend the appointment of both *"Stationary Agents*, to receive
and solicit, within their respective districts, donations and
subscriptions, and to aid in circulating the reports and documents of the Society.....and *Travelling Agents*, to pass through
the U. States and their territories, soliciting donations and
subscriptions, reporting on the state of morals and religion,
collecting information for the Board, and establishing
Auxiliary Societies...." However the final Board action merely
authorized plans "to appoint travelling Agents to organize
Auxiliary Societies, and otherwise to promote the objects of
this Society..." These itinerants were provided with sample
printed constitutions and with "hints for the formation of
Auxiliaries and other Bible Societies." The omission of
emphasis on collections and subscriptions may have represented

a growing recognition that Auxiliaries themselves should solicit funds, without competition from outside Agents. However the value of mutual information and encouragement, between local citizens and the national Society, was clearly emphasized.

Henceforth a number of Agents were employed in various regions: in Nantucket, New Bedford, and ports of Rhode Island; in Georgia and the Carolinas; but "mostly in the Western States." Contrary to the original proposal of a percentage of subscriptions and donations received, most of these men seem to have been paid at agreed rates (usually about $600 a year, plus expenses). Their specific task was to establish new auxiliaries and "excite greater activity" among old ones, providing for the Society "larger funds and more friends." If invited to preach, they were to focus on the importance of the Bible cause and stimulate liberality, above all being "careful to avoid any of the peculiarities of denomination, and dwell on those great essential truths of religion in which all the evangelical unite." According to the 1830 "Instructions of the Auxiliary Society Committee of the American Bible Society to the Agents:"

> The Bible cause has no sectarian character, and its Agents should give it none, either by their preaching or conversation. All metaphysical, sectional, or political topics, which divide the opinions even of many good men, are to be avoided by those whose great business is to circulate the Word of God as it was received from Heaven. Try to produce harmony, forbearance, and kindness among different denominations, by treating all who have the Christian spirit as members of the same great family and expectants of the same inheritance in their Father's house on high. You cannot feel too deeply the importance of your work, and the importance of looking continually to the Great Author of the Bible for wisdom and strength....

Where new societies were getting under way, Agents were expected to stress the "indispensable provisions:" distribution of the Bible without note or comment, placing surplus funds at the disposal of the ABS, membership dues low enough to attract participation from the entire community. But they were to remember that furnishing Scriptures to all the destitute within a given region should take precedence over the appeal for funds. "Are there not some wealthy and benevolent laymen who will become life directors or life members?.....Aim to give a permanency to all Auxiliaries--to make them feel that they are to act from year to year.....No society must think of relaxing its efforts, for a single year, until the *world* is supplied with the Bible."

Official instructions to the Agents specified that the Society would not furnish transport conveyance, but simply "necessary traveling expenses." However these ordinarily included "horse-keeping" and shoeing as well as tolls and meals and postage. There were occasions when the committee had to authorize the purchase or repair of a wagon, or acknowledged the sale or death of a horse. "It is recommended"--according to advice from headquarters--"that Agents, like the primitive disciples, live as much as can be done without waste of time, with the people of God." The implication that such hospitality, from local ministers and warm-hearted church members, might sometimes be costly in time and concentration reflects a familiar experience of many travelers.

In some instances harsh weather or illness delayed the journeys. An Ohio Agent spent ten days in the home of Former Governor Thomas Worthington, a Vice-President of the Society, confined to his room with "a bilious fever, contracted by passing over a country very subject to it." Yet he feared that he might be "deemed indecorous" to "look upon the kind hand of God in granting me such friends in such a time of need." On another occasion the same man, "very unwell" for four days, "ventured out" on the Sabbath to administer the Lord's Supper and preached morning and evening in the Methodist Church, only to find that "these two pulpit sweats perfectly relieved one"--so that he could meet the Board of Managers of the Bible Society on Monday morning.

Such personal visits in various parts of the country provided invaluable insight and information regarding the state of the church and of Bible societies, which could never have been obtained through official reports or formal correspondence. By 1822 the Kentucky Bible Society, once so eager to borrow stereotype plates and supply the entire western region, was adjudged in "a drooping state." Of Lancaster County, Pennsylvania, it was noted: "The state of vital piety is, I believe very deplorable in this section of country. Great ignorance of divine things--and darkness prevail, consequently, great vice and immorality." In Carlisle, Pennsylvania, an Agent reported that "a large audience, 'all but their attention dead' were present." In Warren, Pennsylvania, where "a languor prevailed too much," the Agent sought to dissolve inactive local associations and promote a stronger county auxiliary instead. Noting the scarcity of money and the depreciation of paper currency, as well as disastrous financial speculation, which were crippling many worthy causes, the Rev. R. D. Hall was moved to comment:

I hope our countrymen are beginning to learn wisdom at last, and hereafter will see the propriety of getting rich gradually & moral honesty--when men make wings and

fly to riches, how often riches make wings and fly away
from them! This has always appeared to me to be the
order of Providence, that the cupidity of mankind may be
checked, and if possible destroyed....

Noteworthy among the journals of these Traveling Agents is the
spirit of Christian brotherhood and cooperation in disregard of
denominational lines. Mr. Hall, to take but one example, appears
to have been an Episcopal priest. Yet on Bible Society business
he visited most cordially with Lutherans, Baptists, Methodists,
Friends, Presbyterians, Congregationalists, Swedenborgians, and
Shakers ("certainly the most singular of any in our land"). He
would preach in a Methodist Church at 5 a.m., in a Presbyterian
Church at 11, and for the Methodists again that evening, or to
Episcopalians in the afternoon and Baptists in the evening.
Furthermore, he was convinced that "those Bible Societies which
have been formed by *any particular* religious Society" failed to
secure general support because of suspicion--whether justified
or not--of "a sectarian spirit." Hall wrote:

> The propriety of sending out Agents to form Societies by
> calling together *all* sects is also more evident to me every
> step I take in my duties. I trust the happiest effects
> will follow the agency not only to religion in general,
> but to the Bible cause in particular, by securing the
> co-operation of all parties through the catholic measures
> pursued by the Agent.

Nevertheless Hall--and others like him--discovered that joint
organization did not guarantee harmony. Of the Bible Society in
Washington County, Pennsylvania, he reported: "The leading cause
which appears to have paralysed its efforts and reduced it to its
present state, is as I was informed the unhappy divisions which
have existed among the professors of religion who have been its
chief supporters. In consequence of disunion every good thing
has suffered a bad declension." Elsewhere in his travels he
deplored Socinianism, Arianism, "something like antinomianism"
and "what are called B i b l e c h r i s t i a n s .....By
this sect is meant persons who have no creeds or confessions."
In Ohio, too, "the asperity of feeling and local jealousies among
the different sects appear detrimental to the Bible cause here
and in this section of country." On the whole, however, Hall
reaffirmed his conviction "that among the numerous incidental
advantages growing out of Bible societies, that of promoting
unity of affection under diverse and irreconcilable opinion
obtains a prominent place."

At least fifty Traveling Agents were employed by the American
Bible Society during the 1830's, but several of these worked for
only a few days or weeks. In 1830 there were fourteen on the

payroll at one time; by 1837 this had risen to thirty-six during
the year. Most salaries ranged from $600 to $1,500 annually,
depending on family obligations, distance travelled, length of
service, etc. As the effectiveness of the Agents became more
obvious and their number gradually increased, the directives
issued from New York became more explicit and more systematic.
A formal document circulated in 1839 gave this precise commission
for Agents:

> ...to revive Auxiliary Bible Societies where they are
> languishing; to form new ones where none yet exist, and
> to endeavor to persuade all to take effective measures
> for supplying every destitute family within their
> bounds with the Bible, and every Sunday School scholar
> with a New Testament. He will also endeavor to procure
> Life Directorships and Life Memberships, Subscriptions,
> and Contributions in aid of the Parent Society, to pro-
> mote, in all proper ways, the great interests of the
> Bible cause.

To this end the Society provided its Agents with a kit of
books and materials sufficient to counterbalance a saddle-bag
full of Bibles: a blank book for use as a Journal, with separate
sections for "Books Sold," "Donations Received," "Traveling
Expenses and Postage," and "Letters Despatche ;" a portable map
to "study the geography and general character" of the territory
to be occupied; the Annual Report of the Society, plus the
Appendix and Monthly Extracts to supply information on the
character and condition of the institution--both national and
local. Detailed instructions were to be read "until you *perfectly*
understand them," Agents were warned, for "neglect of this advice
will cause your labors to be unsystematic and fruitless, and your
correspondence confused and unintelligible."

Since their main business would be with Auxiliaries, Agents
were advised to investigate each one carefully--state, county,
village, or district--to "learn its exact present condition."
Some would be found much in debt, others little. If the local
society was in debt, the Agent was to ascertain why?...what were
the prospects for payment?...was there a likelihood of recouping
financially through a donation of books to be sold? Agents were
further advised to restudy destitute areas "in a systematic,
thorough manner," but to visit various parts of a territory
before forming new auxiliaries, lest a single community prove
unduly zealous, overoptimistic--or pessimistic--about the
prospects for cultivation and support. In most cases a public
meeting for clarification and exhortation, across denominational
lines, was recommended as more productive than relying solely on
committed individuals.

In American history the Methodist circuit rider has become the acknowledged symbol of the Gospel on the frontier. Yet a kindred brother in the Lord, the Traveling Agent cf the American Bible Society, has left a comparable record of achievement and of fascinating history. One of these stalwart representatives estimated that in a year he "traveled upward of 8,000 miles: about one half the distance in steam-boats, flat-boats, skiffs, &c; and the other half on horseback, upon my own, and thirteen borrowed and hired horses." The Rev. John Wilson, a Baptist Agent in Kentucky, reported that during the year of 1833 he had delivered 305 sermons, distributed 6,688 Bibles and Testaments, traveled 2,356 miles, collected $2,782, visited forty counties and "provided for" seven others, and stimulated Scriptural supply in twenty counties and one city. "Beyond this," he concluded, "the value of my labors has consisted in the moral influence, or happy revolution of sentiment in relation to the Bible cause, which I have had evidence to believe has been produced." Still another Agent, from Washington County, Arkansas, claimed that he had reached "the extreme boundary of the United States, and of civilization."

Dr. Samuel Robinson, a dedicated physician, was made a Life Member by the Society for his work in organizing Auxiliaries in North Carolina. At the end of one five-months' journey he wrote:

> Notwithstanding the cold, fatigue, danger, and all the difficulties I had to encounter during my last tour in this state in the Bible cause, the success with which my weak labours have been crowned, and the kindness and Christian hospitality with which I have been in many places received, have rendered all my exertions pleasant, and my paths delightful. In those places where I met with that welcome reception and Christian benevolence, which is so characteristic of the people of the south, and of the practical Christian; the language of their conduct seemed to say, Welcome stranger; thrice welcome those whose message is to diffuse the glad tidings of the Gospel of peace.

Annual Reports of the ABS during the first two decades are filled with detailed travelogues—complete with "constant rains, swollen streams, and impassable roads." They are also filled with personal accounts of individual encounters: men and women in desperate need of the Scriptures, men and women in bitter rebellion against the Word of God. From Kentucky in 1832 came two such stories, of fathers who angrily refused to permit a Bible within their homes, of Agents and wives who quietly per- sisted. In one instance the man's curiosity and growing interest finally prompted him to pay for the once-forbidden book, but the Agent admitted that he had "not yet learned whether it has

produced any permanent and saving effect upon [the husband's]
heart." In the second case, the father had been enraged at the
mere offer of a Bible but had finally yielded. Here, according
to the Agent, a man who had been "profane and extremely dissi-
pated...soon ceased to take the name of God in vain, became a
sober man, a regular attendant with his wife and family upon the
ministration of the word, and...now a member of the Methodist
church."

Thus the Traveling Agents of the American Bible Society
supplemented, encouraged, and supported the efforts of local
Auxiliaries, both in the circulation of Scriptures and in the
raising of funds for the "Parent Society." During the 1830's
the Agency system cost, on the average, between five and six
thousand dollars a year. How much these itinerant representatives collected for the cause is impossible to estimate, since
many of the contributions which they inspired were channeled
through Auxiliaries.

But the value of Agents and Auxiliaries--or of direct mail
solicitation--cannot be measured in strictly monetary terms.
Alexander Proudfit, a delegate to the founding convention of the
ABS in 1816 and later President of the Washington County (New
York) Bible Society, traveled extensively on behalf of these
organizations. At the end of one of his tours as an Agent he
concluded:

If there was not a single dollar added to the public
treasury, nor a single copy of the scriptures thrown
into circulation in consequence of these agencies, there
are other considerations which amply compensate for all
the expenditure of time and money which they occasion.
The members of the spiritual family, from various parts
of the christian world, are thus brought into intimate
and delightful fellowship; they form that acquaintance
here which is introductory to an eternal intercourse in
their Father's kingdom; the bond between the different
constituent parts of the church universal, is strengthened; each becomes more deeply interested in the prosperity of the other; their gifts and their graces, by
this interchange of every expression of love, are
improved and expanded.....

4

The General Supply

The population of the United States, potential readers of the
Bible, multiplied rapidly during the first few decades of the
nation's history. In 1790 there were 3,929,214 Americans,
5,308,483 in 1800, 7,239,881 in 1810, and 9,638,453 by 1820,
representing a growth rate of approximately one-third each
decade. Most of this increase came from a natural rise of
births over deaths, for the great flood of immigration from
Europe did not begin until after this period. But already great
numbers were traveling westward to open up new territories. From
1800 to 1820 the population of the West, beyond the original
thirteen states, jumped from 400,000 to two million.

Samuel J. Mills' account of the appalling Scriptural "famine"
on the western and southern frontiers of the United States had
contributed substantially to the establishment of the American
Bible Society. The Agents who followed in his footsteps along
the Mississippi, deep in the Appalachians, and among the bayous,
reported--as he had--thousands of settlers without the printed
Word of God. As the Bible Society approached the end of its
first decade, it encouraged its Agents and Auxiliaries to investigate the spiritual poverty of the entire nation. Statistics were
gathered not only by concerned churchmen, but by census takers
and tax collectors in various localities. The conclusions were
shocking.

A woman in the nation's capital inquired, "What is a Bible?"
"She could read," one Agent explained, "but could not tell
whether they had such a thing in the house; but her husband told
me they had not."

"Ohio comprises about 100,000 families & I should not be surprised if one-fifth were found without a Bible in their tenements. What a state of things!" another Agent exclaimed.

Nine counties out of thirty-six in Alabama in 1825 counted 2,695 families with Bibles, 2,378 with none, an estimated total need throughout the state for nearly 100,000 copies.

On the very doorstep of the Society, two wards in the city of New York were found to have 588 families, 1,778 persons over ten years of age who could read, without any Scriptures.

In North Carolina there "cannot be less than 10,000 families... living and training up their households without the Bible."

"...Not more than half of the families in the County [of a Western state] possess the heavenly gift."

"[There must be] between 600 and 700 families...without the precious Volume of inspiration."

Fired by such deplorable conditions, even in populous centers of the East, students at the College of New Jersey in Princeton adopted the following resolution in 1827: "that the Nassau Hall Bible Society will this year if possible, relying upon the blessing of God, supply every family of New Jersey that is destitute of the Bible, with the cooperation of the other Bible Societies in the state." Thus challenged by its junior neighbor, the Philadelphia Bible Society voted in September of that year to "make the effort to supply every destitute family in the State of Pennsylvania with a copy of the Sacred Scriptures."

Robert Ralston, a founder and Treasurer of the Philadelphia Society since 1808, a Manager of the ABS from 1816 and a Vice-President from 1828-36, promptly made two inquiries of the American Bible Society Agent. First, he asked, would the national organization be able to furnish a large quantity of stereotype plates, and if so, "in what period of time and the price?" Second, he sought advice as to whether a time limit should be set for such an ambitious undertaking. On one hand, if the organization were committed to a deadline, it might "hereafter appear inconsistant;" on the other hand, "without a limitation...there may be less exertion." Whether the Agent or ABS headquarters proffered such assistance or advice is not recorded, but during the following year the Philadelphia Bible Society paid the national body over $1,500 for Scriptures, indicating a significant effort at total circulation.

Early in 1829 Dr. Alexander Proudfit, a founder and part-time Agent of the ABS, reported that there was now "scarcely a family

in the County of Washington (New York) without a copy of the
Sacred Oracles." Eager to extend such blessings to "destitute
families throughout the United States and its territories," the
Salem Bible Society pledged five thousand dollars "towards the
execution of this magnanimous purpose...within two years."

> We are persuaded [the officers added] that there is not
> only ability, but liberality enough in the friends of our
> Master, and of these perishing thousands, to aid you in
> the achievement of this mighty and magnificent project.....
> This, we are fully assured, would be a greater pledge of
> prosperity to our highly favored nation, and of perpetuity
> to our civil institutions, than all the purity of our
> patriots, or all the wisdom of our statesmen, or the
> prowess of our armies and navies.

With such examples and encouragement the American Bible Society
could hardly remain indifferent. So daring was the proposal that
it was not only referred to committee but also subjected to
thorough examination by the Board of Managers in at least four
sessions during March and April. At the 1829 Annual Meeting of
the Society the following resolution, already approved by the
Board of Managers, was moved by the Secretary for Foreign
Correspondence, James Milnor, and seconded by Lyman Beecher, the
famous preacher from Connecticut:

> That this Society, with humble reliance upon Divine aid
> will endeavor to supply all the destitute families in the
> United States with the Holy Scriptures, that may be will-
> ing to purchase or receive them, within the space of two
> years, provided sufficient means be furnished by its
> Auxiliaries and benevolent individuals, in season to
> enable the Board of Managers to carry their resolution
> into effect.

In his supporting speech Milnor, rector of St. George's
Episcopal Church in New York, who served on the Bible Society
staff for twenty-one years without salary, reviewed fully and
frankly what would be required to place the Bible "in every
house, in every cottage of our wide-spread country, from Maine
to Georgia, from the shores of the Atlantic to the Rocky
Mountains, whose doors shall be opened by their owners to its
admission." The achievements of New Jersey "entirely," Maryland
and Vermont "nearly," and a large number of county Bible
societies which have "faithfully and fully accomplished the
work" gave hope that it could be done, although two years before
"its authors would have been smiled at as Utopians."

Mechanically, the enormous task could be accomplished, the
speaker explained. Eight steam presses were already in

operation, eight more to be installed during the summer. Where
stocks a year earlier had numbered about 18,000 books, there
were now 100,000 bound and an equal number unbound or partially
completed. It would soon be possible, Milnor declared, to print
5-600,000 copies annually and to increase that figure by another
200,000 when building space for printing and binding became
available.

Thus the immediate problem was financial, the responsibility
almost entirely of Auxiliaries. Already these local societies,
numbering over six hundred, owed the ABS $30,000 in accounts due,
but a vast increase in remittances and donations would be
necessary to finance the maximum output envisioned. To provide
Scriptures for 800,000 destitute families would cost $480,000,
or $800 from each Auxiliary: "But this of course is not to be
expected. The deficiencies of the poor must be supplied by the
abundance of the rich." Finally, Milnor reminded his audience,
the Bible Society's task would not be over even *when*--not *if*!--
they met two years hence "not to boast of the fulfilment of this
great work, but to give God the praise for its completion." A
rapidly expanding population would require that the projected
efforts be sustained permanently to meet the regular demand and
to "circulate among new millions of inhabitants, the uncorrupted
Word of God."

To launch immediate plans for implementation, the Board
approved a printed "Address to the Public" from the President,
Vice-Presidents, and Secretaries; the cultivation of clergy,
influential laymen, and other friends through a general meeting;
and strong encouragement to Auxiliaries to meet their debts,
raise new funds, carefully survey their districts, and make plans
for distributing Scriptures to the destitute. The General
Supply--as this effort for total coverage came to be called--
attracted great enthusiasm in many parts of the country. To
encourage local responsibility the Society offered a system of
"special sale" in which Scriptures would be supplied to
Auxiliaries and other societies on the understanding that they
would remit to New York the entire proceeds from any sale of
such books, as well as any collections received. Particularly
large grants were made to North Carolina and Virginia on this
basis, and in two years a total of 42,975 Bibles and 4,425
Testaments were distributed under this particular provision.
However the resultant income, the prices asked and accepted for
Scriptures, even the degree of effort on the part of local
groups, all proved completely unpredictable. Therefore in 1831
the Board returned to a policy which differentiated between
sales on credit (for a specific amount) and books which the
"Parent Society" itself could designate as donations, either for
sale (to the benefit of the local auxiliary) or for free distribution.

The "Address to the Friends of the Bible of every religious Denomination in the United States" (dated June 4, 1829) described the General Supply as "one of those bold, but not presumptuous measures, as harbingers, we believe, of the latter day glory of of the church." The preacher of saving doctrines, the "indefatigable missionary," "the pious Sunday School teacher," and "the compiler of the useful Tract," all must derive their message from one "pure and sacred source," it declared, "but the Bible, as an immediate revelation from God himself, is an unerring guide,-- the common and conclusive standard of faith and practice, prescribed to the whole family of man."

Therefore, it was argued, Bible societies should be enlisted, revived, reorganized, newly instituted--as the situation might demand--to ascertain the needs (for purchase at cost, for purchase below cost, and for "gratuitous donation") and the resources available to meet those needs. Special appeals for active support were directed to ministers, theological students, female Bible societies, and "youth of both sexes." "The widow's mite will be acceptable, while wealthy Christians should feel constrained to devote a liberal portion of their substance to an undertaking on which the salvation of thousands may depend." The magnitude of the task thus set forth was clearly recognized. Dr. Milnor in his original recommendation acknowledged that:

> The Society does not engage positively to supply every destitute family: that would be presumptuous, for the inscrutable Providence of God might permit unanticipated and insuperable difficulties to arise, and prevent it. It looks primarily to God for his benediction. It will endeavor to supply, in dependence on the blessing of God.....

As in all such campaigns, the very scope and nobility of purpose inspired great and little deeds of genuine sacrifice. On the day the resolution was adopted by the Board of Managers, sixty-one girls employed in the bindery pledged seventy-five cents each, and the manager of the bindery doubled their gift; twenty-six men in the bindery gave as many dollars, and fifty-two in the printing office pledged $46. From all sources the first year's total receipts for the General Supply amounted to $44,480.30.

At the Annual Meeting in May, 1831, at the end of the designated time for the campaign, the following resolution was adopted:

> Resolved that while a delay of Funds and the severity of the past winter have prevented the full redemption of the pledge to supply the United States with Bibles, in two years, there is still occasion for unfeigned gratitude

to God that so much has been done towards the accomplishment of the enterprize, and also encouragement to expect,
in the continued exertions of Auxiliaries and Friends,
that the entire supply contemplated may be soon effected.

A year previously the Bible Society of Philadelphia, which
had initiated this kind of effort at total coverage in 1827,
celebrated its twenty-second anniversary by announcing "the
completion of the great work of supplying every destitute family
in the State of Pennsylvania with a copy of the Holy Scriptures,
within the space of three years." Through an ample supply of
books and funds, published addresses, commissioned agents,
extensive correspondence with each county, every application for
assistance had been met. According to the Philadelphia Society's
review:

> The committee do not say nor believe that every family in
> the State is in possession of the Sacred Scriptures; for
> some have been unwilling either to buy or receive them as
> a gratuity; and in so large a field of inquiry as this
> State has presented, it is probable some have been over-
> looked, and perhaps some individuals have not completed
> their distribution.....The work is done. In less than
> two years and a half the destitute families in this large
> State, possessing a population of 1,200,000 have been
> supplied with the Heavenly Oracles. Every family willing
> to possess the privilege, may now read the glad tidings
> of salvation, and learn the way to everlasting happiness.

In 1831 the American Bible Society made no such claims. To
be sure, they had met the demand for books from all the cooperating societies--at the cost of a very substantial debt. They had
been prudent and cautious wherever there was doubt that the
Scriptures would be really welcomed or responsibly distributed.
They retained confidence that many districts would be completely
supplied by the end of the summer--after a winter of deep snows,
rains, and swollen streams.

Thirteen states and territories reported the work "substantial
completed:" Maine, New Hampshire, Vermont, Massachusetts, Rhode
Island, Connecticut, New York, New Jersey, Pennsylvania, Maryland
Virginia, Mississippi, and Michigan Territory. In eight others
about three fourths of the goal had been achieved: Delaware,
North Carolina, South Carolina, Georgia, Kentucky, Tennessee,
Ohio, and Louisiana; about half in Indiana and Illinois, less
than half in Missouri, Alabama, Arkansas and Florida. However
it was recognized that in some of these places a "general supply"
accomplished a few years earlier had probably been out-run by
subsequent population growth.

Neither bare statistics nor florid rhetoric can convey the
impact of this effort in human terms, for families receiving
their first copy of the Holy Scriptures, or for volunteer workers
discovering materials and spiritual poverty. Maine distributed
at least 13,000 Bibles in three years. New Hampshire endeavored
to supply every adult reader with his own Bible and every Sunday
School scholar a New Testament "with his own name affixed."
Vermont found that "many, and some of them among the poor," were
willing to pay for their Scriptures at a reduced price. The
Massachusetts Bible Society "with the utmost cordiality" agreed
to make a donation of $500 and to loan the national Society
$3,000 at five per cent interest, payable annually in Bibles.
For New Jersey it was proposed that a reorganization might
profitably replace small township auxiliaries with county
societies. From Pennsylvania came a report that a deputy
marshal in one county had "discovered *fifteen* or *twenty* families
destitute."

"The quotations are made," the Annual Report of 1831 explained,
"to show not only, that Auxiliaries which have once supplied
their destitute ought to be kept in *existence*, but ought to make
efforts every year to circulate the Bible at home, as well as to
aid in Foreign distributions."

Illustrations of purpose--and sometimes of success--were
equally varied. Maryland aimed to give Bibles to all pupils on
leaving the Sabbath School, "especially to those who are to
become *apprentices*." A Juvenile Association of Baltimore contributed $26.50 to aid in the printing of Tamil Scriptures in
Ceylon. In Virginia, "one of our largest States in universal
possession of the word of God,....Christians of different
denominations are becoming more and more united, and more active
in the Bible cause than they have ever been at any former
period." In North Carolina, cited as a praiseworthy example,
a newly married couple bought two Bibles "and agreed to read
them through together, that we may assist each other in understanding and remembering them." New York claimed a Bible Society
in every single county, except for three counties forming one
Auxiliary on Long Island. "In no part of the Union," according
to another boast, "has a better spirit been manifested toward
the Bible cause than in Georgia."

A story appearing in that same 1831 Annual Report came from
an Agent in the mountains of New Hampshire:

[He] entered the unfrequented hovel of a hermit, and though
the tenant was at the time absent, the Agent did not leave
his lonely habitation destitute of the sure guide to
Heaven--the word of God. The next Sabbath, soon after the
services of the sanctuary had commenced, to the astonishment

of the whole congregation, 'the hermit of the mountain,'
as is supposed for the first time in his life, entered the
house of God, and through the day gave earnest attention
to the word dispensed.

Many state and district reports, at the end of the two years
set for the General Supply, expressed the hope--or the firm
conviction--that total coverage in the area would be achieved
within the succeeding year. It is therefore of interest to refer
to the 1832 Annual Report as a sort of postscript--both to achievement
and to unfinished business. That summation voiced less
solicitude about the few portions of the country where supply was
incomplete than about areas where re-supply was already needed.
One county in New York, for example, thoroughly canvassed and
supplied in 1826, discovered 990 families four years later without
a Bible, five hundred of them without even a New Testament.
An Auxiliary in Illinois found 128 families without the Bible in
a county which had been fully covered as late as 1830. Only
continuous re-investigation "in a systematic manner from year to
year," the Managers concluded, would "*keep* the word of life in
every dwelling, or prevent thousands of our countrymen annually
from going, unenlightened and unwarned, to the grave."

In statistical terms the accomplishments of the General Supply
were obvious. Circulation for the year 1827-28 had been 74,428
Bibles and 57,427 Testaments--and it is noteworthy that the
entire Bible continued at this period to outdistance the separate
New Testament. During the two years of the General Supply these
figures took a dramatic leap upward: 129,996 Bibles and 93,170
Testaments in 1829-30, and 171,967 Bibles and 70,058 Testaments
in 1830-31. For the next five years, however, distribution
registered a sharp decline, though not to the level before 1827.
In fact, for the two decades from 1821 to 1840 circulation of
Scriptures increased at a rate faster than that of population
growth, despite a severe financial panic in 1837.

Of equal importance in the wake of the General Supply was the
Society's retrospective evaluation of policy. "That good and
evil both have resulted from the undertaking, they [the Managers]
are fully convinced." For most Auxiliaries the General Supply
inspired powerful new impulses and efforts. In some the result
was increased pledges, in others more thorough exploration of
neglected areas. Nearly half a million copies of Scriptures
distributed during the period represented a not insignificant
influence, especially on the western and southern frontiers.
"Another good effect of this undertaking," the 1832 Annual
Report pointed out, "has been to show the religious community
the degraded state of those around them who can live without the
Bible, and thus to lead on to other efforts for their moral
improvement." Communities which engaged in comprehensive and

conscientious surveys found an alarming shortage of schools and churches as well as Bibles, a distressing prevalence of "intemperance, profanity, falsehood, and Sabbath-breaking." Further on the positive side stood a fresh appreciation of the Bible among those who already owned it, a renewed commitment to its study and circulation.

On the other hand, the Managers recognized certain evils attending the General Supply, related both to the "Parent Society" and to many of the Auxiliaries. In an effort to make a vast quantity of books available quickly to many parts of the country, the Society borrowed heavily for paper and for printing operations, and there were months of acute "pecuniary pressure." Admittedly, in "the hurry of supply," many books were poorly printed and poorly bound, many local surveys were superficial and inaccurate. In their eagerness to provide all the destitute with Scriptures, societies encouraged too many people to expect donations without compensation, thus weakening the motive to buy among some who could afford to do so, and consequently raising the cost for the total venture. "But the most serious of all the evils attending this work," the Annual Report warned, "was on many of the Auxiliaries themselves, the apathy which followed the season of high excitement and great exertion." Indeed this apprehension seemed to be fulfilled by an estimate five years after the General Supply that between 250,000 and 300,000 families were without Bibles in 1836.

Yet this apathy and neglect were not universal. As supporters of the Bible cause returned to more normal and regular pursuits, they discerned other areas of special opportunity. One of these was among "Colored Persons and Slaves." Negroes had always been recognized among the destitute in need of Scriptures, and at least three African Bible Societies had been formed—to minister to blacks in the United States. In 1834, perhaps inspired by the spirit of the General Supply, the American Anti-Slavery Society proposed to the American Bible Society that $20,000 be appropriated for the purpose of providing every Negro family, not already supplied, with a copy of the Bible within two years. Toward this goal the Anti-Slavery Society pledged a quarter of the estimated cost.

With a caution unlike its earlier enthusiasms—a caution born in part of frustrations from the General Supply but also, perhaps, of diplomatic sensitivity to the racial problem in American society—the Managers affirmed their appreciation and willingness to help. But, they declared, they must leave "the direct labor of distributing these books as well as the responsibility of selecting the proper families and individuals within their respective limits who are to receive them,...wholly to the wisdom and piety of those who compose these local associations in the different States and Territories."

Unrebuffed, the Anti-Slavery Society renewed its offer of $5,000 and "earnestly entreated" the ABS to request its Auxiliaries to see "that every colored family in the United States be furnished with a copy of the Bible." The Bible Society replied that it had nothing to add to its previous policy statement, that it had in the intervening year made a number of efforts to provide Scriptures for slaves, and that it would do more "in conformity with the rules which subsist between the Parent Society and its local auxiliaries."

In this dilemma the ABS found itself caught between two increasingly determined, even fanatical, forces. Within four months after the Anti-Slavery Society made its second appeal, the President of the Newberry (South Carolina) Bible Society forwarded to New York a newspaper story charging that four steam presses of the "Parent Society" were being used night and day to print abolitionist tracts. Added the Newberry president:

> No southern society can remain auxiliary to, nor can any southern man continue to assist, a society capable of perverting, in this fraudulent manner, the contributions to purposes so dangerous not only to their property, but to the peace and even to the lives of the people of the south. If the Bible Society has been guilty of hypocrisy so base as to cajole southern christians out of their money under the pretense that it was intended to propagate the gospel of peace, while it was really intended to employ it for the purpose of scattering publications inciting the slaves to cut the throats of the generous but deluded contributors, the fact should be known. But this will not readily be believed. Justice forbids that a conclusion so harsh; (one which must set the friends of the Bible in opposition to a society established supposedly for the exclusive purpose of spreading the word of God over the whole earth;) should be irrevocably drawn from a charge which may have originated in that disregard of truth which generally accompanies settled infidelity. It may be that the author of the extract is an enemy of the Gospel, and that he is actuated by hatred of the instruments of its propagation. Or it may be that he has been misinformed....

The writer concluded that his Auxiliary would not forward any further contributions until they were given some explanation with which to refute these charges or to "direct us in the future, if the charge is well founded."

The reply from the "Parent Society" expressed astonishment that any friend of the Bible cause could write "nearly a whole letter as if it [the charge] might be true." It cited other accusations, previously received, as equally preposterous: making six dollars on each book sold, or even "having written and sent out the Bible as a Yankee speculation." In this instance, for the first time, the Society agreed that a correction was demanded and would be forthcoming. John C. Brigham, Corresponding Secretary from 1828 to 1862, added this further assurance: "Meanwhile, I will state to you that the ABS does not own a press of any kind. Our work is done by a worthy religious printer on contract and who assures us that he never printed a line for the Abolitionists."

Thus even the "simple, noble object" of dispensing Scriptures without note or comment suffered between opposing pressures and prejudices. As late as 1848 the Annual Report quoted Agents in Virginia and North Carolina to the effect that they found no obstacle to distributing Bibles among slaves who could read, and that they could remember no instance of a Bible being refused to any Negro. Yet the very fear that furnishing every Negro family in America with a Bible might threaten the institution of slavery suggested once again the power of the Gospel.

Another movement which gained momentum in the wake of the General Supply was the growth of Sunday Schools. Although the Bible Society consistently rejected any involvement with tracts or commentaries, it early recognized the importance of placing Scriptures in the hands of children. It did this first by issuing a Sunday School Bible at fifty-five cents, less twenty per cent discount for school use. It did this by donating twenty thousand New Testaments to the non-denominational American Sunday School Union, established in 1824, which sought "to establish Sunday Schools extensively in the Valley of the Mississippi." It did this also by encouraging the Auxiliaries to emulate Strafford, New Hampshire, in supplying every child in the county with a New Testament. To this end the Society lowered the price of the Sunday School Bible to forty-five cents and published a Sunday School Testament at nine cents. Beyond this, it encouraged Auxiliaries which had exhausted their own resources for this youth supply to "make known their remaining wants to the American Bible Society for the purpose of obtaining gratuitous aid."

Reaffirming denominational impartiality and the importance of Auxiliary cooperation, the 1835 Annual Report declared:

It is obvious to every moral observer that our free institutions, civil and religious, depend for perpetuity on a
pure public sentiment, which nothing but the Bible can
preserve and keep in healthy action. It is equally
obvious, that to create a love and respect for the Bible,
a familiar acquaintance with it must be early formed.....

> Under our political system, the moral training of the
> indigent is no less important than that of the affluent;
> all have power which may affect that system for good or
> for evil, and all are alike in need of that holiness which
> the Bible inculcates, and without which no man shall see
> the Lord.

The most active partner in this enterprise was the Methodist
Episcopal Sunday School Union, which in the eighteen-forties
circulated 3,500 Bibles and 20,700 New Testaments, over one-half
of the total grants made for Sunday Schools.

The Board of Managers could also call attention, by 1837, to
a rising interest in the use of the Bible in the public schools
of the nation. A group of professional teachers in Cincinnati,
for example, urged "that the B I B L E - no selection from the
Bible, but the B I B L E itself - *ought to constitute the class-
book* in our common schools. Only the Bible can spread over the
whole ground."

Still another special emphasis of the American Bible Society
over the years, service to the blind, began in the eighteen-
thirties.   The first school for the blind was incorporated in
Boston in 1829; others appeared shortly in New York, Pennsylvania,
Ohio, and Virginia. At a meeting in Boston on May 31, 1833, a
recommendation that the ABS print an edition of the New Testament
in raised letters for the blind was adopted--and supported by a
collection of $190. Aware of the great bulk and great expense of
such an edition, the Standing Committee heard with interest a
report that various individuals were in the process of devising
"some practicable shorthand system" and "that great improvements
in the Science may be anticipated within probably the ensuing
year."

Nevertheless the Managers immediately expressed willingness
to investigate this field, and two years later appropriated
$1,000 to the New England Institution for the Education of the
Blind to further Dr. Samuel G. Howe's method of raised printing.
By the fall of 1836 Dr. Howe had reduced his four-volume New
Testament to two volumes, and was distributing them selectively
to blind persons who had learned to read sample passages. Meanwhile the British and Foreign Bible Society contributed ₤150
toward a raised-letter edition of the Psalms. At the time it was
estimated that, among over six thousand blind persons in the
United States, perhaps one third could be taught to read. However, in addition to those distributed by Dr. Howe, including
some to Great Britain, the Bible Society itself issued only
fifteen sets of the New Testament for the blind in the years
1838-40.

Whether it was ever true that, in any single locality, *every* person who would accept a copy of Scriptures had received one, the massive goal of General Supply did set in motion many vital developments. Some of these, for Negroes and the blind, have already been reviewed.

In an effort to reach all military personnel, permission was granted by the War Department "to put Bibles in the bundles of clothing destined for the different posts." Smith Thompson, one of the original Vice-Presidents of the ABS and later an Associate Justice of the Supreme Court, served as Secretary of the Navy from 1819 to 1823. In this position he arranged for the distribution of 3,500 copies of Scripture for every seaman and petty officer in the U.S. Navy. Wherever possible, books were supplied for the crews of ships and barges on the Great Lakes, the Ohio and Mississippi Rivers, and other inland waterways.

To French, German, Spanish, Welsh, and a handful of Dutch Scriptures distributed in earlier years, the Society in the late 'thirties reflected a new tide of immigration by adding Bibles and Testaments in Portuguese, Italian, Swedish, Danish, Polish, and Irish. In 1836 grants were made to provide Bibles for "Portuguese pirates in prison" in Virginia. On the west coast of South America a naval officer handed out two hundred books to Peruvian sailors and marines, "where I doubt very much if a Bible had ever been seen." In its first venture with single Portions, the Society provided five hundred copies of the Gospel of Luke in the Mohawk tongue and 750 in the Seneca language, during the eighteen-twenties. At the same time the ABS provided 545 English Bibles, 1,215 English Testaments, 55 French Bibles, and 10 French Testaments for use in Indian schools, the French editions primarily for Canada.

Thus, through its first quarter century of operation, the American Bible Society strove with fervent dedication to reach all sorts of conditions of men, within the boundaries of the United States and beyond. There were great achievements and great spiritual rewards, not only for the officers and members and agents, but for thousands of humble Christians whose prayers and donations helped to disseminate the Scriptures. Yet looking back ten years on the ambitious and far-reaching General Supply, the Board of Managers in 1840 made some sober appraisals. Half apologetically, they recalled that they themselves did not propose the enterprise and had referred it to their constituents "not without misgivings." Despite these reservations (which were by no means so apparent in earlier documents), "never, perhaps, did an object of benevolence meet with more universal approbation." Unquestionably, the distribution of nearly half a million Bibles in two years "was of incalculable value."

Nevertheless, the Managers confessed that "they were afraid
of the syncope which should follow such a high state of excitement, afraid of the long drought which should succeed such a pro-
fusion of rain." In retrospect they concluded "that more, on the
whole, would have been gained by a steady adherence to the mode
in which the Bible cause was carried on when this great two years'
effort was proposed." In many areas a systematic "general supply"
was already under way, and a more gradual process might have
avoided the "general excitement, to be followed by a general
apathy...the prevalent impression that our Bible work was finished
and a time for rest had come.....The result was, very many of the
Auxiliaries fell into a profound slumber, from which some have not
awaked to this day."

During its first twenty-five years the American Bible Society
felt its way toward enlarging responsibilities. Largely preoccupied with domestic needs, it sent shipments of books to scattered
missions abroad whenever a suitable occasion arose. Yet, as the
next chapter recounts, increasing involvement with other countries
led to increasing problems: in texts and translations, in
potential competition with other societies, in administrative
complexities.

Within the United States, however, certain trends were becoming clearer. One was the importance of retaining direct supervision of printing operations, to uphold quality and economy.
Stereotype plates, the effective new process for mass publication,
guaranteed a large measure of uniformity. Most printing and
binding contracts were made with individual operators, but these
private companies were drawn closer and closer to the Bible
Society by a preponderance of orders, sometimes by loans from
the ABS for the purchase of presses, and by renting space in
Bible Society premises.

As the volume--and variety--of business grew, so did the paid
staff. Volunteer secretaries for foreign and domestic correspondence became full-time employees, designated after 1833 as
Corresponding Secretaries. Participation in Board meetings by
officers of Auxiliaries, or in annual meetings by all ordained
clergymen, had to be curtailed. From the beginning Elias
Boudinot, the first President, had favored formal incorporation
of the Society, but did not wish to push the matter against considerable opposition--presumably by those who believed a religious
organization should remain as informal and "voluntary" as possible.
In those early days the single purpose of publishing and circulating the Scriptures without note or comment met almost universal
acceptance. Nor did anyone question that within the larger partnership of Christian laymen and clergy, the former should compose
the Board of Managers.

How should the expanding budget be raised? How should the
widespread destitution of Scriptures be alleviated most rapidly
and effectively? These were the major problems which beset the
officers and directors. Although scores of local societies had
joined the national organization as Auxiliaries, many of these
were preoccupied with needs in their own regions. Others
tended, as the Philadelphia Society had warned, to relax their
efforts and leave responsibility to the "Parent Society." In
vast areas of a new country population was too sparse to encourage
organized activity.

For these and other reasons, therefore, Agents were appointed,
initially to stimulate the formation of new Auxiliaries and
renewed efforts on the part of old ones. Eventually they found
themselves also raising money for the national Society, either
directly or indirectly. The decision to charge nominal prices,
wherever possible, for Bibles circulated was in part psychological,
to instill greater respect for the Scriptures, in part economic,
to utilize financial resources more widely. Quite naturally,
donations for the benevolent work of the Society came chiefly
from areas where long-established churches possessed greatest
wealth and strength. For example, during the Society's first
four years, income for the Bible cause came--through churches,
auxiliaries, and individuals--in the following percentages from
principal geographical areas:

New England	34.6%
New York, New Jersey, Pennsylvania, Delaware	29.3%
Virginia and North and South Carolina	18.9%
Georgia and Florida	5.9%
Ohio, Indiana, Illinois, Michigan	5.4%
Kentucky and Tennessee	3.6%
Maryland and the District of Columbia	2.2%

On the other hand, from the frontier settlements of Alabama,
Mississippi, Louisiana, and Missouri, where the need was greatest,
financial support was minimal. Here lay the principal missionary
opportunity of the American Bible Society in its infant years.

Very early in its lifetime the ABS recognized, specifically
and deliberately, the need for the Word of God among special
groups: slaves, blind, soldiers, sailors, migrants to the west,
immigrants from the east, children, prisoners, Indians. Despite
the phenomenal population growth during the nineteenth century,
the proportion of church members increased even more rapidly, as
the following figures(1) indicate:

1810	7.0%	1840	14.4%
1820	11.2%	1850	15.5%
1830	13.3%	1860	22.7%

It is not unreasonable to assume that the vigorous activity of
the American Bible Society was one significant factor in this
burgeoning church life.

Yet these manifold challenges merely emphasized the perpetual
nature of the task--and the need for steady, continuous effort.
"On sober review," the Managers acknowledged in 1840, they would
be "very reluctant" to encourage a repetition of the intensive,
speedy, universal General Supply. "Not that Bibles are not
again wanting by thousands in every State, and should be speedily
furnished," they realized, "but that the work of supply should be
done in a less exciting, public manner." In the light of experience the Society concluded further, not only that the deliberate
systematic canvassing of needs and resources should be done by
Auxiliaries, but that it should be done by local members rather
than paid Agents. "This course will require labour and self-
denial, but is it greater than the cause demands? Is it not
doing that, in a measure, for our destitute at home, which the
missionary is called to do abroad? Is it not a sacrifice of
personal labour which the friends of the Bible should cheerfully
make?"

With this renewed dedication the Society moved into its
second quarter century; with this expanded horizon the Society
moved beyond its own national boundaries into the world.

NOTES

1. Herman C. Weber, *Yearbook of the American Churches* (New
    York, 1933), p. 299.

5

First Steps Abroad

Resolved that whilst the Society are zealously engaged in
supplying the wants of the inhabitants of their own country,
they esteem it a distinguished honor and privilege to be
permitted to co-operate with kindred Institutions in this
and other countries, in procuring the Holy Scriptures to be
translated into every language, and distributed in every
region of the habitable globe. (Annual Report, 1830)

With an expanding frontier and immigrant population, with
hardly ten per cent of its citizenry enrolled in churches (in
1816), the youthful United States offered a challenging mission
field for the still younger American Bible Society. Yet the ABS
was constantly reminded--by missionaries, by Auxiliaries, by its
own officers--that although its title did not specify "and
Foreign," its Constitution did pledge, "according to its ability,
[to] extend its influence to other countries, whether Christian,
Mahometan, or Pagan."

The Bible Society came to birth exactly twenty years after
William Carey, the acknowledged pioneer of modern Protestant
foreign missions, sailed from England for India. As early as
1805 Robert Ralston, a founder of the Philadelphia Bible Society
and later a Vice-President of the ABS, had been receiving donations for the work at Serampore. In 1810 Samuel J. Mills, who
was soon to portray so vividly the desperate need for Scriptures
in the United States, had encouraged the formation of the
American Board of Commissioners for Foreign Missions. The New
York Missionary Society, organized that same year, included
among its leading supporters John M. Mason, John Romeyn, Divie

Bethune, men who were also instrumental in inaugurating the
Bible Society. Jedidiah Morse published in *The Panoplist*, along
with pleas for the Bible cause, reports from the embryonic
missionary movement in various parts of the globe.

No wonder that William Jay began his influential "Memoir"
with an account of Scriptural destitution abroad before he turned
to the North American continent. No wonder he affirmed that "to
love others besides ourselves, is the peculiar characteristic of
Christianity." No wonder he inquired "to what extent we have
diffused the light of Revelation beyond our own borders:"

> The society is to be a *foreign* as well as an American
> society; and why should it not be? Are the Christians of
> America under fewer obligations than their brethren in
> Britain to extend the blessings of their Religion beyond
> the confines of their own country? If it be said that we
> ought first to supply the want of Bibles at home, it may
> with equal justice be said, we should send no Missionaries
> abroad, while we have vacant Pulpits at home. Had the
> apostles never travelled from one city to another, till
> they had converted all in the first, slow indeed would
> have been the progress of Christianity.

Thus it is no mere coincidence that the enthusiasm and commitment
for the distribution of Scriptures--and the corresponding problems and discouragements--have paralleled the Great Century and
a half of foreign missions.

At the outset of Bible Society work only a small fragment of
the world was open to the Gospel as Protestants understood it.
In all Latin America and at least half of Western Europe,
Christianity was represented by the Roman Catholic Church.
Africa was not only unevangelized, but largely unexplored. Only
a handful of missionaries had touched the sub-continent of
India. The ABS had been functioning for twenty-five years
before the so-called Opium War of 1839-42 opened a few ports in
China to the foreigner and made Hong Kong a British possession.
Japan fiercely repulsed all intruders except an annual Dutch
trading vessel until the second half of the nineteenth century.
The first mission to Hawaii was authorized in 1819 and reached
the islands the following year. Very little was actually known
about the people, customs, religions, languages throughout much
of the globe.

The acceptance of responsibility for world-wide circulation
of the Bible was not achieved without controversy. In the
debate over including the Apocrypha for Latin America (discussed
in Chapter VI) Professor Luther Halsey of Princeton went far
beyond the textual argument to charge that foreign commitments

of the Bible Society caused critical shortages at home. "Why
leave a field half tilled to force your way through briars to
some new employ?" he queried. After suggesting that there were
other missionary and tract societies which could serve the needs
of South America, the professor asked rhetorically: "In this
most interesting period of exertion at home, the American Church
has *ever seen*.....must all be checked for the sake of a *debatable
charity*?.....For I do know, do your *best*, you cannot do more than
meet domestic exigencies." (Letter to the ABS, December 26, 1827)

Even the Board of Managers was not unmindful of the tension
when funds were being solicited and when allocations were being
decided. When they sent $1,000 to William Carey in India in
1822, they expressed regret that the amount was small in relation
to the vastness of the need there, "but [these gifts] could not
have been enlarged, perhaps, without some restrictions upon the
gifts to the destitute in our own country." On the other hand,
the committee which recommended this appropriation called attention to the fact "that the public mind is at this juncture, more
than commonly interested in behalf of the destitute Heathen,"
and expressed the hope that new objects of benevolence abroad
might well expand the resources available at home.

> The communications of many of our auxiliaries give support
> to this anticipation, and one from a respectable Female
> Society...earnestly exhorts us to listen to 'the touching,
> imploring appeal of the destitute Heathen, which, they
> say, has excited their sympathy and called forth their
> prayers.'

What the realistic businessmen on the Board of Managers
needed to ascertain was whether the plight of distant lands
would also inspire measurable philanthropy and call forth tan-
gible contributions. The committee believed that it would, that
the "vast expansion" of the British and Foreign Bible Society
beyond its own shores had greatly "contributed to swell [its]
resources," that foreign missionary projects would provide "a
new spring to some of our less active auxiliaries...a powerful
excitement to individual munificence."

The Corresponding Secretary of the American Board of Commissioners for Foreign Missions declared flatly in 1823:

> The experience of the British and Foreign Bible Society
> has abundantly shown, that a liberal use of the resources
> of that institution, for the benefit of the distant
> heathen, has been a powerful means of augmenting these
> resources.....So it will be in every similar case.

A subsequent appeal for further assistance to the mission at
Serampore, India, remarked pointedly:

While we with joy witness your unwearied concern to give
the Bible if possible to every one of your own countrymen
...our experience of your past liberality repels the
idea, that you wish to confine your...help to your own
shores.....And we cannot believe that a Society instituted
for the express purpose of rendering America, like Britain,
a blessing to the remotest nations of the earth, ever
intends to narrow the streams of Christian liberality and
confine them to the shores of America.....

Despite the growing commitment of the ABS and its supporters
to distribution overseas, the actual appropriations seem
incredibly modest by present standards. Although early statistics are undoubtedly incomplete, the following figures cover
most grants made during the Society's first fifteen years
(1816-30):

	Bibles	Testaments	Funds
Chile	175	1,478	
Uruguay	174		
Argentina	421	960	
Peru	225	1,000	
Venezuela	325	862	
Surinam	24	12	
Colombia	1,021	561	
Brazil	20	40	
Panama		30	
Guatemala	12	132	
Mexico	1,052	2,653	
West Indies	864	2,266	
Spanish America, Gen.	885	1,125	
Latin America Total	5,198	11,119	
France			$ 500
Spain		25	
Greece	50		2,500
Russia	22	10	
Africa	261	450	
Ceylon	267	456	1,100
India			1,000
Burma			1,200
China	274	12	
Hawaii	562	475	
Cape Verde	100	210	
Canada	816	650	
BFBS	2	2	
Grand Total	7,552	13,409	$6,300

Added to this were 15,791 Portions, almost all of which were
Gospels of Matthew published in Hawaiian for American Board missionaries in the Sandwich Islands. It will be noted that more
than three quarters of the volumes shipped went to Latin America.
Monetary grants were used primarily to subsidize translation and
printing overseas, but occasionally to purchase books from the
British and Foreign Bible Society.

The American Bible Society took its global stand decisively
in 1837, when the Board of Managers *defeated* a motion that after
a certain date "all appropriations for distribution of the Bible
in Foreign lands be made from such moneys only as shall have been
expressly contributed for that purpose." As the unsuccessful
motion implied, the Society had for some years been spending
considerably more money for translation and distribution of
Scriptures overseas than had been designated for such work. In
fact, during the preceding year $38,570 had been allocated for
foreign projects, although only $31,004 had come in for that
purpose in 1835. And in 1839, when enthusiasm for a World Supply
had dropped sharply (see below) and produced gifts of only $3,554
for overseas work, the Society expended $19,735--more than five
times the designated income--for grants of books and money abroad.

Part of this commitment to a world outreach was inherited--
and imitated--from the British and Foreign Bible Society. Although
serious differences in policy arose from time to time, the staffs
in London and New York maintained a courteous and usually cordial
relationship. Just a year after the formation of the American
Society, Dr. John Mason attended the Annual Meeting of the
British Society in London, and similar visits, official and
unofficial, have taken place in both directions ever since. The
deaths of early presidents (Elias Boudinot and Lord Teignmouth),
but also of much humbler officers in either Society, brought
resolutions or letters of sympathy and respect.

This is not to imply that there were never any clashes between
the two Societies: in policy, in territorial comity, in rival
efforts. Although they had accepted an initial contribution from
London with genuine appreciation, the Americans in 1819 declined
an offer of ₤500 from the "Parent Society," believing that it was
based on an "erroneous apprehension of the state of the finances
of the American Bible Society." William Jay, quite literally a
son of the American Revolution, warned against regular or full
use of the "Monthly Extracts" (news and activities from Britain),
as it would be "unwise and undignified for the American Bible
Society to engage to reprint *here* whatever the other Society see
fit to publish in *London*."

In general, however, there was polite deference to the position of "the other Society," a deference based on mutual respect

and courtesy as well as on efficient stewardship of resources.
As will be seen, many policy decisions were made in consultation
though not necessarily agreement with officers across the Atlanti
Shipments of books, supplies of paper or stereotype plates, cash
contributions to subsidize translations, were often made to
supplement or complement the program of the other distributor.
In a reciprocal gesture the ABS relayed Bibles to the Cape Verde
Islands for the BFBS, while the British delivered books for the
American Society to Malta.

This mutual respect was expressed by the British and Foreign
Society librarian in 1823, in a letter commending the purchase
of land by the ABS as "a pledge of the permanence and stability
of your Institution:" "Surely, though modesty and humility may
lead you to speak of walking in *our steps*, we may well ourselves
admire and receive instruction from your example."

Throughout its history the American Bible Society has relied
heavily on cooperation not only with other Bible Societies, but
with mission boards. Missionaries, scattered in increasing
numbers in far-away places, took for granted that the Scriptures
were the most important single instrument for spreading the Good
News of Jesus Christ. The Society recognized just as clearly
that missionaries would be the most effective agents for translation and distribution.

As early as 1819 the American Board of Commissioners for
Foreign Missions requested two or three hundred English Bibles
for the Sandwich Islands. The Society also instructed its
representative to prepare an elaborate volume of the Scriptures
for Tam-Ah-Am-Ah-Ah, "King of Owyhee," and one for Tan-o-ree,
"the other sovereign on those islands." As this "public relations" enterprise developed, the presentation included not only
two Octavo Bibles (worth $6.50 each!), but also diplomas granting
these royal personages honorary membership in the American Bible
Society. Four more modest volumes (at $1.75 each) were sent for
the local helpers who had arranged this ceremony, plus two
hundred Bibles and one hundred Testaments for general distribution. In similar fashion the Bible Society provided the Americar
Colonization Society with special copies of the Scriptures for
the Governor and chiefs in Sierra Leone.

When William Ward, the printing partner of the Serampore Trio,
visited the United States in 1820-21, he was given copies of the
Bible Society's "best edition" for himself, for William Carey,
and for Joshua Marshman, the teacher. Four years later Carey
himself attended a meeting of the Society in New York (although
he was erroneously recorded as "Rev'd E. Cary"). On other
occasions the ABS sent "similar expressions of their esteem and
approbation" to Robert Morrison in Canton and William Milne in

Malacca. Morrison, the first Protestant missionary to China, had been refused passage on East India Company ships from England, so he first crossed the Atlantic to America. There Robert Ralston and other shipowners who actively supported foreign missions helped to arrange transportation to China in 1807 and letters from Secretary of State James Madison to the American consul in Canton. Despite the importance of Morrison's translation work, in completing the Old and New Testaments in Chinese by 1819, there is no record of direct financial aid from the American Bible Society. Milne, a Scot also sent to China by the London Missionary Society, initially joined Morrison in Macao and Canton but eventually settled in Malaya and engaged in the translation of Scriptures in various dialects among Chinese emigrants there.

Samuel J. Mills, in the first year of ABS operations, had urged substantial assistance to the Serampore Baptist mission, but expressed anxiety that "the Constitution of the Society in its present form would not permit the Board to make this appropriation." *If* this were the case, *if* the non-sectarian emphasis were interpreted to prohibit direct donations to a denominational mission, *if* there were "an article of a restrictive kind," Mills very gently proposed "an alteration in the Constitution."

Although the Board did not construe its policy so narrowly, the committee examining Carey's appeal in 1822 did recognize that all the missionaries at Serampore belonged to the same denomination and that "it is of great consequence to the union and harmony of our operations, to adhere inviolably to the principles of indulging no Sectarian preferences." Nevertheless it expressed the confidence, endorsed by the Board in its first $1,000 grant, that the outstanding achievements and devotion of the Serampore missionaries assured the impartial use of any appropriations. Certainly the Society could hardly overlook the fact that in twenty-five years of labor in India, William Carey and his associates had translated the entire Bible into five languages, the New Testament and parts of the Old into ten more, parts of the New Testament into another six, and one or more Gospels in an additional ten languages or dialects.

Yet the concern about denominational partiality persisted. Because of its head start, the American Board of Commissioners for Foreign Missions expanded into more fields more rapidly than any other religious agency at the time, and consequently forwarded to the Bible Society more appeals for help. American Board missionaries arrived in Ceylon in 1816, very shortly after the island had been transferred to British control as a result of the Napoleonic Wars. There they found translations of the Bible already made by eighteenth-century German missionaries, but the Americans requested funds to purchase Tamil Scriptures from the BFBS. For this purpose the American Bible Society granted $500 in 1822 and another $600 in 1829.

In addition to the spectacular success of the Serampore Trio, great interest in England and America focussed on the work of Adoniram Judson in Burma. Having collaborated with Samuel J. Mills to initiate the American Board of Commissioners for Foreign Missions in 1810, Judson and his wife Ann sailed three years later as the first American missionaries to Asia. In anticipation of working with William Carey, they studied Baptist doctrine on the long sea voyage, became convinced of its Biblical validity, requested baptism by immersion when they reached Calcutta, resigned from the Congregationalist board, and went on to inaugurate Baptist missions in Burma.

During the Anglo-Burmese War of 1824 Judson was arrested as a suspected spy and spent twenty-one months in prison, part of that time in the death house. A faithful Burmese convert, visiting one jail just after Judson had been moved elsewhere, rescued his pillow from the courtyard ad a treasured momento. Months later the freed missionary was overjoyed to locate his lost pillow, for in it was hidden the Burmese translation of the New Testament ready for printing. The original of that version can now be seen in the library of the New York Bible House. For Judson's faithful and scholarly translation work, despite wars and imprisonment, the American Bible Society appropriated $1,200 in 1829. But the following year a storm of controversy broke on the Society over Baptist translations of Scriptures (see Chapter VI).

In actual fact, grants of books and funds to overseas missions were remarkably well dispersed. In its first fifteen years the Bible Society contributed the most money to the Baptists in India and Burma, the most Scriptures to the American Board of Commissioners for Foreign Missions, which at that time represented Congregationalists, Presbyterians, Reformed Churches, and some others. Ironically (since certain Episcopalians had feared that the Society would be dominated by Presbyterians), the third largest financial grant in this period, made through other organizations, ($500 for Greece) and the fifth largest shipments of books overseas (after the American Colonization Society and the American Seamen's Friend Society) went to the Domestic and Foreign Missionary Society of the Protestant Episcopal Church. Methodists and the United Foreign Missionary Society were also beneficiaries from the very meager foreign appropriations of the ABS.

Despite these facts--and the limited possibilities for circulation abroad under any auspices--denominational questioning and grumbling still reached the ears of Bible Society officers. In 1831 the Committee for Foreign Distribution spoke directly to this problem, among others. Acknowledging the interdependence of the missionary enterprise and the Bible cause "as inseparable associates" and the fact that most missions are related to

particular denominations, nevertheless "your Committee are not
disposed to depart in the smallest degree from the unsectarian
spirit of our Institution." If on this account, however, the
Society were to refuse direct support, in the form of books or
financial grants for translation and circulation, it would be
denying itself the most fruitful channels for achieving its own
ends. Obviously some groups would have wider areas and opportunities for service than others, the Committee recognized, but
its report continued:

> If equal favor is shown to all in proportion to the scope
> of their operations and their consequent ability profit-
> ably to disseminate the Scriptures, surely all true
> Christians will see in their employment for this purpose
> no cause for jealousy, but on the contrary abundant reason
> to bless God for opening to us such salutary channels for
> our beneficence, such a happy means of effectuating the
> noble work which he has committed to our hands.

Just as it depended on Auxiliaries for distribution at home,
the Bible Society was conscious of its indebtedness in the
foreign field, not only to missionaries, but to merchants and
sea captains, sometimes to consuls and chargés d'affaires. But
as the vastness of the need became apparent, matched--or often
unmatched--by the desires and resources to undertake the effort,
the values of supervision, coordination, direct communication,
and single-minded purpose became evident also. Missionaries,
even in those days, were busy people, torn in many directions by
the endless variety of challenges. Scholars who understood the
laborious process of translation were unfamiliar with the complexities of shipping and finance. The British and Foreign
Bible Society appeared to have general--if not universal--success
in the employment of Agents for an assigned territory.

Thus, from time to time, even in its first few decades, the
American Bible Society considered hiring Agents in a given area,
"men who shall co-operate with missionaries in preparing and
distributing the Scriptures, and yet be responsible to this
Board for their operations." The Managers adopted this procedure as official policy in 1836, although foreign Agents had
been employed for brief periods earlier. At the recommendation
of the American Board of Commissioners, the Managers added two
guiding principles at the same time: "that the Bible agent at
each station shall be of the same religious denomination as that
to which the missionaries on the ground belong, [and] that they
receive the same compensation or support which is received by
the missionaries in similar circumstances."

Agents came and went, in assorted styles and assorted manners.
It is clear--a few disastrous failures notwithstanding--that the

New York Board and its appropriate committees scrutinized men
very carefully before making official appointments. A number of
volunteers were courteously but pointedly rejected--or ignored.
One was a foot-loose missionary in the Middle East, who had
transferred, for undisclosed reasons, from one mission board to
another several times and found himself unemployed in the region
that he knew and loved and did not want to leave. A brother of
a respected missionary was passed over in fear that his Russian
citizenship might expose him to more persecution and pressure in
his own country than an outsider would experience. Even when
nationals were paid to perform certain services for short periods
of time, the Society was seldom willing in early days to bestow
the title of Agent on them.

On the whole, the Board was much more inclined to ask of
leading theological seminaries whether they had recent promising
graduates with an avowed interest in foreign missions. Expectations were high. A China missionary pioneer of the American
Board of Commissioners, Elijah C. Bridgman, responded to an
inquiry about establishing an Agency there:

> If you can obtain a young man of sterling abilities and
> ardent piety, who will devote his whole life to the cause,
> come among the Chinese, learn thoroughly their language,
> and give himself to the work of manufacturing and circu-
> lating Bibles, you will do well to send out such an agent
> and he cannot come too soon. Probably in no other place,
> or in any other way, could a man be employed with a fairer
> prospect of extensive usefulness. He would be a direct
> organ of communication between your Society and the mis-
> sionaries in this wide field, and a most welcome fellow-
> laborer.

Investigating one candidate at Andover Seminary, John C.
Brigham, Corresponding Secretary of the Society, wrote in 1836:

> Tell him we want a man of good scholarship, pious, provi-
> dent, energetic, and who likes the missionary work. He
> will be with the missionaries and must sympathize with
> them. He must help translate, read proofs, see to print-
> ing, distribution, travel some. He must be the A.B.S. in
> miniature. He must be a superior man.

Measured by such standards, it is not surprising that few
Agents were appointed by the Society during those early years.

The United States' interest in Latin America grew not only
out of geographical location, but from sympathy for revolutionary currents which began early in the nineteenth century. The
U.S. Government recognized independence movements or appointed

diplomatic representatives in Mexico in 1822, in Chile and La
Plata in 1823, in Brazil and the Central American Confederation
in 1824, in Peru in 1826. The Monroe Doctrine, proclaimed as
Executive policy in 1823, warned all European powers that the
Western Hemisphere was no longer open to fresh colonization.

Despite liberal, sometimes anti-clerical, regimes in many
Latin countries, circulation of the Scriptures was handicapped
by intermittent political and military turmoil and by resistance
from the Roman Catholic Church. The pioneer Bible distributor in
South America, James Thomson, was sent by the British and Foreign
Bible Society in 1821. Before long the Young Men's Bible Society
of Baltimore shipped twenty-five Bibles and fifty New Testaments
for Thomson to use among English-speaking residents of Montevideo,
Uruguay. Yet John C. Brigham, then a missionary of the American
Board of Commissioners and soon to join the Bible Society staff,
wrote in 1823 that in the cities of Spanish America "the
Scriptures sold rapidly for a time and then the demand entirely
ceased."

The Annual Report for 1824 announced that the Board of Managers
had "availed themselves of every practicable method of obtaining
an accurate knowledge of the various channels through which the
Scriptures might be introduced into every part of Mexico and
South America" and had "accordingly appointed a Standing Committee
for their distribution in foreign languages, whose efforts will be
particularly directed to the wants of the newly established
republics of the South." The next year the Society made an
appropriation of $500 to expedite translations into Peruvian,
Quechua, Aymara, and Moxa languages.

All kinds of difficulties continued to plague distribution
efforts. The government of Peru banned all Bibles "except with
commentaries of the Roman Catholic Church," although one missionary managed to secure the release of four cases of books, which
he offered for sale in his home. A correspondent in Venezuela
told of a shipwreck in which the volumes of Scriptures on board
were "plundered by Indians...who forthwith brought them hither
and sold them for a goodly sum." A case of Bibles in Valparaiso,
Chile, was reported to be badly damaged by water, either on ship-
board or in the customs house. But a major obstacle to Scripture
circulation in predominantly Roman Catholic lands was the decision,
by both British and American Societies, *not* to publish the
Apocrypha (see Chapter VI).

The first official action authorizing a representative of the
ABS to go to Latin America came in late 1827. The Rev. Robert
Baird of Princeton, New Jersey, had indicated his interest in
making an "exploratory" trip to Mexico or Colombia and then,
after settling his family "in some accessible place,...to spend

my life in the service of the Bible Society, and in South
America." His qualifications, including his Christian dedication,
were extravagantly praised by those who knew him; he was given an
advance of $250, plus the assurance of $100-$200 for the mainte-
nance of his family during his absence; Secretary of State Henry
Clay promised to furnish him with a general letter of introduction
In fact, the President of the United States, John Quincy Adams
(1767-1848), a Vice-President of the Bible Society from 1818 to
1848, "said that he would cheerfully have complied with the
request of Mr. Baird, but for a Rule established & strictly
adhered to by all his predecessors, that of never giving either
public or private letters to any but official characters."

Baird had his passage booked from Philadelphia about Christmas
Day, 1827. But this was at the height of the dispute over use of
the Apocrypha in Scriptures for Latin America (see next chapter),
as bitter a debate in the United States as in the Southern
Hemisphere. Believing that it would be unwise to expand or even
to call attention to its work in South America until this issue
had been settled, the Society requested a postponement of Baird's
sailing. The candidate had previously offered to engage in other
work, or to yield his place to a single man if that would reduce
the financial and personal responsibility of the Society. But on
February 16, 1828, two months before the formal decision about the
Apocrypha was reached, Corresponding Secretary John Brigham wrote
Baird that he saw "no propriety in his going to South America
under existing circumstances."

Meanwhile the proposal to send an Agent to Latin America
generated considerable public interest. In July of 1828 the Yale
College Auxiliary, unaware that Baird had not sailed, requested
that its funds be invested in Bibles for Colombia, out of "a
deep interest for the moral, and political welfare of our South
American Brethren." In Maine the Rev. Daniel Merrill had started
raising money for South America, "Mexico, Cuba, and any other
part of the world where the Spanish language is spoken." However
the Bible Society expressed some apprehension that such a campaign
might be regarded in Latin America as offensive patronage, and
that it might also infringe on the right and responsibility of
Auxiliaries to raise funds. Merrill graciously acceded to this
advice and agreed to turn over all money he had raised for the
Society.

Not until 1833 was the first foreign Agency of the American
Bible Society actually established, and even this was a travelling
assignment in Latin America rather than a fixed residency. Isaac
W. Wheelwright was appointed "for the Western Coast of South
America," although the committee proposed an itinerary covering
the principal towns of Chile, Peru, Ecuador, Colombia, and "if
practicable" parts of Guatemala, "and that he then revisit all

the places above specified should circumstances indicate that further distribution of the Sacred Scriptures can be advantageously made." He received a $300 clothing outfit allowance, travel expenses, and living costs rather than a fixed salary. Uncertain when or where letters and additional books might reach him, he took with him eight hundred Spanish Testaments and several hundred English Bibles and Testaments. These he was to make "strenuous efforts" to sell, but when the market was exhausted, the Agent would be at liberty to distribute them free to schools which agreed to adopt them as reading texts, or to families likely to "make a wise and faithful use of the same sacred gift."

Wheelwright found the process of distributing Scriptures depressingly slow and living expenses distressingly high, $100 a month. He himself was undecided as to whether free donation or sale at a nominal price produced the more appreciative acceptance, but he felt that one policy or the other should be adopted, since gratuitous circulation tended to undercut any possibility of sales. Despite his admitted discouragement, the Society reappointed him for another year in June, 1835. In November officers in New York learned, by exceptionally delayed mail, that Wheelwright had relinquished his Agency in August to direct a school in Ecuador. Attacked by Catholic clergy for "disturbing the public tranquility, and exciting a general commotion among the people," he had apparently become convinced that only through the acceptable medium of education could the youth of Latin America be reached by the Bible and the Evangelical (Protestant) faith. Wheelwright continued to correspond with New York, and to distribute Scriptures in schools and elsewhere, but this first Agency lasted officially just seventeen months.

A more successful venture was launched in the Middle East in 1836, when the Board appointed Simeon K. Calhoun, a tutor at Williams College, to go to Smyrna, in western Turkey. Since the British and Foreign Bible Society already had Agents and depots in Greece, European Turkey, and Asia Minor, and since "Syria, Egypt and more remote countries, do not hold out great immediate encouragement," there was some uncertainty as to the most strategic location. Yet the need of Scriptures and the increasing number of American missionaries in the area proved persuasive. Calhoun came to the Board's attention with extraordinary recommendations:

> I know of no young man equally promising, and as well qualified so far as I can see to be 'a Bible Missionary' ......He has a good constitution...is in the habit of a good deal of bodily effort...Walks considerable distances-- chops wood...has a strong vigorous mind--particularly that quality which is called 'good common sense'...is a thorough scholar...possesses deep consistent piety...has a desire to

spend his life abroad in missionary operations...has an
unusual talent in gaining the love and esteem of others and
of swaying their minds...owing I suppose to his good sense--
scholarship--kindness--and desire of the best interests of
those with whom he has to do in time and in eternity.....
He is an enterprising energetic man--bold, not rash--decided,
not violent--persevering, not obstinate...the very man for
you. (David D. Field to Corresponding Secretary John C.
Brigham, June 20, 1836)

Despite attractive invitations by the American Board of Commissioners to serve in Constantinople or in Russia, Calhoun finally
accepted the Bible Society offer and sailed in November, 1836,
studying Hebrew and becoming ordained in the intervening months.
In addition to his passage and an outfit allowance of $300, the
new Mediterranean Agent was offered an expense account "not to
exceed eight hundred dollars per annum" in lieu of salary. Later
he requested that this be changed to a fixed salary, even of the
same amount, because he did not feel free to make his own financial decisions, including personal benevolences and board payments
to missionary hosts, when he was on an expense allowance.

Calhoun promptly won high esteem from his fellow missionaries,
and handled a number of delicate problems with maturity and
sensitivity. He did have one major quarrel with the Bible Society
however. The Board's financial policies seemed to Calhoun to
imply a lack of trust, both in the Agent and in other missionaries
Although he agreed that major items over $1,000 should be referred
for approval to New York, he found that innumerable smaller
expenditures (e.g. $100 for a storehouse for Scriptures, or a
quarter of the wages for "a pious Greek" helping in the depot)
were not covered by his regular draft. Unless he were willing to
wait months for official authorization, he had to choose between
overdrawing his account or using his own meager salary to cover
such payments.

Furthermore his instructions required that the Agent obtain the
approval of at least two missionaries in Smyrna before giving
Scriptures to American missionaries elsewhere. This not only
made it impossible to allocate books while Calhoun was traveling,
but seemed to suggest that the judgment of Smyrna missionaries
was somehow more reliable than those in the hinterland, an
especially touchy point if denominational differences were
involved. Denying any intended discrimination in favor of Smyrna
missionaries, the Corresponding Secretary nevertheless replied
that "the testimony of any two or three missionaries is of course
as good...[but] we want some besides his own;" in other words,
that the Agent was not to proceed arbitrarily in making grants
of Scriptures at his own discretion.

Bible Society officers in New York generally agreed that the
next most strategic Agency would be Singapore, from which port
Scripture distribution might be extended to Malaya, the East
Indies, China, and even--hopefully--Japan and Korea. Except for
brief consideration of sending Simeon Calhoun to Singapore,
apparently no candidate with sufficient qualifications could be
found. Thus through its third decade the American Bible Society
dealt with one of its potentially greatest fields, East Asia,
through slow, vague, and sometimes contradictory communications
with missionaries there.

Despite the incomprehensible scope of the "heathen world"--
or perhaps because it *was* incomprehensible, geographically,
numerically, religiously--the hope of world-wide proclamation
continued to inspire Christians in the West. Encouraged by the
response to the General Supply within the United States, William
Plumer of Virginia wrote to the Bible Society headquarters in
1833 proposing a "universal distribution of the sacred Scriptures
in 20 years." With immediate recognition that any such effort
could be undertaken only in conjunction with the British and
Foreign Bible Society and others like it, the Board of Managers
voted to confer with other societies, by correspondence or a
personal delegation if expedient, to ascertain:

> ...what countries on the face of the earth are destitute
> of the revealed Will of God, into what languages the Scrip-
> tures have not been translated; what are or may be the
> probable facilities of access and distribution among the
> destitute portions of our globe, what division of labor
> between the existing Bible Societies may probably be
> secured; and what assistance in this great enterprise may
> be expected from other lands.

A year later the Board pledged itself to cooperate with other
institutions in "the work of distributing the Bible among all the
accessible population of the Globe within the shortest practicable period." In response to a public pamphlet, to other
communications, and to Agents' inquiries, thirty-five Auxiliaries
and fifteen ecclesiastical bodies endorsed the plan, some with
"thrilling interest" or "unequivocal desire for its success."

Meanwhile, however, the two most active and experienced allies
across the Atlantic expressed reservations. The British and
Foreign Bible Society and the French and Foreign Bible Society
both considered it "impracticable" to set any definite time limit
for such an undertaking. But the BFBS cautioned more explicitly
that a) persons accessible to Scripture circulation at one time
may be "quite otherwise in a short space of time;" (b) the number
of languages and dialects in the world is unknown; (c) even if
they could all be ascertained, it would be impossible to predict

the time required for translation and distribution; (d) such
world supply would require an amount of gratuitous distribution
totally beyond the means of all the Bible Societies combined;
(e) the work of Agents in these foreign fields is still too
experimental to warrant any radical expansion of the enterprise.

With such sober advice from "Parent Societies" abroad, and
with caution learned from the General Supply at home, enthusiasm
for this crusade quickly waned. To be sure, such coverage of the
world with the Scriptures remained a paramount goal not only for
the Bible Societies, but for every Christian. The reaffirmation
of this goal in "the shortest practicable period" had positive
value in reminding missionaries of the importance of translation
in their work, and in quickening the zeal of Auxiliaries in this
country. Yet by 1840 the Board of Managers frankly questioned
"whether this sudden impulse given to the cause was of permanent
utility...[or whether it had] a tendency to divert the Auxiliaries
from those regular enduring efforts which produce in the end the
most satisfactory as well as the greatest results."

Although political and religious circumstances have drastically
changed, though the world population has outrun the growth of the
Christian Church, the dream of a World Supply of Scriptures cannot
die. Plans for the sesquicentennial celebration of the American
Bible Society included a resolution, in 1963, to join with twenty-
two other national Bible societies in renewed effort to provide
a Bible for every Christian home, a New Testament for every
individual Christian, and a Gospel for all who could read, in
their own languages, anywhere in the world.

6

"Without Note or Comment"

In defining the "sole object" of the American Bible Society, the first article of the Constitution included two brief but crucial phrases: "without note or comment" and "the version now in common use." Over these two simple conditions, their interpretation and their implementation, sharp controversies have raged, in part precisely because they are central to the unity and purpose of the Society. Chapter XIV will indicate changes in the Constitution and in policy and practice necessitated in the twentieth century by various revisions and new English texts.

"The version now in common use" was taken for granted by the Founding Fathers; it was the King James Bible completed in 1611, the "Authorized Version" in the English language. As various publishers printed various editions, some careless errors and some casual emendations inevitably crept in. These took many forms: punctuation, orthography, verb tenses, italics, paragraphing, typography, etc. In an effort to insure accuracy, the Society from its inception sought professional proofreaders and as early as July, 1817, invited "ministers of the Gospel, resident in the city, who are members of this Society, together with the Standing Committee" to examine the proofs of the stereotype plates used. But the version itself was never in question at that period.

When the Board of Managers decided, in January of that first year of operation, that they could at least consider publishing and/or distributing Scriptures in all languages, "provided the same can be obtained without note or comment," the problem of authentic versions seems not to have arisen. In the first place,

they trusted any edition which the British and Foreign Bible
Society approved as "standard copies"--a trust which led to conflicts in Latin America, Greece, and India within a very few
years. In general, the ABS was content to purchase Bibles and
Testaments in Gaelic and Welsh, German and French and Spanish,
through the "Parent Society" in London rather than to print for
the limited foreign language market in America. When an appeal
for aid in financing a French edition came from a German in
Paris, Frederic Leo, discussion centered on whether to encourage
a translation of the New Testament rather than the whole Bible.
But when John Mason returned from a trip to Europe, warmly
commending Leo for the sacrificial, dedicated service he was
giving to the Bible cause, the ABS readily despatched $500 with-
out even questioning the version, though there was no Protestant
"authorized edition" in French.

Equally early the Society confronted similar problems in
serving "our brethren of the woods"--as the Minutes often called
the American Indians. Even the missionaries working among them
could not agree on policies. Some considered it urgent to supply
the Scriptures in tribal languages, as rapidly as those languages
could be reduced to writing. Others argued that it would be
quicker, easier, and of greater value in the long run if the
Indians were taught to read English; thus more missionaries
could provide more consistent instruction in the Christian faith
than the few who learned the indigenous tongues. A committee
report for the Bible Society declared in 1817: "With the Gospel
must go civilization.....Hunting grounds are shrinking, forcing
new ways of life, necessary and useful arts and cultivation of
the soil must be learned." But whether the Good News of Jesus
Christ should also be presented in Anglo-Saxon terms, rather
than in the "language of the forest," was not so clear.

In 1817 Rev. Frederick Denke, a missionary of the United
Brethren, submitted to the Society a translation of the Epistles
of John in the Delaware tongue, offering it without charge but
admitting that he would appreciate a donation toward his
expenses. The translation was checked by another missionary of
the same denomination, and a few explanatory additions were
deleted as unjustified "note or comment." In publishing these
Epistles in Delaware and English, the ABS issued (in July, 1818)
its first diglot or bilingual edition and its first non-English
Scriptures, yet no question was raised about accepting one man's
unauthorized translation.

Other considerations arose, however, when a woman from the
Cincinnati Auxiliary Female Bible Society offered $100 toward
producing a "harmony" of the Gospels in the Delaware tongue. The
translater-transposer, David Zeisberger, had lived with the
Delawares for forty years, and his Indian assistant had reportedly

been a member of a congregation organized by David Brainerd
(1718-1747) in New Jersey. The arrangement *seemed* to be free of
error and composed solely of Scriptural verses. But Zeisberger
had died, and there appeared to be no one else qualified to
evaluate his work, certainly no editorial committee able to
review it. The project was rejected, therefore, by the Society
and eventually issued privately—but by the ABS printer and on
paper supplied by the ABS at cost.

In the case of the Mohawk-English Gospel of John, an edition
prepared much earlier by the British and Foreign Bible Society
was assumed, *ipso facto*, to be authoritative if not authorized.
Without checking with the London office, the American Bible
Society printed a thousand copies of the British version, complete
with the original typographical errors and list of errata at the
end of the book. Quite understandably, the BFBS sent a polite
letter of reproof at the lack of consultation, for they still
had five hundred copies on hand which they wanted to dispose of,
and claimed to have heard nothing from the thousand copies sent
to the translator in 1804 (though their Annual Report for 1808
mentions an acknowledgement of five hundred of them). One reason
for the eagerness of the American Society to produce Scriptures
for the Indians may have been Elias Boudinot's long-standing
concern for those people. He had once been considered by George
Washington as principal negotiator with the tribes, and had
declared in 1792, when Congress proposed to increase military
appropriations to subdue them: "The Indians are with difficulty
to be reduced by the sword, but may easily be gained by justice
and moderation."

As with later wars of other kinds, the "Battle of the
Apocrypha," which engaged the British and Foreign Bible Society
in Europe during the 1820's, spread inexorably, with regional
differences, to the Western Hemisphere. Almost as unfamiliar as
Americans with Continental usage, the BFBS had accepted traditional European forms of the Bible, which continued to include
the Apocrypha, although designated as non-canonical writings.
Martin Luther had declared in his 1534 translation: "These books
are not held equal to the sacred scriptures, and yet are useful
and good for reading." Though it had no intention of printing
the non-canonical books in new editions, the BFBS received
occasional complaints when they were omitted. Conscious too that
its Anglican constituency, represented by one half of the
Managers, accepted the Apocrypha, the Board voted in 1813 to
leave the decision to each individual Auxiliary.

Under protest from the Edinburgh Bible Society and the
Scottish Presbyterian Churches, however, the BFBS began a search
for acceptable alternatives. It decided consecutively: in 1822,
that *its* funds could be used only for Bibles without the Apocrypha,

but other societies might do as they liked with their own funds;
in 1824, that no BFBS appropriations could be applied to printing
or distributing editions with the Apocrypha, *and* any such grants
should be scrupulously applied to publishing canonical books
only; in 1825, that all grants to societies or individuals should
conform to these principles, totally excluding any part of the
Apocrypha; in 1826, that "no pecuniary aid can be granted to any
Society circulating the Apocrypha;" and in 1827, that all books
sent to societies which circulated the Apocrypha must be distributed "without alteration or addition" and the proceeds held at
the disposal of the BFBS.

The Scots were still dissatisfied, demanding the withdrawal
of BFBS officers from Scotland, and most of the Scottish Auxiliaries seceded. Meanwhile, on the other side of the debate,
twenty-six Cambridge scholars expressed their opposition to
this "violation of one of the grand and fundamental principles
of the Society, namely, that of uniting in one common work the
efforts of all Christian communities," since it would bar the
distribution of the full Bible in some areas. Many European
Auxiliaries, regretting the British policy, announced that they
would continue to circulate the familiar form of Scriptures--
with Apocrypha.

Across the Atlantic those who knew of the debate in Great
Britain hoped that it would not impede the work of the American
Society. A few Christian periodicals carried occasional reports.
Even references to "difficulties" in the Foreign Operations of
the British and Foreign Bible Society seldom specified the nature
of these difficulties, whether from ignorance or unconcern or a
deliberate effort to avoid stirring controversy. An officer in
New York wrote to London in 1826 that there had "not yet appeared
any disposition here to agitate the subject." In 1824 the ABS
Board of Managers had approved publication of a Spanish Bible
based on the Madrid text, an approved Roman Catholic version,
and eight thousand copies were issued by 1829.

From Latin America the opinion was almost unanimous that "we
cannot sell Bibles without the Apocrypha." As far apart as
Mexico and Argentina Roman Catholic priests were denouncing the
abbreviated version as "a Protestant cheat," as "selections"
from the Scriptures, or as a "mutilated Bible." William Torrey,
a clergyman visiting in Buenos Aires, voiced his "feeling that
a man had better be anywhere else, than in this country trying
to circulate the Bible without the Apocrypha at present." "I
am fully persuaded," he continued, "as are also most of those
...who have any acquaintance with the subject that the quickest
&...best way to introduce the 'sincere milk of the word' among
this people is to give it to them mixed with the water of the
Apocrypha so long as the remains of prejudice & ignorance render
them 'not able to bear it' in any other way."

But the subject could not remain "unagitated"--not when professors and other pious Protestants became extremely agitated.
In December, 1827, the Rev. Luther Halsey, a Ministerial Director
of the ABS, wrote from Princeton, New Jersey, rejoicing at the
Society's concern for "the spiritual welfare of South America"--
but "rejoicing with trembling" because he believed that the
Spanish Bible with the Apocrypha represented "an unholy compromise" with "servants of corruption...in upholding an apostate
and antichristian Church." The Bible Society, he declared, must
make sure that their publications "speak exactly and unequivocally the Mind of the Holy Spirit...his perfect and most sacred
Law...which shall fairly and exactly represent to immortals [sic]
what *God hath spoken*." Otherwise, Halsey warned, the "disastrous
divisions" in Great Britain would be repeated in America and
would destroy "the peace and prosperity of the 'National Society.'"

Although he himself would "sincerely deprecate the issue of
an *open* assault on the National Bible Society," he continued in
subsequent correspondence, "some of the first men of the country"
considered the printing or distribution of the Apocrypha as a
violation of "fundamental principle" and would demand that it be
done--if it *must* be done in Latin America--"by a *separate Society*
organized for that purpose."

> There are many christians in this Country, (call them weak
> or bigoted if you please)...who consider it a *sin* for the
> Bible Society to send the catholic version & its apocryphal
> mixtures to the Catholics of the South - Others I know, who
> would revolt on the ground of expedience - Add them all
> together, & if their opposition be called forth, it would
> issue in a lamentable confusion-.....It would embarrass the
> *future proceedings* of the Am.B.S. - It would give a dreadful
> *check to public confidence* in Other Benevolent institutions
> of the age - It would bring into the field under the name
> of religious zeal, much that was hellish.....A war at home
> for the sake of being charitable abroad?....

Halsey was joined in his protest by Moses Stuart, Professor
of Sacred Literature at Andover Seminary from 1810 to 1848.
During his long teaching career Stuart made two notable contributions to Biblical scholarship: to plead for American recognition of German scholars and research, and to establish Hebrew as
a major subject in American seminaries. Finding that few
Americans knew enough Hebrew to teach it effectively, Stuart
compiled the first Hebrew grammar in the United States, then had
to import the type and set it himself because compositors were
totally unfamiliar with the language.

In his communications with the ABS about the Apocrypha,
Stuart appealed to the decision already reached in Europe, and
deplored any policy which might seem to contradict that of the

British and Foreign Bible Society. Fearful of jealousy, mistrust
and dissension among the ranks of Christians, he insisted that
"one and all here - say, NO." Yet he went on to admit, in a
letter of February 7, 1828:

> I must add, for myself, that if the question were to be
> debated, *de Novo*, I should take the other side. I view it
> [the Apocrypha...as] an accompaniment which, though not
> Bible--does not contradict nor counteract it. I cannot see
> any wrong in this.....The apocryphal books have childish, &
> some superstitious, things in them, - but nothing that con-
> traverses sound doctrine.

Nevertheless, in light of the Catholic view that the Apocrypha is
a *bona fide* part of the canon, in respect for the policy adopted
in London, and in view of the threat of vehement opposition or
even secession on the part of some Auxiliaries, Stuart maintained
his adamant position against including the disputed writings.

The pressures were not all on one side. As late as September,
1827, the Board of Managers had approved a massive campaign to
raise $100,000 for printing the Scriptures in Spanish and other
foreign languages. Uninformed or unconcerned about the Apocrypha
controversy, Daniel Merrill, the Maine clergyman already mentione
(in Chapter V), inquired about a Spanish Bible "that evangelist
Protestants can conscientiously approve of its general circulatic
in the new republics at the South," and later offered to raise
funds to establish a Bible depository in every Latin American
country. The Board of Managers acknowledged that they had
"received several communications [from Spanish America], all
purporting that no Bibles without the Apocrypha would find
acceptance."

At home criticism rested on the twin pillars of "fundamental
principle" and financial threat. On April 3, 1828, the special
committee recommended:

> That without deeming it expedient to detail the reasons
> which have influenced the decision of the Committee, they
> have unanimously agreed that the Apocrypha ought not to
> be printed and circulated with the canonical Scriptures
> by the Managers of the American Bible Society.

The Board of Managers promptly resolved:

> That the principles on which the American Bible Society
> is founded, which limit its operation to the circulation
> of the Holy Scriptures without note or comment, be fully
> and distinctly recognized as excluding the circulation of
> the Apocrypha.

They further ordered the immediate alteration of any stereotype plates which included the Apocrypha and the withholding of any Spanish Scriptures on hand in the depository "until the Apocrypha Books be removed therefrom." In explaining the policy to the public, in the Annual Report of 1828, the Managers reviewed their previous distribution of "the Catholic Bible" containing "the uninspired relic" in Latin America.

> They have discussed and deliberated with deep interest, and with some diversity of views, (as to the lawfulness of such distributions,) yet always with perfect charity and Christian forbearance. They have sought the advice of the wise and prudent, and found likewise among them a difference of opinion. To perpetuate that harmony which now so happily prevails among their Auxiliaries, and to prevent an evil which has shaken the mighty Society of England, as with the heavings of an earthquake, your Board have with great unanimity resolved, that no Book containing the Apocrypha shall henceforth be issued from your Depository.

In none of these statements was the prohibition as absolute as that imposed on the British and Foreign Bible Society, especially in regard to funds, although it became so in practice. A few murmurs of protest arose from Latin America, but the "Protestant Bible" without the Apocrypha was not totally spurned, and certain independent Bible Societies, in Colombia for example, continued to circulate Scriptures with the Apocrypha included.

In January, 1827, the Board of Managers appointed a Special Committee to examine various editions of the Bible and compare them (for punctuation, spelling, etc.) with correct, authentic, standard British editions. After the debate over the Apocrypha they realized that this committee should encompass more than technical, scholarly competence. In the new committee appointed in 1829 all the denominations currently represented on the Board were included: Presbyterian, Episcopalian, Baptist, Methodist, Quaker, and Dutch Reformed. By the end of the next decade even this procedure proved insufficient to deal with editorial, linguistic, and theological complexities. In 1836 George Bush was employed to serve as editor for problems of translation (excluding English editions after 1839). He in turn requested a committee to aid and counsel him, and in 1840 this was made into a Standing Committee on Versions, one of the most important branches of Bible Society operation in decades to come.

Close on the heels of the Apocrypha issue came the far more bitter "*Baptizo* Battle." The former had reflected largely anti-Catholic bias; the latter was an internecine struggle within Protestantism, a struggle which split the American Bible Society itself and dragged on for more than a decade.

From their respective inaugurations the Bible Societies in
England and America had demonstrated admiration for William Carey
and the Serampore Mission in many ways: partly because of his
courageous pioneering in a distant place, partly because of his
contributions to Bible translation. Without apparent question
both Boards of Managers had accepted translations made in
Serampore, as in Burma and Hawaii, as "faithful" versions of the
Holy Scriptures. The first serious doubt reached the United
States in 1835 in the form of an appeal from the British Baptist
Mission in Calcutta, for assistance in publishing a second
edition of the New Testament in Bengali. The request admitted
frankly that the British and Foreign Bible Society had declined
such help because the word used for *baptism* clearly implied
immersion. Asserting that "our version is approved & used in
its present state by all denominations" (including "many native
schools of the Church of England"), the Baptist missionary complained that a BFBS committee, allegedly "ten-twelfths pedo-
Baptists, has declined to extend to us its aid," adding:

> We think this illiberal--not Catholick--that they should
> aid *all acknowledged good versions*--that the plan they
> adopt will end in rendering the Bible Society a denomina-
> tional not universal Society & if not altered will lead
> the Baptists to withdraw from the Society & to form a
> Bible Society of their own as soon as they find their
> translations are impeded for want of funds-- If the
> Society interfere about the word Baptism it will be only
> to interfere next about Bishop, deacon, church &c.....
> We look to America for more liberality than at home....

Further investigation revealed that the issue had not arisen
in London until 1827. Then, after several years of slow correspondence and negotiation with Carey, the British and Foreign
Bible Society had voted to provide financial assistance only
when "the Greek terms relating to Baptism were rendered either
according to the principle adopted by the translators of the
English Authorized Version, by a word derived from the original,
or by such terms as might be considered unobjectionable by the
other denominations of Christians composing the Bible Society."
In other words, unless there was an appropriate word in the new
language which did *not* suggest any particular form of ritual
(sprinkling, pouring, or immersion), then the Greek *baptizo*
should be "transferred" or transliterated into the language of
the new translation.

In September, 1835, the ABS appointed a special committee to
study the problem, with one representative from each member
denomination. To forestall any discriminatory action by the
Board of Managers, a Baptist member proposed that "when in any
translation any deviation is made from [the authorized English

version], which affects the articles of belief in which the
denominations...differ," the Board will approve aid (presumably
for translation, publication, or distribution) only by unanimous
consent. This too was referred back to committee. Meanwhile
some uncharitable remarks, including the insinuation that
Baptists had long and deliberately been accepting Bible Society
support for a sectarian text, gravely hurt and offended certain
individuals, including Dr. Spencer H. Cone, a Baptist and
Corresponding Secretary of the Society.

Proposals and counter-proposals were drafted and redrafted,
argued and tabled, over several months. One resolution sought
to redefine the constitutional restriction of "the version in
common use," when applied to foreign languages, as one "that all
religious denominations represented in this Society can consistently use and circulate...in their several schools and communities." Added to this, to be sent to all mission boards likely
to request "pecuniary grants," was a proposition that such
applications for aid must be accompanied by this kind of assurance regarding the edition in question. In a minority report
Secretary Cone declared that Baptists had never understood the
Bible Society to be organized upon this "neutral principle,"
and that if it were to be so enforced, the Society should return
to the Baptist General Convention an unspecified sum (presumably
equal to all previous Baptist donations to the ABS) for their
own use in supplying Scriptures "to the perishing millions of
the East." Since a rough calculation would quickly disclose
that appropriations to Serampore and other Baptist missions had
far surpassed specifically Baptist gifts to the Society, this
demand hardly strengthened his case.

The decisive vote--on "versions..that all the religious
denominations represented...can consistently use and circulate..."
--came on February 17, 1836. Twelve of the fifty-six Managers
present abstained; among the fourteen voting against the
resolution were most of the Baptists--and William and Peter Jay,
Episcopalians. If, as one of the Secretaries later wrote, the
only other courses open were to stop foreign distribution or let
all denominations translate as they pleased, then clearly the
"neutral principle" had to be enforced in all translations
receiving Society support.

Although the meeting "was conducted on both sides with
commendable spirit," the Baptists attempted at several subsequent
meetings to present "a respectful remonstrance," which was eventually rejected on the ground that it was "inexpedient to receive
any protest from a Minority on a question which has been discussed and decided by Ayes and Noes recorded." At the same time
the Baptist Board of Foreign Missions declined an appropriation
from the Bible Society of $5,000 for Scriptures in foreign

languages, implying that "certain conditions" were unacceptable. Instead they called on Baptist churches to supply the needed funds and advised their missionaries engaged in translation to ascertain the exact *meaning* of the original text, and not to "transfer" any words capable of literal translation.

Rebuffed once again at the Annual Meeting of 1836, Spencer Cone resigned as Corresponding Secretary of the American Bible Society (as did most, but not all, of the Baptist members from the Board) and organized the American and Foreign Bible Society. Among other innovations the AFBS printed a New Testament with a supplementary page giving Greek, Authorized Version, and "Proper meaning" of such words as *angel, baptist, bishop, overseer, churc congregation,* and *passover*. As the ABS tried repeatedly to make clear--to constituents, to missionaries, and later to politicians --the issue was not a denial of immersion, but an unwillingness to translate an ambiguous Greek term with an *un*ambiguous foreign word. The editorial superintendent of the British and Foreign Bible Society expressed its parallel policy unequivocally:

> If...any body of Christian translators should choose to express it by a native word, the Committee will not object, provided always that the word selected be one that simply implies a religious rite in which water is employed, without defining the mode or extent of its application. Dipping Versions, and sprinkling ones, if such there be, will never obtain the sanction, I am assured, of this society.

Despite this clearly defined position, some embittered and overzealous Baptists continued to attack the American Bible Society. On one hand, they charged that transliteration was a "popish practice," "an unintelligible language to the laity" introduced by "the arbitrary act of King Jas.;" that a translation meaning "dip" had actually been used in Welsh, Dutch, Russian, and other versions which the Baptists had not protested. As a matter of fact, it was discovered later that the term used in the Seneca Gospel of Luke did mean "sprinkle" or "pour;" the ABS in 1841 acknowledged, explained, apologized--and did not republish that edition. On the other hand, Baptist critics claimed that donations from Baptist churches had been deceitfully diverted into anti-Baptist causes (e.g. $40,000-50,000 in legacies, which turned out to amount to only $18,000, all of which had been spent in the United States during the General Supply of 1829-31).

The legislative campaign proved to be still more virulent. In 1841 the American Bible Society was incorporated under the laws of the State of New York. At the same time the rival American and Foreign Bible Society attempted to incorporate in the same state. For two successive years the latter application was rejected, but a renewed effort in 1844 set off a series of maneuvers and counter-maneuvers, a tidal wave of lobbying pro and con, and a flood of letters and "remonstrances." Although complaints were registered that the similarity in names caused legal and postal confusion, not only with the American Bible Society but also with the British and Foreign Bible Society, ABS forces concentrated their efforts on the demand that the schismatics should include the term "Baptist" in their title. This they refused to do, on the ground that members of some other denominations were participating in the AFBS. Unholy pressures were applied to "pious members" of the legislature and its Committee on Religious and Charitable Societies; lobbyists for each side spent weeks in Albany soliciting votes; pamphlets were printed to inform officials and the general public of the issues involved; petitions were sent in from all corners of the state.

Finally the Baptist Bible Society (as the ABS always called it) was granted a charter of incorporation as the American and Foreign Baptist Bible Society, only to have the General Baptist Convention refuse the name and renew the campaign for an American and Foreign Bible Society. By 1845 the politicians--and many of the advocates--had grown weary of the controversy. Yet the ABS representative in Albany reported that the battle was "hotter and hotter," and one legislator told another that if the Baptists did not succeed on this occasion, they would bring the matter into "Politicks" next year. (This suited ABS supporters admirably, since Methodists alone in New York State outnumbered Baptists by almost three to two.) Rumors of compromise or concession soared and then collapsed. The observation that no new charter could be granted until the 1844 one had been repealed seemed to disturb no one, politician or protagonist.

The vote was finally taken in late April, when "the House was uncommonly thin," and resulted in a two-thirds majority *of those present* favoring the AFBS charter, but incorporation required two-thirds of the *total elected membership*; the American and Foreign Bible Society had failed by six votes.

In September a member of both the AFBS and ABS Boards proposed that the American Bible Society should remain passive in the next attempt to secure incorporation, that Auxiliaries and friends should cease all opposition to the rival organization, and that both societies should cease publishing anything perpetuating strife or contention. Although the ABS Board courteously tabled the resolution, it renewed its resistance the following year, and the Baptist effort failed again by five votes. By 1848 provisions for incorporating charitable institutions had been simplified in the State Legislature, and the American and Foreign Bible Society was finally chartered. By then both sides were exhausted, the Baptists so much so that in 1850 they decided *against* publishing

an English version which would use the word *immerse*, but to
remain instead with the "commonly received version without note
or comment" (namely, the King James Bible).

However this decision produced still another schism. In order
to publish a truly "Baptist Bible," actually a new English translation, an American Bible Union was organized, with Spencer Cone
as president. This further split contributed, indirectly at
least, to a "growing friendliness" between members and officers
of the first two societies. Men like Dr. Francis Weyland,
President of Brown University and a Life Member of the American
Bible Society, labored continuously for a reconciliation, which
he believed would "begin at the south and move northwardly."
Urging patience and Christian feeling, he suggested in 1856 an
invitation to the AFBS President to read the Scriptures and pray
at an Annual Meeting of the ABS (an invitation not received in
time, but warmly appreciated), and the appointment of a prominent
Southern Baptist layman, Judge John Belton O'Neall, as a Vice-
President of the American Bible Society. Judge O'Neall graciousl
accepted the appointment in the hope that "if I could be instrumental, *in restoring union*, I should rejoice in it."

Such gestures of goodwill, together with time and the Holy
Spirit, brought gradual healing. After much deliberation the
ABS in 1856 declined a request from the AFBS to print an edition
of the Bible with a joint title page, since it did not grant that
privilege to its own Auxiliaries. As late as 1865 some dissident
Baptists revived ancient accusations against the "Parent Society,
but it is noteworthy that most of these belated and belabored
charges came from the mid-West. The extraordinary efforts of the
American Bible Society to supply Scriptures to Southern Baptist
Sunday Schools during and after the Civil War did not go unnotice
Eventually Baptists in various conventions resumed their earlier
place among the most loyal supporters of the ABS. To a large
degree, as President Weyland foresaw, reconciliation did "begin
at the south and move northwardly."

While it lasted, the controversy, ironically stemming from the
doctrine of Christian baptism, was painful and deplorable. Not
only did it violate the basic spirit of Christian harmony and
cooperation on which the American Bible Society was founded, but
it provided a shocking public example of Christian people reduced
to settling their conflicts in a secular arena. Yet the Managers
of the American Bible Society never really doubted, since the
Baptizo issue first broke upon them, that a sectarian translation
of any disputed doctrinal word in any language would violate *both*
constitutional provisions: "the version in common [i.e. universally accepted] use...without note or comment."

This uneasiness about acceptable versions lingered on, as an
understandably sensitive area. Although many scholars regarded

the Latin Vulgate as one of the most accurate editions of the
Bible, there were critics who considered it too "Catholic" even
with the Apocrypha removed. When someone asked if the founders
of the Society would have approved of the Vulgate, the answer
was clearly, Yes, yet the Board of Managers acted quickly in 1842
to substitute a Protestant version of the Spanish Bible to avoid
giving offense.

Somewhat ironically, having helped to precipitate the *Baptizo*
controversy, the British and Foreign Bible Society wrote in 1848:
"We always ventured to think that you gave up the point of
versions from the Vulgate rather too easily." The reasoning was
that Spanish-speaking Protestant scholars, in Europe or Latin
America, were so scarce that both their theological understanding
and their linguistic competence would presumably be less reliable
than the Catholic translation from the Vulgate. Even the Society
for the Propagation of Christian Knowledge, long a bellwether of
missionary policy in England, had accepted a new Spanish translation from the Vulgate by the Bishop of Barcelona.

Questions of what constituted "note or comment" were more
easily settled than a "common version" in some new language. Yet
the Society over the years made these determinations with equal
care.

Although a committee in 1816, in the first six months of ABS
operation, had deemed it "inexpedient" to publish separate
Testaments "at present," the Board never voted this as official
policy. Exactly a year later it appropriated $500 for a French
New Testament, as already noted. A proposal to print English
Testaments from the full Bible plates was postponed "indefinitely"
in March, 1818, because of divided opinion, but when Boudinot,
Bayard, and other influential officers renewed the appeal a
month later, the matter was reconsidered. It was then decided
to prepare a New Testament in large type for elderly people and
a New Testament in smaller type for learners, manufacturing new
plates lest additional usage of plates from the whole Bible
should make them wear unevenly.

In an editorial comment 145 years later, long-time General
Secretary Eric M. North pointed out that "the issue was manifestly a religious rather than an economic one," as indicated by
the use of the term *propriety* in regard to a separate New Testament edition. It is difficult today to comprehend any reservation
whatever on this point. As North continued, "the victory of
Christian common sense over dogmatic scruples was of immense
importance to the Society's missionary task, for with the New
Testament millions upon millions were to come with directness
to the Gospel and to the Redeemer of mankind."

As editions multiplied, with different sized pages and different sized types, it was discovered that chapter summaries and running guides which had been taken for granted in the King James Version did not always fit the new formats. Their elimination would appear a simple economy of space, yet they constituted a problem for editors for the next forty years. Pleas came into the Society for and against these headings. Unitarians warned that such notations represented a violation of the fundamental basis on which they had consented to cooperate with the Society. Proponents demanded not only chapter headings but a table of contents, bound between the Old and New Testaments, for the benefit of those many readers who did not own concordances. They even offered to pay more for this editorial aid. Declaring that the only previous omission of such headings had been "for the sole purpose of saving expense," the Board of Managers in 1830 reaffirmed that it "would not feel justified" in publishing any other headings than those found in the King James Bible, still the English Version "in common use," to which the Society was constitutionally restricted. Not until 1931 did the Committee on Translations authorize a revision in "running heads," which should be "simple summaries, without doctrinal bias and as far as possible in the words of the text."

From several churches in the Reformed tradition came appeals for the inclusion of the Scottish Metrical Psalms. Advocates urged persuasively that such an edition would greatly increase distribution and hence more than cover additional costs, and that it would be an opportunity for the American Bible Society to "go far to harmonize the different branches of the Christian Church on the important subject of Psalmody, the most delightful of divine institutions." Refusal, on the other hand, it was argued, would be "exceedingly unpopular in our neighborhood," might lead to the formation of a new Bible society, and, some feared, would "place the gravestone upon the Inspired Songs of Zion. We think otherwise however." To this entreaty the Board rendered a firm decision: "inadmissible."

A missionary request for binding the Bible with the Catechism and some hymns in tribal languages for American Indians was rejected as "inconsistent with the principles of the ABS." A separate edition of the Psalms was judged "inexpedient"--although millions of these have been issued in later decades. An appeal from Singapore in 1836 to include explanatory notes to aid the heathen was turned down sharply. Despite the fact that a few Portions had been printed for Indians, Hawaiians, and Latin Americans, when the Young Men's Bible Society of New York proposed Portions in English, French, or German for immigrants, the Board of Managers doubted the wisdom of such a move. Even the distribution of unbound pages to other societies was discontinued in 1818, not only because it upset bindery schedules, invited

poor quality without the ABS embossed stamp, and often resulted
in greater instead of less expense through use of insubstantial
covers, but *also* for fear that unauthorized persons might bind
other materials of note or comment along with the Bible.

With petitions of this kind, especially after the "battle of
Baptizo," the Board of Managers naturally sought to clarify and
regularize their policies. The Annual Report of 1844 reminded
missionaries and contributors that "when engaged in a common
united work, every thing of a sectarian character must be laid
aside." Article IV of the 1846 By-Laws, reaffirmed in 1853, set
forth the position adopted in 1836 (which had led to the Baptist
withdrawal): that appropriations for translating, printing, or
distributing should encourage "only such versions as conform in
the principles of their translation" to the common English
version, so that all participating denominations "can consistently
use and circulate said versions in their several schools and
communities." The revised By-Laws of 1858 specified, at the
request of the Versions Committee itself, that it "shall examine
all new translations thereof in foreign languages presented for
the consideration and action of the Society, especially in regard
to their catholicity and the fidelity of their translation...."
And the Managers announced in 1860 that the Society could support
translations, corrections, and editing, "subject to the action
and decision of the Committee on Versions and the Board."

Thus, as the number and scope of foreign translations expanded,
the American Bible Society endeavored to safeguard the purity not
only of the texts which it published and/or distributed, but also
of its constitutional commitment to circulate the sacred Scriptures in the "version in common use...without note or comment."

7

Changing Patterns in
the United States

Methods of operation that answered our purposes thirty or
fifty years ago are not sufficient now. Our system should
be made flexible enough to meet the altered condition of
things in this age; and this involves no real change of
principle, but new applications of our power in practicable,
safe, and tried forms of Christian enterprize.

With this ringing affirmation "Upon the Enlargement of the
Work" the Secretaries of the American Bible Society called in
1869 for a series of new policies and experimentations. The
second half of the nineteenth century brought accelerated change
to every facet of American life. Even the records of the Bible
Society, without going into political and social documentation,
reveal how fundamentally and drastically the Civil War shook the
very roots of society: psychologically and culturally as well
as economically. The growth of the United States in its first
ninety years had been relatively mild and leisurely. But after
1865--as after 1945, far more than after 1918--the transformation
was deep and pervasive. The nation would never be the same again

Most obvious, of course, were the scars of fratricidal war,
the political wrenching of attempted secession, and the social
upheaval which began in the 1860's and continues to convulse the
nation a century later. The industrial revolution gained
unimaginable momentum. Fresh waves of immigration, from Asia as
well as Eastern and Southern Europe, turned quiet Anglo-Saxon
cities into polyglot and polychrome cities. The single decade
at mid-century saw the territorial boundaries of the United State
push far westward to embrace Texas (1845); California, Nevada,

Utah, Arizona, parts of Colorado, New Mexico, Texas, and Oklahoma (1848); Oregon (by boundary agreement of 1846); Arizona and New Mexico additions (Gadsden Purchase, 1853). Communications, too, kept stretching toward the Pacific with the opening of the Erie Canal in the mid-twenties, the invention of the telegraph in the 'forties, the completion of the transcontinental railroad in the 'sixties.

Earlier chapters on the initial activities of the American Bible Society carried the story through the first twenty-five years. In succeeding decades the percentage of church membership in the United States continued to grow slowly but steadily, reaching 22.7 per cent before the Civil War. Under the inspired preaching of Lyman Beecher, his son Henry Ward Beecher, and the evangelist Charles G. Finney, churches along the Eastern seaboard experienced a series of great revivals. On the frontiers circuit riders were replaced by camp meetings as settlements became more numerous and less isolated. Tensions over the slavery issue split the Methodist Episcopal Church, the Presbyterian Church, and many local congregations. Of greatest effect on Bible societies, the growing size and strength of the churches led to increasing concentration on denominational programs and budgets, including home and foreign missions.

By the middle of the century Scripture circulation had settled into a steady, seemingly dependable pattern. In the decade of 1840-1850 distribution of Bibles had increased three and one half times, of New Testaments five times, with only two years not showing a gain, in contrast to the "waverings in the twenty-four years preceding." Auxiliaries were still regarded as "indispensable," although the "Parent Society" offered alternative provisions, especially the hiring of Agents and Colporteurs, where local societies were not fulfilling their task. Depositories had been established at Chicago and Alton, Cleveland, Detroit, Louisville, Madison and New Albany (Indiana), Memphis, and Milwaukee. But these had proved to be a costly concession: tying up capital, delaying payments, and sometimes encouraging inertia. Omitting this system entirely from its 1845 By-Laws, the Board of Managers restricted Depositories to $1,000 worth of stock and authorization from the Committee on Distribution.

Up until this time Auxiliaries had been entrusted with the major share of collection and distribution. Agents were appointed primarily to establish and encourage local societies; in 1846 permission was granted for them to carry supplies of books *for sale*, but not for gratuitous distribution without express approval, and "not to interfere with the regular Auxiliary system." By mid-century this emphasis had drastically changed. The 1849 Annual Report declared flatly: "The agents of the Society have two objects distinctly and constantly before them: the

distribution of the Bible, and the collection of funds." The
1850 Report revealed even more fully the failure of the Auxiliaries: "We are satisfied that over the whole country new
societies will not be formed, funds will not be collected, nor
the work of exploration and supply prosecuted to any adequate
extent, or in any way equal to the wants of the country and the
cause, without the influence of active, enterprising agents."

In that year some twenty-seven Agents were employed, from
four or five different denominations, "liberal and catholic men,
of piety, activity and zeal; men who engage in the work from
sincere love of the cause." Their salaries ranged from $500 to
$1,000 per annum plus travel expenses. Several worked for the
Society as long as ten years, many from four to six years. One
Auxiliary reported that without an Agent it collected about $700
a year in the county, with a partial agency $1,100, and with all
the townships visited receipts were $2,000. An itinerant in
Michigan rejoiced at--

> ...the spirit of benevolence and philanthropy that is mani-
> fested towards this noble cause, the cordiality with which
> the agent is received in every place, and by Christians of
> different denominations, and the interest manifested by
> many who make no profession of religion, but who desire the
> universal circulation of the Bible for its beneficial
> influence in a moral and civil point of view.

Agents supplied most of the human interest stories used for
emotional appeal in the Annual Reports or *The Bible Society
Record*.

From Alabama: "I am a widow; my husband was a drinking man,
and I have had hard work to support my children, and we have no
Bible. If you can give me one, I shall thank you as long as I
live." Told that the Agent had just given away his last copy,
"she took a little boy by the hand, sobbing, *'O, how shall I get
a Bible?'*" And the Agent added:

> I have heard many passionate exclamations, but never one
> that so filled me with sadness, and so continued to ring
> in my ears, and to thrill my heart, at those tears and
> that--*'O, how shall I get a Bible?'* People of God, will
> you not come to our rescue, and help us by your liberal
> contributions, to extricate from this wretchedness the
> poor for whom the Saviour died?

From Georgia: the account of a drunkard who clutched a Bible
under his arm, "where it continued, during all his intoxication,
for two days and nights," but the fact that this miraculous gift
was neither injured nor soiled during that ordeal was accepted a

"Divine interposition in its behalf," with the result "that he has quit the use of ardent spirits."

Or the "hard-working German men and women" in Ohio, who in 1850 subscribed $2,500, principally in Life Memberships, "most of it, to be earned by weaving, spinning, sewing, and selling butter and eggs. One German Lutheran, owning 110 acres of land-- with six small children, from any of whom he can yet receive but very little assistance--has undertaken to dig out of the *natural soil* seven life-memberships--$210."

And a Tennessee Agent voiced his conviction that "there are thousands of planters in the South West, who could easily do the like, and God would no doubt bless them in the deed, by making their fields yet more fruitful, and their hearts glad in the consciousness of having performed a noble charity."

Gradually the Agency system was supplemented, though never replaced, by colportage. Missionaries and Christian travelers (like Samuel J. Mills) had often carried "wallets" or saddle-bags full of Bibles and Testaments. Apparently the Louisville and Vicinity Bible Society in 1838 employed the first colporteur-- whose dictionary definition ("a hawker or distributer, esp. of religious tracts and books") came from the French: to peddle, to carry around the neck, to carry around, or (appropriately) endure. The Lexington and Vicinity Bible Society, seeking a similar employee, rejected one Abolitionist whose "usefulness would be marred to say the least" but found another man, John G. Simpson, who became in 1840 the first colporteur on ABS salary, $1 a day and travel for six months. By 1843 there were fifty-six colporteurs in nineteen states, in the 1880's over 300.

During the next few decades, however, it was impossible to estimate the number or the effectiveness of these salesmen. Many were employed by local Auxiliaries. Although the "Parent Society" would not pay, on constitutional grounds, for any colporteur who distributed other books, it did encourage local societies to join forces with the American Tract Society and other similar groups for joint colportage. The primary task was selling Bibles and Testaments, at cost plus transportation; colporteurs were not to collect donations or subscriptions, and only reluctantly did the Society give permission for free dis- tribution of books. Occasionally debates arose as to whether colporteurs should be self-supporting, accepting book donations from the ABS but covering their expenses out of the sale price.

Not until 1869, in their Special Report "Upon the Enlargement of the Work," did the Secretaries propose a formal "system of *Bible Colportage*, which shall be supplementary to the Society's present method of operation through its Agents and Auxiliaries,

and various benevolent institutions."   Immediately the South
Carolina Agent wrote his acclaim:

> The friends of the Bible will rejoice at the introduction
> of the long *desired, wise* & *timely* system of Colportage
> into South Cardina. This will infuse new life into the
> Auxiliaries & enable them to send the Bible to the poor
> and needy in *hundreds* of obscure remote neighborhoods
> where the people are only accessible to the colporteur.

Although the new organization did not universally "infuse new
life into the Auxiliaries," it did provide for the rest of the
century a useful, even essential, substitute for declining local
societies. Colporteurs became, in a sense, the post-Civil War
circuit riders, and their journals glowed with the same commit-
ment--and the same hardships.

One in Kentucky resolved "to *visit in person every family*
that could possibly be reached by any human being, either on
horseback or on foot. In carrying out this plan, I more than
once endangered my life, and lost a favourite and faithful horse"
(from eating poison ivy). Another, however, urged his fellow-
ministers of evangelical churches--

> ...who may be burying their talents in our larger cities
> and towns, amid the profusion of Gospel privileges, to go
> out into the mountains of this State, where they will find
> a calm and safe retreat, a kind and hospitable people, a
> wide field for usefulness, and an effectual remedy for
> dyspepsia and all sedentary diseases.

When some colporteurs were called Distributing Agents and
others were specifically encouraged to establish "Bible organizations," labels and functions became increasingly blurred. Yet
for most of this period, 1840-1900, it appeared to be true, as
the Secretaries had prophesied, "that colportage produces '*the
largest results with the smallest expenditure of means.*'"

Some of the movements which were to transform the nation--and
the American Bible Society--during the next half century were
already under way by 1850. One of these was the opening of the
West, although vast, uninhabited regions still stretched between
the Mississippi and the Rockies. Much of the new territory was
acquired by occupation, negotiation, or purchase. But the
Mexican War of 1846-48 represented the first military engagement
of the United States since the Bible Society had been founded.
Determination to provide Scriptures for the armed forces had been
made clear in time of peace. In time of war the effort was
intensified with the same despatch which characterized the Societ
in later, larger conflicts. The Annual Report of 1847 claimed

simply but proudly: "It may well be questioned whether any army ever went forth before so amply provided [with Scriptures]."

The cession of California to the United States, followed almost immediately by the discovery of gold there, opened up a cosmopolitan new field for Bible distribution. In early July, 1849, the Board of Managers instructed its Committee on Agencies to "send an efficient Agent to California...and send him forth immediately." Six weeks later Frederick Buel sailed from New York to be "Our Agent at California." His letters, reprinted in *The Bible Society Record*, provide a fascinating--surprisingly contemporaneous--glimpse of the suddenly bustling Pacific coast. Buel traveled by way of Panama, where he contracted the Isthmian fever which killed six of his fellow-passengers. When he arrived on October 8 in San Francisco Bay, the town, still without any wharves, was in a "drizzly fog" that soon turned into unseasonable torrents of rain.

To Buel "the strange mingling of faces, complexions, garbs and dresses" represented an evangelistic opportunity like that of Pentecost. "Such a field," he wrote, "is not open to my knowledge in any part of the globe." From Asia had come Malays, Japanese, and "the overflowing population of China...pouring itself on American soil." "The islands of the sea brought tribute to us in their sons"--Sandwich Islanders, New Zealanders, Marquesans, and Society Islanders. People from every nation in Europe were there, Buel declared, with Germans most numerous. Mexicans, Chilenos, and Peruvians provided merchants, mechanics, and some laborers. But the "native Californians...the oldest inhabitants...are known by their dress and appearance; their dark and swarthy countenances are overshadowed by broad sombreros and partially concealed by their unshorn locks and beards. In place of cloaks they wear coloured ponchos...."

Just three weeks after landing, Buel brought together representatives of all religious denominations in San Francisco except Baptists and Roman Catholics. Aware that the Gold Rush, the Pacific trade, the agricultural resources of the West, all would make of the port city a rapidly growing center strategic for the nation and the globe, they "determined that it was expedient to form a Bible Society" auxiliary to the ABS. The original officers included John M. Finney (Presbyterian), Dr. J. L. Ver Mehr (Episcopalian), William Taylor (Methodist), and Fred Hawley (Congregationalist)--names still known and honored in their respective denominations. *The Bible Society Record* (September, 1849) may have been too optimistic in declaring that in California the Holy Scriptures were "more to be desired...than gold, yes, than much fine gold," but it was correct that "while the foundations of civil government and social order are laid, it is of indispensable importance that the Word of God should be the corner stone."

While the lure of gold glittered far away on the Pacific
coast, the shadow of slavery lay over large portions of the
United States and threatened to spread into new territories. As
Abolitionist sentiment increased in mid-century, the offers of
money to supply the slaves with Bibles became in some instances
bitter accusations: that the Society neglected the distribution
of Scriptures among the colored population or that it yielded
to local prejudice in actual opposition to supplying Negroes. In
1847 the Board of Managers adopted a detailed report "On the
Subject of Distributing the Scriptures Among Slaves." This
reviewed previous resolutions of the Board and grants which had
been made for this purpose, but it also presented, more fully
than ever before, two major, inhibiting factors.

One such obstacle to supply was the illiteracy of most slaves.
Insisting that "few, very few, have that ability [to read the
Bible]," the Report concluded that "there is a previous work to
be done by the schoolmaster or other teacher." But, despite the
demands of many zealous Abolitionists, the Board of Managers
rejected this role of social reform for the Society. "It is an
institution for one great, simple object. It is not formed for
purposes of education, or missions, or the correction of civil
laws; but it is formed for the purpose of circulating the Word
of God without note or comment, *as far as practicable*, among all
classes and conditions of men who are capable of using it."
Acknowledging that more might and should be done, by the "Parent
Society" and by Southern Auxiliaries, to get Scriptures into the
hands of colored people who could read, the Report gently
questioned the motives and misapprehensions of those in the North
so intent on raising money for a special purpose.

The other restrictive factor was the Auxiliary system. Some
of these societies were "large State institutions, organized
before the American Bible Society;" most of them were bound to it
only by simple promises to circulate the Scriptures without note
or comment and to remit their *surplus* revenue to New York. In
local matters of procedure, agents, coverage, budgets, policy,
etc. they were completely independent. "And this is a state of
things which the Board, on account of its important bearings,
would by no means disturb, even if they had the power." In
conclusion, the Report pledged the Society to use every opportunity "to further the distribution of the Bible among the slave
population at the South," but it also inquired of all partisan
donors "whether it would be wise to *restrict* their contributions
to an object which can only be obtained gradually, and the funds
for which must remain in part unexpended, while others of the
human family equally destitute, and more accessible, are left
unsupplied with the Word of God."

This policy statement did not allay criticisms. Was it true:
(a) that the ABS did not supply Scriptures to slaves? (b) that

Agents were instructed to pass by slave homes? (c) that the
Society declined a grant (of $1,000? or $10,000?) for use among
the slaves? (d) that there was an Agent in the South assigned to
slaves, but the ABS ignored him? To critical, analytical eyes
today, many of the replies--mostly from Secretary Joseph Holdich--
may appear evasive. The Society had made numerous grants, in
books and money, for slaves and colored people, but distribution
was *always* left to Auxiliaries, in keeping with policy. Certainly
Agents had never been instructed to ignore the blacks. But
Holdich declared that he *knew* of no law forbidding Scriptures to
the slaves, and that *if* the Bible Society had been offered donations by Abolitionist groups, it had been before his time.

Actually (as indicated in Chapter IV) at least two substantial
offers from the American Anti-Slavery Society had been declined,
on grounds that very few slaves could read, that some slave-
holders would object, that any such supply should be handled by
local Auxiliaries, and that so large a restricted designation
would tie up funds or stocks which could more readily and promptly
be used elsewhere. Yet false charges of deliberate discrimination
continued for years after the Civil War. On the other hand, it
must be admitted that the figures for circulation among Negroes
in the entire decade before the War were dismayingly small: 246
Bibles, 689 Testaments, 78 Portions, 380 Bibles and Testaments--
many of these to New York, New Jersey, Ohio, and even Canada,
with only North Carolina, Virginia, and Kentucky mentioned among
Southern states.

When the Civil War did break out, the Bible Society immediately
recognized three crucial areas of need: Southern civilians,
freedmen and escaped slaves, and the armed forces North and South.
Contact with the Confederate States and the Auxiliaries located
there was severed almost completely, with the partial exception
of Virginia. In June, 1861, ABS Secretary James McNeill resigned
from the New York headquarters and returned to his native North
Carolina, serving later in the Confederate Army. The following
year a Confederate States Bible Society was formed in Augusta,
Georgia, but the two editions of New Testaments which it had
printed in Atlanta were totally inadequate for the need.

In a bold, dramatic gesture Dr. Moses D. Hoge, a Presbyterian
minister from Richmond, slipped through the Charleston blockade
to Nassau, arriving in England in February, 1863. There he
appealed to the British and Foreign Bible Society for a purchase,
on credit, of 10,000 Bibles, 50,000 Testaments, and 250,000
Portions. This the BFBS readily granted without conditions,
although stressing to Dr. Hoge "their deep and conscientious
feelings with regard to the impartiality that should be observed
in the distribution of the Bible." The British also declined to
accept any responsibility for transporting these books, and hope

of a direct shipment through the blockade under a flag of truce
had to be abandoned. Therefore packages trickled into various
Southern ports along with "medicines, gunpowder, and other
contraband" over a wide span of time. Some were captured some
were sunk, some appeared or disappeared at odd places like
Havana, but most of them reached their intended destination,
and were distributed "almost exclusively to the soldiers."

This appeal, duly reported from London to New York, confirmed
the destitution of Scriptures in the South and intensified efforts
of the ABS to meet that need. As early as July, 1861, the Board
of Managers announced that it saw no reason "to make any alteration in their practice and policy in regard to supplying the
Auxiliary Societies," which continued to be listed in all Annual
Reports. The problem was one of communication and transportation
through the lines. Although an early shipment of Testaments
apparently got into Kentucky, later packages were stopped as
contraband by the Union commanding officer in Cairo, Illinois.

One door did remain surprisingly and consistently open:
Maryland. Repeatedly the Agent there appealed for "full and free
donations" to the Maryland Bible Society. Wagons traversed the
roads from Baltimore to Virginia with comparative freedom; U.S.
customs and military permits were readily granted; and Southern
pride accepted donations from Maryland that would have been
spurned directly from New York. The Annual Report of 1863
estimated that some 30,000 volumes had been sent into the South,
chiefly by that route.

Later that year the Maryland Bible Society received from the
Virginia Bible Society a request for 25,000 Bibles and 75,000
Testaments, to be paid for eventually, not accepted as charity.
A rather petulant letter also complained that the "Parent Society"
had not replied to earlier requests and was presumably unwilling
to correspond with the South, also that Bibles had been declared
contraband by the United States authorities. Thomas Quinan, the
resourceful Maryland Agent, pointed out that this order was
obviously too large for the Maryland Society to fill, and furthermore, "I have letters showing that the VA Bi So well understood
where the largest portion of the books come from." Nevertheless
the ABS somewhat defensively instructed Quinan in a rather
"pointed way" to notify the Southerners that it had been supplying Bibles to the Confederacy all along, and this "aroused their
political animosity," in Quinan's view. However this wartime
exchange ended with an apology from the Virginia Society for the
"unfortunate wording" which may have caused misunderstanding, and
with appreciation for all efforts to supply the South with
Scriptures.

One other major appeal reached the New York headquarters
through the Maryland Bible Society "by flag of truce" in the

summer of 1863: an order for 25,000 New Testaments for the
Southern Baptist Sunday School Board. "The condition of paying
after the war ends" caused fewer reservations than the prospect
of catering so largely to a single denomination. When the grant
was made, and forwarded by the United States government "free of
cost," Agent Quinan, one of the sceptics, admitted that "the
impression upon the Baptist body generally is most happy." Where
"hitherto we could not do anything among that denomination," he
was now invited to a Baptist pulpit (in Baltimore?) "to present
the Bible cause!!! This is a remarkable innovation." The
magnanimous gesture may, in fact, have been a vital "breakthrough"
not only in North-South relations, but in Baptist attitudes
toward the American Bible Society.

During the War itself distribution of Scriptures among Negroes
probably declined rather than advanced. The Emancipation
Proclamation of January 1, 1863, was of course operative only in
territories occupied by Union troops. Even in many places in
the North, escaped slaves were regarded as "contraband of war"
to be used like other captured property. Although many freedmen
and white sympathizers recognized the importance of learning to
read, little could be done to combat illiteracy during the
conflict. Yet an Agent on tour in Virginia and North Carolina
immediately after the War reported "bright...prospects of a
future harvest:"

There is an eager desire among all this people to possess
the Word of God. Even while they cannot read, they have a
kind of superstitious reverence for it. To have it lying
on the table of their humble cottage, would be a comfort
highly prized, and even some of their former masters quite
demurred at my position, that the ability to read should be
a condition of giving them a copy of the Bible. The whole
Bible is one of the first objects of their desire when they
begin to gather around them the conveniences of a self-
regulated house.

Meanwhile contributions came from as far away as Constantinople--
from Greeks, Armenians, and one Mohammedan--to supply ex-slaves
with Scriptures.

Provision for the armed forces, North and South, became the
top priority for the American Bible Society. Much of the distribution among Union soldiers was carried on by the U.S. Christian Commission, a service agency of the Y.M.C.A., actually
organized in the Bible House at New York in 1862. Hundreds of
thousands of New Testaments were distributed by chaplains,
Auxiliaries, regular Agents, and three special Army Agents, in
hospitals and camps, on battlefields and ships, in prison camps
and naval stations. "In common with millions," declared the

Chairman of the Christian Commission in October, 1862, "we thank God for the American Bible Society."

> ...Never before did its value seem so great. A million of men, enlisted to save the nation at the peril of life, lift up their voices and stretch out their hands for the Word of God.....The Testament is small and slips into the soldier's pocket. It is light and he can carry it. Its words go straight down into his heart, and make that light too.

Altogether the Christian Commission alone, not to mention the Society's normal channels, handled "1,466,748 volumes of the Sacred Word...amid those scenes of war and carnage."

How many more copies reached servicemen on the Southern side can never be accurately counted. An appeal for 25,000 Bibles and 75,000 Testaments for Army colportage in North Carolina offered to pay for at least part of the order in cotton, which would be shipped north if possible or "religiously held for the Society" until the war was over. A shipment of books to the Confederate Army through Memphis was approved by the Secretary of the Treasury in Washington, provided it could be packed and sealed by U.S. Customs agents, since "disloyal or unscrupulous persons" had been known to transport percussion caps and other contraband goods in innocent-seeming bundles.

At the close of hostilities the Bible Society moved promptly to bind up the wounds with its particular resources. In answer to allegations of discrimination and neglect, the Secretaries issued in August, 1865, a major document entitled "The American Bible Society and the South." It reviewed the efforts, general and specific, which had been made to supply Bibles to Confederate soldiers and civilians. Now that "Providence has plainly ordained that we shall be one people, with one government, one civilization one Bible, one Christian faith and destiny," the officers pledged: "Our purpose is to supply the entire population of the South, irrespective of colour, just as rapidly as Providence shall open the way and give us the means and the men for its accomplishment."

Despite some resentment at charitable gifts from the North, most of the Auxiliaries which had survived the War reopened communication with the "Parent Society." By 1867 ABS Agents were at work in every Southern state except Louisiana and Maryland, where the State societies had their own employed agents. At the height of war-time destitution Bibles had even been taken from churches and Sunday Schools to supply the armed forces, and these had to be replaced. Once Emancipation was conceded, the importance of Negro education and evangelization became self-evident. Regarding freedmen the 1867 Annual Report declared:

All the unsolved problems, and hopes, and fears, connected
with their future, may well determine the whole nation to
work at once with zealous wisdom for their education and
elevation in mind, morals, and religion. The question of
their civil rights is indissolubly bound up with their
possession of the Bible, and their strong religious sus-
ceptibilities, limited knowledge and experience, pre-
eminently demand that they have the Bible as a school book
and in their families...

By 1869 the Board of Managers concluded "that the restoration
of the American Bible Society in that whole region may now be
regarded as accomplished," and neither the "Parent Society" nor
the Auxiliaries henceforth made racial distinctions in their
reports. Yet exactly thirty years later *The Bible Society Record*
admitted that "the future of the negro population of this country,
especially in the southern states, is an even more important
question that that of Mormonism, and a more difficult one." A
proposal for the establishment of an agency for distribution
among blacks was not adopted until 1901, on the threshold of a
new century.

Other dramatic changes besides those of race and war were
taking place on the American continent. The revolution in transportation became an opportunity for the Bible Society. In the
first half of the nineteenth century Auxiliaries had found a
receptive clientele among passengers and crews on the lakes,
canals, and rivers, generally heading West. During the brief
but colorful years of the Pony Express (1860-1862) the Overland
Mail Company supplied most of its riders and station masters
with copies of the Bible. To meet the challenge of mass migra-
tions the Secretaries' report "Upon the Enlargement of the Work"
spoke of mining regions, of streams of immigration and of travel,
of new centers of population, asserting:

This form of distribution must necessarily precede more
permanent efforts, such as the organization of Committees
and Auxiliaries.....We cannot discharge our duty by waiting
until the destitute bring their appeals to this house. We
should take the Bible to their own doors, and thus follow
Him who came to 'seek and to save that which was lost.'

The transcontinental railroad was completed in 1869. An
Article reprinted in *The Bible Society Record* in 1873 reviewed
the advantages of placing Scriptures in special receptacles in
railway cars: people have leisure to read; Portions will
"antidote...vicious literature" of other kinds; they may preach
the Word "in the constant presence of peril;" this method will
reach neglected emigrants and employees; "the want of the soul
[is] no less in the coach than in the chapel;" and "the

beneficent purpose of the American Bible Society" will be widely
advertised. By 1875 an estimated 3,484 volumes were "riding
the rails" in some 1,300 cars. With what results? The earlier
article already cited claimed that people do read, that conver-
sions do occur, that "demand for low literature [is] perceptibly
affected," that the books are well-treated and seldom "abstracted,
that the attention of "thoughtless or curious" persons is caught,
and that fresh contribution and cooperation for the Bible Cause
is stimulated.

Another fruitful field for Scripture distribution during
these post-war decades was the influx of immigrants, Asians in
California, Europeans on the East Coast. As the Atlantic tide
shifted from Northern to Southern Europe, more volumes were
needed in Portuguese, Spanish, and Italian. The New York Bible
Society assigned an Agent to meet incoming ships and distribute
books donated by the ABS; by 1874 this particular project was
recognized as "national work" whose cost should be shared by
other Auxiliaries. In 1893 total immigration through the port
of New York amounted to 353,885 from twenty-five nations--and
the American Bible Society was able to provide some books in
twenty-one of those languages. Colporteurs were assigned to
German, Hungarian, Swedish, and Chinese districts in the city
for additional circulation, sometimes of diglot Scriptures, which
proved helpful for newcomers learning English.

Meanwhile the Society continued to supply Bibles and Testaments to benevolent institutions and handicapped groups. Although
earlier policy--never adopted as a written rule--prohibited
gifts to charitable or penal institutions supported by national,
state, or local governments, the 1869 Report of the Secretaries
charged that civil authorities were not keeping these institutions adequately supplied with Scriptures, and recommended
therefore that any such restrictions be rescinded and "all such
applications be considered and decided upon the merits of each
case." Said one prison warden: "I should as soon think of
going to sea in a ship without a compass, as to attempt to conduct a prison without the Bible."

From 1835, when the Bible Society first supported the "line
letters" of Dr. Samuel Howe, Scriptures for the blind had been
of central concern. Even prior to that date a blind Frenchman
by the name of Louis Braille had devised a simpler system of
raised dots or points, but it was slow to spread to America,
and assorted forms of Braille led to controversial debates. In
1868 William Wait developed the New York Point print, cheaper to
produce and easier to learn to read than Howe's raised letters.
After careful investigation (and the receipt of a $30,000
legacy whose income was to be used to provide Bibles for the
blind) the Society began to produce books in New York Point

print: the Gospel of John in 1874 (at a publishing cost of
$3.08 per copy, but sold for $2), the Psalms in 1885, then the
other Gospels, and finally the full Bible in 1894 (11 volumes
for $7).   By this time a request was made for assistance in pro-
ducing the Bible in American Braille, one of several forms still
being developed, but the Society decided that "it was not
advisable to publish another system until the New York Point
print had been thoroughly tested."

In ignorance or disregard of its own dubious 1840 evaluation
of the General Supply, the Bible Society during the second half
of the nineteenth century undertook three more similar campaigns.
The aim was partly to remind its constituents of the basic
purpose of providing the destitute with Scriptures wherever they
are to be found, partly to bolster the declining income from
Auxiliaries.   The Second General Supply, 1856-1860, was initiated
by the secretaries in New York, whereas the first had been proposed by concerned Auxiliaries.   Urging the use by local
societies of "self-denying volunteers" for survey and distribution, the ABS issued Bibles for poor families at fifty cents
each and New Testaments for children at a dime.   Special emphasis
was placed on youth, seamen, inland waterway boatmen, railroad
hands, stage drivers, soldiers and sailors, westward migrants, etc.

During the Second General Supply the number of Bibles circulated increased over the previous four-year period from 951,431
to 972,253, but the sales and gifts of New Testaments actually
dropped from 1,786,079 in 1852-1856 to 1,664,637 in 1856-1860.
Despite satisfaction at the distribution of full Bibles, the
Second General Supply did little to move beyond the regular, on-
going program of the Society and its supporters, in part because
of a "sudden collapse in commercial and pecuniary affairs throughout the country."

The Third General Supply, coming just a decade after the
Second, was designed to celebrate the fiftieth anniversary of
the Society by meeting the acute destitution of Scriptures left
by the Civil War.   Resolutions adopted by the Board of Managers
in May, 1866, included these challenges:

Whereas, God in his gracious providence has conducted this
Society from small beginnings to a degree of strength and
capability which fit it for accomplishing a greater work
than ever, and has signalized our Jubilee year as a year
of peace and universal freedom throughout the land;

Whereas...multitudes throughout our older States are found
destitute of the word of life; and...great want of the
Scriptures exists in the South and Southwest, and the means
of supplying it by former Bible organizations, there
existing, have been almost swept away; and

Whereas, Millions of freedmen now thrown upon their own
efforts, and passing through a most critical formative
state, need the great Charter of duty and privileges, and
are anxiously asking for it.....

Therefore, without neglecting "its obligations to the world...in
its work abroad," the Society acknowledged a duty to undertake
the supply of "this vast field of want [as] the first work of our
second semi-century."

The Address of the Board of Managers "To the People of the
United States" reviewed the nature and extent of destitution,
the growth of population, the responsiveness of those to be
supplied, and the importance of the Bible to the welfare of the
nation:

It should be universally distributed, that our statesmen
may have it as their infallible and authentic guide in the
legislative, judicial, and executive departments of the
government; that our citizens may all possess it as the
divine charter of their civil and religious immunities,
and an exposition of their duties and obligations to the
state; that a religious element may be diffused in the
education of the nation, in all our institutions of
learning, from the lowest to the highest, and thus promote
the moral and spiritual as well as the intellectual power
and progress of society; that the vicious influence of the
press may be antagonized and counteracted, and a sancti-
fied literature furnished to a reading nation; that our
civilization may be refined, progressive, and Christian,
and that our morality may be authoritative and adequately
sanctioned....

Although estimates during the campaign suggested an average of
one-fifth of the population lacking Scriptures, the final
figures show less than one-tenth:

Number of families visited (in five-year period)	2,990,119
Number of families destitute of the Scriptures	283,186
Number of destitute families supplied	228,807
(the discrepancy attributed to "the fact that Romanists so generally refuse the Scriptures")	
Number of individuals also supplied	91,811
Number of soldiers and sailors supplied	121,491
Number of Sunday and other schools supplied	5,537

Notes remind the readers of this 1871 Annual Report that grants
to other institutions and certain special categories have not
been included in this table. Nevertheless the figures seem to
suggest that, while the supply to those *found* destitute was

commendable, the coverage in terms of families visited across
the nation was deplorably small. This in turn highlights the
tragic decline of effective Auxiliaries, even though a committee
report as late as 1888 reaffirmed that "the Auxiliary System
[is] thoroughly imbedded in the history of the Society and can
not be abandoned without seriously impairing the efficiency of
the Society."

Seven years earlier, however, it was claimed that more
families were being supplied with Scriptures by direct Agencies
of the American Bible Society than by all the Auxiliaries
reporting to it. During the 1880's paid colporteurs, presumably
travelling in remote areas, found one sixth to one seventh of
families visited without Bibles, whereas Auxiliaries found only
one in ten destitute. This continuing need prompted a Fourth
General Supply from 1882 to 1890. In addition to the "alarming
rate" of population growth, the Proposal said, "we are no longer
a homogeneous people, but have gathered here representatives of
almost all the nations of the earth. This country is therefore
eminently missionary ground."

For all the energetic colportage; for all the books at last
being read "by the lumbermen in the deep forests, by the cowboys
on their lonely ranches, and by the miners in the rude hovels;"
for all the eight years of this longest General Supply; for all
the unity and prosperity claimed by the nation during that
period; the results were not spectacular. The entire distribution of Scriptures was 8,146,808, in twenty-seven different
languages. Approximately 757,581 families (about one ninth of
the total visited) were found to be without Bibles; copies were
provided for 473,804 of these, plus 299,053 individuals. Again
the figures indicate a perpetual challenge, a continuous task,
rather than a "crash" achievement.

The Fourth Supply was followed almost immediately by concentration on young people, a Sunday School Supply inaugurated in
1891. The Fourth Supply had sought to reach every destitute and
accessible child. Colporteurs were instructed to sell Testaments
and Portions at list price, "in no case to credit." Churches,
individuals, Auxiliaries, Sunday Schools, Young People's
Societies, Agents or District Superintendents, all were reminded
of thousands of "children on the frontier and the multitudes of
poor children in our large cities." Bibles were priced as low
as twenty and forty cents. At the end of three years the Annual
Report admitted that "the expectations of the Society have not
been realized [despite] an increase of interest as well as an
increase of effort." Two years later, by 1895, "the demand for
Bibles for the children has not come up to the expectation of
the Managers."

By the end of the century the Society found itself barely able to keep pace with the movement and growth of population in America. Both the Auxiliary and the Agency System had declined in effectiveness and in adaptability. A proposal to institute a separate Business Department to supplement the Benevolent work was flatly rejected as inconsistent with the Society's purpose, but the rule prohibiting sale of Bibles to private dealers was repealed, and by the 1880's the Society was frankly seeking booksellers, offering commercial discounts, and advertising.

Similarly a suggestion to establish a Standing Committee on the Bible Cause in major denominations was vetoed in 1886 from fear of denominational conflicts and jealousies. Yet the hopeful new direction at the end of the century was to turn to the churches (see Chapter XVI). Ironically the rise of denominational agencies, mission boards, and benevolence budgets had been one of the blows to Bible collections through individual gifts. In 1898, however, a report to the Board of Managers referred to the "wretched failure" of Auxiliaries as collecting agencies, and the uncertainty of private legacies, "as a providential interposition, to drive us to the only proper & sure way of maintaining the work, the direct & systematic contributions of the churches." In God's Providence a wide door, a new door, for effective work had opened.

8
Nineteenth Century Outreach:
Latin America, Europe, Africa

Despite the Constitution's concern for "other countries, whether Christian, Mahometan, or Pagan," the American Bible Society for many years gave minimal attention to Scripture circulation abroad--or relegated it to the women to support. Reaffirming that "the home field has always, in view of the Board, a primary claim," the Managers in their Annual Report for 1842 added somewhat condescendingly: "The Providence of God, at this juncture, has opened in the foreign field a broad channel for all the sympathies and the benefactions of these female Associations." In that same year expenditures for work abroad had been *reduced* by thirty-three per cent, even though appeals for assistance overseas had *increased* by sixty-six per cent, "most of them of an urgent character."

Yet by 1858, with the Second General Supply nearing completion and economic prosperity outshining political storm clouds, the Society turned its attention to a systematic survey of the foreign field. A circular sent to missionaries of all related boards declared that, although "we shall still have much home work to do every year,...the time has come when we must look out upon Papal, Mohammedan, and Pagan lands, and inquire earnestly, What can we now do to give the Bible to the suffering millions beyond our borders?" Then a series of questions sought to determine: the most needy and the most accessible people in each area; the stage of progress and the "character" or acceptability of existing translations, in order "that different denominations can use them, as they do the English Bible;" the availability of local facilities for printing, proofreading, and circulating books; what funds could be *wisely* used in Bible work during the next year or two.

The second half of the century saw a substantial growth in
the number of permanent Agencies established by the Society.
Meanwhile, however, important policy decisions of 1860 greatly
strengthened collaboration with missionaries in many parts of
the world. Funds from the ABS could henceforth be used not only
for printing and binding, but also for transportation and storage
"when needful;" for native colporteur service "by believers...
confined to the distribution of the Scriptures, and when the
missionaries have not time to perform this work for themselves;"
and for translations and corrections by "persons of competent
learning and skill...subject to the action and decision of the
Committee on Versions and the Board."

As the Society expanded its foreign work, it came increasingly
into direct contact with the British and Foreign Bible Society
in the field, not simply in cordial communication from headquarter
In this process both minor frictions and major policy differences
became apparent from time to time. Some of these conflicts arose
from territorial competition in Central America and parts of the
Middle East. The extravagant popularity of Harriet Beecher Stowe,
when she visited England soon after publication of *Uncle Tom's
Cabin*, coincided with reports that ABS policy toward Negro supply
was cautiously conservative, and this created some tension and
suspicion. Relying almost exclusively on local Auxiliaries, the
British Society had used few agents or colporteurs or distributor:
in its home islands, although some had been employed in France,
Belgium, and Holland, where there were no Auxiliaries. Furthermore, the BFBS had no manufacturing department, preferring to
place orders with commercial printers rather than to "make books"
itself. British Auxiliaries seldom accumulated any sizable debts
to the "Parent Society." As early as 1853 the BFBS opened certain Bible depots to general sales, a practice the American
counterpart long resisted.

In an effort to explain some of these discrepancies the ABS
Agencies Committee Report for 1859 contained a rather remarkable
evaluation which betrayed America's sense of inferiority even
eighty years after Independence:

It should be remember'd that England is a small country with
a dense compact population, embracing a territory so small
that an Agent could reach any part of it in about a day's
travel. Then again the population of the country differs
materially from that of ours; it is permanent, homogeneous,
intelligent, in every community having available talent and
resources to carry on their auxiliaries themselves; ours
besides being sparse, is fluctuating, heterogeneous, in
many places quite incompetent without the help of an Agent
to direct and carry on their affairs, and in many places
too much absorbed in procuring means to live or in amassing

wealth, to give sufficient time and attention to the Bible work.

Differences which developed between the two Societies were usually bridged, sooner or later, by gestures of personal good-will and official cooperation. Fraternal delegates were often present at Annual Meetings--though more often in London than in New York. In accordance with its title the BFBS Constitution required six "foreigners" on its Board of Managers, and these posts were occasionally offered to Americans resident in England. A special delegation sailed from the United States in 1853 to honor the Fiftieth Jubilee Year of the British Society--but one of them encountered such bitter criticism as a slave-holder that he withdrew his name after reaching London, in order to avoid embarrassment to all concerned. Overseas, Britishers and Americans occasionally served on the same board, as in the Constantinople Bible Society. Versions and plates were exchanged, at least once without permission, until an agreement was reached in 1860 under which either Society could print any version financed by the other, *providing* no changes whatever were made without the other's consent.

In sketching the work of the American Bible Society abroad, it is impossible to review each country or each decade in detail. Whole books could and should be written about the personal experiences of Agents and colporteurs and about transformed lives in many lands. These pages can only touch occasional highlights-- significant and sometimes disastrous policies, unusual adventures, rare personalities, and a few quite insignificant incidents--in the hope that such fragments may give more of a "feel" for the times and for the true meaning of Bible distribution than pages of statistics or lists of names and dates.

The American Bible Society accepted a divine commission more than 150 years ago, but its execution has been a very human blend-ing of drudgery and danger, discouragement and dedication, self-ishness and saintliness. Some of the physical and spiritual destitution, some of the courage and romance, *sound* more exciting against the backdrop of a far-away foreign field and a seemingly simple century, but actually recapitulate opportunities and human conditions already familiar in the home field.

LATIN AMERICA

In the mid-1800's Latin America, the neighbors to the South, still received more books from the American Bible Society than other parts of the world, though not as much money as some. New editions of Spanish Bibles and Testaments were produced, and Portions of John and Acts for use in schools. A few earlier versions in Indian tongues were being reprinted, but surprisingly little effort was being made to alphabetize and translate indigenous languages.

As Secretary Edward Gilman pointed out on a "trouble-shooting" expedition in 1879, "the circulation of the scriptures in *Mexico* antedates by many years the sending of Missionaries there." In 1848 a former Methodist missionary to Argentina was appointed to work among Mexican civilians and American soldiers during the Mexican War, but his term was cut short when the U.S. Secretary of War expressed fear that a Bible Agent would hamper peace negotiations by seeming to undermine the dominant Roman Catholic faith of the people. Ten years later another distributor worked along the Rio Grande as assistant to the Texas Agent until, after three years and a raise in salary from $600 to $1,000 per year, he simply disappeared, presumably back into the wilds of Texas. Two other Agents served during the 'sixties, experimenting with colportage and balancing precariously during the alternating regimes of the supposedly liberal Benito Juarez (1861-1864, 1867-1872) and the more or less tolerant Emperor Maximilian (1864-1867). One of these Agents, James Hickey, a convert from Roman Catholicism to the Baptist faith, left Texas because his sympathy for the Union cause in the Civil War made him unpopular there. But he was a beloved and effective Bible Agent until his death in 1866. His successor, Thomas Westrup, resigned after three years for--by his own confession--preaching more Baptist doctrines than the non-sectarian Bible Society could approve.

For ten years the post lay vacant until the Board sent a dentist to open the Society's first permanent Agency in 1878. Aside from renting a strategically-placed but extravagant store-front, the doctor proved so lazy and unsatisfactory, so "partisan, careless, and inefficient," that one of the New York secretaries, Edward Gilman, went down to investigate--and to fire the man. Gilman also took charge of some 14,000 books (regarded as a wasteful over-stock, even though 10,000 of them were Portions) which the British and Foreign Bible Society consented to sell for $800 when they withdrew from Mexican work. Finally, in 1879, Hiram Philetus Hamilton, newly graduated from Union Theological Seminary in New York, was appointed as ABS Agent in Mexico and served until his death in 1905.

Despite the fact that the Mexican Constitution of 1867 rather ambiguously prohibited the burning of Bibles or even their banning by hostile priests and local officials, colporteurs were harassed by hired or incited "banditti;" Mexicans who accepted "Protestant" Scriptures were often excommunicated; poverty, illiteracy, and civil war left a desolate country in which to peddle books. In the familiar debate over whether to give books away free or enhance respect by a nominal price, the Mexican

Agency leaned toward the latter policy, based on advice from
China and India. But prices were reduced to six cents instead
of sixteen cents for a Testament, two cents instead of six cents
for a Portion, and sometimes commodities were accepted in lieu
of cash: cloth, rosaries, even machetes, to be resold eventually
to tourists. In the face of such assorted problems, Hamilton
enlarged the colportage staff to fifty by 1894 (though it dropped
back to twenty-two in the depression three years later) and
increased average circulation from 10,000 to 25,000 volumes a
year. By 1893 a typewriter was approved for the Agency in
Mexico city!

*   *   *   *   *

On his way to California Frederick Buel, first Agent on the
Pacific Coast, had written of the need for Scriptures in Panama,
especially among Americans sick and stranded. Some Bibles had
been distributed in Honduras through the American Consul there,
but an Honduran Bible Society organized by missionaries disinte-
grated because of interdenominational frictions. An ABS Agent,
D. H. Wheeler, was appointed to Nicaragua in July, 1856, but was
shot by native troops three months later. Another, sent to
Panama and *Central America* in 1863, lasted less than a year
because of ill-health, though he had previously worked in both
Argentina and Mexico.

In 1892 Joseph Norwood, temporarily forced out of Venezuela,
and Francisco G. Penzotti, Sub-Agent in Peru, were asked by the
Society to make a tour of Central America. This they did,
travelling separately with assistants, but meeting occasionally
to exchange observations. As a result Penzotti was transferred
to Guatemala, although four years elapsed before the permanent
Agency was opened, covering Guatemala, Costa Rica, Honduras,
Nicaragua, San Salvador, and Panama (politically part of Colombia
until 1903).

Here in Central America, as in Mexico, the American Bible
Society Agent ran into competition with the British Agent. In
Mexico nearly two decades earlier the British had protested the
sending of Bibles from the United States to American missionaries
as an infringement of BFBS territory and had sought to keep a
rival Agency out of the capital city. But they had finally
conceded the argument of propinquity and had withdrawn from that
field--not before quibbling at length about the value of the
books to be transferred. In Central America the BFBS appointed
a Spaniard as Agent without knowing of the ABS Agent in Guatemala.
In subsequent correspondence the London office seemed to apolo-
gize and agree that such duplication should be avoided in the
future, but to New York's surprise and Penzotti's dismay another
BFBS man was sent to replace the Spaniard. Thus the rivalry for

the Central American isthmus continued until 1913, when the
British withdrew (except for British Honduras), while the Americans simultaneously ended their work in Persia.

*   *   *   *   *

Meanwhile Bible distribution had been increasing in the
Caribbean islands to the east. The first Agent sent from Florida
to Cuba was adjudged "a good Christian man...amiable, friendly,
and cautious," but lacking in linguistic ability, good health,
"Northern energy and despatch." An investigator, who later became
a Temporary Agent for the Society, reported Cuba "about as ready
and accessible for Bible work as any entirely new field can well
be." He recommended the use of colporteurs, commercial booksellers, newspaper advertisements, volunteers, warning however
that "it will be a great mistake to make a practice of giving
away either Bibles, Testaments, or Portions." He also urged the
use of tracts, arguing that they would be useful in interpreting
the Scriptures and would no more violate the non-sectarian, "sole
purpose," "without note or comment" clauses than did the sermons
of many Bible Society representatives.

In 1884 Andrew J. McKim established the first permanent
Caribbean Agency in Havana, and labored conscientiously throughout the island for a dozen years. Early reports spoke of areas
where "only one person in five was able to read" and of "the
Sabbath being spent in drinking, dancing, cock-fighting, and
other wickedness." Later reports told of disappearing colporteurs, the requisition of all horses, "military law...arbitrary
tyranny," and other manifestations of civil war. In March of
1896 the Agencies Committee decided to close the Cuban work
temporarily.

The Spanish-American War in 1898 was brief but bloody--and
required thousands of Testaments for Yankee soldiers. It also
produced, from Secretary Gilman to Agent Penzotti, a typical
example of prevailing sentiment in the United States:

> We are in for the war, unitedly and vigorously,...on the
> ground that motives of humanity demanded that our nation
> should intervene for the independence of the Cubans. We
> do not want to annex it or any other Spanish territory,
> but we do not know what responsibilities will devolve upon
> us in the final settlement.....A great victory at Manila
> ...has made it imperative that we send an army of occupa-
> tion to take possession of the Philippine Islands.....Some
> persons are urging the immediate annexation of the Hawaiian
> Islands, as necessary for the demands of war. We may also
> attack Puerto Rico and take it.

Francisco Penzotti reopened the Cuban Agency in 1899 and found it "the most hopeful field I have ever visited in Latin America." J. M. Lopez-Guillen took charge the following year, while McKim opened a separate office in Puerto Rico; both territories were consolidated into a *West Indies* Agency in 1905. During this period some books were sent to Jamaica, Haiti, and Santo Domingo, but for the most part those islands were "well cared for by the British and Foreign Bible Society." Penzotti's famous summary of the Central American Agency may well apply to the entire area during this half-century. After three stages of "novelty, crisis, and re-action," he wrote in late 1898, "we have now reached the best part--triumph, although it must be admitted that we may be mistaken."

*   *   *   *   *

In South America the Scriptural scene, like the political picture, was in even greater flux. Some of the republics which revolted from Spain in the 1820's had slipped into dictatorship, others into chaos. Despite laws for religious freedom in many countries, the hostility of Roman Catholic clergy toward Protestant missionaries and the Bible remained the major obstacle. The ABS decided not to open an Agency in *Venezuela* in 1850 because "they can't buy the Bible," but four years later sent a converted Spaniard, Ramon Montsalvatge, as Agent for South America. He soon discovered, as a missionary had written fifteen years before, that "the Christian laborer, to effect much here, must begin as would a farmer in the wilderness--clear and prepare well his field before sowing the wheat." Within a year Montsalvatge had been excommunicated and banned from all the churches in Venezuela. As an ex-Roman Catholic, he met vicious insults everywhere. On the other hand, as a Spaniard who still drank brandy and played cards, he was condemned by many Protestant missionaries. "It is necessary," wrote one of the milder critics, "to be very careful in one's actions in a country like this where every little inadvertency is noticed."

After a brief return to the United States, Montsalvatge shifted his Bible headquarters to New Granada (Colombia) from 1855 to 1857, but apparently found similar difficulties. A proposal to send him to Argentina was vetoed by missionaries there on the ground that the treaty between that country and Spain would permit extradition if he got into further trouble with political or ecclesiastical authorities. Eventually, after shipwreck and other misfortunes as a part-time Agent of the Society, then a would-be colporteur in Algeria, the unfortunate convert became a missionary of the American and Foreign Christian Union.

Meanwhile the Rev. J. dePalma was sent to appraise the Venezuelan situation in 1877. Convinced that the country's location, climate and resources destined it to be "one of the greatest nations of the South American continent" and that the government had "humbled and vanquished" the Roman Curia and the Romish priesthood with a "terrible blow," dePalma urged the immediate despatch of evangelical missionaries. "The gospel," he felt confident, "leavening the souls of the people, will give them, with the hope of eternal salvation, sure foundations and stability to the prosperity of the nation."

When Andrew Milne, Agent in the La Plata region, again recommended an Agency for Venezuela, William M. Patterson was appointed in 1888. Finding that "no Protestant church has yet entered the country" and that the people were "more ready to listen than to buy," he reiterated dePalma's plea for evangelical missionaries. Patterson died in Caracas and was succeeded by Joseph Norwood, who on his arrival received assurance from the President of the republic that he would have "the same liberty and protection" for the distribution of Scriptures as he had known in Mexico. When Norwood was imprisoned by an overzealous local police chief, he appealed to the United States Minister to Venezuela. Promptly the Venezuelan Minister of the Interior instructed the state governor that "the propaganda of religious matter and the questions of conscience in general, are not legal causes for imprisonment under any consideration" and ordered "the punishment of those who for ignorance or abuse of authority have proceeded against the liberty of that individual." Nevertheless, although Norwood claimed that "the whole matter has been a blessing to the cause," persecution of colporteurs and purchasers continued, and in 1898 he transferred the Agency to Colombia.

*   *   *   *   *

When the American Bible Society in 1828 joined the British and Foreign Society in refusing to circulate the Apocrypha, an Argentinian Bible Society was established independently in Buenos Aires. The comparative toleration of religion in *Argentina* attracted various missionary groups, and the American Bible Society entrusted them with many shipments of books. In 1849 one small band of missionaries took a collection of $93 for "that best of Institutions," the ABS. The Roman Catholic Church was declining in influence, although one missionary wrote in 1849: "Politically it is a mere shadow. Yet it is the estab-lished religion, & it is the policy of the government to humour it, in its petty interferences with Protestantism."

As previously indicated, one of the most effective and beloved missionaries in all of Latin America in the mid-1800's was James Thomson, a Scottish Baptist Agent for the BFBS and for the Lancastrian Educational Society. For some years he and missionar associates handled most of the distribution of Scriptures in South America. Increasingly, however, North American mission- aries requested shipments of books from New York. From 1864 to 1907 Andrew Murray Milne (1838-1907) served one of the longest, most dependable—and least spectacular—of all Agencies in American Bible Society, that of *La Plata*.

Milne, a Scottish Presbyterian, had dedicated his life to Christian service at the age of twenty, while listening to the future Prime Minister William Gladstone at a Y.M.C.A. meeting in London. Nevertheless, Milne arrived in Argentina not as a missionary, but as a businessman with a fruit company. The enthusiasm with which he devoted his free time to Bible colpor- tage led to his recommendation as an Agent for the ABS. In accepting the appointment, the young Scot made three resolutions: to circulate Scriptures throughout Latin America, to provide Scriptures in the Indian dialects, and to distribute a million copies of Holy Writ. By the end of his lifetime the continent was well organized and covered by both British and American Societies; translations had been undertaken in many of the Indian tongues; and Milne's Agency had disposed of 854,812 books.

If the administration of La Plata (which during much of this period included the west coast and part of Brazil) was quiet and steady, the social and political environment was not. Milne lived and worked and often traveled through a revolution in Uruguay (1865), a war between Paraguay and Argentina (1867), the War of the Pacific (Chile, Bolivia, and Peru, 1880), a revolution in Argentina (1890), and innumerable lesser uprisings. Occasion- ally he was arrested; frequently book shipments were confiscated or delayed; epidemics of cholera and yellow fever disrupted travel; serious depressions struck the struggling new nations in 1876 and 1894; especially on the west coast hostile Roman Catholic priests incited attacks on Bible colporteurs.

Through all these tribulations Andrew Milne continued to "go round with my books from house to house." Describing his work more fully in the Annual Report for 1870, he wrote:

In the evenings, from seven P.M. to ten, I go to the coffee houses and billiard rooms, where the people are congre- gated, and thus have the opportunity of speaking to them when they are at leisure to listen. In this manner I some- times sell more books in one hour than I have done all the day long.....I am happy that I can say that my work is undoubtedly taking effect. Here the Bible is no longer depreciated on account of its connection with Protestantism.

Milne was one of the first Agents to use a magic lantern (stereopticon projector) "with good results" not only in sales,

but in persuading people "to read it [the Bible] with more
attention." Unlike some other representatives, he did not
believe that the printed word was sufficient in itself. In 1874
he reported:

> The Bible has done and is doing much for South America;
> this is plain to every one; but in order that the good
> effected be fostered, it is necessary that the Church in
> general prosecute the work of evangelization, of which the
> circulation of the Scriptures is but the preliminary step.

*   *   *   *   *

The *West Coast* of Latin America was less hospitable to the
Scriptures. Peru in its early years of independence simply
refused to allow any imports of Bibles whatever, and one distributor in Chile grew so tired of trying to deal with people and
governments who possessed so little honesty and punctuality that
he decided to open a distillery. Some were not so easily discouraged. David Trumbull, missionary of the American and Foreign
Christian Union and the Seamen's Friend Society of New York,
served for over forty years (c.1849-1889) as Chile correspondent
for the American Bible Society. In fact, he founded a Valparaiso
Bible Society and personally labored so faithfully among sailors
in the harbor that the ABS gave him a gift of $500 in compensation
for "valuable services" rendered. However a regular Agent
appointed in 1857 encountered such great hostility to Scripture
circulation that he decided (without permission) that it was
easier to occupy a local pastorate during Trumbull's absence
than it was to sell books. That man was summoned back to New
York the following year.

David Trumbull continued to press for a full-time Bible Society
Agent and finally persuaded Milne to make an inspection tour of
Chile, Bolivia, and Peru. This led to the employment of Francisco
Penzotti as sub-agent for the west coast in 1888. Chile was the
freest country in which to work, but to avoid competing with the
Valparaiso Bible Society Penzotti settled in Callao, Peru. There
in 1891, he was imprisoned for eight months for holding "public"
religious services, even though his preaching was behind locked
doors with admission by ticket only, and even though the law had
not been enforced against Anglican worship or Chinese Buddhist
rituals. The Penzottis, father and son, appear repeatedly in
Bible Society history in almost every part of Latin America far
into the twentieth century.

*   *   *   *   *

In *Brazil*, as elsewhere, early Bible distribution had been
carried on by missionaries. Not only were German and other

European colonists eager for the Scriptures, but Portuguese settlers also demanded full Bibles--despite a Pastoral Letter from the Roman Catholic bishop directed against Evangelicals (the term customarily used for Protestants in Latin America). Two Agents appointed to Brazil in the 1850's valiantly distributed books to soldiers and slaves, traders and immigrants and school children, but lasted less than a year and a half each. The second dreamed of traveling up the Amazon by steamer, leaving stocks of books at key towns along the route, and then floating down the river in a canoe from the Peruvian border--alone if he could not hire paddlers. He died before he could accomplish that particular mission, but his associate made a similar trip the following year, distributing a thousand volumes on the way.

For twenty years southern Brazil was administered as part of the La Plata Agency. For the rest of the country, after two shorter terms, the Board of Managers appointed a young missionary of the Methodist Episcopal Church, South, whose work will be cited more fully in Chapter XI. From 1887 to 1934 the names of Brazil, of H. C. Tucker, and of the American Bible Society were to form a spendid triad, known throughout the hemisphere.

* * * * *

Latin America during the nineteenth century was a tumultuous field, marked by wars (from the struggles for independence to the Spanish-American War), political instability, resistance to social change, poverty, and illiteracy. But the greatest obstacle to Bible circulation in that period remained a brand of Roman Catholicism which was often corrupt and exploitative, whether its power was expressed in national laws, intimidation of the people, violence against colporteurs, or the traditional preference for the Apocrypha. Yet with support from hundreds of Evangelical missionaries, with a growing desire for education and intellectual freedom, with infinite patience and determination, Latin America was opened to the Word of God. In that process the American Bible Society was served by three of its most faithful and influential Agents anywhere in the world: Andrew Milne in La Plata, H. C. Tucker in Brazil, and Francisco Penzotti in Central America.

EUROPE

Europe during this period was over-churched, perhaps over-missionized, but certainly not over-supplied with the Scriptures. Yet the active presence of the British and Foreign Bible Society in almost every area where the Roman Catholic Church would tolerate Bible work left little room for direct activity by Americans. The ABS therefore concentrated on supplying Bibles

and Testaments to American missions and on providing limited
funds for local printing. Even within this narrow scope, competition with the BFBS proved unavoidable.

In *France* a French and Foreign Bible Society and a Protestant
Bible Society of Paris had been formed before the American Bible
Society, but they had fallen on hard times politically, financially, and religiously. During the Revolution of 1848 the ABS
sent two gifts of $10,000 each to aid the French in purchasing
new plates and hiring colporteurs. For the international
expositions of 1867 and 1888 the Bible Society of France
(reorganized from the French and Foreign Bible Society in 1865)
appealed to New York for Scripture exhibits as well as funds.
During the Franco-Prussian War of 1870 grants totalling at least
$5,000 helped to provide Testaments for French troops. The
substantial gifts ABS also made to the Evangelical Society of
Geneva, which carried on extensive work in southern France as
well as Switzerland.

*   *   *   *   *

As early as 1831 Secretary John C. Brigham reported on a
visit to *Germany* that zeal for the Bible cause was looked upon
as "Methodism" in contrast to the more moderate Lutheran
"religious temperature." Whether this judgment was warranted
or not, most American Bible Society work in that country was
administered through the Methodist Episcopal Church (625,898
volumes between 1860 and 1900) and the American Baptists.

Thus the ABS avoided setting up a German Agency in competition
with the BFBS, but the two Societies did come into conflict over
pricing policies. On one hand, the Methodists gave discounts of
ten to twenty per cent to ministers, colporteurs, and certain
other missions when the British did not (although after 1890 the
BFBS allowed some twenty-five per cent discounts and the National
Bible Society of Scotland as much as fifty per cent). On the
other hand, the British sold their books so cheaply that some
were being bought up in Germany and shipped back to England for
resale at a profit there. Wrote a Methodist missionary indignantly in 1867: "Their whole system to sell to rich and poor
below cost is wrong; but they are the BFBS and we certainly have
to do as they do.....We are obliged to sell as cheap as the
British and Foreign Bible Society does, and in this way much
money is lost."

Through the Methodist Mission also went many Bibles and Testaments to German Sunday Schools and, during the Franco-Prussian
War, not only to German soldiers but to French prisoners of war.
With typical loyalty to the country of his residence and service
the same Methodist missionary wrote in 1871: I hope our America

Christians will now acknowledge, that the French are not yet ripe
for a Republic. We should all try to deliver them from the Papal
yoke, that is the only help for them."

*   *   *   *   *

In *Belgium, Scandinavia, Austria,* and *Hungary* the American
Bible Society sent assistance into areas already occupied by the
British. Most of the grants were for modest amounts, generally
administered by Methodist or other American missionaries, but
the trespass was obvious enough to produce recurrent friction.
At least once, in the case of Hungary, officers in New York
insisted that the British could administer the work more economically and advantageously and that it was "hardly necessary for
the two Societies to occupy the same ground." When a Congregationalist missionary requesting Scriptures from the United States
cited British intrusion in Mexico and South America, the ABS
promptly corrected his "facts:" i.e., in the cases mentioned
the British had entered Latin American fields earlier than or
with the Americans, once at American invitation. Hence, prior
claims were not as strong or as valid as in Europe. Six years
after this stern defense of the comity principle, however, the
ABS was still supplying Scriptures to Austro-Hungary through
the American Board of Commissioners for Foreign Missions, and
by the end of the century that project had amounted to contributions of 165,130 books and $18,434.57 in money.

Italy offered a new and challenging opportunity, as it moved
from a heterogeneous assortment of city states, tightly dominated
by the papacy, to a unified nation by 1870. To be sure, opposition to Scripture distribution (including the highly-praised
Diodati version) continued to vary widely. In some places for
a colporteur to sell nearly a hundred copies in three months was
acclaimed as "unexpected success." Declining to open an Agency
in Italy, despite several applications, the Managers repeated in
1860 that "the books thus circulated be the Holy Scriptures only,
without note or comment, and that Colporteurs...avoid those
ecclesiastical and denominational topics on which Protestants
may entertain different views, while cordially united in this
great Bible work."

*   *   *   *   *

As a closed society, political and ecclesiastical, *Spain*
seemed to provoke Yankee determination to achieve a Scriptural
"breakthrough." In 1856 Signor Angel H. deMora was appointed to
Madrid as the first--and only--ABS Agent in Europe. He was to
have a salary of $800 and $1,350 toward his transportation,
$1,000 of it by special gift from the Massachusetts Bible Society.
Soon after his arrival, he was arrested as a Spaniard and

imprisoned. The ABS promptly appealed to the U.S. Minister,
although the U.S. Treasury Comptroller doubted if his government
would intervene, since America did not tolerate interference
from other countries in regard to her citizens or policies.

Meanwhile the ingenious deMora escaped to England, but the
Acting British Consul who had aided him expressed grave doubts
about his questionable activities and considered him "a clever
rogue, who finds *professing* the Protestant religion a good trade."
As a former priest in charge of a Catholic college, deMora had
allegedly falsified some documents before fleeing abroad and
abandoning his past connections. For such a man to return to
distribute "Protestant" Scriptures in Spain was an affront to
both Church and State. Although appraisals of his sincerity
differed widely, the Bible Society was apparently well rid of
deMora, who taught Spanish at Oxford for two years and then
migrated to Honduras.

Not only did the Roman Catholic Church oppose the circulation
of any religious books in Spain, but the government prohibited
operations by any foreign society. The Annual Report of the ABS
in 1861 stated flatly: "Nothing favorable or encouraging can be
said in regard to the dissemination of the Holy Scriptures in
these countries [Spain and Portugal]. The Bible is still a
prohibited book. We must wait for the opening of Divine
Providence." Although a few copies were smuggled over the
Pyrenees, Spaniards might be imprisoned even for reading them.
In appealing for a colporteur to be assigned along the Franco-
Spanish border, a missionary cautioned not to give any publicity
to such activities, for "the prison and the gallows are still
part of the Spanish Code and...the first condition of all work
in this country, after prayer and the aid of the Lord, is prudenc
and secrecy."

Yet gradually the pressures lifted; Scriptures could be
printed within Spain long before they could be imported, and the
British and Foreign Bible Society issued several editions in the
late 1860's. In 1869 5,000 Bibles sent by the ABS were admitted,
"the first which has ever passed through a Spanish customs house.
I need not assure you, that every official eyes these boxes of
Bibles with bitterest malignity." But others did not; the books
were promptly sold and thousands more were supplied in the next
few decades, largely through the American Board of Commissioners
for Foreign Missions, leaving the major activity still to the
British and Foreign and the Scottish Bible Societies.

*   *   *   *   *

Russia, too, was a field approached "with difficulty" but with
eagerness. The British and Foreign Bible Society had initiated

work there in 1806 and had helped to launch the Russian Bible Society in 1813. Perhaps, as some critics charged, it was "instituted for mere show" and did nothing for the really destitute, even though ministers were required to collect money from poor parishioners for the Bible cause. Perhaps, as others implied, "clergymen who are servants of Government here" had no interest in the Scriptures for largely illiterate worshippers. Perhaps, as still others inferred, Roman Catholic encroachments in Russian territory forced the state to adopt tighter restrictions on all non-Orthodox religious groups. In any case, a change of Czar and a strengthening of Holy Synod control over all religious activities led to the suspension of the Russian Bible Society in 1826. Even when it was re-established as the Evangelical Bible Society of Russia in 1863 (chartered 1869), it could circulate only such Scriptures as had been approved by the Holy Synod, and only among non-Orthodox peoples.

Nevertheless Protestants in the West continued to manifest concern: for "the poor Fins," for convicts in Moscow and for prisoners in Siberia. A supporter donated a Life Membership for a missionary in Esthonia to encourage Bible work there. Yet Russia was hard to reach, administratively as well as politically. With Scripture distribution limited to Protestant groups, the German colonists in southern Russia around the Black Sea were served from the Levant Agency (sometimes counted in statistics for Asia), to the jealous indignation of the BFBS Agent. Some volumes were sent to the Baltic provinces through Scandinavia and Finland. In still other areas the ABS, working through the Russian Society, could distribute books more easily than the BFBS, as a foreign organization.

Ironically, the strict policy against publishing the Apocrypha, supposedly settled fifty years earlier, aroused antagonism not only among the Russian Orthodox, but among Baltic Lutherans as well. Similarly, when concerned Christians were rejoicing over a new translation of the Bible into modern Russian, prepared by the Greek Synod, it was discovered to contain a calendar of readings. A missionary pleaded for the Bible Society to acquiesce in this modification in policy, on the ground that it was "much valued by the Russian people" especially in preparation for their long liturgical services, but the Society remained adamant that this calendar represented unacceptable "note or comment." Eventually the Russian Bible Society secured copies of the New Testament without the calendar, presumably of more limited usefulness and popularity.

With such difficulties imposed by the Christian community itself, the dangers of robbers and highwaymen (who murdered one colporteur), the hardships and expense of travel and transportation across the Siberian wastes, the barriers of growing

nationalism and ethnic prejudices seemed relatively minor. In
1865 one of the faithful American laymen who composed the Protestant Committee (or "Agency") in St. Petersburg wrote to New York
that "the work of distribution goes on steadily through the
agency of the local pastors. And it appears unnecessary to
employ any other means." Except for the appointment of a few
hardy colporteurs across the vast distances of Siberia, this
remained the predominant pattern for Bible circulation in Russia.

AFRICA

Africa was an unknown, unpenetrated continent for most of the
nineteenth century. Even the British and Foreign Bible Society
did not begin regular work there until 1847, although the ABS in
1820 had made contributions, through the American Colonization
Society, for the settlement of former slaves in Liberia.

During the first half of the century there were few white men
preaching the Christian Gospel, few black men who could read it,
few travellers to make the area known. Yet by 1864 the British
had organized nearly fifty Auxiliaries or other Bible organizations in their newly-opened colonies.

The American Bible Society limited its activity almost
entirely to the *West Coast* and, toward the end of the century,
to Zulu Scriptures for Natal in South Africa. Grants of books
and occasionally of money were made to the Colonization Society
and to missionaries. During the two decades of 1841-1860
approximately 6,649 books (*none* in native languages) and $2,364
were contributed by the ABS, according to somewhat incomplete
statistics. Most of the monetary grants were used to support
translations in Liberia, Gabon, Gold Coast, and South Africa.
Books went to colonists from America, sometimes to slaves rescued
from ships along the coast, seldom to illiterate villagers in the
jungles. One missionary accepted payment in silver dollars, red
flannel, gunpowder, beads, or foolscap paper. Another was paid
for books with fish, fowls, cassava, and building materials,
estimating a (cash?) intake of $50 in eight years.

From 1882-1889 (or beyond) the Mayor of Monrovia, who was
also representative of the American Colonization Society, served
as unsalaried "Agent" for the Bible Society. During that period
the total recorded grants from New York amounted to 2,991
volumes and $135. The meager circulation is all the more note-
worthy in view of the rapid deterioration of books in the
tropics. Wrote one Presbyterian mission executive to the ABS:
"Losses are numerous, not due to neglect or carelessness of the
owners, but the humid climate dissolving the binding, roaches
eating the starch, and white ants the paper, and especially rain

and leaky canoes, for our people carry their Bibles with them on their constant journeys and visits."

In *South Africa* the American Bible Society sometimes found itself subsidizing one missionary translation of the Bible at the same time that the BFBS was supporting another. Only with the Zulu Scriptures for Natal, therefore, did the ABS make an all-out effort to meet the demand. Between 1871 and 1891 it financed the printing of books in Africa (12,000 copies in 1883 alone). From 1891 until 1916 some 220,179 volumes of Zulu Scriptures were printed in New York and shipped across the Atlantic. Unlike many fields, Natal reported no need to give any of these Bibles away because they sold so rapidly. Yet less than twenty years earlier a missionary had warned that, on account of poverty and illiteracy, "our sales must necessarily be for many years to come small."

Indeed they were small in comparison to other parts of the world. But in South and West Africa they were growing by the end of the century, whereas on the coast of *North Africa* Bible distribution had flared hopefully, sputtered, and died. In the 1850's Chester Righter of the Levant Agency had visited Egypt, called on the Greek and Armenian and Coptic Patriarchs, and found some prospect of using Bibles in the schools. What little demand continued in Egypt was supplied thereafter from the Levant.

After his somewhat abortive efforts in Latin America, Ramon Montsalvatge arrived as a colporteur in Algeria in 1859. He and another Spaniard, Bautista Mauri, were to receive $400 each plus travel expenses and the cost of the government license to distribute Bibles. What they did *not* receive was that essential government permit to sell--prompting Montsalvatge to quip that the only way he could distribute Scriptures would be to *lend* them "forever." The French and Foreign Bible Society, regretting that the half-civil half-military colony of Oran was "averse to every effort of religious proselytism," offered to try to help Mauri as a layman but dared not jeoparadize their own standing by intervening on behalf of a minister. Monsalvatge returned to America. Mauri was arrested on a contrived charge of forging a deed for a coal mine. When, three months later, he was absolved, still without a colporteur's license, he became a blacksmith near Oran, and the American Bible Society sent him heartfelt thanks and 300 francs for his services.

No further grants were made to Algeria during that century, apparently none to any other territory in North Africa.

*   *   *   *   *

The financial depression in the United States during the mid-1890's seriously curtailed many Bible Society programs, especially the number of colporteurs who could be hired. At the risk of distorting a parable with broad generalizations, it might be said of the seeds sown during the nineteenth century that in Latin America "they fell along the path, and the birds came and devoured them;" in Europe "the thorns grew up and choked them;" in Africa "when the sun rose they were scorched, and since they had no root they withered away." In the Middle East, traditionally most resistant to the Christian Gospel, and in Asia, heartland of ancient religious cultures, a few "seeds fell on good soil and brought forth grain...."

9

Nineteenth Century Outreach:
The Middle East and Asia

> Looking at the country and its condition with reference to
> Bible distribution, the chief impression made upon me was
> that it was the most utterly hopeless region I had ever
> known.

The time was 1878. The place was Palestine, although it might
have applied to all the Middle East. The writer was Edwin Bliss,
second-generation Assistant Agent of the American Bible Society.
Yet the *Levant* (covering a vast arc from Bulgaria and Greece
through Turkey and the Caucasus to Persia and back to Egypt)
continued through the nineteenth century to be the largest and
most important foreign Agency, chiefly under Edwin's father,
Isaac G. Bliss, from 1857 to 1889. Although official records
show about twenty-five per cent less (1,421,886 volumes in the
forty years of 1861-1900), the Agencies Committee in 1884
estimated Levant distribution at nearly fifty thousand books
annually, about one-tenth of total ABS foreign distribution.

As earlier chapters have indicated, American Bible Society
appropriations for "that oppressed country" of Greece began in
1828: $500 worth of books and $500 for a Distributing Agent,
followed by $1,000 for translation and printing. Here, in
connection with Bishop Hilarion's Modern Greek New Testament,
loomed the first debate over what constituted an "authorized
version" in foreign languages. Here an ABS translation with
slight changes from the BFBS version caused confusion and suspicion without obvious improvement--thus hinting at the need for
closer collaboration. Here missionaries advised against assign-
ing a regular American Agent to Greece, because of illiteracy,

restrictive laws, and the operations of the British Society.
Yet when, in 1836, the ABS Board of Managers appointed Simeon H.
Calhoun as Agent in the Levant, his territory included Greece,
perhaps because that country had previously been part of the
Ottoman Empire.

After a year in the field the new Agent deplored the meager
fruit of missions and acknowledged that we are "looking altogether too much to the numbers sent out, to the funds raised etc.
etc., and too little to God." During two terms (1836-40, 1841-4)
Calhoun wrestled with the relative roles of Bible Societies (for
the BFBS was at work in most of the same areas) and missionaries.
He confronted "ecclesiastical opposition in all quarters," from
Orthodox hierarchies and Muslim authorities and most of the
Middle Eastern sects. Finding that Scriptures could be distributed to some priests and bishops without papal or patriarchal
permission, he concluded: "It is best to carry on our plans
without seeming to have any." Under various regimes, from Athens
to Jerusalem, from Constantinople to Cairo, he found "a mingling
of politics and religion...to conciliate the favor of the government...and to secure the assistance of the secular arm in
repressing any spirit of religious inquiry."

For a decade the Levant Agency stood open, although the
Society continued to send money and books to missionaries,
especially under the American Board of Commissioners for Foreign
Missions. In 1852 the Sultan of Turkey issued an edict "confirm-
ing and increasing" the protection given his Protestant subjects.
For two years, which happened to coincide with the Crimean War
(1854-56), Chester N. Righter served the Levant Agency, claiming
to find more freedom in Turkey than in "the whole of Catholic
and Russian Europe." During the fighting, Scriptures were distributed on both sides, 20,000 copies under the supervision of
Florence Nightingale and her staff. On a visit to Jerusalem
Agent Righter called upon the Latin and Armenian Patriarchs, the
Greek Archbishop, and the Grand Rabbi, observing: "Intolerant
bigotry, almost rising to fanaticism, that characterizes all
religions including the Moslem in the Holy City, renders it a
most unfavorable field for Missionary effort, yet we rejoice to
find at present an increased spirit of harmony prevailing among
the different Christian sects."

Righter died on a tour of mission stations in Asiatic Turkey,
to be replaced the following year by Isaac G. Bliss, who had
already served as a missionary in the area for five years. In
his instructions Secretary John C. Brigham told Bliss: "The
work to be done is solemn, and the field of labour full of
interesting memories. You are to distribute the *Word of God*,
and in the land where it was first promulgated but where its
light is well nigh blotted out." Over the next 31 years Isaac

Bliss, later aided by two of his sons, did just that. If
methods of Bible circulation, like political circumstances,
changed less in the Levant than in other parts of the world during the 19th century, nevertheless the scope of the work expanded
and its impact was significant.

Bliss was an efficient administrator whose very independence
and determination led to frequent clashes with the home office.
For ten years he complained that his salary of $1,500 was less
than that of any missionaries in the field--and in 1868 it was
raised to $2,500, on a par with the British Agent. Repeatedly
he hired student colporteurs, paid missionaries directly for
services to the Bible cause, employed a Sub-Agent in Greece who
had been working for the BFBS, proposed to divide contested
fields along geographic boundaries, etc.--without waiting three
months or more for round-trip correspondence with the Board. He
protested the shipment of books directly to Persia and money
directly to Greece without his knowledge or handling. Most of
all, like Simeon Calhoun before him, he resented the lack of
trust implicit in New York's demands for prior consultation:

> I do not wish or intend to do wrong or act contrary to the
> wishes of those who sent me forth. I seek only the good of
> the cause & the honor of the society & seldom act in any
> vital matter without consulting the missionary brethren in
> whom you all have so much confidence.....I am constantly
> acting without special authority for I have supposed that
> you trusted me & wished me to do so.....If the Board do not
> wish me to do anything of this nature without first asking
> their approbation they have only to instruct me to that
> effect & I shall follow instructions, even though it may
> prove sometimes detrimental to the work....

When an advisory committee of missionaries was proposed in
1874, Bliss inquired minutely as to its authority, whether if the
committee and Agent agreed they might proceed without waiting for
further Board approval. Many of his stands drew from the
Secretaries not only endorsement, but apologies for delays or
for ignorance of immediate conditions. On a few, however, the
Board was adamant. Bliss argued that if the Society could pay
missionary translators, colporteurs, sub-agents, dealers, and the
like, it should also compensate missionaries for time spent in
supervising Bible distribution. New York headquarters took the
position that such participation in Scripture circulation should
be a normal part of mission activities, that donors in America
would criticize the sectarian use of Society funds, and that
problems of authority and responsibility were bound to arise.
Similarly, Bliss maintained that hiring Bible *Readers*, native or
missionary, would greatly enhance the understanding and sale of
Scriptures in public places. The Managers believed that this

practice would open a dangerous crack of "comment" in its single-
ness of purpose. But Bliss hired some Bible women and Readers
on his own initiative.

Another project which Isaac Bliss carried through by his own
efforts was the construction of the first foreign Bible House.
Supporting the need for an adequate, cooperative mission headquarters in Constantinople, one missionary wrote:

> The proposed Bible House would not only prevent much loss &
> many serious inconveniences, but its *moral effect* upon the
> population, both native & foreign would be very great, and,
> by affording a permanent & conspicuous center of operations,
> it would at once give a character of permanency & efficiency
> to the work of the distribution of the Holy Scriptures, as
> in fact to all evangelical labors, which years of continued
> effort have not as yet accomplished.

Bliss could understand, if not fully accept, the view of the
Managers that "it is not the policy of this Society to hold any
real estate outside of our present premises." But in his private
campaign to raise $50,000 for such a building he pleaded for
months before securing even an official, public endorsement to
the effect that the Board, "believing such a measure would be of
great advantage and benefit to the Bible work in the East, approve
of the object, and hope the friends of the Cause will esteem it
a privilege to share in so worthy and important an undertaking."

The Bible House in Constantinople (now Istanbul), Turkey, was
completed in 1872, an imposing building containing offices,
bookshops, a bindery, a chapel, and a residence apartment
(pictured and described in *Harper's Weekly*, August 9, 1873).
Over succeeding decades its usefulness justified all the effort.
Despite numerous controversies in the Middle East, the British
and Foreign Bible Society expressed gratification at having the
two Agencies under one roof. Although it had given minimal
support to the building campaign, the ABS complained about the
time Bliss spent in managing the building, and suggested that
any surplus from rents should go to the Levant Agency instead
of the legal owners, the Bible House trustees. A question was
raised subsequently as to whether the Bible Societies should be
so closely identified with a single missionary organization (the
American Board of Commissioners for Foreign Missions, who had
offices in the same building) if they wished to maintain equal
relations with all denominations. "The Bible Society can make
its way faster than the Mission with the multitudes," Agent
Marcellus Bowen concluded as late as 1895.

Throughout this period the British and Foreign Bible Society
resisted ABS expansion and sometimes threatened to crowd it out.

In Bulgaria, in the Caucasus, in Persia, and elsewhere, efforts
to divide the territory or to collaborate in the work failed
repeatedly. An indignant letter from Secretary Joseph Holdich
to Isaac Bliss in 1867 summed up the American attitude: "The
continents of Europe, Asia & Africa are their fields also, but
this was not to exclude us entirely.....The truth is that where
there are American missionaries we must go, and wherever we can
find an open door & a demand for our labors." Bliss figured
that a division of territory on the basis of preponderant national
missionary personnel would give the British over two-thirds of
the foreign Bible work--but whether this meant in the Levant or
world-wide was not clear.

When Secretary Edward Gilman visited London in 1879, he was
told flatly that the British and Foreign Bible Society "could
not be debarred from any territory where they chose to go to
disseminate the Scriptures." On the other hand, when Marcellus
Bowen, Isaac Bliss' successor as Levant Agent, proposed a clear
demarcation of fields based on "fitness" and "equitability,"
Gilman rejected the plan in these words:

> We feel under obligation to give our hearty co-operation to
> the American missionaries who are in active possession of
> that field. It is a cardinal principle with us that mission-
> aries from the United States, whether they are in Bulgaria,
> Austria, Egypt, or anywhere else, are not to be sent to the
> British and Foreign or the Scotch Bible Society for aid.
> This does not mean, of course, that we feel called on to go
> independently and put down our stakes *ad libitum*; but we
> recognize the duty of going where our country men go to
> evangelize the nations; and if this principle sometimes
> leads to duplicating agencies, we are in the same boat with
> the great missionary societies.

In 1898, when the ABS closed its Persia Agency for lack of funds
and the British offered to continue the work, the American
Agencies Committee replied with equal bluntness: "It will, in
our judgment, promote a more satisfactory care of Bible work in
North Persia for the American Bible Society to have undivided
responsibility for it." Not until 1913 was Persia finally
"surrendered" in "exchange" for Central America.

Friction also developed over competing price policies. As in
Europe, the British often sold Scriptures so cheaply that other
publishers could not even cover costs. For example, the BFBS
in Egypt lowered its price for the large Arabic Bible ten piastres
below that of the ABS--though the latter Society had paid for the
translation and the plates and *given* the plates to the British
as a grant. Missionaries in Egypt, Syria, and West Turkey
petitioned for a standard price list between the two Societies,

but the British did not have a uniform system of calculation on
which to base a common price. Furthermore the BFBS, by including
in distribution figures books purchased from or sold to the ABS,
tended to duplicate and distort statistics for both Societies.

Through these years the number of colporteurs, often hired
and supervised by missionaries but paid by the Levant Agency,
multiplied: 12 in 1861, 26 regular and 14 part-time in 1867, 75
in 1879, 129 in 1881, but in the last decade of the century the
figure dropped from 111 to 32 due to shortage of funds. Through
rebellion in Bulgaria, uprisings in Persia, cholera epidemics,
and the Russo-Turkish War (1877-78) (of which Edwin Bliss
commented, "We should like to see both sides pretty thoroughly
whipped."), these colporteurs journeyed boldly--but often well-
armed. Wrote Bliss of one such traveling companion: "He was a
perfect arsenal of weapons. With his double barreled gun over
his shoulder, and pistols and hangers [holsters? pouches?] in
his girdle, he looked as little like an apostle of peace as could
well be imagined. Yet from some of his experiences...I could see
that these were an absolute essential to his safety and success."

Some threats could not be handled so directly. When government pressures, semi-official harassments, and clerical persecu-
tions grew too severe, missionaries were not averse to appealing
for American government intervention. Since "Bibles are more
dangerous than powder" (as the Annual Report for 1884 noted
casually), books to be sold had to carry a stamp of approval from
the Turkish Ministry of Public Instruction. When even this was
repeatedly ignored by petty authorities, who seized Bibles and
imprisoned colporteurs, protests were delivered to U.S. consuls,
to the American Minister in Constantinople, and at least once
(by a joint delegation from several missions including the ABS)
to the President, Chester A. Arthur, in 1884. These requests,
both from Bliss and from Bowen, his successor, were very
specific: protection of "the business enterprises of American
missionaries," redress in the form of a "lesson-giving" indemnity
for "flagrant outrages," and the stationing of an American gun-
boat off the coast of Turkey as a reminder of American strength.

Isaac Bliss expressed his views on international politics as
well. Just prior to the Congress of Berlin, called in the
summer of 1878 to settle the issues of the Russo-Turkish War,
the Bible Society Agent wrote directly to Prince Otto von
Bismarck to stress the importance of religious liberty in the
Middle East. "Religious animosities more than anything else,"
Bliss informed the German mediator, "have embittered the relations of the different nationalities & interfered with the
material prosperity of this country [Turkey].....The present
state of this question of Religious Toleration has a most injurious influence both upon Mohammedans & Christians." Whether

this appeal had any direct influence or not, the Congress of
Berlin did secure--on paper at least--the political equality of
the many religious faiths in the area.

No wonder Caleb T. Rowe, General Agent of the American Bible
Society from 1854 to 1898, wrote on a tour of the Middle East in
1874: "My visit here has already given me a much higher estimate
of the various duties...which Agent Bliss has to perform--both as
to their extent and kind--than I think we have placed upon them.
He is a most devoted worker and with great ability fills up every
hour of time." No wonder a missionary wrote to the Society from
Central Turkey as early as 1864: "You have done a great work
towards filling this land with [the Scriptures], by your co-operation...in translating and publishing the Bible in [ten or more]
languages of the people of the East."

                              ASIA

As American missionaries penetrated the sub-continent of
India, they frequently appealed for Scriptures from New York.
Indeed, in the opening years of American Bible Society activity
abroad, 1831-60, appropriations for India were greater than for
any other portion of southern or eastern Asia. When the early,
enthusiastic support for William Carey's Serampore Mission
culminated in the *Baptizo* controversy (chapter VI), the ABS
shifted some of its assistance to the American Board of Commissioners in Madras and Madurai. Most of its contributions in
mid-century, however, went to mission presses at Lucknow and
Ludhiana, leaving to missionaries and their helpers the actual
task of distribution.

But total American involvement in India remained small. If
only one in fifty of the Mahrattas, for example, could read
(according to one estimate in 1834), they would need 240,000
copies of Scriptures, and the number of readers could be expected
to double in five years. An adequate Tamil supply would cost
$20,000 a year, in the opinion of John Scudder, first of a dis-
tinguished missionary family in India. And he added urgently:

We must go forward, and you must, in connection with the
British Society, come up to our help, or our hands *must
hang down*.....Your Society...should put forth your whole
energies, and resolve...that you will supply all the *calls*
at least which may be made by those who will...resolve to
distribute what they ask for....

The most acute problem was personnel. Distributors handed out
Portions at *melas* (religious fairs) and wedding feasts, to village
head men and to accountants during the annual tax collections.

They opened "reading shops" and supplied Bibles as textbooks in
schools. "My dear sir, we want money, but we also want *men*,"
one missionary begged; "O! that we had this moment some thirty
or forty faithful and devoted men, who should go through this
land in its length and breadth to distribute the word of God to
those who are willing to receive it." To be sure, free circulation had its dangers. As another missionary warned:

> The distribution of the Scriptures among a heathen popula-
> tion, whose only motive in applying for them...is the
> gratification of curiosity...or the desire to possess a
> book, who are quite well satisfied with their own religion,
> and who suppose that the Scriptures are given with the same
> motives, with which supposed meritorious actions are per-
> formed among themselves, requires...the exercise of much
> caution and judgment.

Forty years later, however, other missionaries reported that
"we seldom see any signs of hatred of the Scriptures. All the
Hindus have a reverence for sacred books." If there were
occasional exceptions, they came from three sources: conservative
Brahmin priests; "those who have been in contact with western
skepticism and have caught their ideas from the West;" or mili-
tant devotees encouraged in their hostility by "the excessive
and criminal deference of the British Gov't & officials to Hindu
idols & superstitions" (as one indignant missionary, Rev. Royal
G. Wilder, wrote to the Society in 1866). So strict was this
British policy of religious neutrality that Bibles were prohibited
in the schools for a considerable period, especially after the
Sepoy Mutiny of 1857 and before Queen Victoria was proclaimed
Empress of India in 1877.

As British rule over India became more official and more
inclusive, the British and Foreign Bible Society expanded its
operations until, by 1860, it had active Auxiliaries in Allahabad
Bombay, Calcutta, and Madras, with numerous branches elsewhere.
Even American missionaries themselves could not agree on whether
they needed an ABS Agency in India or whether (as one wrote in
1866) "the British auxiliary here answers every purpose for our
missionaries as well as for those of British societies." The
Board of Managers in New York decided unequivocally against
opening an Agency in India, "a part of the British Empire [and]
a proper field of another Bible Society," but reaffirmed in 1869
its right to serve "in certain localities, where there are
American missionaries who depend upon us for their Bible work,
where the places are remote from the Societies in the country,
or where we have been requested to supplement the labours of
those Societies that are feeble."

In the mid-1870's ABS circulation hit a drastic slump. In
addition to British competition and occasional Hindu opposition,

the decade included a severe cholera epidemic, a critical drought, a cyclone and tidal wave which killed 200,000 people, *and* a rather abrupt decision by the Society and missionaries to *sell* Scriptures, even if below cost, rather than to give them away free. The closing of printing presses in Madras and Ludhiana further reduced available supplies. The only translation subsidized by the American Society in the last four decades of the century was a revision of the Telegu Bible, issued in 1881. As a result of these various retrenchments, between 1861 and 1900, amid the vast and needy population of India, the American Bible Society spent only $111,666 in printing 245,745 volumes of Scriptures and distributing 473,608 copies.

* * * * *

"The Bible in *Ceylon* is, I am satisfied, working a great change in the views and feelings of the heathen." So wrote a missionary from Colombo in 1834. That same year the American Board opened its Jaffna Press and appealed to the Bible Society for five hundred reams of paper. Nor did the zealous Congregationalists hesitate to specify how much money the Society "may very properly" donate to the Ceylon Mission--or to complain if a grant fell short. But appropriations were well spent, and in those early days it was possible to supply every seminarian, every teacher in mission schools, even every member of the church, with a copy of the Tamil Bible. Most of these books were purchased from the Mission Press or the BFBS Agency in Madras, or through the British Auxiliary in Jaffna. As in India, the institution of sales instead of free donations caused a sharp drop in circulation in the mid-seventies. Although the American Board pioneered very successfully in the employment of itinerant Bible women, there is no record of any protest from the Bible Society against this policy--perhaps because, over a forty-year period (1861-1900), the total ABS appropriation for Ceylon was only $3,810, total distribution only 22,821 books.

* * * * *

With the exception of $5,000 to subsidize Adoniram Judson's New Testament in Burma, the American Bible Society steered clear of other British colonies in Southeast Asia.

Thailand was a totally different situation. Siam (as it was then called) presented few if any of the obstacles to Bible distribution encountered elsewhere. Its rulers were open to modernization and Westernization, in railroads and communications and education. Its dominant Buddhism was easy-going and tolerant. It possessed the highest literacy in Asia "except perhaps Japan." Its missionaries were almost entirely American. Ann Judson in Burma and Karl Gützlaff, en route to a famous

career in China, both worked on Bible translations into the
Siamese language.

The Presbyterians, who had started work in Siam in 1840 and
had become the largest Protestant mission in that country,
established a press in Bangkok in 1861 and received small annual
grants from the ABS. Missionaries rather than colporteurs
handled most circulation of Scriptures, and like colleagues elsewhere they concluded that a nominal sale price enhanced the value
of the books. In 1886 the China Agent, Luther Gulick, added Siam
to his territory and traveled extensively through Southeast Asia.
On this journey he came to an understanding--which proved to be
a misunderstanding--with the British and Foreign Agent in
Singapore regarding the Malay-Siamese isthmus, where little or
no work was being done by either Society, but where the populace
spoke largely Siamese.

In 1889 John Carrington, a former Presbyterian missionary,
became American Bible Society Agent for Siam, with marginal pene-
tration into Laos and Cambodia. Like Bliss in the Levant, he
was later assisted by his son. During his first year Carrington
tripled circulation to over 9,000 copies, quadrupled the number
of books printed in Bangkok. Over the next decade *average annual*
figures jumped from 3,600 to 24,000 volumes distributed, from
5,000 to 35,000 printed, and from $1,250 to $4,500 appropriated
by New York.

Yet it must not be assumed that receptivity to the Scriptures
meant openness to conversion. Despite "uniform kindness"
Carrington characterized his first ten years as "a time of seed-
planting pre-eminently.....There has been little reaping." By
1914 Siam had a smaller percentage of Christians than Burma,
Ceylon, Malaya, or French Indo-China. "We do not encounter
hostility or active opposition," Carrington reported, "for the
people are peaceable and friendly. They [difficulties] come
rather from inveterate formal attachment to the Buddhist religion,
stolid indifference, and inordinate pleasure-seeking on the part
of the people."

*   *   *   *   *

The ubiquitous giant of Roman Catholic missions, Francis
Xavier, died on an island near Hong Kong, waiting in vain for an
opportunity to penetrate the "Forbidden Kingdom" of *China*.
Robert Morrison, who reached Canton in 1807 as the first Protestant missionary, spent many years in virtual hiding, learning the
language and producing a somewhat elementary translation of
Scriptures into Chinese. Not until 1842, following the first
so-called Opium War, did the British force China to open her
treaty ports not only to foreign trade, but to missionary

residence and activity. It took further "disciplinary" action by the Western powers in 1856-60 to knock down the flood gates for a great wave of missionary immigration. In 1858 there were eighteen Protestant missionaries in China; thirty years later the number had reached 1,889, and by 1905 there were 3,445.

Elijah C. Bridgman arrived in 1830 as the pioneer representative of the American Board of Commissioners. Within two years he appealed for a massive supply of Scriptures. "There is, probably, no one language on earth," Bridgman wrote, "in which the Bible, were it universally distributed, could be read by so many millions, as in the Chinese language." With that claim he precipitated a lengthy debate on the fundamental efficacy of the written Word by itself. The argument, based on traditional Chinese respect for the literati, was that "Buddhism...has worked its way into every nook and corner of the empire, through all the grades of Society, by means of books, without the aid of teachers." Surely Christianity could do likewise.

Bridgman belonged to a distinguished line of advocates for that point of view. Robert Morrison's Chinese assistant, Liang A-fa, "made a selection of chapters & verses...from the Sacred Scriptures.....These I have explained & illustrated, & so composed a set of tracts, entitled...'good words to admonish the eye'." Karl Gützlaff, brilliant scholar of the Netherlands Missionary Society, admitted the widespread motivation of curiosity among the Chinese, but was nevertheless convinced of the potent impact of the Bible. *"No country of Asia*, ruled by native princes," he declared, *"is so easy of access."*

Years later, in 1863, Henry Blodget of the American Board raised the pertinent question: "Is it well to circulate the Scriptures among a heathen people in advance of missionary effort?" or "Can an unaided heathen mind derive light from the Bible?" His own answer was affirmative: "that he can, and often does... [that] the moral precepts, the miracles, the death, the resurrection, are there, and may be easily understood." Supreme faith in this unaccompanied Word appeared in *The Bible Society Record* for November, 1850: a proposal for "Missionary Balloons" to cover the vast country, each carrying 2,000 Portions and tracts and dropping them one-by-one. "Thus, the Word of God would fall literally like a refreshing shower over the incredulous 'Flowery Land'."

Others disagreed. S. Wells Williams--printer, scholar, diplomat--declined an invitation to exchange the U.S. Legation for the ABS Agency. But at great length he discussed policies and methods of Bible distribution in the Celestial Kingdom, regretting that Society rules forbade the use of tracts and notes, paraphrases and pictures, which he thought would be extremely helpful

to the unfamiliar reader. Circulation figures, he pointed out,
showed at best a willingness to receive the Scriptures, not
necessarily to read them, and in some instances "hundred of
copies were eagerly taken by the people, who could get them
gratis, to sell to shoemakers to fill up the thick soles of
boots, or to druggists to wrap medicines in."

Other missionaries described whole rooms "filled with books
to be devoured by worms," or "sometimes as many as a dozzen"
volumes collected "to ornament the shelves," or "nine out of
ten...bought simply as *curios* from the hand of the foreign devil,
this last circumstance giving them all their value." In one
outrageous scandal, while Gützlaff was raising money in Europe,
his colleagues in China discovered that many of his colporteurs
and preachers were dishonest frauds, falsifying their reports,
squandering their funds, and reselling to printers the books
they supposedly had distributed.(1)

The lesson, of course, was not only to provide closer supervision, but to place more emphasis on personal evangelism than
on books as sheer commodities. Free and forthright in their
advice to the New York office, missionaries stressed repeatedly
that China circumstances differed from other places, and that
modifications in rules and procedures might well be necessary.
Among such recommendations were these: the employment of Bible
Readers, both male and female, as the British Society did; paying
expenses for missionaries to travel on Bible-distribution tours
(apparently granted by 1864); the formation of local committees
composed of *all* interested missionaries and native Christians,
instead of dealing with each denomination separately; "the
propriety of rigidly adhering to the *sale* of books, and the
perniciousness of *giving* them away here in China."

Bridgman, Williams, and scores of others gave generously of
their time and energy and counsel for the Bible Society cause,
but repeatedly they urged the appointment of a China Agent. The
BFBS had stationed a representative in China as early as 1836-39,
then permanently after 1860, and the National Bible Society of
Scotland had sent an Agent soon afterwards. The Board of
Managers of the ABS as early as 1847 expressed their desire to
act, "if we could find exactly the right man" to superintend
finances, printing, circulation, translation, reporting. As
late as 1870 the proposal was dismissed as too expensive so long
as missionaries were distributing Scriptures effectively. But
in 1875 Luther H. Gulick was appointed as Agent for China and
Japan, with the latter split off as a separate territory in 1881.
In less than ten years Gulick built up a staff which included,
at its peak, nine Western colporteurs as well as forty-eight
Chinese. In 1884-85 they traveled 68,653 miles, visited 5,873
places, and circulated 177,689 copies of Scripture, most of them
Gospels or Portions.

One problem neither Gulick nor his successors ever resolved: the term for God. Early Roman Catholics had divided over whether to translate God as *T'ien Chu* (Lord of Heaven) or *Shang Ti* (Supreme Ruler) but had finally settled on the former. Protestant Evangelicals, in search of a word to emphasize the Divine Immanence, chose *Shen* (Spirit). If the earlier terms suggested Confucianism, the later one carried animistic connotations. Henry Blodget called for a committee of theologians and seminary scholars to consult with linguists and even Roman Catholic experts and to settle the issue. But no such Protestant Council was ever convened; missionaries within the same denomination heatedly argued the point, and the China Agency continued to publish both *Shang Ti* and *Shen* Bibles for its divided constituency.

China's cultural unity has often been attributed to a universal written language, despite the diversity of spoken dialects. But nineteenth-century missionary scholars soon discovered that the styles of classical literature and colloquial speech were vastly different. Literati scorned writings in the vernacular (*Kuan-hua*); simple literates could make little sense of the ornate, classical *Wen-li*. The Bible had to be produced in High *Wen-li*, Easy *Wen-li*, the predominant northern Mandarin, and scores of colloquial dialects.

Major work on the Mandarin Old Testament, and later on the Easy *Wen-li* Bible, was carried on by Bishop Samuel Schereschewsky, one of the most colorful--and courageous--characters in the history of Bible translation. Schereschewsky began his pilgrimage as a Lithuanian Jew. His heart was opened to the truth of the Christian Gospel during rabbinical school, but only after years of study in Germany and America did he publicly proclaim his conversion. As an Episcopal missionary to China, Schereschewsky made use of his linguistic skills and his knowledge of the Old Testament in particular, encouraged the establishment of St. John's University in Shanghai, and was elected bishop over his modest protest. While he worked on Mandarin translation, the American Bible Society contributed $10,500 over a four-year period toward his salary and that of assistants. In 1881 Schereschewsky was paralyzed by sunstroke. Yet for another twenty years he labored to the limit of his strength to produce or revise further translations, pecking out tortuous letters on a typewriter with one finger or a short stick. In 1900 the American Bible Society published the bishop's entire Bible in *Easy Wen-li*.

Only brief mention can be included here about the other events of that turn-of-century year, "the most disastrous ever experienced by Christian missions in China since their establishment." Facts and speculations about the Boxer Rebellion of 1900

have been debated in many quarters ever since. Briefly, the
shrewd Empress Dowager, an approximate contemporary with Queen
Victoria on their respective thrones, managed to incite or to
deflect against foreigners a massive uprising compounded of
frustration and defeat (by Japan in 1895), of aborted modernization, and of inefficient autocracy. The result was widespread
pillage and massacre, focussed most dramatically in an eight-
week seige of two thousand Europeans and Chinese Christians
within the Legation Quarter in Peking.

One of the few China missionaries wise enough and fair enough
to recognize *at the time* the complex elements and meanings of
the Boxer Rebellion was ABS Agent John R. Hykes. In a prompt
and extensive report from Shanghai he acknowledged that the
target of attack was everything foreign, "that the crusade was
not specially anti-missionary." With remarkable candor he
pointed a finger at Western territorial encroachments and at
foreign greed for mines and railroads and other profits, as
contributing causes. At the same time, he conceded that "the
influence of the missionaries had undoubtedly been a powerful
factor in the line of reform in its best and highest sense, and
in so far has contributed to the bringing about of a crisis in
China."

The 183 Protestant missionaries killed were concentrated in
four of the eighteen provinces, and included none of the ABS
staff. Eighteen Chinese colporteurs working for the Agency set
out from Peking in May after a sober conference with the superintendent; only four returned. "Of the colporteurs under
missionary supervision I have not heard of one who escaped,"
wrote Hykes in his Annual Report of 1901. The Agent also
estimated the loss of 100,000 volumes at the hands of the Boxers
and imperial troops. Had the Boxer tragedy not occurred when it
did, Bible distribution in 1900 might have reached three-quarters
of a million, as the first six months surpassed the totals for
all of 1899. Excerpts from the Agent's eulogy to Bible-reading
and Bible-selling Christians bear double poignancy seventy years
later:

Our mission premises have been looted, Scriptures and
Christian books burned, many Christian homes destroyed and
the owners beaten, and, in some cases, killed.....The con-
stancy and heroism of the whole native church ought to
forever dispose of the cavil as to the possibility of
converting a Chinaman to Christianity. No one ought to
have the temerity to again ask the question, 'Are there
any native Christians in China?'.....The Churches at home
dare not abandon the Church in China; it has proved its
right to exist.

*   *   *   *   *

Protestant missionaries first entered *Japan* in 1859, less than a year after U.S. Consul Townsend Harris signed a commercial treaty with the hitherto closed Empire. Unlike the agreements with China, however, no provisions assured religious freedom to evangelists or potential converts. Not until 1873 were the edict boards against foreign religions removed. Although Western influence brought greater toleration and "a more liberal spirit of enquiry," the death penalty for conversion to Christianity remained officially in effect until late in the century.

Karl Gützlaff, S. Wells Williams, B. J. Bettelheim, and others had already undertaken Japanese translations; in fact, a Gospel of John had been printed in Singapore in 1837. But once missionaries penetrated Japanese society, they quickly realized that most of these "outside" efforts were "entirely unfit for circulation." Some early arrivals brought with them ABS Bibles in English, Dutch, or Chinese, which could be read by a few scholars, and the American Bible Society provided subsequent shipments for Episcopal, Dutch Reformed, Presbyterian, and later Methodist missions. In early years any attempt at printing Scriptures within the country had to be "with the greatest secrecy and at the risk of life to everyone engaged in it."

In correspondence with missionaries in 1866, ABS Secretary Joseph Holdich urged prompt joint action to translate the Scriptures, adding: "It seems to me that until native Japanese begin to think Christian thoughts and conceive accurately Christian ideas, you will hardly be sure that you will succeed in conveying correct Scriptural view to them." In 1872 representatives of the Presbyterian, Dutch Reformed, and American Board missions initiated an informal translation committee (made more permanent in 1878) and invited the Anglicans, the Protestant Episcopalians, and the Greek Orthodox to join them. The Gospel of John in Japanese appeared the next year (too hasty for quality), followed by Luke and Romans (the two most satisfactory translations). The entire New Testament was completed in 1879 and printed in 1880.

As the chairman of the Translation Committee wrote in 1872, appealing for financial assistance from New York:

The Scriptures are much needed now, in the native tongue. Ancient systems of religion are going to decay, and many minds in this country are looking for something to take their place.....[After thirty-four years in Eastern Asia] I am persuaded that no heathen nation at the present day offers more encouragement to the friends of Christ as a sphere for evangelistic operations. It looks as if the set time has come.

In 1875 the American Bible Society appointed, as Agent for Japan and China, Luther Gulick, an ordained medical doctor born of American Board missionaries in the Sandwich Islands, a former missionary to Micronesia and mission secretary for the Hawaiian Evangelical Association. Gulick, incidentally, favored having the ABS pay the salaries of missionaries who were giving full time to translation, and this was done in several instances. Gulick expressed admiration for the spectacular material progress Japan had made in less than twenty years: "...telegraph wires, & puffing trains of cars.....The science of the Western nations is being eagerly sought, & the nation is in an intellectual ferment." But he was also apprehensive. "How important that the conservative influence of a Biblical Christianity should be rapidly poured into Japan, to meet the evils otherwise inevitable! he wrote in 1876. And a year later:

> Japan has not yet accomplished the proposed assimilation of western life and civilization. The attempted adoption of some of the material advantages of western science, while shutting out, in large degree at least, the vitalizing religion of that science and civilization, will prove abortive. Not till Japan receives the conservative element of Christianity, as well as the radical tendencies of its scientific thought and practice, will she be fairly launched on the new departues of progress and peace.

While deploring "indiscriminate giving" of Scriptures, early missionaries ignored Bible Society policy against free donations, explaining that salesmen were despised in Japanese society and that all "commerce" was assumed to be for private profit. Furthermore they discovered that a fixed price, in a book or on a list, was alien to Japanese concepts of trade. Eventually, perhaps, the "peculiar nature" of Bible distribution would be understood, and the Society's rule could be observed. For these and other reasons the system of colportage had failed in Japan prior to Gulick's arrival. After five years he had five colporteurs in direct Agency employ and eighteen at work under missionaries but partially paid by the ABS; their effectiveness, their dependability, and their conditions of labor remained controversial issues for decades to come.

When Gulick moved to China in 1881, Henry Loomis, a Presbyterian missionary, took over the Japan Agency. Secretary Edward Gilman's detailed instructions about correspondence, reports, and Board policies included a reminder that "you are not sent out as the rival or competitor of any one in the field, and... you will...as a matter of comity but not of obligation, consult the agents of the British and Scotch Societies when you are planning to put new editions to press."

The foreboding was justified. Although early American Protestant missionaries carried Scriptures furnished by the ABS, and although the first few British missionaries had not entered Japan until 1870, the China-Japan Agent of the British and Foreign Bible Society arrived about the same time as Luther Gulick, followed shortly by a representative of the National Bible Society of Scotland. Both immediately made plans to publish--and sell at reduced prices--the individual New Testament books which were being translated by American missionaries and subsidized by the American Bible Society. In an effort to keep peace and avoid duplication, some plates were prepared under joint ownership. Under the mistaken assumption that the ABS planned to issue the book of Exodus without consultation, the Scottish Agent seized the joint plates and locked them in his office. In January, 1888, by precipitously binding the newly-completed Old Testament books with the previously prepared New Testament, the NBSS preceded by one month the "earliest complete one-volume" edition of the Bible issued by the ABS.

Various approaches to this intense competition were proposed--and rejected. The British opposed a geographical division of territory. An 1887 inquiry about uniting the British and American Societies and excluding the Scots came to naught. The next year the Scottish Agent announced his resignation, his convictions "that there was no need of three societies [in Japan] ...that much money had been wasted and a great amount of evil had resulted," and his preference for turning over NBSS work to the ABS rather than to the BFBS. In 1884, again in greater detail in 1889, plans were suggested for a Japan Bible Society, to be administered one-third by Americans, one-third by Japanese, one-third by Britons and Scots. This would give to each Agent a distinct department (e.g. publishing, colportage, finance) and to each Society an equal share in the budget and in distribution (thus greatly enlarging the British and Scottish proportions). The chief objection among missionaries seemed to be that the Japanese were not yet ready to assume such major responsibility.

Yet some solution had to be found. Rival colporteurs walked the same streets; books lay idle because each Society had separate stocks in some places; competitive discounts and price cuts were adopted. A committee of missionaries petitioned the three Agents to find some form of cooperation which would reduce rivalry and jealousy. Loomis wrote to New York saying: "It is the opinion of some of the best men in Japan that the competition between the Bible sellers has been a most serious obstacle to the spread of the gospel, as well as a constant source of trouble in the churches." The "obvious answer"--that such a small country with so few British missionaries and so many ties to the United States should be left to the Americans--could not be pressed in the light of ABS "intrusions" and avowed policy in India, Ceylon, the Middle East, and elsewhere.

The Bible Societies' Committee for Japan was designed in 1889 and inaugurated the following year. Its composition included the three Agents (or a substitute for the Scottish representative, who soon departed), five American missionaries, three associated with the BFBS, and two from Scotland. Somewhat surprisingly, all three home offices "were of opinion that the native Church should be represented," but the Tokyo Committee and the missionaries in Japan were "adverse to this policy." Nevertheless "the desirability of such a representation" and the ultimate "transfer of the entire work to a native Society" were clearly affirmed. Concentration of stock at one depository in Yokohama, hard-wrung agreements about prices and colporteur wages, unified communication with the various missions, all represented worthwhile economy and efficiency.

But constant friction marked the first decade of the Committee' operation. The Constitution stated explicitly:

> The whole work of publishing and circulating the Bible and portions thereof shall be under the direction and control of the Committee.....The Committee shall have power to determine the various editions and styles of its publications; the work and place of residence of the Agents; all matters connected with the purchase or renting of buildings for offices and depositories; the appointment, work, and compensation of colporteurs and sub-agents, prices, commissions, and all other matters connected with the publishing and circulating of the Bible.

Yet the American Bible Society constantly stressed the superior wisdom and experience of its Agent and of its long-standing policies, implying that the right of *appeal* by any two minority members of the Committee constituted the right of *veto* by any of the "Parent Bodies." Clearly many of the controversies arose from the clash of stubborn personalities, sometimes from ignorance, sometimes from undisguised national prejudice. Issues were often minor: sending Scriptures to Japanese emigrants in Hawaii, publishing the Sermon on the Mount as a separate tract, moving the Tokyo headquarters to a cheaper location. But principles and prerogatives were staunchly and often bitterly defended. So consistently did ABS Secretary Edward Gilman support the positions of Agent Loomis, though occasionally with a gentle personal reprimand, that the Committee at one point endeavored, unsuccessfully, to appeal over his head to the President of the American Society.

Loomis and Gilman may have been right in most of their practical, objective positions, but it can be argued that, having acceded to a committee form of government to resolve an intolerable competition, they should have yielded more gracefully to "majority rule." On several points only Loomis' brother-in-law voted with him, although there were four other Americans on the Committee. In 1893 the ABS sent one of its vice-presidents, Augustus Taber, to Japan to investigate the causes of tension. He exercised tact and business acumen, refused to examine old wounds, assured the Committee "that there was not the least doubt the Union would be preserved," and "endeavored to encourage sociability and kindly feeling" by treating the entire Committee and their wives to dinner at the Tokyo Hotel ("out of my own pocket"). But he did not settle any fundamental policies, and the next year the ABS tried--in vain--to reduce the required "notice" for terminating the Japan Committee from one year to six months.

At the very same time, however, as Secretary Gilman (perhaps from Taber's report) was beginning to suspect that the ABS Agent might be unwittingly "obstructing" the work and perhaps should be recalled, Loomis himself described a new atmosphere of congeniality, mutual trust, and agreement. In the latter half of 1894 he wrote:

> The spirit of God has been at work upon the hearts of us all. I trust it may be manifest in the future even more than in the past.....There is now the apparent beginning of a new era. Since my return from the South I have been shown such consideration as never before. I think the change is real and gives promise of a brighter future. I shall certainly do all that I can to promote 'peace and work'.....I am most happy to report that the Committee and myself are now in perfect accord in regard to the present conduct of the work.

The Committee continued through 1903, when a territorial division went into effect (see chapter XIII). But when it came, the "break-up" was agreed upon for greater effectiveness in a rapidly growing field, not because of the jealousies and frictions which had so severely threatened its survival a decade before. In fact, the ABS Annual Report for 1901 soared to this high note:

> With the month of July, 1900, closed the first ten years of joint Bible work in Japan. The importance and value of this method of conducting the work of Bible publication and distribution has been demonstrated in many ways.....
> It was evident that there was a universal feeling of oneness in this department of Christian effort that was not only gratifying to all, but the very fact that there was no division of sentiment or spirit of rivalry made the

meeting above referred to one of special impressiveness
and power. As far as is known there is no desire in Japan
for any return to a division of the work.....There is not
only economy of money and of labor but more systematic
methods and satisfactory results. It has been the lot of
Japan to set an example to the world in many ways that
ought to be helpful. The union of different bodies of
Christians of the same faith has been a great object
lesson, and the gain in the work of incalculable value.

*   *   *   *   *

Missions were slow to get under way in the Hermit Kingdom of
Korea, closed until 1876, long distrustful of the outside world.
In 1883 the country was added to the Japan Agency under Loomis,
while the British and the Scots were eyeing it from China.
Within three years of their arrival the early missionaries,
mainly Presbyterians and Methodists, organized a Permanent
Executive Bible Committee to coordinate and supervise the vital
task of Bible translation. Support for publication and distribution was to be divided on the basis of two-fifths each for the
American and British Societies and one-fifth for the National
Bible Society of Scotland, although the latter had been at work
longer, and Loomis once suggested leaving Korea to the Scots if
they would withdraw from Japan.

In 1890 the ABS declined a request from the missionaries, a
majority of whom were American, for an ABS Agency in Korea,
but Secretary Gilman suggested that the missionaries themselves
take responsibility for publication and colportage, perhaps to
"head off" the British. Yet when the missionaries urged ten
years later the formation of a Bible Committee of Korea, the new
Secretary, William I. Haven, expressed grave reservations. He
may have had in mind Japan's unhappy experience, but the Japan
Committee had been appointed by the respective Societies,
whereas the Korean missionaries intended to keep control in
their own hands. According to the proposal, five representatives
from the three Societies (two-two-one) would be supplemented by
two from each Protestant mission having fifteen workers or more
in Korea, one from each smaller group which had been in the
country at least three years. Despite Haven's doubts, ABS
officers regarded the Committee as preferable to other alternatives; namely, to concentrate on translation and publication,
leaving distribution to the BFBS; to organize a joint Agency of
the three Societies; to establish a separate ABS Agency in
competition with others; or to withdraw from Korea completely.

Korean translations of Scriptures made outside the country
had proved to be poor, but the missionaries on the Bible
Committee completed a New Testament in 1887 and an improved

version by 1900. These had to be published in three scripts
and, as in China, with two editions using different terms for
God. Yet in five short years, 1895-1900, the American Bible
Society distributed 51,728 volumes of Scriptures and sent
$5,950 to Korea. Barely fifteen years earlier the king's edict
approving trade with the West specifically warned against
religious contamination: "While we learn to use their machinery,
let us repel their doctrines; and if some stupid fellow secretly
attempts to diffuse his teachings, we have a law of our state by
which all such shall be destroyed without mercy." By the turn
of the century Korea was on the way toward having the largest
Protestant population in Asia.

                    *   *   *   *   *

Far out in the *Pacific*, the Hawaiian Mission, outpost of
America's westward expansion, gave birth to little missions and
little Bible shipments in Micronesia, Samoa, Pitcairn's and
Ellice Islands. For example, Hiram Bingham, Jr., son of one of
the first missionaries to Hawaii, reduced the language of the
Gilbert Islands to writing and produced a translation of the
New Testament in 1873. Some of these books were printed in New
York, others in Honolulu.

Gradually, with the inclusion of other denominations than
those of the American Board of Commissioners, and eventually with
the inclusion of laymen, the Hawaiian Board (Board of the
Hawaiian Evangelical Association, 1863) assumed major responsibility not only for publication of Scriptures, but also for
distribution among European seamen, Asian immigrants, and Pacific
islanders. The American Bible Society established Auxiliaries
in Honolulu and Lahaina (including four chiefs among the members)
but focused its aid mainly on translation and printing.

Attending the Annual Meeting of the ABS in New York in 1841,
Hiram Bingham, pioneer and veteran of Congregational missions in
the Pacific, expressed the gratitude of his colleagues thus:

Great reliance is placed by missionaries in their efforts
for the evangelization of the islands, upon the influence
of the pure word of God. It is their great care to bring
it into contact with the native mind, and to place it
within the reach of every family.....The produce of fifteen
years of anxious and laborious toil, [this Hawaiian Bible,
presented to the ABS] was printed by native hands; and has
already found its way to thousands who are able intelli-
gently to read it. It is proper that I should here
publicly say, that it is to the aid of this Society that
these labours have been made available.

                    *   *   *   *   *

When the American Bible Society first got under way, its resources were naturally and necessarily concentrated on supplying the needs of the United States. During the two decades from 1821 to 1840 only three per cent of the budget went for donations of books or money overseas. In the next twenty years, however, this proportion jumped to ten per cent. The phenomenal growth of distribution abroad began after the Civil War. Highest circulation figures in the latter part of the century were 200,000 in 1871, 400,000 in 1886, and 630,000 in 1896, but these were peaks with much more meager years in between. Through financial and political administrative problems at home, the American Bible Society was laying foundations, developing organization, exploring procedures for the world-wide expansion of Scripture distribution in the twentieth century.

NOTES

1. Kenneth Scott Latourette, *A History of the Expansion of Christianity*. (New York: 1944) Vol. VI, p. 305.

10

The Home Front

Changing conditions of life affecting the approach to
people require the Society to be ever alert in adapting
its methods to new opportunities and, at the same time,
steadfastly seeking by these methods to achieve the same
fundamental spiritual results which it has already
sought. (1928 Annual Report)

Repeatedly the Bible Society has declared its readiness to
meet changing circumstances by adjusting policies and procedures,
without ever losing sight of its central commitment. Repeatedly
a world in transition has forced major alterations in program
and administration, but the purpose has remained constant in
every age: to share the Good News of reconciliation and redemp-
tion.

It has become an obvious—but none the less significant—
cliché that the life of man on earth has changed more in the past
twenty-five or fifty years than in all the previous centuries of
human history. In terms of indirect, often unrealized, but
influential environment, this is true for the peasant in an
Indian village or a jungle tribesman in Africa as well as for a
sophisticated Occidental. Not only has the sum total of human
knowledge multiplied astronomically, but electronics and
satellites have produced a far greater awareness of other
people and circumstances. The complexity of man's decisions and
the scope of their consequences have created an interdependence
never experienced before.

The twentieth century brought to the United States--as to all
the world--unprecedented challenge and opportunity. The
Spanish-American War and the Boxer Rebellion heralded this
country's involvement as a global power, although the American
people did not fully acknowledge this until 1917--and tried to
turn away again in the 1920's. Two world wars and major military
action in Korea and Vietnam, severe economic depressions in 1894
and again thirty-five years later, the racial and social turmoil
of the past twenty-five years, decisively affected every area of
American life.

But other movements were taking place in the religious and
spiritual climate of the nation--movements which sought to recon-
cile continuity and change. As the twentieth century opened, the
so-called Social Gospel was permeating many churches, but its
early leaders (Walter Rauschenbusch, Washington Gladden, Josiah
Strong, Frank Mason North) sought only to apply to society and to
human institutions the love and brotherhood, the justice and
unselfishness, which they found in Jesus Christ and in the
Scriptures. Although many organizations, including the Bible
Societies, had manifested inter-church cooperation for a century,
the modern ecumenical movement may well be dated from the formation of the Federal Council of the Churches of Christ in America
in 1908 and the Edinburgh Missionary Conference of 1910 on the
world scene.

It would be impossible to trace the impact of every new event
on Bible production and distribution. Clearly, during the
twentieth century, the ABS confronted its greatest challenge and
opportunity in the recurrent military mobilization at home and
in the phenomenal missionary expansion abroad, which reached its
numerical peak in the 1920's. Into the next few chapters must be
compressed developments in the circulation of Scriptures which
were, on the contrary, explosive in terms of translation, administration, technology, cooperation, and commitment.

As the tempo of change accelerated in the twentieth-century
world, so did the pace of Bible Society experimentation. In no
area was this more apparent than in organizational structure.
The Bible Society found itself caught up in a series of administrative adjustments on the home front, designed to apply the most
effective structures under current conditions to meet "eternal"
needs. By the turn of the century, both Auxiliary and local
Agency systems had outlived their usefulness, at least within
the United States. In fact, the Auxiliaries Committee reported
to the Board of Managers in 1904 that "whereas, the Auxiliaries
of this Society were once an arm of power, we believe that, with
notably honorable exceptions, they are today a serious drawback."
Recurrent depressions in the national economy, the failure of
many local societies to engage in active distribution or to remit

any funds to central headquarters, the elimination of District Superintendents from direct cultivation, above all the growth of denominational budgets and appeals--all these factors contributed to the decline and fall of the nineteenth-century "arm of power." Even the District Agencies had become more costly than their proceeds justified.

Convinced that "our hope for success rests in having the churches of our land in living and cordial sympathy with the great work which we are doing," the Managers in 1898 disbanded the older system and replaced twenty-one District Superintendents with seven Field Secretaries--carefully chosen from at least five denominations. These men, all but one assigned east of the Mississippi, were expected to "come into vital touch with those... who are the leaders of Christian thought and enterprise...[in] conferences, associations, and presbyteries," but also with those in seminaries, universities, and colleges who would be in the future such leaders. Said the Managers in 1902:

> The Field Agents have no responsibilities connected with the auxiliaries. They are occupied wholly in bringing to the attention of churches, public gatherings, ecclesiastical bodies and individuals the interests of the Society in order to increase the offering on the part of the people for this home and foreign missionary work.

In an effort to evaluate this system and the role of surviving local societies, a conference of Auxiliaries was called in October, 1900. Out of some 1,500 Auxiliaries listed on the roll, less than fifty sent representatives. They came--including at least three bold women--mainly from the East, but one each from Iowa, Minnesota, Missouri, and Virginia, none from farther South. According to the official report, they were "a goodly company... whose very looks bespoke them to be broadminded, intelligent, fervent lovers of God's word and of the Society charged with its circulation in the world." Their agenda concerned expectations of the Auxiliaries in terms of fund-raising, distribution, relationship to churches, foreign mission work, and "special communities and exceptional populations in this country."

In all these areas the representatives acknowledged with admirable candor that "the system...[which] has worked successfully in the past...has become unsuited to the present requirements." More systematic business procedures, more concentration of facilities now that transportation and communication were so improved, a corporate rather than local approach to home and foreign mission needs--all these called for centralized administration. An active Auxiliary, for its part, should arrange for an annual collection for the Bible cause in each Protestant congregation within its territory, and to request donations by public appeal, by house-to-house visitation, or by such other means as may be deemed advisable." On the other hand, delegates agreed that local groups which neither contributed nor reported to the American Bible Society for three successive years should no longer be regarded as Auxiliaries. By 1911 the number of societies listed had been reduced to 332, but 72 of those had maintained no communication with the ABS for three years or more.

Another change, what might be regarded as further refinement of the Field Agency plan, was introduced in 1907 with the establishment of Home Agencies, eventually ten in all. This latter system grew out of an effort to serve the Negro population, expanding rapidly in numbers and in literacy. Quoting Professor W. E. DuBois of Atlanta University, *The Bible Society Record* (June, 1901) recognized "a problem which concerns not only the destiny of 'the nine million men who are the dark legacy of slavery,' but also of the ideals and life of the Republic." In that same year the Society established the Agency among the Colored People of the South, and appointed Dr. John Percy Wragg, a graduate of Claflin University and Gammon Theological Seminary, as its first and only Secretary.

With Agency headquarters and a depository in Atlanta, with a staff sometimes numbering as many as sixteen colporteurs, Dr. Wragg and his wife conducted a ministry which went beyond Bible distribution to missionary evangelism and pastoral care. In recognition of their effectiveness as well as of Negro migration, this first Home Agency became in 1920 the Agency among the Colored People of the United States, administered by Wragg from New York, with sub-agencies in Atlanta, Charlotte, Cleveland, Houston, and Memphis (until 1924). When the Board of Managers held a Silver Jubilee Testimonial Dinner for Dr. and Mrs. Wragg in 1926, they spoke not only of 1,300,000 volumes of Scriptures circulated among Negroes, not only of scores of colporteurs trained and inspired, not only of support for the Society among black denominations, but also of Dr. Wragg's "example in industry, fidelity, enterprise, integrity and consecration to all his workers and to all his associates."

On his retirement in 1929, in the midst of another reorganization, Dr. Wragg donated a fund from his own savings to perpetuate the work, under the title of the William Ingraham Haven Memorial Agency among the Colored People of the United States, in memory of the ABS Secretary who appointed him in 1901. At the same time the sub-agencies became Divisions directly under the Agency in New York: for Atlanta, Charlotte, Cleveland, and Houston, with New England, the Northwest, and the West handling their own work among Negroes.

In the early years of this first Home Agency, "contrary to what happens in almost every other field in the world, Mr. Wragg

and his colporteurs have sold more Bibles than they have Testaments, or even portions," a total of 95,212 volumes in four
years. The spirit behind that record may be expressed in the
words of a Negro colporteur in 1906: "I know you are going to
tell me to leave until winter, as I lost my strength here last
summer [from malaria], but how can I when the people are asking
for the Word?"

Impressed by the success of the "Colored Agency," the Board
of Managers decided in 1906 to inaugurate geographical Home
Agencies in place of the previous Field Agencies. These,
initiated successively, covered the following areas: Northwestern
(1906), South Atlantic (1907), Central (1907, called Western from
1909 on), Pacific (1907), Southwestern (1907), Eastern (1908),
Middle (or Central, 1909), Atlantic (1910), National Capital
(1925). In 1911 the Managers expressed their confidence that--

...the Society is now organized, with a degree of efficiency
probably without parallel in its history, for a unified and
therefore efficient administration of its work among the
many peoples of this country.....It seems to be almost an
established fact that the development of the Home Agencies
has been one of the wisest movements on the part of the
Society throughout its history.

Many of these Home Agencies were formed in conjunction with
an existing Auxiliary or independent Bible Society; e.g.,
Northwestern with the Chicago Bible Society, South Atlantic with
Virginia, Pacific with California and Washington, Atlantic with
Philadelphia, National Capital with Maryland and Washington, D.C.
Each of the Auxiliaries explicitly retained its organization and
title, as well as its local responsibilities; most of them
nominated the Home Agent and selected the advisory committee.
A few miscellaneous items from Agency reports may indicate some-
thing of the problems and attitudes in various regions.

Northwest: Despite active collaboration from only one-third
of the churches, over 1,000,000 copies were distributed in 1930,
and Universal Bible Sunday had become a regular observance.
Scriptures were circulated in hospitals, soldiers' homes,
orphanages, Indian schools, and even at football games (with the
endorsement of Coach Amos Alonzo Stagg: "This little volume
will help us all to win in the Game of Life.").

Western: "Exceptional populations" (called minority groups
today) included miners, immigrants (Scriptures in seventy-four
different languages were distributed in 1929); Mormons (81 per
cent of Utah towns had *no* Protestant residents whatever); Roman
Catholics (New Mexico was regarded as "practically a foreign
country" in this respect); in fact, in 1908, with the exception

of Missouri and eastern Kansas "the territory of this Agency is yet under pioneer conditions, and so is a real missionary field."

Pacific: As in the Gold Rush days of Frederick Buel (see chapter VII), California remained a polyglot mission field (circulating books in eighty-two languages and dialects in 1930). After the 1906 San Francisco earthquake and fire, a new Bible House was built--and freed of its mortgage by 1912. Volunteer groups with cars and trucks and bulletin boards and daily Bible readings on radio spread the Word to residents, while others provided Scriptures for crews aboard trans-Pacific liners, the Japanese Fleet, and the German dirigible, the Graf Zeppelin. Hawaii, brought under the Pacific Agency in 1920, as was Alaska in 1926, continued to be "one of the greatest interracial mission fields under the 'Stars and Stripes.' It is a veritable ethnic whirlpool. Perhaps nowhere else have there been such strong influential movements in civic and public life flowing out of the Bible, manifested among all classes, as in the Hawaiian Islands."

Central: From Lake Erie to the Gulf of Mexico, even in 1909, "we are finding a younger generation that have little interest in or knowledge of the Bible Society work." Begun in cooperation with the Young Men's Bible Society of Cincinnati, "one of the oldest and most loyal of the auxiliaries of the American Bible Society," this Agency circulated Scriptures "to penitentiaries, prisons, workhouses, reform schools, Gospel wagons, Y.M.C.A.'s mission work, in city and mountains, hospitals, and the poor and needy." Twenty years later volunteers in Kentucky prepared "neat little boxes that hold ten or twelve books. These are placed in the county courthouse, the dental offices, the barber shops, the Union bus station, and the hotel; and a number are left with the jailer to give to the prisoners in the jail."

At twenty-five year intervals two further structural changes took place in the Society's administrative pattern. In 1935 the Home Agencies became Districts, with the addition of a Southern District and a reallocation of some of the states. The Haven Memorial Agency for Colored People continued with four divisions, but the Society reduced its depositories for shipping books to six: New York, Atlanta, Chicago, Dallas, Denver, and San Francisco. District Secretaries and their staffs were to concentrate on four principal tasks: supervision of distribution of books, promotion of the use of Scriptures, education of the churches regarding the Bible cause, and cultivation of financial support.

Perhaps the latest reorganization since World War II should be attributed more to modern technology than to recent attitudes and social change, although the latter undoubtedly enter in.

Systematic analysis revealed that the largest distribution of books could be handled at the lowest cost from central head-quarters, that the second largest distribution took place through commercial (including denominational) bookstores, and that major campaigns of education and cultivation (for churches or the general public) could be administered most effectively from the New York office. District Secretaries with large territories to supervise could not reach the "grass-roots" towns and churches any more personally than could national headquarters. In the mid-twentieth century the "separate but equal" structure of a Negro Agency had become an anachronism. Half a dozen depositor-ies, with supplies which were adequate in quantity and diversity, represented much idle stock, waste storage, and duplicate operations.

Therefore, in 1959, the American Bible Society consolidated its domestic work under the National Headquarters into three Regional Offices: Eastern (at New York), Central (in Chicago), Pacific (in Los Angeles). In each Regional Office was a Secretary for Church Relations, for Community Relations, and for Special Ministries. Activities involved under these titles will be sketched briefly later in this chapter.

The construction in 1962 of a Central Depository in New Jersey, highly mechanized and linked by computer to the home office, together with the completion in 1966 of new headquarters in New York, made possible a consolidation undreamed-of even a decade earlier. Some staff members insisted that "the heart of the system is the Regional Office; National Headquarters exists to serve the regions." Others would reverse the emphasis--or point out the significant shift from "Regional Office" to "regions"-- presumably under a centralized administration.

*   *   *   *   *

If organization and reorganization loomed large on the internal scene of the American Bible Society during the past seventy years, war and threats of war dominated the world pic-ture. In Bible distribution, as in many other areas of human life, the tragedy and suffering of armed conflict seemed to draw forth man's greatest benevolence--and his deepest awareness of spiritual need.

Three days after the German declaration of war in 1914, a telegram reached New York from the Christian Tract Society in Germany: "For charity work among soldiers we need urgently German, Russian, French and Polish Testaments, parts of Bibles, and money. Help us for Christ sake." Two days later, before this appeal could be printed on the inside cover of *The Bible Society Record*, the Board of Managers adopted the following resolution:

> The Board of Managers is deeply moved and distressed by
> the horrors of the war in Europe, and deems it fitting to
> give expression to its sympathy for all those of every
> nation who must suffer anguish and bereavement. It is
> the earnest desire of the Society to do whatever it can
> to help them either directly or through our sister socie-
> ties in Europe.

Bible Societies in England, Scotland, France, Netherlands, as
well as other religious organizations sent similar pleas. The
ABS was facing a financial crisis of its own, requiring increased
income or serious retrenchment of its program. Nevertheless it
promptly appropriated $1,000 for Scripture distribution among
armed forces across the Atlantic, and launched a European War
Fund Campaign for additional donations.

More dramatically, however, it pledged cooperation with the
World's Sunday School Association, an international, interdenominational agency claiming 30,000,000 members in many countries.
The American Branch of that organization proposed to raise
$50,000 (a nickel from each of a million Sunday School pupils)
if the Bible Society would print a million Testaments in the
various languages needed and distribute them to soldiers in
nations at war, through societies and churches in Europe. Three
aspects of the undertaking were quite unusual: first, commitment
to such a mammoth project under one organization; second,
publicity for the "Million Nickel Fund" in the Bible Society's
own promotional literature; third, the inscription on the title
page, "Presented by an American Sunday-school Scholar." Of the
last point especially, the Managers emphasized that it constituted "a wholly exceptional procedure and [was] not to be a
precedent."

Statistics of this kind cannot be precise, but contributions
through the World's Sunday School Association came to an estimate
$27,051.33, of which the Bible Society spent $26,936.33 on some
565,833 volumes, most of them Gospels rather than full Testaments
These figures were in addition to $3,328 granted by the Society
for other Scriptures, largely manufactured in Europe.

Meanwhile, in 1916-17, thousands of American troops were
mobilized on the Mexican border. The Southwestern Agency made
a valiant effort to supply these men with khaki-bound New Testaments, but called on the national Society both for books and for
permission to raise extra funds. The Managers, lacking any
financial reserves, authorized a nation-wide campaign for
$10,000. Records do not indicate the monetary response, but
several other Home Agencies supplied 5,000 Testaments each for
distribution among men in their own "recruiting stations,
hospitals, barracks, wireless stations, ships and camps," and

through the Y.M.C.A. Thus the Society estimated that ten thousand copies were given to American soldiers in 1916 alone. The Southwestern Agent made this additional observation:

> When the United States declared war on Germany it was then seen how providential was our Bible work on the Mexican border; for these were the troops which were sent first to France, and they were prepared. They not only had the military training, but they were equipped with 'the sword of the Spirit,' which is the Word of God.

At a meeting of the Federal Council of the Churches of Christ in America, called in May, 1917, to discuss the churches' role in the war, Secretary William I. Haven asked "sympathetic support" for ABS plans to give a Bible to any chaplain requesting it "and to make the Scriptures available for every soldier and sailor of the Army and Navy." Mindful of its own empty treasury, the Board of Managers initially offered special editions of the Scriptures "to any approved agency at one-half the cost of such editions...so long as the money received for this distribution shall make it possible." In July the Board created a Committee on War Work to conduct an Army-Navy Fund Campaign. But in August, at the request of the National War Work Council of the Y.M.C.A., the Society over-rode its previous cautious policy and undertook to provide a million pocket-sized New Testaments for distribution free of charge through chaplains and the Y.M.C.A. This was an act of faith. No grant of such magnitude had ever been made by any Bible Society. In reporting this momentous decision, the Society admitted that "our reserve funds are all exhausted and our world-wide operations are seriously menaced," that it would have to let contracts with three responsible printers because its own presses were already running sixteen hours a day. "It is furnishing the plates, the paper, the printing, and the binding and pays all the bills.....Nevertheless, we have taken this step because we could not do anything else. The American people will expect the ABS to furnish what is so urgently demanded, and to do it quickly."

The production process itself made a dramatic story. Because these books would suffer hard usage, the Society insisted on "good print, small size, and strong, appropriate binding." Many commercial firms did not have the requisite grade of paper or the special machinery necessary. The Schlueter Printing Company (founded by German immigrants, *The Bible Society Record* pointed out) ran four presses twenty-four hours a day "except for the Sabbath rest," from Labor Day to St. Patrick's Day, 164 days in all, to print 1,150,000 complete New Testaments. But other phases of the operation had greater difficulty. With unprecedented cold, which stalled trains and ships, and with a critical three-months coal shortage, workers grew too numb to work

rapidly; glue and paste were too frozen to use. During the
summer, on the other hand, extreme heat actually melted some of
the rollers. Transportation of essential machinery was delayed
for months. Despite these handicaps the time losses were
counterbalanced, and the million Testaments were ready in six
and a half months instead of seven.

Initial cost estimates were $200,000 for these Testaments,
another $200,000 for other war needs. Agency Secretaries were
given primary responsibility for raising these funds, and the
task grew more difficult as the Red Cross, Y.M.C.A., and many
other service organizations made their appeals. To encourage
donations the Society agreed to accept Liberty Loan Certificates
(war bonds)--and promised not to redeem them until the war was
over. At the end of 1919 the following distribution figures
were announced: for American armed forces 4,920,543 volumes of
Scripture; for belligerent forces of other countries 1,887,758;
total *6,808,301*. By an almost miraculous conjunction of faith
and stewardship, total expenses for this effort came to
$264,578.25 and contributions amounted to $247,121.57, leaving a
"comparatively small deficit of $17,456.68."

Miscellaneous by-products of this massive war-time campaign
provided indirect clues to Bible Society policy.....The Paulist
Press offered to supply free copies of the Army and Navy edition
of the (Roman Catholic) Douay New Testament for distribution
through ABS Home Agencies. Aside from reporting this offer
through the central Bible House, no official response was
indicated.....Contrary to traditional policy against "note or
comment," the Maryland Bible Society pasted inside its books a
letter from President Wilson, the Massachusetts Society a letter
from the Governor, and the New York Bible Society a letter from
Colonel Theodore Roosevelt. Others proposed to include additional
reprints of the Lord's Prayer or the Sermon on the Mount. But the
ABS, maintaining its historic position, refused to add anything
whatever to the text of its own editions, simply providing a page
for identification (name, address, "service") and a blank page
for "memoranda".....Throughout this period military and naval
facilities supplied free transportation for books shipped to
chaplains.

When the first 100,000 Testaments emerged from the press,
token presentations were made to representatives of the Y.M.C.A.
and the Army and Navy. Hailed as "a unique occasion in the Bible
House," the ceremony in New York featured martial music,
patriotic anthems, abundant speeches, and "the most beautiful
silk American flags" that John Wanamaker's store (just across
Astor Place) could provide. In his address ABS President James
Wood recounted one reaction to these gift Testaments: "This is
a good thing," a doughboy told his buddies, for the books were

printed on nice paper just the right size for rolling cigarettes and he had already "smoked through to II Corinthians." "In spite of this, perhaps at the appointed hour," President Wood remarked, "he may read one little verse in II Corinthians before he smokes it up that will change the entire course of his life. This is our hope, and that is our prayer accompanying every one of these precious books that we send forth."

Instead of being shocked by such candor, several speakers picked up the theme. Brigadier General Eli D. Hoyle dismissed it as a witticism, braggadocio or carelessness, dwelling instead on the more prevalent "superstition among soldiers that the Bible is a physical protector, as well as a spiritual inspira-tion." The naval chaplain assured the audience that "our men will not use the Bible or the Testament" in that fashion. The chaplain from Governor's Island recognized that "the fact that the President was not afraid to tell that story--concerning the soldier who smoked his way through the Bible--teaches this, that religion is not a thing you can hurt." When one soldier grumpily accepted a Bible because "it may stop a bullet," the chaplain assured him that "a pack of cards will stop a bullet better" since it is thicker and looser, but "don't take the Bible for that sort of life preserver. It may protect your heart for you, but I pray God it may save your life in and through your heart." It was that kind of hope and faith and prayer that inspired millions of Bible Society friends to meet the sudden and enormous needs of the armed forces, at home and abroad, in the First World War and in each succeeding conflict.

On the other hand, the Bible Society reaffirmed the importance of the Holy Scriptures in building a peaceful world. To the Peace Conference at Versailles the Board of Managers sent a cablegram urging the statesmen "to further their great object by making ample provision for securing and maintaining complete religious freedom throughout the world," and adding:

We would not restrict this freedom in any manner so as to exclude any creed or profession of faith. We believe that no other foundation can be laid than that which is laid in the Holy Scriptures known as the Christian Bible, but we would leave all peoples free to follow God's leadings in their comprehension of His Truth.

At the same time the Society donated to the Peace Conference a specially prepared Bible, in red morocco slip cover with the seal of the Society in gold and "boxed in a handsome blue morocco covered case, with blue silk padded lining."

On a more mundane level the ABS faced innumerable post-war problems. In 1919 the Managers reported a forty per cent

decrease in national distribution, attributed to demobilization,
to the scarcity of books published abroad, to inflationary
printing costs, labor troubles, and material shortages. Furthermore, the "weakening of evangelical churches," which had been
noted in the Eastern Agency report in 1909, had gained momentum
during the war. Major missionary appeals for world-wide
rehabilitation (such as the Methodist Centenary Fund) collapsed
disastrously or sputtered away. When economic recession combined with political isolationism and spiritual apathy, benevolent causes had to be sharply curtailed, even in the early
'twenties. With the onslaught of the Great Depression in 1929,
practically every Agency Report mentioned bank closures,
unemployment, bread lines, dwindling contributions, even
Scripture sales for "59¢ worth of beans" or "one nice fat hen."

The following table illustrates some of the effects of the
Depression:

Year	Sales	Gifts	Total	Auxiliary Contributions
1929	$305,081	$19,402	$324,483	
1930	281,970	18,683	300,653	
1931	245,153	15,218	260,371	$13,993
1932	178,397	13,304	191,701	11,760
1933				9,645

The Society's appropriation to its Home Agencies in 1934 was
thirty per cent below what it was in 1930. Circulation dropped
from over 4,000,000 volumes in 1929, the largest in peacetime
history, to approximately 3,000,000 each of the next three years.
As one contribution toward lifting the nation out of its
Depression, the ABS, in a major campaign along military lines,
provided 140,000 free Testaments to men in Civilian Conservation
Corps camps, an effort unprecedented in time of peace.

By the end of the 1930's both Europe and Asia were at war
again, and America's armed forces were mobilizing. Across the
Atlantic the changing political map of Europe necessitated
innumerable adjustments to continue American Bible Society work
and to assist or take over the disrupted activities of other
societies. It took nearly three years, for example, after Nazi
Germany absorbed Austria in 1938, before ABS Treasurer Gilbert
Darlington and many other negotiators arranged the transfer of
eighteen tons of stereotype plates from Vienna to Geneva. There

in neutral Switzerland the Society opened a liaison office for Europe, cooperating with the Bible Work Department and the Ecumenical Commission for Chaplaincy Aid to Prisoners of War and Refugees under the still-unofficial, embryonic World Council of Churches. Between 1940 and 1945 the Geneva office issued the following books: for prisoners of war 51,378 Bibles, 111,416 Testaments, 163,563 Gospels, totalling 326,357 volumes; for European civilians 32,780 Bibles, 42,440 Testaments, and 49,972 Gospels, totalling 125,192 books.

To meet these needs as well as the rapid military mobilization at home, the American Bible Society commenced a War Emergency Fund in 1940, offered free Scriptures on request of chaplains, and in four months distributed 14,106 Testaments and 22,600 Gospels *above the normal circulation.* When the United States became fully embroiled after Pearl Harbor, the ABS repeated its massive supply, with separate bindings for the various "services." It also offered to provide Douay New Testaments for Roman Catholic servicemen and Old Testament Selections for Jews. This time, in contrast to earlier policy, military Testaments included a page for identification, a letter from President Franklin D. Roosevelt "commending the reading of the Bible to all who serve in the armed forces," and nineteen pages of selected Psalms, hymns, prayers, the National Anthem, plus references to "favorite passages." During the first two years of the War Emergency Fund the churches of America contributed barely one-third of the amount expended by the Bible Society.

When in 1942 Captain Eddie Rickenbacker and his flying crew were rescued after twenty-one days in a life raft, they credited their motivation for survival to the daily reading of a New Testament. This heroic testimonial dramatized the importance of Scriptures for the armed forces, but it also led the Bible Society into an intricate--and costly--experimentation with waterproof containers (made of lead foil, cellophane, and asphalt cement) so that every life raft carried on the sea or in the air might have a watertight Testament. Said one airman assembling equipment for medium bombers: "I have been ordered not to pack these rafts until a New Testament goes in each one of them."

In Japanese Relocation Centers, in Italian prisoner-of-war camps, in refugee compounds, and "liberated areas" Scriptures were needed in assorted foreign languages. For the Japanese and Americans of Japanese descent who were evacuated from the Pacific Coast, it was necessary to reproduce books by photography, since all editions in Japanese had previously been imported. Between July 1, 1940, and December 31, 1945, the American Bible Society provided 7,420,910 volumes to men and women in U.S. armed forces (455,251 Bibles, 4,407,005 Testaments, 2,558,384 Portions). But this represented slightly over half of the expenditures under the War Emergency Fund. Toward a total of nearly two and a half million dollars, $962,110 came from individual donors, $958,219 from denominational funds, $309,770 from local churches, $186,117 from Auxiliaries and other sources, $50,048 from ABS General Budget.

Peace was short-lived. The outbreak of war in Korea in 1950 brought orders from the chaplain at United Nations Command in Tokyo for Testaments in nine different languages: French, Turkish, Siamese, Tagalog, Korean, Chinese, Spanish, Portuguese, and English. To meet the unusual request shipments poured in from New York, Rio de Janeiro, Istanbul, Bangkok, Manila, and Tokyo itself. Again the Society, through its Advisory Council, anticipated "the service of chaplains in the armed forces in distributing the Bible, the New Testament, and Scripture portions in quantities which approximate millions." Again war-connected needs overseas spread rapidly beyond the fighting forces to prisoners of war and civilian refugees, spilling over into foreign distribution. Again, as so valiantly in the past, the Bible Society assumed the entire cost for such supply, and then appealed for special donations to replenish the treasury.

And again, even in a sophisticated post-World War II world, the testimonials poured in. The methods and terrain of fighting might change. New modes of distribution appeared. At lonely outposts Thanksgiving Day packages were dropped by plane, containing "turkey with all the trimmings, letters from home and Bibles." But the correspondence from chaplains and men could have been written at Antietam or Belleau Wood or Tinian, instead of (for example) by a naval chaplain in Japan ministering to Marine casualties from Korea:

> It would have thrilled you...to see the boys pull out their Testaments from their pockets, most of them smeared with mud and often blood-stained, as they testified to the power of God's Word to strengthen and sustain them in combat and particularly as they were wounded, some of them lying for a considerable time in a filthy rice-paddy or out under the hot sun of a parched hillside.
>
> Their Testaments were all they brought back. Pictures of wives, children, parents and sweethearts would be carefully placed inside of the cover. When I would offer them a new clean copy for their old one, they would refuse, saying that the old one had been with them through thick and thin, and they wouldn't think of parting with it.
> (*The Bible Society Record*, January, 1951, p. 7.)

As the Korean War simmered to a stalemate, the Bible Society showed another impressive record of distribution in three brief but critical years: 941,241 volumes in 1951, 904,000 in 1952, 1,301,145 in 1953. But the draft and international tensions did not subside. Scripture distribution among the armed forces of the United States went up instead of down: 1,360,604 in 1954, 1,397,101 in 1955. Never before in peace-time had chaplains requested so many books for their men. On April 14, 1955, the Bible Society presented to Admiral Arthur W. Radford, Chairman of the Joint Chiefs of Staff, "the 40-millionth volume of Holy Scriptures provided by the American Bible Society for the Armed Forces and for populations liberated by the Armed Forces."

In 1959, in special ceremonies at the U.S. submarine base, New London, Connecticut, presentation copies of the New Testament symbolized for the first time military distribution on vessels without chaplains. The following year an agreement was reached between the ABS and the Chiefs of Chaplains by which the Society would provide Bibles and Testaments in the King James Version and Testaments in the Revised Standard Version. Estimated costs for the "average figure" of 250,000 copies ran to $81,250, or $18,750 above the Society's "military budget" for the following year. Then came Vietnam, creeping up on the Scripture supply as it did on the nation. Just as the American Bible Society ended its 150th year, the 250,000 Gospels expected to meet military needs for 1966 gave out, and another 250,000 had to be printed.

That omen can be taken in many ways. Some will regard America's military engagements as otherwise unequalled opportunities for Bible distribution, ministering to the spiritual and emotional needs of civilians and servicemen alike. Others will see them, like war itself, as a tragic waste of resources which might otherwise be poured into wider, more diversified evangelistic efforts. The record of the American Bible Society in these periods of war has been heroic, like the record of the men and women it has served. But the enormous burden of supplying free Scriptures to the armed forces has threatened repeatedly to decimate the regular budget, making more imperative than ever a dependence on denominations and local congregations. In 1954 representatives of fifty-five denominations who then comprised the ABS Advisory Council adopted a statement affirming this obligation:

The providing of the Scriptures for the Armed Forces is a responsibility of the *Churches*. The *Churches*, through the American Bible Society, are determined to provide such Scriptures as may be needed by the Armed Forces. Furnishing Scriptures to men and women in national service presents a link which local churches will want to maintain. (italics added)

*   *   *   *   *

Such a pledge highlights once again the shifted focus of Bible
Society operations during the twentieth century: the new
reliance on the churches. As the Agencies and Auxiliaries
declined, structural reorganization could streamline some administration but it could not guarantee an essential base of
support. As early as the 1860's certain denominational bodies
had criticized the ABS for "a very cumbrous kind of machinery,"
for uneconomical use of Agents, and even for "its entire system
of business and financial management." Yet the body which first
voiced "a degree of distrust of the practical management of the
American Bible Society" acknowledged "after full investigation...
no occasion for a want of confidence"--but also that "the duty
rests with the Christian people of this State to bring the
sacred Scriptures within the reach of the whole population."

Ironically, succeeding decades witnessed a steady erosion of
that sense of responsibility. When the Bible Society was
founded, concerned individuals and groups initiated and supported
all manner of benevolent causes. A century later, as the Annual
Report for 1928 admitted, "the centralizing trend of denominational life tends to direct the interest of local churches, and
particularly their contributions, into the channels of the
denomination rather than to local religious causes"--or national
ones. Where the original Agents had worked primarily with
individuals and families, where District Superintendents sought
to stimulate and counsel Auxiliaries, the Home Agents concentrated
their attention on church conferences, synods, associations,
presbyteries, councils, and congregations. In 1927 the Northwestern Agency Secretary reported that "practically every foot
of this area is under the direct supervision of some organized
church or missionary endeavor"--which ought, therefore, to be
replacing colporteurs, "searching out the unchurched and carrying
the printed volumes to those beyond the reach of the preachers."
Yet in fact he regarded orders for Scriptures from 2,000 out of
12,000 organized churches as "a wonderfully encouraging response
....at least twenty-five per cent more than in any previous year
of the Agency's history."

Although a few volunteers travelled from house to house or
devised creative schemes for publicizing the Bible cause, both
cultivation and circulation came increasingly to depend on
denominational agencies, on the 10,000 professional home mission
workers throughout the United States, and on direct promotion
from headquarters. Where ninety per cent of Bible sales in 1913
had been made through colporteurs, in 1927 eighty-five per cent
came by mail through Home Agency offices. By the early
'thirties, quite apart from the financial crisis, indifference
or preoccupation or the absence of organization had eliminated

at least three-quarters of the local churches from "any definite
work toward supplying the Scriptures to either their own constituencies or to their communities." Some of the "slack" was
picked up by denominational bookstores and by home mission workers
and institutions. The remaining portion of the task reverted to
the central Bible Society headquarters and to individual contributors.

Nevertheless this hard fact did not alter the basic principles
on which the Society rests. A significant conference of Home
Agency Secretaries, held in 1933, reaffirmed the conviction that
"responsibility for the distribution of the Scriptures rests
primarily upon the whole Christian church, and is implicit in
the nature of the Bible, of the church, and of the Christian
message. It does not rest upon the Bible Societies alone."
The Conference therefore challenged the churches to use their
own resources, personnel and institutions, to further distribution of Scriptures, *and* to support the Society's "indispensable
...specialized service, which they could not separately do so
effectively and economically."

In other sections of the 1933 report, subsequently approved
by the Board of Managers, the Home Secretaries reaffirmed a
number of fundamental policies, sufficiently important to
warrant direct quotations:

> The Society rightly calls Christians of all communions
> into fellowship. As it does not undertake teaching and
> interpretation...nor prescribe 'doctrinal tests' for its
> staff or members, it is free to summon to its support all
> persons who hold in common the Society's sole purpose. It
> will not so relate itself to any body of Christians as to
> prevent others, holding its central purpose, from support-
> ing or serving it.....

> As the objective of the Society is not merely distribution
> of Scriptures in large numbers, but a development of inter-
> est and conviction as well as of possession...the Society
> may justly, therefore, undertake the encouragement of the
> reading and study of the Scriptures by such means as
> appear suitable.....

> [Although] distribution by sale avoids that disrespect
> toward the Scriptures which generally attaches to widely
> spread free propaganda literature,...the principle of sale
> to those who can buy [at a price suitable to the multi-
> tudes] is paralleled by the principle of partial or outright
> donation [to indigent persons or institutions or in time
> of war and other emergencies].....

The missionary purpose of the Society requires that first consideration in distribution be given to areas and groups not served by the normal opportunities for possessing the Scriptures...to those financially unable to supply themselves; and to those indifferent to the meaning and use of the Book.....There is an obligation upon the Society to give particular attention to areas and groups in which distribution is made difficult by ignorance, prejudice, or hostility......

In an effort to fulfill "the missionary purpose of the Society," national and regional staffs have sought to identify "people in need" and then to devise strategies for serving them. In a survey document on "The Task of the American Bible Society in the United States" Secretary Eric M. North listed twelve categories of persons: (1) those in institutions (prisons, hospitals, welfare homes); (2) groups in similar employment or occupation (e.g. manual laborers, industrial workers, tourists, campers); (3) people in transit; (4) students attending schools or colleges; (5) men and women in military or naval service; (6) the blind; (7) linguistic and cultural minorities; (8) those reachable through churches and missions; (9) people in residential areas; (10) members of distinct organizations; (11) those within reach of mass media (radio, TV, advertising); (12) victims in disaster areas. Ostensibly representing people to whom the ABS has a "distinctive missionary obligation," such a list obviously should, in one category or another, include every inhabitant of the country who does not possess the Scriptures--or it is an incomplete summary of Christian responsibility.

*   *   *   *   *

Some of these groups have long stood in the forefront of Bible Society concern, most notably the blind. Previous chapters indicated the development of publications in Samuel Howe's Boston Line Letter (1836) and William B. Wait's New York Point (1894). Amid competing variations, the ABS printed some American Braille in 1911, but finally concentrated on Revised Braille Grade 1½, taught to blinded servicemen after World War I. These books-- and others in the older systems for those who could not relearn-- were distributed largely through schools and agencies. Gradually Scriptures for the blind were produced in other languages: Portuguese, Spanish, Korean, Siamese, Japanese, Armenian. In 1924, largely through ABS effort, Congress authorized the mailing of Braille materials for one cent per pound. Although circulation was always limited (62,528 volumes between 1901 and 1930), Braille books were sold far below cost. As a result, the Society spent for these Scriptures approximately $10,000 a year from 1921 to 1928, increasing to $11,250 in 1929 and over $12,000 in 1930, reimbursed in part by legacies and designated gifts.

Still more important, perhaps, the particular needs of the
blind led as early as 1921 to a modification of hitherto strict
constitutional policy. A volume of selected portions was prepared and published in New York Point Bipage and in Revised
Braille Grade 1½. This "Small Volume of Scripture Passages"
contained excerpts from Genesis, Exodus, Psalms, Isaiah, Matthew,
Luke, John, Mark, Acts, Romans, I Corinthians, and Revelation.
Selections from John, I John, and Hebrews were added to fill the
requisite number of pages. Whereas most Braille editions run
between 100 and 300 copies, this one sold over 2,000 in the first
five years (at fifty cents for blind persons, $1 for others),
necessitating further printings. Although these combined
excerpts obviously represented far more than a single book, it
violated previous strictures against "arbitrary" selection of
Biblical passages, which might be interpreted as editorial
"note or comment." Though not regarded as a precedent, this
"Small Volume for the Blind" did open the way to later extracts
or "teasers" in regular print.

The most sensational development for the blind, however, came
in the use of sound recordings. In 1931 the entire output of
the Bible Society for the blind took the form of Braille volumes;
by 1966 only seven per cent was in books, ninety-three per cent
consisting of 115,515 records. Helen Keller, the great spokesman
for the handicapped, paid frequent tribute to the American Bible
Society. "The Bible," she declared in 1934, "seems to me like
a river of light flowing through my darkness; and it has kept
my hope of accomplishments bright, when things seemed too
difficult to overcome." Despite growing interest on the part
of the public, and despite international agreement on a uniform
system of Braille, over eighty per cent of blind people were
still unable to read Braille as recently as 1966.

Into this situation back in 1934 came a providential invitation from the Library of Congress Talking Book Service to the
Blind, a request to provide the four Gospels and Psalms on
records. An audio-version of the "Small Volume of Scripture
Passages" appeared in 1935, the centennial of ABS work for the
blind. The entire New Testament and twelve books of the Old
Testament (King James Version) came out in 1938 on seventy-three
discs at twenty-five cents each. When the complete Bible was
issued on records in 1944, 169 discs running 84½ hours, they
accounted for 7,879 volume sales in comparison to 5,400 Braille
books. The next year the Managers appointed the first full-time
Secretary for the Blind, and the work expanded at almost geo-
metric rate. Individual records carried seasonal or thematic
passages: The Bible Story (1964), Festival Record (Christmas,
Easter, Pentecost: New English Bible, 1964), Thanksgiving
Record (24 Psalms: KJV, 1964), The New Commandment (Love
passages: Phillips, 1965), Bible Prayers (Revised Standard

Version, 1965), The Kingdom of God (Today's English Version, 1965), Good News for Modern Man (TEV, 1966), and an Anniversary Album (50 favorite chapters: RSV, 1966). In addition, the Revised Standard Version and Today's English Version New Testaments were issued on tapes in time for the Society's sesquicentennial.

Meanwhile promotion for the blind kept remarkable pace with these new materials. Braille bookmarks for Thanksgiving-to-Christmas Bible Reading were prepared as early as 1952. In 1960 a 28-minute color film, "So Great the Light," publicized the plight of the blind dramatically. Braille alphabet cards were distributed at the New York World's Fair, attracting wide interest. The impact of technology, promotion, and concern proved spectacular. In the first century of work for the blind the Bible Society distributed 122,000 copies; in the quarter-century from 1935 to 1960 it sold 669,000 books and records. This included publications in forty-two systems or languages abroad, although foreign work had by now been assigned to regular overseas offices instead of a separate department for the blind.

Appropriately, therefore, the first "Specialists' Desk" projected by the Committee on National Distribution was that of Secretary for the Blind. These offices at headquarters were designed to supplement and undergird the functional programs in the three Regional Offices. Their purposes: to marshal resources and experts, to develop programs, to produce new materials, to devise experimental methods, to stimulate creative ideas in specific fields.

The second area of emphasis and concern was Campus Ministry. With over four million college students in 1963, and ten million projected in 1975, the Society recognized that "of all the 'special ministries' with which we are concerned, this one has been one of the most neglected and is one of the most needed." In cooperation with denominational and interdenominational campus programs, this "desk" sought to develop new formats of appeal to students, arrange campus visitations, provide some 64,000 international students with Scriptures in their own vernaculars, and acquaint seminarians with the program and facilities of the Bible Society. Other "giant steps" into the future will be sketched in a subsequent chapter.

This is not the place for an overall evaluation of 150 years of National Distribution. Many crises and triumphs of the past have had to be omitted from this survey. No accurate appraisal of the American Bible Society can be made without at least a glimpse at its world-wide outreach during the twentieth century. Yet perhaps the domestic scene may be summed up here in the words

of Dean S. Collins, Executive Secretary of the Western and
Pacific Region, on the eve of the Society's 150th anniversary:

Much has happened that is excellent. Some of the achievements which under casual study had seemed to be excellent,
were found wanting when exposed to a more careful and
thorough study. Needs continue to be staggering, and the
opportunity beyond adequate description. The present
program which has achieved so much must continue, but to
it must be added other programs so that the total program
may be more balanced and that the sale of Scriptures may
be increased. This, with God's help, we will try to do.

11

Into All The World:
Latin America

Even before the American Bible Society came into being in 1816, rebellions against Spanish rule began popping like fireworks all over the South American continent. Through the nineteenth century, revolutions and reversals took place at a rapid rate, enthroning and dethroning emperors (in Mexico and Brazil) as well as presidents, dictators, and military juntas. With the overthrow of the Portuguese succession in Brazil (1889) and the transfer of Cuba to the United States (1898) the liberation of the hemisphere from European control was complete--except for a few tiny colonies along the Caribbean shores. But the political picture changed very little. Assassinations and coups and border conflicts continued intermittently.

Gradually, however, in the twentieth century, Christianity in Latin America began to develop new patterns of social responsibility, new relationships between Protestantism and Roman Catholicism, between Church and State. In some countries anticlerical intellectuals demanded complete religious freedom; in others secular governments ignored acts of persecution and oppression by local authorities. An influx of evangelical missionaries from North America brought a warm-hearted spiritual atmosphere into cold formalism and tradition. In this changing climate of Christian influence, the Scriptures played a significant part.

Among Bible Societies, as among nations, the great new trend of the twentieth century, especially after World War II, was independence. One by one, Agencies and even Sub-Agencies reached the point of autonomy, of self-government. Sometimes the

pressures were primarily political; at other times the demonstrated competence of national leadership had to be recognized
and utilized; in some instances autonomy seemed the best solution to harmful competition. Somewhat surprisingly, the
fundamental *principle* of national responsibility, or even of
joint operation, seldom appears in ABS records before 1932,
although Secretaries and Agents and committees and boards all
around the world spent countless hours over many years working
out the pragmatic details in each situation.

The procedures and the sequence of events varied from place
to place. Most often the first step was appointment of a
national as Agent (or Sub-Agent or Acting Agent), directly
responsible to the home office in New York. Then came selection
of an Advisory Council, composed primarily of Christian laymen
or representative ministers and missionaries of cooperating
denominations. Many of these advisers did, in turn, become
members of the Board of Directors for the national Bible Society.
In at least one case, nationalization produced legal problems
and tax liabilities which the ABS Agency had not faced; elsewhere the principal change might be the removal of the resented
label "American" from a salesroom window.

Obviously the process was not uniform, but the individual
stages--occasionally quite intricate--cannot be reviewed for
every country. Nor did they take place in a vacuum. If the
United States seemed to confront a series of crises--economic
and military and social--during the twentieth century, how much
more so the rest of the world! Revolutions simply punctuated
almost continuous political turmoil. One should read the
detailed, documentary story of the American Bible Society with
a parallel textbook in modern world history, fully to appreciate
the trials and tribulations. Similarly, only first-hand
experience can truly visualize the difficulties of travel and
communication sixty years ago. Against such backgrounds one
marvels at the accomplishments of Bible distribution, accomplishments which cannot be expressed either in bare statistics or in
isolated, individual "human interest" stories.

Latin American countries have always stressed their diversity,
against the "Yanqui" tendency to lump them in stereotyped uniformity. For that reason the following sketches seek to indicate,
however inadequately, some of the distinctive characteristics of
different areas. Yet to avoid repetition reference must be made
to certain Bible Society policies which affected the entire
hemisphere.

One of these was the establishment of the Penzotti Institute
at Mexico City in 1956. Designed as a training school for
colporteurs under mission auspices as well as those hired by the

Bible Societies, the center provided such a range of practical
instruction that some inexperienced new Agents or Sub-Agents
were assigned for a year of study there. As an extension service, Penzotti Workshops, so-called, were held in schools and
seminaries and Bible institutes throughout Latin America, to
train pastors and laymen not only in Bible circulation techniques, but in many aspects of evangelism. The course, sometimes repeated year after year in the same institution, included
personal witnessing and Bible study on one hand, house-to-house
visitation, sociological and psychological analyses on the
practical side.

When the Mexico Bible House was dedicated in 1963, it provided accomodations for the Latin American Service Center, a
non-administrative coordinating headquarters for all the Agencies
of the hemisphere. The Center included Departments of Information and Promotion, Translations, Colportage Training and
Recruitment, and the Study of the Place and Use of the Bible in
Latin America. From it went all sorts of pamphlets, magazines,
audio-visual materials, and other supplies which individual
Agencies could not have produced for themselves. To it came
reports of novel experiments, community surveys, denominational
programs, and other aids for future development. Frequently
during this period the home office would sponsor conferences
for all the Agents (and sometimes selected colporteurs, correspondents, missionaries, and other helpers) to evaluate the
field and to share common problems--and solutions.

*   *   *   *   *

When Hiram P. Hamilton died in 1905, after twenty-six years
as ABS Agent in *Mexico* (see Chapter VIII), his wife offered to
continue the work. Although officers in New York were extremely
hesitant to give official appointment to a woman, her "temporary"
status continued for a decade without formal action, but with
repeated reference to "our Agent in Mexico City." During her
tenure Frances Snow Hamilton proved herself to be as courageous
and determined as she was efficient. Among many noteworthy
events these few stand out.

The Mexican Agency published a Gospel of John in Braille,
complete with a Braille map of Palestine. Senora Guadalupe
Rosillo, a blind Bible-woman, who helped prepare the edition,
remarked that she could now understand as never before the
Saviour's life and work, "because she can trace his life and
journeyings by means of the [Braille] map." This same Bible-
woman continued her work without interruption during the
Revolution, when most missionaries, including Mrs. Hamilton,
had withdrawn in 1914.

Earthquakes and floods, locust plagues and droughts, afflicted the country--and indirectly but inevitably Bible distribution. On a trip to New York Mrs. Hamilton, like St. Paul, encountered shipwreck and lost all her belongings.

For the centennial of Mexican Independence in 1910, the Bible Society published a patriotic edition of the four Gospels, bound in red-white-and-green, and a Modern Version of Proverbs also bound in the national colors. Wrote Mrs. Hamilton: "An interesting feature of the year was the proposal that the ladies of Mexico should each undertake to teach some illiterate person to read. Even the young girls took up the task.....No truer patriots are to be found in Mexico than the evangelical Christians." The following year Mrs. Hamilton accompanied a committee (one member from each Protestant group in the capital), to present to new President Francisco I. Madero a special edition of the Spanish Bible.

But she soon concluded that his policies were too weak and lax, and she did not hesitate to make her political views known in letters to the home office. On one hand, she was convinced that "the country has shown itself utterly unfit for self-government;...a strong, military, despotic government is needed here in this present crisis." On the other hand, she argued even more firmly that the United States should not interfere, except to "demand full indemnity for all pecuniary losses." "Where will it all lead?" she worried. "We simply pray that it may not lead to intervention, as that would mean such a terrible sacrifice of American lives all through the country.....How I wish I could talk for an hour with President-elect Wilson!"

But intervention did come, and after three years of revolutionary pressures Mrs. Hamilton finally left the country in April, 1914. This time the Managers would not send her back to Mexico, preferring to place the Mexican Agency under the West Indies Agent, with Mrs. Hamilton designated as Assistant "at the same salary." She died while doing research in the New York Bible House the following year, without having gotten back to strife-torn Mexico.

In 1922 General Secretary William I. Haven reported to the State Department a serious attack on Miss Elizabeth A. Streater, a Bible worker connected with the Mexico Agency. "She and her companions who were distributing the Scriptures were severely set upon in Durango, stoned and beaten with sticks and thrown into a ditch for dead, at the instigation of the Mayor of the city and the Parish Priests." Such Roman Catholic opposition to Bible circulation fluctuated widely, often appearing *more* acute when a liberal government policy threatened to undermine Catholic power through religious tolerance. In his Annual

Report for 1927 the Agent presumably reflected the Society's position of strict political neutrality:

> The missionaries and the colporteurs are not trying to understand about the disputes over oil rights and mining claims. The Bible Society, and all those who are trying to represent our Lord in the world, are none of them taking sides in the agrarian question, no matter how some of the poor people want land and how the rich land-owners feel about it. All they are trying to do is to see that the whole people really know Jesus, and this is the only way such questions can be fully and finally settled.....
>
> [Roman clerics in Mexico are having to choose in allegiance between the Pope and the President.] But Jesus had questions equally hard presented to him, and the only way is to study his entire life and the whole range of his teaching. Not only Bible reading, but Bible study, and continued from one generation to the next, this is the only solution of these troubles and the wars of the world, and the Bible Societies are the prime movers in doing this.

Hazael T. Marroquin was not only the first Mexican Agent appointed by the Society, but the first "national" Agent installed anywhere. A few Spaniards had served brief terms in Latin America, and Francisco Penzotti, though Latin American by lifelong residence, was born of Italian parents in Switzerland. Marroquin, a Presbyterian layman, had joined the Agency staff in 1920, and had visited the United States for consultation and study. In 1925 he devised a significant plan for more effective utilization of colporteurs. The proposal was simply this: that missionaries would select men to work in their districts under their supervision with their wages "as much as possible in cash" (Marroquin suggested $25 per month), while the Agency would supply books to be sold on commission "and so help them to make up enough money to live on."

To this end Senor Marroquin suggested to some thirty-nine missionaries of seven denominations what qualities a colporteur should have:

(a) He should be a thoroughly converted man, and full of love for his fellow-men, and filled with the spirit.

(b) He should know how to read and write.

(c) He should know how to use his Bible to the best advantage.

(d) He should be a psychologist in a practical way.

(e) He ought to know how to preach the gospel in public.

(f) He should be polite, cleanly in person, honest and faithful in the discharge of his duties.

(g) He ought to be able to devote his entire time to the work.

(h) If he happens to have a small family, so much the better; for the pay of the colporteur will be very small.

In response to this proposal put forward by Marroquin came one telegraphic reply: "We accept offer, please send books." Two other denominations promptly adopted the plan; three more expressed wholehearted approval but found themselves financially unable to participate immediately. In Mexico, as in many other parts of the world, colporteurs carried the brunt of Scripture distribution—and the satisfactions. Traveling for weeks away from their families, over difficult and sometimes dangerous terrain, they suffered constant verbal assault and sometimes physical attack. Yet many Annual Reports of the Bible Society glow with examples of the dedication, the compassion, the courage of these men and women.

Often, as Marroquin realized, they had to show themselves not only preachers and Bible-readers (if not Bible scholars), but also "psychologists in a practical way." One Mexican doctor, for example, vehemently demanded proof for the existence of God until a colporteur led him to acknowledge the existence of unseen pain—and then to purchase a copy of the New Testament. At another time, a crowd doubted that a small volume could contain the whole Bible, until a Christian woman came to the aid of a colporteur with a simple hyperbole:

That watch which you wear on your wrist is not complete. I consider, however, that big clock up in the parish tower is complete....That little boy is not complete, although they tell me that he is a man; the man I would consider complete is that big, tall gentleman back yonder.

Despite such constructive contributions as the colportage plan, despite warm endorsement from many missionaries, the New York office hesitated a long while before appointing Marroquin as full Agent. For over a year he served as Temporary Agent, a period which included harsh Roman Catholic persecution, the transfer of Agency headquarters to Mexico City, the development of lantern slide presentations, the donation of a special Bible to President Plutarco Calles, and the inauguration of plans for the Agency's Golden Jubilee. Marroquin became Mexico Agent

officially in March, 1928, while he was in Jerusalem attending
the International Missionary Council.

The Marroquin term extended over three decades. It witnessed
an organized Roman Catholic "Crusade Against Protestantism"
(1944) and left-wing anti-clericalism. It experimented with
radio advertising, book fair exhibits, literacy campaigns, and
dropping Portions from airplanes for volunteers to distribute.
A staff officer in New York sharply criticized this last project,
sponsored by an independent missionary group, as wasteful of
books, risky in potential damage suits, intrusive on colportage,
and lacking in vital follow-up.

Under Marroquin the Mexico Agency suffered stock shortages
during World War II but raised $1,000 for the Society's War
Emergency Fund. It collaborated with the Wycliffe Bible
Translaters to produce three diglot Gospels in Indian dialects
and Spanish (1946), and the first New Testament in an Indian
language of Mexico, Tzeltal (1956). A selection of thirty
Gospel passages in simple Spanish was published in 1948, with
the approval of the Versions Committee in New York. Yet
thirteen years earlier Secretary Eric North had reprimanded
Marroquin for printing the "short and searching" Sermon on the
Mount:

> I have discovered, somewhat to my surprise, that there is
> not in the Agency Secretaries' Manual a specific statement
> indicating our policy of not publishing less than an
> entire book of the Bible. This has been our rule in all
> cases where there is in existence a translation of at
> least a whole book. You can readily understand that we
> must, on some basis, avoid the selection of special
> passages because of implications as to interpretation,
> that would be the consequence if that process were extended
> too far.

Similarly, to illustrate the growth of trust in national
leadership as well as changing attitudes, Marroquin formed an
Advisory Council in 1950, though Mexico had been adjudged "not
ready" for that step in 1934. Its thirty-six members included
eight laymen and seven missionaries, represented fifteen
denominations and two institutions, and adopted as its primary
purpose "to foment in all possible ways the Bible cause within
the Evangelical Christian Churches in the country." Marroquin
retired in 1957 but continued to serve as consultant, librarian,
and (from 1961) as Executive Secretary Emeritus. In 1966 he and
Senora Marroquin celebrated their golden wedding anniversary.

The year of his retirement brought the first appointment of
a Promoter of Distribution--assigned--like the Home Agents in

the United States--to work with churches and seminaries. In 1958 the Agency weathered a theft by two employees who had falsified bills, but one of them, by way of partial restitution, donated a car, which the Agent found very useful. In 1962 Mexico had the honor to publish the 1,200th language of Scripture, a Gospel of Mark in Zapotec Del Rincon, an Indian dialect spoken by about 14,000 people. In 1963 the Archbishop of York, F. Donald Coggan, President of the United Bible Societies, dedicated the Bible House in Mexico City. In 1964 the Agency sponsored a fraternity of devoted supporters, Amigos de la Biblia, who covenanted to read the Bible and pray daily, distribute a Portion each day, and contribute five pesos (forty cents) per month plus freewill offerings on Bible Day. In the footsteps of Frances Hamilton, Guadalupe Rosillo, Elizabeth Streater, and the literacy teachers of 1910, still another feminine personality pioneered in the Bible program of Mexico when Mrs. Ofelia de Lopez Garza was named in 1965 as Promoter for Women's Work.

On the eve of the ABS sesquicentennial the Sociedad Biblica de Mexico came into existence and two months later joined the United Bible Societies. The country and the Agency had come a long way. Not much earlier Roman Catholics had denounced the Protestant Bible as a subversive book and physically assaulted distributers. But in 1962 the Catholic Church sponsored a National Bible Day and the following year invited the Joint ABS-BFBS Agency, newly united, to prepare an exhibit of Scriptures at the Catholic Seminary. In 1931 the ABS distributed 52,495 books; in 1966 the Bible Society of Mexico circulated 894,004 Bibles, Testaments, and Portions (plus 709,604 selections), 47.16 per cent of them from the ABS. When the Advisory Council was inaugurated in 1950, as a first step toward autonomy, Agent Marroquin wrote triumphantly:

It was stimulating to realize once again that there is one great thing upon which all Evangelical Christians are really united, which they agree to have as the basis of their faith and conduct, and greatly enjoy to propagate: it is the Holy Scriptures without note or comment, as the American Bible Society aids in their translation, publishes and circulates without profit.

*   *   *   *   *

The story of the American Bible Society in the Caribbean reads like a game of musical chairs or fruitbasket-turn-over. *Central America*, including a few lesser islands, became the Caribbean Agency in 1921, only to be renamed Central America in 1946. The West Indies consisted primarily of Cuba and Puerto Rico, alternately conjoined or separate, with Haiti, Santo

Domingo, Guadeloupe, Martinique, and the Virgin Islands hitched on or cast off in a bewildering array of configurations. Colombia and Venezuela moved in and out of both these Agencies, with portions of territory administered intermittently from La Plata or Upper Andes. Mexico came under West Indies jurisdiction for a few years. Headquarters for these assorted groupings included, at some time, Texas, Georgia, and New York, as well as at least six cities of South, Central, or Caribbean America. Add to these overlapping maneuvers the agreements and disagreements, joint agencies and divided territories, with the British and Foreign Society (plus their associates, Canada and Netherlands), and the maze appears insoluble.

This account, therefore, touches only the main features and developments, risking some inaccuracy by omission. In general, Central America covered Nicaragua, Honduras, San Salvador, Costa Rica, Guatemala, Panama, Venezuela and coastal Colombia between 1931 and 1946, plus the Dutch West Indies until they were turned over to the BFBS in 1946. Agency headquarters were in Guatemala City until 1917, in Cristobal (Canal Zone) from 1917 to 1960, then moved back to Guatemala. The ubiquitous Francisco Penzotti was Central American Agent from 1893 to 1907. In 1913, in exchange for American withdrawal from Persia, the BFBS turned over to the ABS its work on the Central American isthmus with the exception of British Honduras. But in 1962 the ABS Central American Agency and the BFBS Jamaica Agency formed a Joint Agency in Guatemala.

Characteristics of the area were remarkably similar (despite previous references to individuality): poverty, illiteracy, superstition, heat, disease, Roman Catholic antagonism, primitive travel, sparse shipping. Most Scripture distribution was carried on by missionaries, but there were few of these. In later years, after World War II, Costa Rica--with the highest literacy, the most missionaries, and the greatest political stability--develope an Evangelical Alliance among the various denominations, and subsequently a Bible Society Advisory Council.

The opening of the Panama Canal in 1914 gave a spectacular boost to the economy and to public interest in the region. ABS President James Wood journeyed to Panama to negotiate with General George Goethals, Governor of the Canal Zone, for a Bible House site and to secure his permission for Scripture circulation on board ships in transit. Gradually Canal Zone residents accepted responsibility for certain neglected areas of society. For example, when the Gospel of Matthew was provided in 1924 for the Valiente Indians less than 100 miles from the Canal, the Agent wrote of the joy not only on the faces of the Indians who had a Portion of Scriptures in their own language for the first time, but *also* among Christians of the Canal Zone who had financ the publication.

Yet on the whole the plight of Panama, adjacent to the United
States' possession, has long been one of the saddest blots on
America's record overseas. In 1931 Agency Secretary Raymond R.
Gregory wrote: "Strange and yet true, Panama, a part of Latin
America directly influenced by the United States, is the last
cared for and missioned by the evangelical churches." Exactly
thirty years later Agency Secretary Reginald H. Wheatly still
described Panama as "one of the weakest links in the Central
American chain."

Expressing his hopes for the newly-formed Caribbean Agency,
Gregory prophesied back in 1922:

> The next ten years will see wonderful changes in Central
> America. The old order is dying, and the new is being
> born. There is unrest and discontent everywhere, but it
> is a healthy discontent. It is that of the growing boy
> who is outgrowing his clothes and feels out of place;
> and he will not feel comfortable until the tailor does
> a neat job. So it is with Central America; her religious,
> political, economic, and school system do not fit into
> this new order; they are of a bygone day, and the need
> is for a readjustment of values all along the line.

By 1966, when this particular account ends, despite the faithful labors of missionaries, colporteurs, and correspondents,
there was still "unrest and discontent" in Central America. The
little boy had not fully grown up; as late as the 1960's his
"Uncle Sam" slapped him in Panama and Guatemala. In twenty years
Scripture distribution totalled 11,805,630 in the fluctuating
territory, but over two-thirds of the 1966 figure represented
Selections, over one-fifth Portions. *Bible* distribution in the
two decades rose from 15,962 to 40,946, Testaments from 14,631
to 66,450. Central America's educational, political, economic,
and religious systems still did not "fit."

* * * * *

The *West Indies* were administered from Havana and San Juan
(1901-05), Havana combined (1905-10, 1923-59), San Juan (1910-12,
1919-23), New York (1912-14), Texas (1914-16), Mexico (1917-18).
Puerto Rico, Haiti, Jamaica, and Cuba were formed into Joint
Agencies with the BFBS in 1962, the latter two to be supervised
by the Canada Bible Society.

Until 1924 approximately two-thirds of the Bibles distributed
went to church members; by five years later the proportions were
reversed, and two-thirds reached new inquirers or prospective
converts: thirty per cent of them children, fifty per cent
young adults, and twenty per cent elderly. In his Annual Report

for 1929 José Marcial-Dorado, the Spaniard appointed as ABS Agent in 1917, quoted a distinguished member of a prominent social club as saying: "We do not wish from the Americans money, nor commerce, nor industries.....That which we do wish is that you do not fail to send us your Bibles."

Unlike the mainland, these islands depended heavily on itinerants and local helpers to circulate the Scriptures. The same 1929 Annual Report from Marcial-Dorado gave a revealing if optimistic picture from four groups of Bible distributers:

Colporteurs: The public has changed in these latter years. Previously we were received in some places with indifference, in others with contempt, in some with hostility, and in very few with sympathy. Today, nearly everywhere we are received with joy and affection.

Correspondents: Formerly it was necessary to do much talking and distribute much printed matter, to interest the people in obtaining and reading the Bible; but today it is not so necessary. It suffices now to show the Bible, to awaken in them the desire to possess it.

Sub-Agents: There is no doubt about the gain we have made in the distribution of the Bible. Before we had to spend much time in studying how to reach the persons, who, on account of their ignorance or being badly advised, did not wish to hear of the Bible; but all that is changed. We go out into the street and always find some one who accepts the Bible with pleasure. We write to whatever unknown person and nearly always secure a buyer and a good reader. We make a call and wherever we speak of, and present, the Bible, we meet with success.

Voluntary Workers: For many years it was thought that the work of proposing and presenting the Bible to the public was difficult and ungrateful. We believe that the times have changed greatly, as, at least in the West Indies, that does not occur at all. We are well received by all, and on numerous occasions are called in by persons who wish to hear the Bible read and commented upon.

Despite these hopeful assurances, difficulties continued and Scripture circulation moved slowly. For the sixteen years from 1931 through 1946 total distribution in the Caribbean came to 1,121,712 (compared to 1,417,666 for the preceeding three decades), and three-fourths to four-fifths of those were Portions At the end of that period the Dutch islands of Curacao, Aruba, and Bonaire were turned over to the British and Foreign Bible Society to be administered by the Netherlands Bible Society, but they rejoined the Joint Jamaica Agency in 1962. The Virgin Islands, purchased by the United States from Denmark in 1917, were attached to the Jamaica Agency in 1962, but because the British had no work there, they returned to the Puerto Rico Agency two years later.

The Dominican Republic, despite the rigid dictatorship of Rafael Trujillo (1930-38, 1942-61), offered greater stability, prosperity, and shipping facilities than most other countries in the area. At the end of World War II "the work in the Dominican Republic is in very good condition," the Agent reported. Following the assassination of Trujillo in 1961 the new Puerto Rican Agent appointed a District Promoter in case an emergency should isolate Santa Domingo. The Sociedad Biblica en Republica Dominicana came into being in 1962, and local gifts for the first five months exceeded those for all of 1961. A separate Women's Department and special projects like Portions in Christmas parcels moved ahead favorably until the disruptive revolution of 1965.

Haiti, the only Negro republic in the Western Hemisphere, was plagued with illiteracy, witchcraft, and difficult travel. As late as 1947 it was estimated that ninety per cent of the population could not read or write. At the beginning of the twentieth century primitive animistic cults in Haiti were said to include not only serpent worship and midnight orgies, but "occasional surreptitious human sacrifices and accompanying cannibalism." Right up to the present, voodoo rituals and spiritualism prevail in many parts of the island. As for travel hardships, the Annual Report of 1913 carried this testimony:

Bible work is certainly very hard in this land.....A colporteur must be ready to eat or drink anything, sleep anywhere, sink in any mud and even swim on the main road (as happened to one of our colporteurs last summer), endure any showers, and lose much time in getting his books from place to place. But in this pioneer work he feels his heart burning with joy so often through the encouragement he gets that great is the compensation.

Out of such devotion the circulation of Scriptures continued to grow. "Evangelical forces which have not hitherto worked together" joined in a Bible and Religious Book organization in 1943. Ten years later the ABS Board of Managers established Haiti as an independent Agency, declaring: "Perhaps no country in all of Latin America presents such a challenge to evangelical forces." Publication of the New Testament and Psalms in Haitian Creole (1960) raised controversy over whether this distinctive local dialect was too colloquial and primitive for use by educated people--or in the Holy Bible.

Nevertheless the tiny Agency promoted literacy campaigns, Bible reading on the radio, Scripture-reading contests, and other special features. In 1964 the Haitian Agency Secretary ran into conflict with political authorities and fled to Guadeloupe, just as the new Bible House was opened, leaving to a missionary the supervision of the work in a time of turmoil.

The Puerto Rico Agency, Sub-Agency, depository, or headquarter (depending on the year) celebrated its fiftieth anniversary in 1932. Two years later, as the world began to emerge from its economic depression, special Scripture drives produced gratifying results. The "Campaign of the Faith Package" sold 1,500 Bibles, 2,000 Testaments, and 11,000 Portions; The "Campaign of the Seamen" resulted in the distribution of 10,000 more Portions. By 1938 the Agency complained that its problem was not sales, but sufficient stock to meet demands.

During World War II, when Puerto Rico served as the principal naval base for the United States in the Caribbean, the supply of available books proved even scarcer than before. Sixty-four cases of Bibles were torpedoed en route to the island and could not be immediately replaced. At the close of the war circulation picked up, though without any spectacular increase. An Advisory Council was formed in 1958, and the following year the ABS and BFBS inaugurated a Joint Agency, including the Dominican Republic and the Virgin Islands. A Puerto Rican took charge in 1960, vigorously pushing the campaign of "God's Word for a New Age," by magazines, radio, and television. He also tried to minister to the revolutionary chaos in the Dominican Republic.

Just at the end of this sesquicentennial period, the Puerto Rican Agency found itself squeezed between two dissimilar religious bodies, jeopardizing its jealously-guarded neutrality. The (British) Trinitarian Bible Society supplied volumes to bookstores already carrying ABS publications, while the Massachusetts Bible Society sent several shipments of Scriptures directly to the Puerto Rico Council of Churches, of which the Bible Society was a "cooperating organization." The resultant competition, with theological overtones, demanded a restatement of traditional, mediating policy. Asked for counsel, the General Secretary of the United Bible Societies replied that the matter in itself was not serious, "but that it underlines the fact that the Bible Societies must always be careful to make clear that they work with and serve not only 'ecumenical' but also 'non-ecumenical' wings of the church, and are not aligned solely with the ecumenical movement."

From the late nineteenth century on, even before the Spanish-American War, Cuba and the Bible Society work there were caught in revolutionary currents. Marcial-Dorado, the Spaniard who

served from 1918 to 1941, was elected to the first Cortes of the
Spanish Republic and took periodic leaves to attend to political
affairs, especially issues of religious freedom, in Europe.
Meanwhile the Havana office found itself, through missionaries
and colporteurs, reaching diverse segments of the Cuban population with the Scriptures: actors, chauffeurs, "professional and
trades people, from the humble cobbler working in the doorway of
some house, the street hawker and wandering lottery ticket seller,
to the doctor or the famous lawyer" (1928 Annual Report).

In the year 1933 Cuba reputedly suffered nine revolutions in
eight months, five consecutive presidents, 145 strikes, and at
least 600 assassinations. That year Fulgencio Batista seized
power and held it, behind seven puppet presidents, until his
flight in 1959. Yet the Bible Society launched a series of
special distribution projects being sponsored throughout the
West Indies. Young people carried out "The Fair of the Holy
Book" in seven towns.

In April, 1940, the Evangelical (i.e., Protestant) movement
gained new momentum from a missionary conference held in Cuba
under the leadership of John R. Mott, Chairman of the International Missionary Council and a Vice-President of the American
Bible Society. Shortly before his death, on the eve of World
War II, Marcial Dorado reported, from visits to the interior
of Cuba, that "the Christian Church [was] growing in zeal and
numbers, and making its beneficient influence felt upon the
social order as distinctly efficient and highly appreciated."

Post-war opportunities appeared to Agent J. Gonzales Molina
as "almost unlimited." Literacy campaigns flourished. Testaments for the blind attracted attention. Circulation for 1953
was the highest in the Agency's history. Offerings came from
1,029 churches, colleges, and Evangelical institutions in 1957.
Fully aware of political stormclouds, Molina wrote at the end
of 1959, even after Fidel Castro took over the government: "Our
statistics give us encouragement, especially in Cuba."

During the Revolution personal testimonies poured in to
the Society: Notwithstanding the circumstances, we
continue to preach the Word. It is the only bread which
relieves our hunger.....We have lost everything...but we
have not lost faith. Our only sustenance is the Holy
Bible, which we guard as a precious jewel, so that no one
will take it away from us.....We do not know how, but the
Bibles came. There is great jubilation in the congregation. People who never read the Book now seek it and read
it avidly.....

There is no money, but do not cease to provide us with these
New Testaments. We will pay for them soon.....Now I have
exchanged my gun for a Bible. Thanks be to God.....

An anonymous donor sent $40 for Bibles to be sent to rebel head-
quarters in the Sierra Maestra; months later revolutionaries
testified that the books arrived, "even good-quality Bibles for
the commanding officers, who received them with sympathy and
respect."

As a matter of fact, the government of Fidel Castro, which
seized power in Cuba on January 1, 1959, promptly lifted taxes
on books in order to encourage reading, thus directly aiding the
Bible cause. In the spring of 1960 a visitor from New York
headquarters reported: "The gravity of the situation in Cuba
is apparently being overstated by the American Press. So far
no restrictions have been placed upon the work of the evangelical churches." Both the Agency Secretary and the president of
Union Theological Seminary at Matanzas felt that "Protestantism
has never had the opportunity in Cuba that it has today."
Whichever came first and aggravated the other, condemnation and
ostracism from the United States or Communist domination in
Cuba, relations rapidly grew worse. On an unhampered visit to
New York Molina was advised to change the name of the Agency to
Sociedad Biblica en Cuba, without the "American" label.

Although the government seized all printing presses in Cuba
and embargoes cut off direct shipments from the United States,
large supplies of Scriptures continued to reach the island from
Mexico, Great Britain, and Canada. Total circulation for 1961
was 906,660 volumes, a gain of more than half a million over
the previous year. But in January, 1962, hounded by police
visits, Molina escaped to Miami, leaving the Agency in the hands
of two pastors and Distribution Promoter Perdomo. Henceforth
official treatment was totally unpredictable. Some shipments
were confiscated and burned; others were licensed and cleared.
Dr. Kenneth George McMillan, general secretary of the Canada
Bible Society, was arrested on arrival in Havana in 1963,
confined to the Canadian Embassy, and deported, though not
before talking with the Bible Society Promoter and an Agency
lawyer. Two years later Perdomo was allowed to travel to London
for consultation. Presumably dislike and distrust of the Bible
tugged within the government against the claim of religious
freedom.

After these experiences, the New York office, through the
Canadians, advised the Bible Society in Cuba to transfer full
administrative control of Agency affairs to the Advisory Council.
The Council, in turn, might continue to function on a self-
perpetuating basis or transfer its authority to "an organ of
the established Christian groups"--in either case with the "hope
that circumstances will one day permit Cuba's admission to full
membership in the UBS [United Bible Societies]." The president

of the Advisory Council replied that "due to legal complications this is not the right time for such a transfer."

Meanwhile, back in 1962, a chaplain at Guantanamo Bay reported that Cuban workers were allowed to carry Spanish Scriptures through the lines, and that some Jamaicans had had Christian literature in English confiscated--not to be destroyed, but to be used in studying English at the local Communist training camp! "Who knows," the chaplain wondered, "what results may come of this or other episodes?"

But those were freer, less hostile days. By 1966, the official end of this story, Scripture imports to Cuba had dwindled to a trickle, and in March, 1968, the government seized the Bible Society's building, its bank account, and its other assets. Perdomo, the Promoter, was sent to work on a collective sugar plantation, from which he finally escaped to Canada by way of Curacao and Madrid.

Bible work in *Colombia and Venezuela*, on the northern end of South America, was frequently described as "meager." As indicated previously, the two countries were intermittently attached to the Central America or West Indies Agency, sometimes linked with Puerto Rico or Upper Andes, joined with each other or apart. From 1946 they were administered as a Joint (ABS-BFBS) Agency under the Central America Secretary, but in 1961 became separate Joint Agencies. Part of the juggling arose from the determination (admitted in 1903) not to let the British assume that the Americans were giving up the field. In 1913 the BFBS proposed an exchange of Colombia (or Colombia and Venezuela) for Korea, but the maximum cooperation generated at that time was joint purchase of a launch to navigate the Magdalena River.

In 1934 the two Societies agreed to divide Colombia, the ABS taking five Atlantic coast departments, the BFBS the interior. More crucial, perhaps, they reached an understanding (which had to be renegotiated five years later) as to common policy on prices and discounts. The Central America Secretary in Cristobal, fearful that the ABS could not participate in a Joint Agency on a fifty-fifty basis, favored a similar division of Venezuela. In response, Secretary Eric M. North at New York headquarters commended the experience of Joint agencies in Chile (under the BFBS) and Uruguay (under Penzotti for the ABS), denying that an equal ratio of support was essential. On the other hand, he declared in a significant policy statement:

It would be exceedingly unfortunate for us if we were to follow the principle of exchange of territory which you outline, for carried to its logical extreme in the effort to avoid duplication of administration we would get to the point where A.B.S. would work in only half of the countries in which it is now working with the British Society, and our story would be correspondingly altered. The steady and generally accepted trend of our program is definitely in the direction of work administered by one Society for both administrations being traded off but not the interest in the work.....We are not particularly moved by anxiety concerning the leadership of one Society or the other, so long as the work itself is put on the most effective basis for circulation and for a clear and non-competitive administration.

According to the Agency Secretary, Colombia in 1936 "constitutes today the most important unevangelized field in South America;" in many areas the Bible colporteur was the only representative of Evangelical missions. Two years later an influx of missionaries drastically changed this picture, and circulation figures for the Scriptures confirm the shift. In 1931 the following books were distributed: 837 Bibles, 936 Testaments, 4,679 Portions, a total of 6,452; in 1941: 590 Bibles, 1,511 Testaments, 126,559 Portions, totalling 134,455 volumes--a substantial growth even though Portions accounted for 94 per cent.

In the Venezuela region mention should be made of the Rev. Gerard A. Bailly, a missionary who from 1897 to 1937 provided continuity and strength to the Bible program in the midst of many upheavals. Although the 1938 Annual Report stated flatly that "we never designated his work as that of a sub-agent yet, in fact, it was that for forty years," and other reports (1920) specifically refer to him as "our sub-agent." On one hand, Bailly stressed the missionary role in distributing Scriptures; on the other hand, his greatest contribution was probably the training of countless colporteurs for both the ABS and the BFBS. "No one but the colporteur," he often remarked, "does so widely contact every creature in his efforts to bring the Scriptures to all peoples of the world in their own language."

Both British and American headquarters agreed on one policy applied to Venezuela: a refusal to sell other books than the Scriptures in stores operated by any Bible Society. "To avoid even the appearance of such arrangement," Secretary North wrote in 1943, "I have recently urged Mr. Penzotti to try to find a way to make a definite separation other than an imaginary line down the middle of the store."

*   *   *   *   *

Like a proliferating amoeba, Bible Society work in Latin America south of the Equator began with one *La Plata* Agency and split into six separate units. Originally the territory included Argentina, Uruguay, Paraguay, Chile, Peru, Ecuador, Bolivia, and part of Colombia, overlapping in practically every instance with the British and Foreign Bible Society. The first Agent for La Plata, Andrew Milne, served from 1864 to 1907, to be followed by Francisco Penzotti, transferred from Central America. In 1920, due to the vastness of the area and the difficulty of travel between east and west coasts, Peru-Ecuador-Bolivia-Colombia were formed into the Upper Andes Agency, administered from Cristobal by W. F. Jordan, former West Indies Agent. Shortly thereafter, in 1921, Paul Penzotti succeeded his father as ABS representative in La Plata.

When Francisco Penzotti died in 1925, having served almost every Agency in Latin America except Brazil, the General Reference and Finance Committees declared in their joint Memorial: "He was like an incandescent light...illuminating many individual souls, and many homes and many communities...shining because of his unbroken connection with the source of spiritual light."

Differences with the British Society arose in most of these South American countries, not only over territorial duplication, but over conflicting practices regarding prices, discounts, colporteur wages, and methods. As early as 1904 the BFBS suggested a division of the La Plata field, where some Bible work had been carried on since 1822. Andrew Milne, among others, retorted that "the Founders of the American Bible Society, contemplated from the very first, Latin America, as the foreign field that had primary and special claims on their attention." He added that "our Spanish revision of the New Testament is superior" and that "nearly all the various mission centers make use of our books, and it is doubtless that they would be unwilling to make a change."

Over the years, as cooperation if not complete merger became imperative in many parts of the world, the two Societies debated whether Agency administration should be exclusively with one Society, a co-partnership, or a primary responsibility of one with secondary relationship to the other. For most Latin American fields the third option was chosen. In 1936 Chile was made a Joint Agency under the British, while La Plata (Argentina, Paraguay, and Uruguay) became a Joint Agency under the Americans. Circulation credit was to be apportioned in the same ratio as financial contributions; usually this was fifty-fifty, although for the first five years ABS participation in Chile never passed one-fifth of the total. Reports were to be sent to both London and New York, but policy decisions rested with the "primary" Society in consultation with the other.

In the early years of the century the principal obstacles to Bible distribution were the common ones of poverty, illiteracy,

disease, climate, terrain. Roman Catholic persecution appeared
intermittently, but secularism often proved a more durable foe.
After touring his entire area for nearly six months in 1909,
Francisco Penzotti wrote: "We notice in these countries a
strong current of progress and liberty. There is no fear from
the lion of the Vatican; but there is another enemy--anarchism--
which mixes up liberty with libertinism." As a result, Agency
reports frequently referred to political and economic instability
to exchange controls and import restrictions, to discriminatory
--or indiscriminate--tax laws, as major problems and preoccupa-
tions.

    In the actual process of distribution conditions varied.
Some places found colporteurs unavailable or virtually useless.
Responding to a questionnaire in 1945, Paul Penzotti observed,
from his boyhood experience on, that "as a rule, our men have
not been a credit to our work" in preparation or even in
personal appearance, that some pastors recommend men "who have
failed in the ministry....They seem to think that ANYBODY can
be a colporteur." Stalwart exceptions, however, compiled an
inspiring record of courage and perseverance: by bicycle, by
horse-and-buggy, by launch, by two-wheeled cart, by horseback,
by foot. Many pastors and missionaries did effective colportage
in remote, inaccessible mountains and forests. A "Bible Coach,"
paid for largely by the Waldensian community in memory of
Francisco Penzotti, carried Scripture supplies, stereopticon
equipment, and living accomodations. So successful was that
first vehicle that other Agencies and missions copied it; one,
operated by a mechanic-evangelist-chauffeur under the Bolivian
Indian Mission, ran for more than thirteen years. In addition
to correspondents (ninety-eight within the La Plata Agency in
1945) and colporteurs, "depositarians" in book-stores and
salesrooms accounted for a surprisingly large percentage of
South American Scripture circulation.

    In 1937, a year after the reorganization of La Plata as a
Joint Agency, the Norwegian Bible Society entered the "consortium
with particular interest in Uruguay. Here the union was pronounced "a great success....Our depository in Montevideo is the
center of evangelical Christianity." Ten years later the three
Societies created the Sociedades Biblicas Unidas (better translated Joint Bible Societies, because United Bible Societies had
come to signify the world-wide association). When in 1959
Uruguay and Paraguay were separated from Argentina, the
Norwegian Society was invited to assume responsibility: first
in appointing a Norwegian Agency Secretary, then in contributing
one-third of the budget, later in providing the Secretary's
salary, and eventually in constructing the Bible House. This
development represented a unique instance of drawing a smaller
Society into responsible administration and mission support.

Whereas Paul Penzotti had felt himself a lone individual serving Uruguay and Paraguay, forty years later the Agency boasted "100,000 voluntarios" in local congregations.

Meanwhile Argentina continued to grow as a field for Bible circulation. Contributions from churches and individuals increased rapidly; for example, from 13,202 Argentinian pesos in 1949 to 55,000 in 1950. The 400,000 "penny" Gospels published in 1944 sold so fast that another printing of 2,000,000 was ordered. By 1948 the Society distributed Scriptures in forty-four languages. The Argentina Advisory Council was the second established in Latin America. Where Andrew Milne had experimented with employing Bible women among the Indians in 1905, Women's Auxiliaries flourished in the post-war period.

Agency Secretary Charles Turner who suceeded Paul Penzotti, stressed three essential factors for Bible Society expansion: (1) "the spiritual purpose of our work...for the sale of a copy of the Scriptures is not an end in itself, but a means to something far beyond: that men shall come to know Jesus Christ as Saviour & Lord;" (2) "active participation by local churches and their membership" in distribution as part of the total evangelistic effort; (3) "the indispensable organizational structure looking toward complete financial support of the work."

As elsewhere in Latin America, Roman Catholic attitudes shifted conspicuously even before Vatican Council II. In his Annual Report for 1929 Paul Penzotti told of Roman Catholics selling 100,000 copies of the combined Gospels on the streets of Buenos Aires. Far from creating disastrous competition, this publicity helped Evangelicals to distribute 40,000 single Gospel Portions in one week during the same period. The Argentine government was often condemned for allowing any such freedom to "the Protestant heresy," whether it be radio evangelism, newspaper publicity, or the importation of allegedly "immoral books." Yet even during World War II Secretary Paul Penzotti recognized:

Nothing helps Bible Society work more than persecution. The more Protestants are attacked, the more people want to know what they believe. The result is that Scripture circulation increases, people are more interested in the Society, evangelical churches are crowded, and people listen to the Sunday broadcasts.

Even earlier a Roman Catholic priest visited the Agency to say: "We must all go back to the Bible. It is the only solution to troubles in this world. I am glad you are doing your share." And another, still in the 1940's, remarked: "Once we were enemies; later we were rivals; now, thank God, we can cooperate." By 1957 Catholics were being urged to form Bible study groups,

and in 1962 they adopted the same time as the Evangelicals for
Bible Week.

In 1961 Argentina's Joint Agency distributed over a million
Selections, and became an Associate Member of the United Bible
Societies. The next year 1,000,000 Gospels were printed within
the country. In 1963 the Overseas Distribution Committee in New
York paid rare tribute to the team of United Evangelical Youth--
students, employees, and businessmen--who engaged in volunteer
evangelism in slum areas, hospitals, parks, and other public
places, "always distributing the Scriptures." Said the
Committee: "The zeal of the early Christians can be seen again
in their kind of dedication."

In 1966, in honor of Argentina's 150 years of independence,
the Society passed out half a million copies of Selections
entitled "The Bible Speaks of Freedom." That same year, the
sesquicentennial also of the ABS, the Argentinian Bible Society
installed a national as General Secretary, received autonomous
legal status and tax exemption from the government, and announced
a circulation of 4,166,905 volumes, among the highest in the
world.

*   *   *   *   *

On the other side of the continent joint efforts moved
smoothly though more slowly. Paul Penzotti had written of
unification in *Chile* under the British in 1935: "We are hoping
that our example will be followed by other evangelical enterprises in these countries. The great need of the hour is for
cooperation. The Societies have led the way." Twenty-five
years later the New York office remarked that "the program in
Chile lacks vigor and imagination, but even so the demand for
Scriptures by the growing Evangelical community is greater than
we are able to meet." Through earthquakes and tight economic
restrictions, the Chilean Agency moved to a 1966 circulation of
951,421, just under its goal of one million.

Government barriers prevented the holding of a Penzotti
Institute in Chile, but those who attended training sessions
elsewhere on the continent returned with enthusiastic commitment
not only to Bible distribution but also to "improvement of the
relationship between the churches and the Bible." In a land
where recent Pentecostal growth has outstripped all other
Protestant denominations put together, the Agency Secretary's
observations may be appropriate. After attending a colportage
school in Buenos Aires, he wrote to Kenneth Bystrom, Director
of the Penzotti Institute: "The lectures which most impressed
me were those on public relations, especially the thought that
we must sell not only the product, but also the 'Firm' and I am

sure that the relations between the churches and the Bible Societies could be a good deal closer if we had more personal contact."

The *Upper Andes*, which became the North Andean Joint Agency under British administration in 1947, divided still further when Bolivia was made a separate Agency a decade later. In the sixteen years preceding that division (1941-56) Scripture distribution in Bolivia fluctuated from a low of 21,804 in 1949 to a high of 87,558 in 1955, those figures representing the ABS half of total joint circulation. By 1966 circulation reached 465,622 in Ecuador and 785,772 in Peru. Of these figures more than three-fourths and two-thirds respectively were accounted for by Selections, yet in the preceding two decades Bible and Testament distribution more than doubled in Peru and quadrupled in Ecuador.

One challenge Bolivia, Peru, and Ecuador shared in common was the need for translations for the Aymara and Quechua Indian tribes. Perhaps because the territories are more compact, perhaps because colportage has proved exceptionally difficult in the Andes, these Agencies have conducted more Penzotti Institutes for training missionaries, laymen, and employees, than have most other areas. Second only to H. C. Tucker in Brazil, Andean Secretaries have proved to be prolific authors. In the 1920's W. F. Jordan published *Crusading in Latin America, Glimpses of Indian America,* and *Central American Indians and the Bible,* while John Ritchie in the 'forties wrote *The West Coast Republics* and *The Indigenous Church, Principles in Theory and Practice.*

From Peru comes one of the Society's most moving testimonials, retold here as it appeared in the Annual Report for 1949:

'Jesus? I don't know Him. Who is He?' was the eager and innocent remark of one woman living high in the Andes mountains. 'But haven't you ever heard of Jesus, God's Son?' I asked her. Was it possible that in the twentieth century, in such a religious land as Peru, there are some who have never even heard His name? And as I endeavored to explain to her in a simple, even childlike way, who Jesus was, the light of understanding and eagerness broke on her face, and she remarked: 'If it is true, why hasn't someone told me before?'

*   *   *   *   *

If any Agency in the entire span of the American Bible Society were the story of one man, it would be Brazil. Hugh Clarence Tucker (1857-1956) served the Society--and the churches and the

world--officially from 1887 to 1934, but his life of service and
influence stretched for a quarter of a century more in each
direction. As a student at Vanderbilt University he had been a
summer circuit rider for the ABS, visiting every home in two
counties to ascertain the supply of Bibles and to supplement the
lacks.

Tucker went to Brazil as a missionary in 1886, at a time when
the remarkable Emperor Dom Pedro II sought to develop the United
States' educational system in his country, freed the nation's
slaves by proclamation, and finally abdicated in favor of a
republican form of government. Before the young pastor completed
his first term, he was asked to investigate the need for a new
Bible in Portuguese for Brazil and to accept the ABS Agency. To
get acquainted with his field (larger than the United States
without Alaska) he traveled extensively and ruggedly, eventually
visiting all but two of the twenty-eight states. At remote
railway stations, where passengers disembarked to buy food, Tucker
would proclaim: "I, too, am selling bread--the Bread of Life....
Here it is, in this book."

Early in his missionary career Hugh Tucker announced that his
goal was "to place the Bible in the Portuguese language in the
hands of the people and to promote the application of Bible truth
and Christ's way of life to the betterment of the social,
economic, and cultural conditions in which people live." For the
latter, social aim he involved himself wholeheartedly in an endless succession of crusades: for social welfare, for public
health programs, for recreation and playgrounds. He established
a Seamen's Home in Rio de Janeiro and the People's Central
Institute, a multi-purpose service institution.

"To place the Bible...in the hands of the people" Tucker
supervised a revision of the Portuguese Bible, which took from
1904 to 1917 and was further corrected in 1926. He devised more
effective methods for training colporteurs. He directed the
construction of a nine-story Bible House in Rio in 1932. In
forty-seven years with the American Bible Society it is estimated
that Hugh Clarence Tucker presided over the distribution of two
and a half million copies of Scriptures.

Only a man who had organized a program, trained able assis-
tants, and impressed his "bosses" in New York could have spent
so many months of almost every year away from his post. With
permission he served for awhile as Presiding Elder of the
Methodist Episcopal Church, South, as first President of the
Evangelical Alliance of Brazil, as President of the Brazil Sunday
School Union, as acting pastor of the Union Church in Rio de
Janeiro at least twice. He attended the Edinburgh Missionary

Conference in 1910; the World Sunday School Convention in
Switzerland in 1913, Glasgow in 1924, Los Angeles in 1928; the
American Bible Centennial in 1916; the Panama Conference on
Christian Work in Latin America; the Federal Council of Churches
in Atlanta in 1924; the Jerusalem Conference of the International
Missionary Council in 1928; most of the quadrennial General
Conferences of his own denomination, and scores of other meetings
and conventions.

But the Brazil Agency is *not* simply the story of H. C. Tucker.
It is also the story of the earliest and most successful agreement
between the American Bible Society and the British and Foreign
Bible Society. In 1903 the vast territory of Brazil was divided
between the two administrations, after careful analysis of current
activities, missionary deployment, population actual and potential,
transportation facilities, etc. Though separated geographically
(except for the capital city, then Rio de Janeiro), the ABS and
BFBS published a joint edition of the Gospels in Brazilian
Portuguese in 1904, with further revisions and additions later.

In 1942 the Sociedades Biblicas Unidas combined their offices
with co-equal secretaries, having functional division of responsibility, continuing to operate through territorial Sub-Agencies,
and dealing directly with both New York and London. Gradually and
naturally, with a minimum of growing pains, the Sociedade Biblica
do Brasil reached maturity in 1948, elected a Brazilian General
Secretary, and subsequently established a network of regional
offices. In 1961 the American and British Cooperating Secretaries
withdrew, turning over the Bible House to the SBB--not only to
honor the principle of devolution, not only because the details
assigned to them could be handled by a Brazilian, but also
because it was reported to the Overseas Distribution Committee
that the last foreign incumbents, less harmonious than their
predecessors over sixty years, "largely cancel each other out,"
in terms of policy.

The story of Brazil covers also a number of pioneer achievements. A Gospel of John in raised letters for the blind appeared
in 1900. The Brazilian version of the Portuguese Bible was
completed in 1914, published three years later in New York; not
until 1956 were the first 75,000 Bibles actually printed in
Brazil. To celebrate the country's Centenary of Independence in
1922 the Societies issued a commemorative Testament with a flag
on the cover, and gave away 10,000 Gospels similarly adorned.
The occasion brought a visit from Secretary of State and former
Chief Justice, Charles Evans Hughes, a Vice-President of the ABS.

In 1924 Tucker pointed out that most free Scripture distribution was going to members of the Protestant community, with
relatively few volumes left for evangelism. Within the next few

years he reported: "The Indians of South America are beginning
to figure more largely in the missionary movement of the continent. There are perhaps nearly a million and a half of them in
Brazil....Only a few...can read.....They present a most
difficult missionary problem." The Society also proposed a
Japanese-Portuguese New Testament for hundreds of thousands of
Japanese immigrants who were entering Brazil.

Even the most enlightened missionaries often have difficulty
adjusting to new currents of thought. Despite his life-long
commitment to the Brazilian people, Hugh Tucker in 1928 questioned
"the rising nationalism in the missionary enterprise of the
world" (presumably including the devolution of leadership into
national hands) on grounds that it was still "experimental" and
that one must "seriously question...what the effect will be on
the supporting constituency at home." Four years later, in
response to an inquiry from New York about a successor, Tucker
expressed the opinion that "it will not be an easy matter to
find a Brazilian with the qualifications desired for the
position of Agency Secretary."

Yet nationalization, like inter-Society consolidation, did
move forward. When the Joint Bible Societies were reorganized
in 1942, the 1-3/4 hour service was broadcast across the nation,
closing with "My country for Christ," a favorite hymn among
Brazilian Evangelicals. The Advisory Council created the following year was hailed as "the first body of its kind to be formed
in Latin America." The Constitution of the Brazil Bible Society,
drafted slowly and cautiously with frequent triangular consultation, proved such a milestone that some of its provisions
deserve to be quoted:

> It is the purpose of the two Societies [ABS and BFBS] to work
> in Brazil solely through the Sociedade Biblica do Brasil.....
> The Brazilian Secretary...is...the General Secretary and
> carries the Senior responsibility with the Board of Direc-
> tors.....Final decisions must rest with the Sociedade
> Biblica do Brasil and its Directors. Neither the British
> and Foreign Bible Society nor the American Bible Society nor
> these two unitedly may exercise a veto.....They must however
> be free to express their judgment...so long as they con-
> tribute materially to the work in Brazil.....The BSB is no
> longer considered to be a joint work, but now becomes an
> entirely responsible and self-governing society.....

Nor did the work falter under the "self-governing society" in
Brazil. The SBB Authorized Revision of the New Testament
appeared in 1952 and the complete Bible in 1959. Popular
observance of Bible Sunday escalated so rapidly that the
Brazilian government issued a commemorative stamp in 1951, the

first country anywhere so to recognize Bible Sunday. The National Bible Society of Scotland donated a launch, the "Light on the Amazon," which carried not only Scriptures but medicine, food, and clothing up the vast reaches of that river. In the year of autonomy, 1948, circulation rose to 82,000 Bibles (up 193 per cent), over 100,000 Testaments, and over 1,000,000 Portions.

Now that the Society belonged to them, Brazilians from every walk of life made their contributions for membership. The poor: a washerwoman who told her pastor, "I want to be a member of the Bible Society, but it is impossible for me to give fifty cents at one time. Will it be all right if I give a nickel a month until my pledge is paid?" The middle-class: "I am a Catholic, but I realize the need my people have for this Book. Here is ten dollars, that I may be a member of your Society." The comparatively affluent: "I was won to Christ through the reading of the Bible. My salary is small, but I want to become a life member with my $500 gift."

The year 1951 brought the first Selections to Brazil, "The Sermon on the Mount" and "The Good News" from Luke. At fairs and bazaars, at expositions and exhibitions, the Scriptures were sold in sixteen languages throughout the country. In 1958 the Sociedade Biblica appointed a Colportage Secretary trained in the Penzotti Institute, and a Secretary of the Women's Department, who promptly organized 7,000 new members and 5,000 renewals (at fifty cents each) into Women's Auxiliaries. With a unique device patented by a Protestant pilot "for Scripture use only" a parachute shower of John's Gospels and invitations to Bible meetings floated down over Sao Paulo.

The United Bible Societies designated Brazil as one of five centers to store international editions in case of war "or natural calamity elsewhere in the world." The First National Conference for Bible Distribution informed, inspired, and instructed 122 volunteers from eleven denominations. In 1965 religious classes in public schools began using Portuguese Scriptures, and the Brazilian Society voted to donate twenty-five per cent of its Bible Sunday receipts for Scripture distribution in Portuguese-speaking parts of Africa. The First National Bible Competition included Jewish, Roman Catholic, and Evangelical judges.

Thus in manifold ways long years of careful planning, sincere cooperation, and creative nationalism bore fruit. The President and Minister of Justice of Brazil signed a decree in 1965 recognizing the Sociedade Biblica do Brasil as an "entity of public utility." Using its constitutional freedom, the Society's advisory High Council recommended that year that "some

Scriptures should also be published *with* notes and commentaries,
limited to clarification of the text, without having any special
denominational characteristics" (italics added). What should
conscientious--and trusting--parents do when their grown children
"come of age" and propose to reject traditional family policies?

A man who belonged to no church was asked why he made a generous
contribution to the Bible Society. He replied: "Brazil has so
many problems and is developing so fast and is so in need of
people of good moral character, of integrity and honesty, that
I decided to offer some money to spread this Book, which in the
spirit of Christ makes people more sane, more honest, and better
citizens." "Way back" in 1948, when the Joint Bible Societies
surrendered their control to the Sociedade Biblica do Brasil, an
Evangelical leader remarked: "We have always known that the work
of the SBU was a good work but never that it was an important
work!" Not only in Brazil but throughout Latin America,
thousands of devoted Secretaries and Agents and colporteurs and
correspondents and missionaries and humble lay Christians are
helping to prove that it is not only a good work, but an
important work.

12

Into All The World:
Europe, Africa, The Middle East

Like most of the rest of the world, Europe in the twentieth
century faced disruption by two major wars and the territorial
and political changes which followed them. A growing tide of
secularism and materialism swept through society, depleting
congregations and diluting the visible influence of the Church.
A powerful theological current, often designated as neo-orthodoxy,
seemed on one hand to emphasize man's finite helplessness before
God's gracious revelation, and on the other hand to inspire bold
resistance to inhumanity in many forms.

Unlike most of the world, Europe altered little, in quantity
or method, its earlier pattern of Bible distribution. The
British and Foreign Bible Society had long before assumed major
responsibility for the Continent, in cooperation with some local
and national societies. ABS participation consisted largely of
grants, in books and money, to a few American missions and to
various European evangelistic agencies. Appropriations went
primarily for printing, supplies of paper, or the manufacture of
plates. When colporteurs were paid with American funds, they
were hired and supervised by other missions. There were no ABS
offices or depositories, except in Bulgaria and Greece as off-
shoots of work in the Levant. Only after World War II did the
American Bible Society collaborate with the BFBS in certain
Joint Agencies and in the United Bible Societies.

In much of Roman Catholic Europe during the twentieth century
opposition to Bible distribution waned with the declining
influence of the Catholic Church itself, although some pockets
of resistance remained. At the turn of the century the Society

of St. Jerome in Italy received papal permission to publish the
four Gospels and Acts in attractive, popular form. After nearly
half a million had been sold, and plans had been laid to publish
the rest of the New Testament, the Pope interposed a seemingly
contradictory note. Addressing the president of the Society of
St. Jerome in 1907, he reportedly praised the organization's
work, since nothing more efficacious than the account of the
life of Jesus Christ "can be imagined for instruction in holiness,
but advised limiting publishing efforts to the Gospels and Acts—
and even those remaining books were apparently withdrawn. Whatever the reason may have been, the papal restriction on Catholic
publications helped to open the door to Protestant distribution
of Scriptures in Italy.

After both World Wars the financial destitution of Europe and
the physical destruction of printing presses and binderies
reduced Bible output drastically. The "Million Nickel Fund"
during World War I (referred to in Chapter X) and the War
Emergency Fund (1940-1945) helped to provide Scriptures for
refugees, for Sunday Schools, for seminarians and many others.
In Scandinavia and Germany, both nominally well supplied, it was
customary to donate Bibles to newly married couples and Testaments
to children in confirmation classes. Both of these stocks had
occasionally to be supplemented by ABS contributions.

The usually self-sufficient Netherlands Bible Society needed
extra books after the disastrous flood of 1953. From late in
the nineteenth century, however, the NBS made a unique contribution to the Bible cause in the field of translation. Convinced
that such work can best be accomplished by nationals rather than
foreigners, the Dutch trained and supported specialists to share
their knowledge of philology and linguistic techniques with
scholars around the world engaged in translating or revising the
Scriptures.

Despite the determination of Bible Societies to serve "both
sides" at all times and places, their work has often been
obstructed by political ideology as well as war. The Nazi
government in Germany discouraged the printing of Scriptures;
donated Adolf Hitler's belligerent challenge, *Mein Kampf*,
instead of a Bible to newlyweds; strictly rationed paper for
religious publications; and eventually urged donation of Bibles
to "waste paper" drives. Immediately after World War II German
churches appealed for at least 1,500,000 Bibles and Testaments,
to be printed locally where possible but at least half to be
shipped from the United States.

One obvious need in rebuilding Scripture work in Germany was
consolidation of local, regional, and sectarian Bible societies.
To this end, a Verband, or central Union, was formed in 1948,

"taking full responsibility for all problems of Bible production and distribution, for planning common policy, and for membership in the United Bible Societies." By the early 1950's it became obvious that many Verband members were unwilling or unable--from traditional policy, ingrown conservatism, or political bias--to share their increasing prosperity in mission enterprises. Therefore the ABS, BFBS, and UBS joined with certain German churches and religious organizations to launch a "Bibelmission in Deutschland," an interdenominational missionary institution to encourage personal involvement through prayer and gifts. Three full-time missionaries worked among refugees from the Soviet Zone, and books were distributed to prisoners, soldiers, expatriates, students, aliens, residents in hospitals and homes. Such an example inspired the Verband, still receiving American aid, to undertake distribution among Roman Catholics, refugees, and the churches of East Germany.

This last problem--responsibility for their brethren in the People's Democratic Republic--deeply concerned all German Christians. Early in 1954, despairing of the Verband, the ABS had authorized $3,000 for the employment of a full-time Bible Secretary in East Germany and $15,000 for publication of Scriptures for distribution there. Meanwhile the British and American Societies joined forces to inaugurate "Bibelwork," "educational in purpose and missionary in character," dedicated even more to Scripture *reading* than to circulation. According to *The Bible Society Record* (April, 1959):

> What Bibelwork is trying to do in East Germany is to focus the attention of the churches, families and individuals upon the power which the Bible can provide for revitalizing the Church, for enabling people to stand up to the persecution from the government, and to provide the hope and determination that will cause the people to carry on according to the fundamentals of their faith during a time of great discouragement.

The "Berlin Wall," reducing to a trickle the flow of people and goods between East and West Germany, cut off direct American association with "Bibelwork." In fact, a large supply of paper intended for East Germany had to be sent to Bibelmission instead. The Verband, financially self-supporting, asked to participate in the United Bible Societies' world-wide campaign, "God's Word for a New Age," and began contributing in 1964 to the global budget. Similarly the Bibelmission, while expanding its home ministry to the sick and aged, to migrants and sailors, made donations for the Bible cause in Japan, Cameroun, Egypt, Algeria, Spain, Brazil, and elsewhere. In the ABS sesquicentennial year the Bibelmission announced its "courageous decision...to try to march on its own financially...[but not without] profound gratitude for your understanding and abundant help throughout

the last years." (In 1970, four years after the official end of
this history, the Bible Society of East Germany was admitted
to membership in the United Bible Societies.)

In other countries of Eastern Europe Bible activities proved
even more erratic than in Germany. A BFBS summary in 1965
reported persecution in Bulgaria, silence from the Baltics,
inactivity in Yugoslavia, "bright prospects" in Roumania.
Poland remained relatively open. In the late 'fifties some
8,000 Russian Scriptures were donated through the BFBS for
refugees in Poland, and in 1964 a Joint (BFBS-ABS) Agency was
opened in Warsaw.

To Hungary the American Society sent paper for 30,000 Bibles
and 60,000 Testaments in 1948. After the 1956 uprising there
hundreds of thousands of Gospels and Portions were distributed
among refugees in adjacent countries. In 1962 the UBS General
Secretary in Europe recommended that the Societies "respond to
any appeals from individuals in Hungary by sending small parcels
of Scriptures directly to private addresses, in plain wrappers,
as we do in the case of Russia and Spain." Yet in 1966 the
Hungarian Bible Society, described four years earlier as
virtually defunct, received government permission to print
2,000 copies of the revised Hungarian New Testament, subsidized
by the ABS and the BFBS.

Back in 1924 a Bible Society visitor in Eastern Europe
reported that "radical Communists in Czechoslovakia often oppose
the work of the colporteurs," but also that there was "very
great demand for the Scriptures." Against a backdrop of comparative prosperity and liberalism since World War II, that
statement may well characterize the situation at the end of
this sesquicentennial history, prior to the abortive liberaliza-
tion in 1968.

In Russia conditions for Bible work have vacillated widely.
As indicated in Chapter VIII, the northwestern and southwestern
borders of Russia were touched from Germany and from the Levant
respectively. The ABS made small gifts to Methodist missionaries in the country just prior to World War I. Since Protestants even then were under pressure and occasional persecution
from the closely-allied Orthodox Church and Tsarist State, Bible
distribution fared badly.

In an unparalleled move, given the political circumstances of
1924, the Soviet Government, having confiscated the entire stock
of bound and unbound Bibles from the Holy Synod but needing the
storage space and planning to burn them, agreed instead to sell
four truckloads to the Methodists--with no ban on circulation.
An ABS appropriation of $1,000 was used for that unexpected

purpose. During this period the Russians forbade import of
foreign books but granted a permit in 1925 to print Scriptures
within the country--at the Soviet Government press. The Bible
Society paid for the plates on condition that "any evangelical
body in Russia" might use them. For a few years smaller gifts
from the ABS enabled expatriates to send in several thousand
books by parcel post.

By 1930, however, the Annual Report announced: "At present
it appears that Bibles can be neither sent into, nor printed
in, Russia." A year later the word was that "the importation
of the Bible into Russia is not only definitely prohibited, but
is strictly prevented." By 1953, after some post-war relaxation,
an old familiar line recurred:

No sure way has been discovered to get Bibles into Russia
.....While we are seeking the opening, we have publicly
offered our [very large stock of Russian] Scriptures free
of charge to any person or organization that can give
assurances that the Books can be got into Russia. To date
no one has responded to the offer.

Despite a visit to the New York Bible House in 1945 by Archbishop Alexei of Rostov, and a donation of 5,000 Testaments and
100,000 Gospels "for transmission to Russia," no direct shipments
were made during the next decade. In 1956 and again in 1961
Russian Church leaders assured the Bible Society that it was now
possible to print Scriptures in the new, simplified alphabet
within the Soviet Union, and--more significantly--that they
could "obtain all materials necessary for the production of the
Scriptures with funds advanced to us by the State." Hence no
imports would be necessary. Apparently freedom for such
publication in Russia has been intermittently restricted and
granted since that time.

One further development in Europe deserves brief mention:
the trend toward unification (see Chapter XV). When the United
Bible Societies came into being in 1946, three or four organizations joined in an Alliance Biblique Francaise. Since one of
these components was heavily in debt, opposed consolidation in
principle, and worked only through churches, the Alliance gave
way in 1960 to a French Bible Society participating in the UBS.
Joint Agencies combined resources after 1960 in Cyprus, Italy,
Poland, Portugal, Austria, Yugoslavia, Belgium, and Germany.
Somewhat strangely, since the ABS role had been so small for a
century and a half, the division between British and American
support was usually set at fifty-fifty. Still, as the Annual
Report for 1956 expressed the situation: "Europe presents a
picture of both light and shadow."

*   *   *   *   *

The Bible in Africa, according to an anonymous writer in *The Bible Society Record* (May, 1925), helped to alleviate four evils in a primitive culture: slavery, polygamy, the rum trade, and a tribal or communal evaluation of individual worth. But the twentieth century brought other, more dramatic transformations in African life. At the close of World War II colonial powers still controlled all of the continent south of the Sahara except for Liberia and South Africa; by 1965, two decades later, only Angola and Mozambique remained under direct European rule.

Because Protestant missions had entered late and sparsely, the ABS policy of Scripture distribution through missionaries and churches did not reach far or deep. Though portions of the Bible had been translated, by 1924, into 225 African languages or dialects, most of them served very small communities and merely emphasized the enormous task which lay ahead. The American Bible Society, therefore, concentrated its appropriations of books and money through missionaries, chiefly to aid in translation and publication. Until the last decade of the sesquicentenary it established no independent Agency in Africa, partly because the British and Foreign Bible Society had work in many areas, partly because opportunities and facilities were so widely scattered. As a consequence, the following picture of ABS activities will consist of isolated snapshots rather than a comprehensive panorama.

In Mozambique, formerly Portuguese East Africa, where the ABS supplied mainly the Methodist Episcopal Mission, sales from 1901 to 1930 totalled 7,334 volumes, mostly Testaments, worth $6,000. Adhering more strictly than most places to Bible Society policy, missionaries there insisted on at least a small price for every book. The full cost of a Testament, twenty cents, equalled two days' typical pay--and sometimes jobs had to be created for the customer. Yet children would walk a day to find work to earn their Scriptures, and old people who could not read would buy for the joy of owning a book "which is making such a change in their country." Wrote one missionary in 1905:

Hundreds of people who will never learn to read, will buy a Testament, or other Scripture, hang it bottomside up on their mud wall, in the dryest place accessible, and their urchin children will learn at the mission school how to set that picture right.....America can read. Africa cannot, and she beseeches you to send her not only the book...[but] agents to light her candle for her till she can learn to manage it for herself.

The problem of illiteracy was complicated further by intermittent insistance from the government that missionaries should

teach in Portuguese and pastors should preach in Portuguese--
though other parts of worship services might be in the vernacular.
This effort to Westernize and "colonialize" drew mission protests
as late as 1929, and required pulpit Bibles in Portuguese for the
churches, Testaments and Portions in Tonga and Sheetswa (now Tswa)
for colloquial home use.

In South Africa, although the BFBS had been there since 1806
and established an Auxiliary in 1815, no Scriptures had been provided for the Zulu population until the ABS commenced translation
in 1863. Over the years the American Society sent occasional
shipments of books, reaching a peak of 22,808 in 1941, when
Britain was hard-pressed by war and the United States not yet in
it. In 1961 the South African Agency of the BFBS became the Bible
Society of South Africa, Auxiliary to the "Parent Society," the
only full member of the United Bible Societies in that part of
the world.

The earliest and most extensive contact of the ABS with the
African continent had been through the Methodist mission in
Liberia. Yet not until after World War II did the British
Society, with a virtual monopoly on the rest of the continent,
suggest that the Americans should have responsibility for
Liberia. An Agency formed in 1954 became a Joint Agency under
the British in 1962, with its own Advisory Council in 1965. Since
Liberians used twenty to twenty-eight languages with only six to
nine of them having any portion of the Scriptures translated,
since illiteracy was reported at 92.5 per cent as late as 1951,
and since ABS shipments from New York (not counting purchases in
London) totalled 2,033 for the entire period of 1931-48, emphasis
has naturally been placed on translation rather than distribution.
Yet exciting proclamation of the Word has taken place through
the Sudan Inland Mission radio station, broadcasting "talking
records" prepared for the blind in forty languages, and through
the use of "finger-phonos," hand-operated phonographs.

Elsewhere in Africa American involvement prior to World War II
was limited to scattered gifts or to filling a few missionary
orders. Early in 1932 officers in New York acknowledged that
"fresh attention should be given to the Continent of Africa,"
but they went on to recognize that "a larger responsibility [with]
adequate plans and adequate funds" would inevitably raise the
problem of comity with the BFBS. Yet twenty-five years later
General Secretary Laton E. Holmgren declared, in a letter to a
prospective Agency Secretary: "Africa is the only remaining
place in the world where our two Societies have not worked out
a complete pattern of cooperation." Within the next three years
three Joint Agencies were established, all under British
administration: Liberia, Congo, Ethiopia.

By 1962, as most African peoples emerged triumphantly but
sometimes tumultuously into independence, the ABS and BFBS held
a conference at Buck Hill Falls, Pennsylvania, to discuss forms
and areas of cooperation. There it was agreed that all Bible
Society Agencies in Africa would be supported jointly. Although
supervision was to be shared, and American, European, and African
personnel were added, the majority of these Agencies remained
directly responsible to London. A year and a half later all the
Africa Secretaries, with representatives from the Home Offices,
met in Kenya to consider the implications of these new relationships. The planners recognized that "the introduction of ABS
methods and philosophy into the Africa scene...[would result in]
a new emphasis...to the Bible cause in Africa." Specifically
they anticipated "the use of Selections, a greater evangelistic
thrust,...a center for production of promotional aids...and
especially....a program to train African churchmen in the
evangelistic distribution of the Scriptures."

A rapid and irresistible trend toward Africanization, however,
far outweighed any fear of Americanization. National Committees
assumed direction of Bible Society programs in most countries;
African Assistant Secretaries took office with clear expectations
that they would soon succeed their British or American counterparts. In 1964 an African Center, modeled after the Penzotti
Institute in Mexico, was set up to plan and execute Scripture
Distribution Training Programs on an indigenous basis. To
maintain ties, other than monetary support, between the "Parent
Societies" and emergent national and regional structures, two
Traveling Field Officers were appointed in 1966: an American
for East Africa and a Britisher for West Africa, *not* with
administrative responsibility, but as advisers to Executive
Secretaries, Advisory Committees, and local staffs.

Under this general pattern it is possible to include only a
sketchy geographical survey of major areas. The West Africa
Joint Agency (1962) included Ghana, Sierra Leone, Nigeria, with
Gambia added in 1964. Sierra Leone became a separate office in
1965. In Ghana, where literacy increased from fifteen per cent
to sixty-six per cent in eight years of independence, an
Advisory Council was formed in 1965. Because of the political
coup the Bible Society of Ghana delayed inauguration until 1967,
outside the official scope of this story, but when it came it
included participation by Roman Catholics--in translation, in
publication without imprimatur, in distribution, and in active
membership on the Council. In the transition to autonomy (1965-
66) Scripture circulation in Ghana passed one million for a
population of approximately seven million. As many as 460,250
Bibles were provided for schools alone in 1966.

At the same time committed Christians initiated a Nigerian
Bible Society under the leadership of Dr. Akuna Ibiam, then a

President of the World Council of Churches, a Vice-President of the United Bible Societies, and Governor of the Eastern Region of Nigeria. This indigenous Society, having no direct connection with the West Africa Joint Agency, welcomed Roman Catholic members and--on the eve of tragic civil war--made confident plans for more polyglot editions of Scriptures to unite its divided constituency, and for widespread distribution of popular Selections on Christmas, Easter, and Pentecost.

Explained one successful Nigerian colporteur when asked about his methods: Beside the table at my "natural and spiritual food canteen" I place an open Bible so that while people eat their food they can read the Word of God; "many people ask questions about the Bible and spiritual life and God has enabled me to help many." "Sometimes," he added, "I stand at the road side and ring a bell, and then sing hymns; the people think I am mad so they come to find out what I am doing. I then show them my Bible."

French-speaking territories of West Africa were formed into the Ivory Coast Agency under American supervision. Here Christianity is weak and Islam resurgent, Roman Catholicism is more hostile to Bible distribution, many tribal dialects have never been reduced to writing, materialism struggles against a lack of natural resources. Without any heritage or experience of Scripture distribution, colporteurs and an Advisory Council equally labor for an understanding and fulfilment of their tasks. In the former Cameroun, where an occasional shipment of French Bibles arrived during the nineteenth century, the Joint Agency administered by the Netherlands Bible Society became in 1965 La Societé Biblique Cameroun-Gabon, an associate member of the UBS.

By rough estimate half the population of the Belgian Congo had been touched, directly or indirectly, by Christian missions, Catholic or Protestant, over a span of eighty years. Yet among two hundred languages or dialects spoken in the Congo Basin and adjacent areas, Scriptures had been translated into only eighty-one by the end of the "colonial era." Les Societés Bibliques au Congo, a Joint Agency under British supervision, was established just prior to the abrupt granting of Independence. Initially it included the Belgian Congo, French Equatorial Africa (Chad, Gabon, Ruanda-Urundi, Middle Congo, Ubangi-Shari) and Angola (Portuguese West Africa). In 1964 Chad and the Central African Republic were attached to the Ivory Coast Agency, but the following year were joined with Congo (Brazzaville) to form Le Foyer de la Bible, and Fritz Fontus moved from the Haiti Agency to direct it. In its first year of separation circulation rose 279 per cent. In 1965 Gabon was linked to Cameroun, leaving Congo (Kinshasa), Rwanda, Burundi, and Angola as a Joint Agency under the ABS--occupying the first jointly-owned Bible House, in

Leopoldville (now Kinshasa). On political as well as administrative grounds, Angola was designated a separate Agency in 1961, but the Secretary who was appointed failed to secure a visa, so the Angola Agency did not open officially until 1967.

The British and Foreign Bible Society, at work in the Rhodesias since 1894, formed a Central Africa Agency in 1939, joined by the National Bible Society of Scotland in 1957 and the ABS in 1963. With the break-up of the abortive Federation in 1964 Rhodesia went to the BFBS, Malawi to the NBSS, and Zambia to the ABS, with a Central Business Administrator for all three.

The Rhodesian National Committee, composed of six Africans, six Europeans, and four others, from eleven denominations, voted at once to invite Roman Catholic participation. An African, Henry H. Kachidza, served for two years as Organizing Secretary "to visit churches, schools and organizations to stimulate the distribution of the Bible and its more effective use [and to] help arrange conferences and study groups and promote the observance of Bible Sunday." But when he was made Executive Secretary, "his predecessor continued to function as though the new appointment had not been made" and the administering Society failed to give him "adequate powers," with the result that confusion and tension had to be ironed out in two successive conferences of Central Africa Secretaries. Since 1965 political and racial tensions in Rhodesia have created a "growing sense of hopelessness," accentuated by a critical drought and by shortages of paper, gasoline, other imports, and funds.

In neighboring Zambia a very different atmosphere prevailed. The National Committee consisted of seven Africans and five Europeans. An African was promoted from Assistant Executive Secretary without recorded difficulty. Headquarters were moved from the more European city of Kitwe to the capital at Lusaka. The Agency circulated Bibles in twenty-two languages and other Scriptures in fifty tongues in 1964. For the country's second anniversary in 1966 the Bible House issued a booklet of Selections entitled "Faith for Every Nation," containing the Sermon on the Mount, a list of daily Bible readings, and a quotation from President Kenneth Kaunda: "Some time ago I read the following words, 'I want to see nations governed by men governed by God. Why not let God run the whole world?' Let us make a start here in our beloved Zambia."

The Bible Society in East Africa (Kenya, Tanzania, Uganda, Mauritius) benefited from relative stability, economic and political, and from a corps of faithful volunteers—such as doctors who distributed Scriptures from their out-patient departments and mobile clinics. The Canstein Bible Society in West Germany donated a book van, thus recalling the very early

contribution to Scripture distribution. As translations into
local dialects appeared, the first Bible in Meru sold 5,000
copies in two weeks, the first Bible in Nkore Kiga sold 3,000
in the same length of time. In 1966 the schools of Kenya,
Tanzania, and Uganda ordered 10,000 English Bibles, and in
Tanzania alone Roman Catholics placed orders for 112,000 Gospels.
On the first anniversary of Kenyan Independence President Jomo
Kenyatta accepted a gift edition of the Swahili Bible; a year
later, receiving the first Kikuyu Bible, he revealed that he had
had a hand in early Kikuyu translation work. With such a
testimonial widely publicized, circulation leaped to 9,000
copies in the first three days, and sales of the Kikuyu Gospels
on which President Kenyatta had worked increased by more than
37,700 copies.

Off the east coast of Africa the island of Madagascar has had
one of the most heroic records in mission history. The Malagasy
Bible, first in any African tongue, was prepared under threat
of violent persecution in 1835; missionaries ordered to
manufacture soap for the queen before being expelled from the
country managed to produce seventy copies of the Bible on a hand
press at the same time. These and additional Portions were
read in secret, on penalty of death, during the next twenty-five
years. In the twentieth century the BFBS administered the work
in Madagascar until the formation of the UBS in 1946. At that
time the Norwegian Bible Society indicated its eagerness to
participate in the circulation of Scriptures abroad and was given
responsibility for administering work on the island until the
inauguration of the Malagasy Bible Society in 1965. In the
first year of the national organization, distribution expanded
by forty per cent, local contributions by thirty-five per cent,
with the use of door-to-door visitation and the mass media of
radio and movies. To the Malagasy budget, the ABS--uninvolved
administratively except through the UBS--gave 47.16 per cent of
the total.

The BFBS handled Bible circulation in Ethiopia under its
Egyptian Agency, until a Joint Agency was established in 1960;
responsibility was transferred to New York in 1965. Emperor
Haile Selassie frequently bestowed his royal patronage on Bible
translations. Modern distribution in Ethiopia has reached out
to hotel rooms (courtesy of an American donor), universities,
seminaries, and other institutions. In adjoining territories
(Somalia and French Somaliland; with Aden on the eastern side
of the Gulf of Suez appropriately transferred to the Arabic
Levant) a 1965 appraisal reported "conditions are rather grim
for Scripture distribution."

Grim, too, was the outlook in North Africa. The American
Society, which had touched the Mediterranean coast only lightly

from the Levant, joined in support of the Algeria Agency in 1962, augmented by the West German Bibelmission two years later. But Libya and Tunisia were virtually closed to the Gospel in the 'sixties; Morocco, more stable and prosperous, was no less fanatically Muslim and nationalistic.

South of the Sahara, as has been shown, national and regional Bible Societies groped and grappled with new responsibilities and new challenges, just as their people did with their embryonic independence. Yet there it might still be hoped, as a missionary wrote enthusiastically from the Cameroun in 1927 in typical African idiom: "never did the ground more readily take in the rain than do the dry and thirsty souls receive the Gospel message."

*   *   *   *   *

"We seem to be living...once more, as it were on a volcano, which may burst at any time." Marcellus Bowen, for twenty-eight years Secretary of the Levant Agency, was writing of Turkey in 1905, but his description fitted the entire Near East during the twentieth century. Frequently the volcano did erupt. Turkey itself, focal point of the oldest foreign work of the American Bible Society, had its revolution of Young Turks, its Balkan Wars its Armenian massacres, its involvement in World War I, its modernizing dictator, Ataturk. Greece, seeking to become a modern European nation, found herself pulled by history and culture, by religion and scattered population, eastward to Cyprus and Asia Minor. Syria, Palestine, and Egypt—despite their growing Muslim and Arab self-consciousness—were still pawns, puppets, protectorates, and then mandates of European colonial powers. Russia reached into the area to absorb three provinces of the Caucasus after the first World War—as she dominated Bulgaria after the second.

At the turn of the century Bible distribution was a relatively simple operation—not in the sense of easy, for Christian sects in the Middle East were often as hostile as Muslims, but in the sense of uncomplicated. When a colporteur in the Sudan in 1900 travelled 1,000 miles by donkey in eight months and sold 651 books, it was considered "fairly successful as a first effort in Bible colportage in such a country." Circulation depended largely on missionary correspondents and bookstores. British and American Societies assumed the right to supply their own missionaries, yet they resented intrusion into historic fields of work. As early as 1903 Secretary Bowen proposed "a clean division" of Syria to the ABS and Palestine to the BFBS; such a partition had been arranged in Bulgaria in 1867 and in Greece in 1886.

Political attitudes were simple too. Missionaries deplored state religions, whether Orthodox or Roman Catholic or Islamic, because they tended to discriminate against Evangelicals. On the other hand, secular governments might uphold religious freedom, against local and clerical prejudice, *or* they might (as in certain periods of Mexico and Turkey) restrict all kinds of religious activity. At the same time, United States Government intervention was not only welcomed, but often demanded by missionaries. A ban on colportage, confiscation of books, even the detention of a national Bible Society agent provoked in those days appeals to uphold the Society's rights, since (as Secretary Bowen wrote in 1905) "our Government maintains [that our work] is a legitimate work fully entitled to its protection." When the American Minister in Constantinople failed to press these complaints vigorously enough, Bowen like Isaac Bliss before him urged that the ABS should exert influence on diplomatic appointments: "What we want is a genuine American, Christian man of ability and force of character who would be in sympathy with what is good and who would find it a pleasure to keep in close touch with his colony here."

In 1922, when the post-war status of Turkey was under negotiation, representatives of sixteen mission organizations including the American Bible Society sent a petition to Secretary of State Charles Evans Hughes, "...that these American institutions with their directing personnel shall be guaranteed their properties, their rights, their privileges and immunities, enjoyed for a century or less under treaties, agreements, capitulations, concessions and precedent." To this an Under Secretary of State replied that the United States would protect American interests and rights in the Near East by every means "short of an act of war."

In an effort to settle accumulating problems of comity, ABS and BFBS officers met in London in 1910, but succeeded chiefly in clarifying issues, not resolving them. The British insisted that Palestine "has been generally understood to be the field of the B.F.B.S.;" the Americans declared that there had been "no boundary recognized by both Societies." An earlier British proposal to exchange the Philippines for Egypt and the Sudan had been rejected, but Egypt was divided geographically, north of Cairo to the BFBS, south to the ABS, with both Societies maintaining offices in Cairo and Alexandria. For Sudan, American representatives noted, "south of Assouan we have no understanding whatever." In this remote desert area, Muslim to the north and primitive animist in the south, British authorities apparently feared that religious proselytism might jeopardize political imperalism.

[But] the Bible colporteur can carry on his legitimate
work throughout these miles of villages without molestation.

His mission is a simple one, to supply the Scriptures to
those who wish the Scriptures. The exigencies of politics
do not seem to demand interference with him. And even the
diplomat finds it difficult to prohibit Bible trade, and at
the same time permit the rum trade. (*The Bible Society
Record*, June, 1902)

By the end of World War I it became clear that the Levant
Agency embraced too great diversity: religiously, politically,
culturally, linguistically. More than turbulent, strife-torn
miles separated Iraq from Bulgaria, Sudan from Turkey. So the
Society's oldest Agency was divided: the Levant (Turkey,
Bulgaria, Greece, briefly the Caucasus) with headquarters at
Constantinople; the Arabic-Levant (Egypt, Sudan, Syria, Palestine,
Arabia and Iraq) with headquarters in Cairo. Each of these
opened several sub-agencies and depots, recognizing national
variations, but the geographical and ethnic consolidations were
obvious. Restrictions and shortages and dangers in Turkey led
the Levant Agency to transfer its printing to Beirut in 1924 and
its administrative office to Vienna in 1928.

Meanwhile, on the outer fringe of the Middle East, the Persia
Agency had been turned over to the British. The office had been
closed in 1896 because of lack of funds, and circulation turned
over to missionaries, who in 1902 urged the reappointment of a
superintendent. In the interim the BFBS had extended its work
into the north, "for many years the special field of the
American Bible Society." Both organizations labored under
difficulties, for importation of books was banned from 1903-1910,
though smuggling and some shipments via Russia did get in.
Rather than surrender its northern supply route the BFBS suggested
in 1912 a Joint Agency, with a territorial division roughly
paralleling mission lines. Bible distribution was further
handicapped by the backwardness of the people. Said the Annual
Report for 1913:

It is an achievement of much hard work and persuasion
every time a copy of the Christian Scriptures is placed
in the hands of a Moslem. It is naturally as distasteful
to him as a bitter pill. He has not the unsophisticated
mind of the African or the open-mind of the Chinaman.
Besides, he is desperately poor, and the ratio of illiteracy must be at least ninety to ninety-five percent.

Before the Joint Agency could be consummated, negotiations
between London and New York resulted in the exchange of Persia
to the BFBS in return for Central America to the ABS.

The London Conference of 1932 (see Chapter XV) represented a
significant milestone in the life of all three world-wide Bible

Societies: the BFBS, the ABS, and the NBSS. To it came Agency
Secretaries from China and the Middle East, resolved to survey
their common task in "a spirit of compromise, mutual respect and
humility." "It is no small thing," as ABS General Secretary
Eric North wrote, "for three great Societies, each with a long
history, each with cherished principles and methods of work, to
come together in common counsel"--and with the explicit intention
of combining efforts, unifying resources, and establishing
harmony in their hitherto separate endeavors. Such a goal was
bound to have global repercussions, in China and Latin America
and elsewhere, but perhaps none more comprehensive than in the
Near East. After a century of Bible work the Levant was far
from ready for autonomy; the scarcity of qualified Christian
personnel, the colonial status of many territories, the inherent
resistance of Arab society, all limited the opportunities for
self-governing Societies. Yet administrative collaboration
could move promptly in certain places: an immediate attempt in
Bulgaria failed because of the sudden death of the BFBS Agent
who was to direct both areas.

The centenary of the Levant Agency was celebrated in 1936
with praise and thanksgiving led by Toyohiko Kagawa, world-
famous Japanese evangelist and social worker, and by ABS
Secretary Eric North, and BFBS Secretary Arthur H. Wilkinson.
Following that occasion the two Secretaries toured the region
extensively, accompanied by the Agency Secretaries. At that
time these five territorial divisions were "fully or generally
observed:" Bulgaria, BFBS north, ABS south; Greece, BFBS in
"old Greece" and the islands, ABS in Macedonia and Thrace;
Arabia, BFBS Aden and the West, ABS on the Persian Gulf; Egypt,
BFBS north of Cairo, ABS south; Sudan, BFBS, Khartoum and
northward, ABS to the southwest. The British published pre-
dominantly in Bulgarian, Ancient and Modern Greek, and Hebrew;
the Americans in Armeno-Turkish, Armenian, Arabic, Judeo-Spanish;
the new Turkish Scriptures jointly.

Secretary North's lengthy, detailed reports touched on several
key factors which can only be mentioned here. One was the need
to cultivate the Orthodox Church more closely, not only in
Bulgaria but throughout the Levant. Another was the antagonism
between assorted Christian Churches: Greek Orthodox, Greek
Catholic, Armenian Orthodox, Syrian Orthodox, Nestorian, Uniate,
Protestant, etc. "These older churches, on the whole," North
reported, "possess little missionary spirit," and are suspicious
and fearful of Protestant evangelism. A third element North
pointed out was the usefulness of the Bible in places like Iraq,
where preaching and teaching would be resented. "The Scripture
once sold can be working where the presence of the missionary
might be undesired or an affront. It can be read in secret.
It states the truth rather than arguing about it--is thus not

polemic. It can go where the missionary--even the colporteur--
cannot go."

"In view of what I have said both of the imperative nature of
the Societies' work and of the effects of Christian disunion,"
North continued, "it would seem that our first duty is the
elimination of every element of duplication, competition, confusion of policy from the combined work of the Societies." To
this end the ABS and the BFBS reached an agreement for the total
amalgamation of their administrative structures, into two large
Agencies, to be supported jointly with circulation figures
shared proportionately. Bible Lands Agency, North (Bulgaria,
Greece, Turkey, Syria, Iraq, and Eastern Arabia) was to be
administered by the American Bible Society; Bible Lands Agency,
South (Palestine, Transjordania, Egypt, Sudan, Western Arabia),
under the British and Foreign. These two Joint Agencies went
into operation in January, 1938.

The immediate years of World War II brought comparatively
little disruption to Bible circulation in the Middle East.
Publishing in Vienna was out of the question. Transportation
and foreign exchange presented problems, but the United States
filled many orders for books which London could not supply.
Astonishingly, distribution figures for 1942 climbed by fifteen
per cent in Syria, sixty per cent in Iraq, and 190 per cent in
Turkey. In Iraq-Arabia the first four years of war, 1939-42,
showed phenomenal growth in circulation: 1,202, 5,389, 8,523,
and 11,074, fairly evenly distributed among Bibles, Testaments
and Portions.

In a touching incident from this period, the sub-agent told
of a poor, aged man who tottered into the Baghdad depot almost
exhausted from the heat:

...He took from his bosom a very much-worn Gospel of St.
John in the Arabic. The covers, which had come apart, he
had tied together with a tape, and almost every page was
loose; they were curled and, in some instances, torn from
constant fingering. Handling it with great care, he put
the little volume in tidy shape, and then rising to beg
us handle it with care too, he held it out with both hands,
and gave it to our keeping, and at the same time requested
another, but as cheap as we could possibly supply it.
....He had bought the Gospel of St. John from one of our
colporteurs some eight months previous. It was the very
first portion of the Scriptures he had had...and as he
was reading it one afternoon while sitting alone, the
light dawned upon him. Salvation and the joy of his Lord
had come out of the pages of the little volume into his
heart.....

The worn-out booklet was carefully wrapped and kept for him in a drawer, but the man would not accept either another Gospel or a New Testament as a gift, preferring to have Scriptures he could call his own. Very reluctantly he agreed to take a Testament on credit.

Since then he has called at the depot three times in five months, and has paid a total of 1 3/4 d in three instalments, and each time has requested a look at his first treasured Gospel of St. John.....Who he is,--what he does,--and where he goes, we know not. He doesn't encourage us to inquire .....We have a *use-worn* Gospel of St. John in the drawer.. as a testimony of the Word of God having been sown by a colporteur in Iraq's scorching desert, and returned to the Bible Society bearing a *hundredfold*.

In Greece during the 'forties guerrilla warfare and its repression closed the Bible depot, scattered the colporteurs, imprisoned the sub-agent in a concentration camp for four months. But when the occupation ended, even in the midst of civil strife, Scripture distribution resumed with increased demand-- and increased supplies, since a wealthy American Greek provided 150,000 Gospels for the Greek army.

Only in Bulgaria, directly in the path of battle, did the war itself bring Bible circulation virtually to a standstill. Between the two World Wars Bulgaria had been "the most fertile" of all Levant fields, despite intermittent opposition from Orthodox clergy on one hand and Communist intellectuals (even during the 'thirties) on the other. Yet peasants had continued to buy Scriptures eagerly, sometimes paying in apples, corn, walnuts, beans and eggs; one gypsy exchanged his precious flint-and-iron for a Gospel.

Under German occupation government law forbade the operation of any foreign agency and cut off communications and transmission of funds from the West. The New York office promptly approved the establishment of a Bulgarian Bible Society, donating to it all stock, printing plates, and cash on hand. Since 3,000 Bibles were burned in a 1944 bombing, along with most printing facilities, an appeal for books followed soon after V-E Day.

By 1947 some 20,000 Testaments and 95,000 Gospels were shipped, on condition that they required no Bulgarian currency export and that funds would be provided from America to cover customs charges. The ABS also sent paper for printing Scriptures, but as Communist controls tightened, circulation dropped in 1949 to 1,210 Bibles and Testaments, 10,758 Portions. Subsequent distribution was spasmodic and unreported; in 1964 the government restricted all independent Bible work other than the meager activity of the churches.

Elsewhere the post-war years of hope opened new doors but
slammed others. In the harbor of Port Said, Egypt, in 1949 a
launch named "Mary Jones" carried colporteurs to 114 ships to
sell 101 Bibles, 39 Testaments, and 98 Portions in twenty-six
languages. The boat was crushed against a quay in 1954,
rebuilt in 1955, burned by an incendiary bomb in the Suez War
of 1956, but the engine was saved and harbor colportage resumed
in 1958.

In Syria a bookmobile operated by the Presbyterian mission
proved to be a fascinating and effective innovation, which the
Bible Society copied some years later. The establishment in
1949 of an Advisory Council for Syria and Lebanon, one of the
first in Bible Lands, marked a major step toward regional
autonomy.....From Lebanon came a bit of whimsy for the Annual
Report of 1945:

The Bible Society Depot in Beirut stands next to the shop
of a well-known purveyor of macaroni and Oriental taffy,
and occasionally his customers enter the depot door by
mistake. So, when a veiled Moslem lady extended some
money and asked for a certain brand of macaroni, she was
offered instead the Bread of Life. She inquired in surprise how the New Testament could be sold so cheaply, and
went her way happy in the possession of a copy. The next
wanderer who demanded half a kilo of the sweetmeat was
encouraged to test instead the sweetness of the Word of
God. He purchased a copy of the Psalms.

To Palestine and Transjordania the late 1940's brought only
bitterness. During months of fighting after British withdrawal
there was no contact with Bible workers, and it was obvious that
separate offices for Israel and Jordan would have to be maintained. Receiving immigrants from all parts of the world,
Israel needed Scriptures in many different languages. Jordan,
trying valiantly to minister to thousands in refugee camps,
increased circulation from 818 in 1950 to 6,657 in 1951 to
14,500 in 1954. After the Suez War of 1956, the British were
unacceptable in the Arab world, and Israel was isolated from the
rest of the area; thus Bible Society administration for Jordan
was transferred to the ABS, for Israel to the London Home Office.
Through the intervening period the Agency Secretary's ironic
comment applied to most of the region: "Jordan passed through
another year of tense calm."

In the "tense calm" which pervaded the Near East during the
early 'fifties Bible distribution made some headway. Greece
celebrated in 1951 the 1900th anniversary of St. Paul's arrival
on the peninsula. Concern for Scriptures among the Greek armed
forces provided incentive for the formation of an Advisory

Committee composed entirely of Orthodox churchmen. Some of the priests, the Agent reported in surprise, were "establishing Bible classes and using Scriptures for teaching purposes." In 1954 the Society began circulation of the Modern Greek Text Bible, reduced photographically from the existing pulpit Bible, so that "for the first time in many years the public could be offered a Bible in a handy size, printed in clear, readable type." By 1957 the American Bible Society was asked to supply 15,000 free New Testaments for the Greek Navy and Air Force, in addition to 40,000 already provided for the Army. The following year a Braille Gospel in Modern Greek was provided for 250 blind persons. Yet in spite of these advances, and apart from intermittent free distribution by a single missionary society, circulation in Greece continued to decline during most of this decade.

Circulation in the Sudan, however, fluctuated erratically: 889, 16,342, 3,251, 22,898 for the four years 1950-53, the variations representing waves of Portions surging around the fairly constant bedrock of Bibles and Testaments. Wrote the sub-agent in 1951:

The Sudan must be viewed in its own light. The thousands of miles that must be traversed, the extreme heat and the torrential rains, the personal contact and witness prefacing every sale, as well as the fanaticism, sickness and illiteracy that are prevalent, provide a picture that must be enlarged by the imagination, if the work of Scripture distribution is to be understood.

Yet the Bible House in Khartoum was rebuilt in 1956, and prospects looked bright until the military coup two years later.

In Turkey a prison warden reprimanded one colporteur for bringing only 300 books for 600 men.....Seven Jacobite youngsters in Anatolia hid their precious Gospels inside their clothes to bring them luck on examinations. Questioned by the Turkish examiners about the strange bulges, the children brought out their talismans, kissing them and pressing them to their foreheads: "This is our Gospel, the Book by which our lives are guided, the Book which stands by us in days of great trouble." "Good," smiled the examiners, "now put them away and get on with the test." The fact that all seven pupils passed carried much weight in the entire community.

After fifteen years of joint operation in Bible Lands, North and South, officials of both Societies realized that "functional rather than geographical" duplication still existed, and that there was "no provision for consultation and coordination." British involvement in the Suez War of 1956 forced the transfer

of all Arab sub-agencies to American supervision and pointed up
the need for more rapid devolution and nationalization, as well
as further administrative realignment. Political and ethnic and
linguistic factors had become far more crucial than geographical
or historical divisions. When the new Secretary for the North
arrived in Beirut, the city was in such chaos that he established
temporary residence in Cairo, and this accident proved "fortuitous"
in re-examining and unifying the work.

In 1958 a Near East Staff Consultation, moved from troubled
Arab lands to Kifissia, Greece, helped to "shatter the complacency
of the Societies, and bring the wheels of change into motion."
The key descriptive word was tension--political, religious,
economic, racial--and there remained little counterbalancing
calm. Greece and Bulgaria, neighbors, stood on opposite sides
in the Cold War. Hostile Arab nations encircled Israel; only
Iraq and the Sudan professed to be non-aligned. Christian
missions were politically and religiously suspect throughout the
area; in fact, as ABS Secretary Paul Collyer put it: "Of the
several Christian institutions and missions in the Arab lands,
the Bible Society is the one and only one that has any liberty
to carry on a Christian mission to Muslims." It was time for
the cooperating Societies to shift attention from administration,
program, and techniques to long-range objectives, strategy, and
creative implementation.

Clearly Bible work in Arab lands would benefit from unified
organization, planning, and development, although each country
needed its own distributing office (for example, Syrian and
Lebanese accounts, previously handled jointly, had to be
separated because of different currency and exchange rates).
Many of the recommendations could not be implemented because of
excessive costs, but the Kifissia Consultation highlighted the
importance of far greater "flexibility," a word which, interest-
ingly, required conference definition:

> The implementation of strategy decisions in such a way
> that finances, personnel, stocks, program development, and
> administrative control can be adjusted with greatest ease
> and effectiveness to meet the demands and exigencies of
> the constantly changing area-wide situation and conditions.

A Strategy Conference for Bible Lands, held in Jerusalem in
1955, placed great stress on cultivating churches and on training
Christians to read, use, live their Bibles as well as to distribute them. In this the Kifissia Consultation three years
later fully concurred, calling it the "first priority." But
where Jerusalem had proposed ministry, in this order, to
Evangelicals, Orthodox, Catholics, and Muslims, Kifissia placed
primary emphasis on serving the Orthodox Churches, which contain

ninety per cent of the Christian population in the Near East, and a new challenge to reach gradually more receptive Muslims. Specifically Collyer recommended the employment of an Orthodox priest on the Bible Society staff as Secretary for Church Relations, and the "necessity" of publishing Orthodox versions. Keenly aware of traditional policy, he nonetheless recognized that encouraging Orthodox use of the Scriptures would lead to a demand for "their *whole* Bible," including the Apocrypha, and "eventually we shall have to meet it."

On a more mundane but essential level, consultants at Kifissia acknowledged that the Bible Societies had been often lax in employment policies and standards, hiring colporteurs and other workers who were uneducated, poorly dressed, inexperienced, or weakly motivated. With full appreciation of the scarcity of dedicated Bible-centered Christians, and of almost unimaginable hardships of travel and persecution, the Bible Societies in "the new day" must revise their job descriptions and qualifications. In the Near East the bulk of circulation has been shifting from colportage to shops and depots; salesmen who are employed henceforth should be able to meet persuasively with professionals and business men, with government officials and teachers, as well as with villagers and refugees.

Modern methods should include posters and advertising, newspapers and radios, display windows and youth programs, reaching into schools, hospitals, prisons, offices, bookstores, and homes. For such ministries staff members, it was recommended, should have secondary school education, some working experience and maturity, evidence of Christian commitment and integrity, pre-service and in-service training, "attractive personality, good manners, polite speech, neat appearance, and an easy friendly way of meeting people." Such men could and should be designated as Specialized Bible Distributors.

From these and other proposals came a new structure for the old Levant. Under the comprehensive title, Bible Societies in the Near East, the region was divided for administrative purposes in 1960 into Arab Lands (Syria, Lebanon, Jordan, Iraq, Egypt, and the Arabian Gulf) under the ABS, Non-Arab Lands (Sudan, Turkey, Greece, Israel) under the BFBS. But Cyprus and Ethiopia remained Joint Agencies; Greece and Bulgaria were recognized as more integrally part of Europe; the Sudan and Egypt are part of Africa. This administrative dispersion was linked under one central Joint Agency, whose staff included functional Directors for publications, publicity, church relations (Orthodox and Evangelical), distribution, promotion of income, personnel. Though political tensions remain acute, some age-old religious animosities are breaking down, as Christians rediscover their unity in the Word of Life. A Maronite bishop,

representing an Ancient Uniate branch of Roman Catholicism in
the Lebanon, remarked at a UBS Conference in Jerusalem in 1962:
"The Bible, which used to divide us, is now uniting us. What a
wonderful mystery."

Appraisal of the Bible Societies in the Near East from 1960
to 1966 is difficult; conditions were confusing, reports meager,
programs in transition. In the Sudan, despite renewed persecution and the expulsion of some missionaries, 1966 witnessed
three spectacular events: One colporteur sold 11,000 copies in
eight months, a far cry from 1900, when 651 in the same length of
time was "fairly successful" or from 1949, when the entire
colportage staff averaged one book per four miles travelled.
A celebration for the centenary of Bible Society work in Sudan
(and the tenth anniversary of the new Bible House, not to
mention the sesquicentennial of the ABS) brought to the Anglican
Cathedral representatives of the Roman Catholic, Coptic Orthodox,
Coptic Evangelical, and various Protestant missionary groups.
And a new Advisory Committee of several denominations agreed to
observe Bible Sunday in all the churches, with the offerings to
go for the work of the Societies.

In 1963 a bookstore was opened in Oman, long one of the areas
most tightly closed to Christian missions.....In Turkey,
observing the tricentenary of the first printed Armenian Bible,
more Scriptures were sold in 1966 than in any of the previous
forty years, due in large measure to a group of young independent missionaries.....

When Arab countries objected even to Bible Society reports of
work in Israel, the Norwegian Bible Society assumed responsibility for directing that Joint Agency. Although an Israeli
clerk, appropriately, won the International Bible Quiz on his
country's tenth anniversary, though new bookstores were opened
in Tel Aviv as well as Haifa and Jerusalem, though scores of
study groups discussed the Hebrew New Testament as well as the
Old, Scripture sales depended in large measure on the very
erratic tourist trade.....

A Lebanese philanthropist proposed to extend his subsidy of
Scriptures for every Lebanese serviceman to "all the hotels of
Lebanon." For the 1966 centennial of the Arabic Bible over a
thousand people, including high government officials and clergy
of many faiths, gathered at American University in Beirut to hear
a personal testimony by Dr. Charles Malik, former Lebanese
Minister of Foreign Affairs and Ambassador to the United Nations,
subsequently named as the first Greek Orthodox to become a Vice
President of the United Bible Societies. Declared Dr. Malik:

As I cannot live without food to eat and water to drink
and air to breathe and friend to love so my soul likewise

cannot get along, my wings cannot fly and soar high, even
I myself cannot exist without the Bible.....I don't know
what will be the judgment of history in the thirtieth
century or in the fiftieth century about the most important
event that took place in the Arabic language and to the
Arabic soul (the Arab person) in the nineteenth century.
But if the Bible is what it is, and Jesus Christ the theme
of the Bible is what He is, I have no doubt that the judgment of history will be that the most important event is
the one we assemble to celebrate at this very day [the
translation of the Bible into Arabic].

A still more apt epigram for the Levant Agency appeared in
the Iraq report for 1935. An Arab boy on family business
stopped to distribute Scriptures to a large group of Bedouins
and fellaheen (farmers), so eager for the books that one sheikh
loaned his horse for the lad to return for more Portions. When
the boy arrived at the depot, breathless but beaming with pride,
the missionary inquired about his family. "Oh, we haven't
arrived there yet," the boy replied, "for we had to give the
gospel to the Arabs." Reviewing the history of the American
Bible Society abroad, Christians, impressed by larger
statistics from other parts of the world, might do well to
reaffirm in this boy's words the commitment to the Middle East
first manifested by the infant Society back in 1836: "Oh, we
haven't arrived there yet, for we had to give the gospel to the
Arabs."

13
Into All The World:
Asia

"Where did you get that page?" asked a missionary of a
fakir, who came to him for instruction with a fragment
of St. John, containing that wonderful 3:16.

"I found it by the wayside under the snows of Badrinath."....

"Where did you find that New Testament, which seems to
have been badly used?"

"One morning, as I went to the Ganges with my net, I
found it lying water-soaked at the river's edge."
                    (*The Bible Society Record*, March, 1909)

These incidents reported by a missionary in North India need
not imply that optimum Bible distribution is accidental or
haphazard. They do suggest that in many parts of the world--
but perhaps especially in Asia--God moves in a mysterious way
through ignorance and superstition, through war and revolution,
through indifference and hostility, to speak His Word of Life
to human hearts.

*   *   *   *   *

Long after William Carey and the unfortunate *Baptizo* controversy (see Chapter VII), the majority of American Bible Society
grants to India helped to subsidize translations and publication
of Scriptures. The British and Foreign Bible Society--with
Agencies in Calcutta, Bombay and Madras--assumed major responsibility for preparing and producing the Bible in most Indian

languages. By the early twentieth century the ABS appropriated
a few hundred dollars annually to principal American missions
(Methodist, Congregationalist, and Dutch Reformed) for the
purchase of books from British depots. These were intended
originally for non-Christians or for new converts, frequently
for pupils in mission schools, but increasingly missionaries
discovered that many church members lacked the Scriptures because
of poverty, illiteracy, or neglect. (A 1965 estimate claimed
that India still had only one Bible for an average of 53 Christian homes, one New Testament for every 212 Christians.)

Hinduism's theoretical tolerance toward any religious
pilgrimage, and Mahatma Gandhi's profound appreciation for the
Sermon on the Mount, might be expected to have opened wide doors
for the distribution of the Gospel in India, but in thirty years
the American contribution amounted to only $12,140 for the
purchase of some 145,846 books. After the London Conference of
1932 (see Chapter XV) recommended "reinforced" cooperation among
Bible Societies, the ABS began to make regular grants directly
to British Agencies in India, gradually eliminating allotments
to missions. These appropriations rose steadily from $500 in
1937 to $20,000 in 1956, and initially were earmarked for
special projects, such as a Motor Caravan, carrying books, a
gramophone, religious records, and a "magic lantern."

The Bible Society of India and Ceylon, formed by the BFBS in
1944, included on its Central Council representatives of the ABS
and the NBSS. Its post-war Advance, for which New York contributed an additional $45,000 over three years toward a print-
ing press, aimed to provide Bibles in twenty-four languages,
Testaments in thirty-nine more, Portions in another sixty. The
Society offered free Gospels-Acts or Testament-Psalms to *all*
students graduating from mission schools, published the Gospels
in serial form in fifteen newspapers, sponsored Bible readings
over radio, encouraged women's work in homes, stocked bookstores,
exhibits, Bible vans, and "wayside cases."

The partition of Pakistan from India in 1947 led eventually
to a separate Agency in 1956, but East and West Pakistan proved
so different in language and culture as well as so remote in
distance that they split into two Joint Agencies in 1962.
Similarly Ceylon, predominantly Buddhist as Pakistan is Muslim
and India Hindu, became a Joint Agency in 1962, exactly 150 years
after the British formed an Auxiliary in Colombo. Three years
later it was recognized as "an autonomous society though within
the framework of our international connections and commitments."

*   *   *   *   *

The Agency for Siam and Laos, established in Bangkok in 1890,
soon found that a climate of gentle, easy-going indolence may be

just as difficult for Bible circulation as outright hostility.
For one thing, Portions were produced in disproportionate
quantity because the Bible in Thai type filled three bulky,
costly volumes; not until 1940 did a single-volume edition
appear. For another, the Epistles of John and such Old Testament
books as Esther and Jonah, whose Oriental flavor is unmistakable,
outsold the Gospels. For a third, so many copies were distributed without charge in the early days that shocking wastefulness
occurred, and in spite of avowed policy to the contrary, free
donations exceeded sales until 1935.

At the start of Bible Society work effective circulation
depended, somewhat in this order, on the Agent, colporteurs,
missionaries (chiefly Presbyterian), and converts.

As for Agents, in the face of "much indifference...some
opposition, and considerable interest," one of them wrote in
1912, "one needs great grace, much tact, and a certain amount
of holy boldness to meet all kinds of people with success."
Those with "holy boldness" and creative imagination were most
successful, and in recent years the Thailand Bible House was
unique in being served by a Chinese of American citizenship
(1956-59) and by a "fraternal worker" from Korea (1962-).

"Lowly colporteurs," whether paddling or chugging through
inland waterways or plodding mountain ledges too narrow for
caravans to pass, were described as "heroes comparable to men
in the trenches. They are laying foundations for preachers,
evangelists, and pastors to build on.....Colportage is a very
human kind of work; it brings us close to our kin. It clears
our vision and warms our hearts."

More and more, however, distribution was to be carried on by
volunteers, by church members, rather than by paid employees.
The very first Agent in Bangkok wrote whimsically but appre-
ciatively: "Our Siamese sisters will not be outdone in their
conversational powers when occasion offers. This will serve us
in scattering the Word and a knowledge of it when they become
converted and the occasion offers for this feature of our
work." On the other hand, missionaries, appointed as colportage
supervisors between 1912 and 1925, proved unreliable in filing
regular reports, and intermittently suspect as aliens and
evangelists.

To be sure, some Christians clearly and sacrificially
recognized their responsibility to share the Good News. Church
members in the leprosarium at Chiengmai, one of the first and
finest in Asia, contributed to Bible Society work as early as
1913. Fifteen years later Thai Christians distributed 12,000
Portions in six months. Although New York headquarters urged

"the national churches in every field to become ultimately responsible for the distribution of the Scriptures in their own territory and to share in the world-wide program," the Siamese Church had a long way to go. A Bible School in the remote eastern section of the country proposed to include colportage training in its program, but the Home Office raised serious question about financing general evangelism, especially under denominational auspices. Not until 1958 did the Bible House sponsor its own highly successful Training Institute on an interchurch basis, for hired colporteurs and volunteers.

The problem of serving tribal groups and Thai people along the borders of Siam plagued the Agency periodically. One early Agent declared emphatically that the boundaries of his work were racial rather than geographic or political, or--as one official put it--he "had the idea that the Siam & Laos Agency has a mission to the Thai people anywhere they were in the world. I verily believe that he would have undertaken work in central Australia if there were any Thai there." The claim had some sound bases. Many of these people were nomadic, roaming back and forth across national borders. Their dialects, especially in Laos, were closer to Siamese than to other languages; preliminary translations had been made in Siam. In some instances, transportation and communication were simpler through Thailand than through adjacent regions. Yet ABS General Secretary Eric North had to warn, on behalf of both major Bible Societies, that "this is not a practical operating basis." To the west Burma was clearly BFBS territory; to the east the British protested indignantly that "our Society is alone responsible...in French Indo-China." Northward in China both Societies were at work, with the British predominant in the nearest province.

Population was so sparse and migratory in these border regions that one Agent despaired of spending money and personnel on translation, publication, and distribution there. In most of the countries involved, he pointed out, governments were trying to enforce education in national languages (Burmese, Thai, Mandarin Chinese) rather than the vernaculars, which might eventually retain only oral use. Against this argument came a plaintive report in 1932 that one hill tribe with 20,000 baptized Christians had "not a word of the Bible in their own tongue." Not even Britain's wartime financial retrenchment, which inspired one proposal that all Scripture distribution in Indo-China should be turned over to the Americans, could budge New York or London to violate comity in this particular region, even when missionaries in the area sent letters appealing for ABS jurisdiction. Burma, Cambodia, Eastern Indo-China (now Vietnam) were indisputably BFBS territory; Yunnan belonged to the China Agencies, British and/or American. Only in 1965 did another war in Southeast Asia force the official transfer of

Laos from the British Agency in Vietnam to the Thailand Bible
House. The same principle, however, reaffirmed Bangkok's
obligation to serve the Chinese people within the boundaries of
Thailand.

For the first three decades of this century annual distribution statistics never passed 430 Bibles, and rose above 1,000
Testaments only three times. Portions, however, circulated at
the rate of more than 100,000 per year from 1913 on. The Agency
celebrated its fiftieth anniversary in 1940 under the new name
of Thailand with the publication of a less bulky single-volume
Bible. During World War II American military action did more
damage to the Bible House and Bible Society personnel than three
years of Japanese occupation, but organization and morale also
required rebuilding. From the Thailand Bible House, which in
1962 became a Joint Agency with twenty-five per cent BFBS
participation, fresh enthusiasm and experimental methods poured
forth. By 1965 and 1966 the ABS share of circulation, seventy-
five per cent, passed a million copies, including Selections.

To meet a rising public interest and stimulate it further
Bible posters appeared on buses, on movie screens, in bookstores.
(One such advertisement was held up because officials could not
believe that any book had really been translated into 1,100
languages!) Churches in the capital initiated a movement to
place a Bible in every Buddhist temple, most of them gratefully
and graciously accepted. Passengers in and out of Bangkok's
airport picked up 27,445 copies of Portions or Selections in
1962 alone, and bookracks in hotels, hospitals, prisons, and
U.S. army bases had constantly to be refilled. Colporteurs and
volunteers on railroads (permitted to distribute in slow trains
but not in expresses) had opportunity for evangelistic conversations; the most successful woman colporteur handed out 5,427
books in one year, mostly on trains. For Thai Christians
realize, as Secretary Ming Chao wrote in 1958, that "Scripture
distribution and evangelistic outreach are inseparable. They
have to go hand in hand. The vitality and the steady growth of
the Christian missionary enterprise in Thailand parallel the
increase in Scripture distribution."

One other important factor had paradoxical effect: the
cooperation of widely diverse missionary organizations and
indigenous churches in Bible work. The closing of mainland
China by the Communists in 1949 scattered hundreds of missionaries, with many different policies and viewpoints, throughout
Southeast Asia. On a visit to Thailand in 1952 ABS Secretary
Paul Collyer was "distressed to find so much ill-will, misunderstanding and jealousy among the missions and mission workers"--
within denominations as well as between them. But he added:
"I can see no organization in the country...that can weld these

many groups into a unified front except the Bible Society." On the Advisory Committee, first inaugurated in 1932, and in circulation of Scriptures these diverse groups labored in a common cause. Ironically the very harmony which did prevail served to prevent establishment of an autonomous Thailand Bible Society: ninety per cent of the Christian community belonged to the Church of Christ in Thailand, which would obviously exert preponderant control in a representative body, whereas the Bible Societies felt that they must represent and be responsive and sensitive to all Christian groups, no matter how small or distinct.

* * * * *

Once a sleeping dragon, China in the twentieth century leaped and twisted and writhed from the Boxer Rebellion of 1900 to the Communist take-over in 1949, through three major revolutions, two international conflicts, one prolonged enemy occupation, almost continual civil strife, not to mention perennial famines, floods, and epidemics. All of these dramatically affected the distribution of Scriptures. Yet in a very real sense the story of the American Bible Society through that period is the story of the largest foreign Agency struggling, as a prototype for other countries, to achieve two sometimes irreconcilable goals: the integration of Bible work under three international Societies, and indigenization (or nationalization) into the hands of the Chinese Christian community.

Although the Society had very early given indirect aid to two Chinese translations outside the country, the Marshman Bible in Serampore and the Morrison-Milne version in Malacca, direct contributions to China did not begin until 1833. For thirty years these appropriations were used exclusively for translating and publishing; missionaries carried on the distribution, increasingly through native colporteurs. In the wake of the Boxer Rebellion it was estimated (in 1902) that the Protestant enterprise in China consisted of 2,950 missionaries, 100,000 church members, a million inquirers and another million under some Christian influence, at a total cost of $3,440,000. When John Fox, the first Home Secretary ever to visit the Far East, came to China in 1907, the Agency report for the preceding year read as follows: six foreign distributors (or Sub-Agents), ninety-five colporteurs under their direction, fifty-five colporteurs under missionary supervision, sold a total of 401,328 books and donated 4,334. But these were years of critical floods, of anti-American boycotts, of the Russo-Japanese War fought largely on and for Chinese soil.

The Revolution of 1911, overthrowing the Imperial Dynasty, caused disruption in transportation and economy and the flight

of missionaries from some stations, yet Scripture circulation
passed the million mark for the first time. Five years later,
as the Society celebrated its centennial around the world, the
China Agency recorded distribution of 12,982 Bibles, 62,951
Testaments, and 2,198,777 Portions. To honor the occasion a
Peking philanthropist, newly baptized and still not a church
member, proposed somewhat ambitiously to place a Bible in every
school in China. In those far-off days supporters of the
Society were less surprised--and perhaps less shocked--to read
of an old Chinese fortune teller who considered his Gospel of
John such a good book that he frequently bowed in worship and
burnt incense to it, than to hear of the hiring of a Roman
Catholic colporteur.

When in 1912 the China Agency offered assistance to American
missionaries in Manchuria, the BFBS warned that the ABS "should
not attempt, as a Society, to do anything in that field." Five
years later, when three other Sub-Agencies were being closed,
missionaries in West China recommended that one office could
handle the Bible business in West China instead of having four,
one British and one American in both Chungking and Chengtu. The
ABS Secretary in Shanghai retorted that such a complaint was
"absurd," that both cities were obviously strategic distribution
centers, and that there was "no friction whatever between the
different Bible Societies." The 1920's, however, brought not
only a new administration, but new attitudes on the part of
missions around the world. The Chinese National Christian
Conference held in Shanghai in 1922, a milestone in many areas
of church policy, recommended greater Christian unity and
cooperation and Chinese leadership, in the preparation of
Scripture texts and in circulation. Six months earlier
Carleton Lacy had announced his "platform" as a new Agency
Secretary:

> Before I entered into the work of the Bible Society I felt
> strongly that there was need for closer co-operation both
> in production and distribution on the part of the three
> Bible Societies.....Its consummation may not be realized
> without the organization of a Chinese Bible Society, but
> there are first steps, and clearly evident steps, which
> we can and must take soon. They are not steps toward
> union, but I trust long strides toward co-operation.

> From every part of China, in every line of work, there
> comes a strong, insistent demand for a larger participation
> in Christian work by Chinese leadership. My impression is
> that few, if any, of the missionary bodies have opened as
> little opportunity to Chinese leadership as have the Bible
> Societies. If we are properly to reach the field, if we
> are not to be outlawed entirely as alien institutions, the

Bible Societies must immediately enlist the co-operation
of Chinese leadership in a much more adequate way.

Some of these "first steps" took place promptly. When the
American Sub-Agent in Canton retired in 1923, the BFBS representative was asked to assume administration of ABS work in South
China--albeit still with separate accounts, separate stock,
separate reports. A proposal for a common title page stumbled
over the Scottish inclusion of interpretive notes and the
British refusal to endorse such an "unconstitutional" practice.
(Apparently the historic scruples of the American Society could
be waived in regard to the title page if ABS funds were not
actually used for such publication, but two decades later the
China Bible House endeavored to compile a new set of annotations
which all three Societies might accept.)

As a "long stride" toward devolution the ABS appointed a
Chinese Field Secretary in 1925--and three more three years
later--with particular responsibility for cultivation among the
churches and the Chinese Christian community. With similar
intent an indigenous committee in Canton formed a South China
Bible Society in 1927, to function much like Auxiliaries in the
United States, and very quickly enrolled over five hundred
members. The request for a Chinese Agency Secretary, as a
co-equal partner in administering the program throughout the
country, was approved by the Board of Managers in 1929 but
repeatedly deferred lest such an appointment obstruct further
collaboration with the other Societies.

To most of these proposals officers in London and Scotland
"turned thumbs down:" the BFBS on the grounds that the Chinese
Church was not advanced enough, in finances or personnel, to
provide this kind of genuine partnership and that support of a
Chinese Secretary from foreign funds would create jealousies
and precedents; the NBSS in apparent fear that their policies
and their circulation would be overshadowed by the larger
Societies. Increasingly missionaries and Chinese Christians
criticized "apparent rivalry and competition." Sub-Agencies and
activities were too closely interwoven (as indicated in Szechwan
province) to permit any acceptable territorial division. The
consolidation at Canton, under an American employed by the
British Society, had succeeded remarkably well, but its actual
unification was superficial and its "lowest common denominator"
prevented any expansion or experimentation beyond traditional
procedures. Some observers felt that the ABS was "stalling" on
indigenization out of expedient deference to the British;
others maintained that encouragement of Chinese responsibility
(as in the South China Bible Society) in advance of Western
agreement would simply result in four Societies instead of
three, with divergent policies and competitive programs.

Meanwhile, however, Bible circulation continued with amazing momentum despite chaotic conditions. The Communist Party in China originated in 1921; within a year it was taking advantage of the popularity of Christianity by removing pages from Gospel portions and using the covers to bind Communist propaganda. The last years of Dr. Sun Yat-sen and the first years of General Chiang Kai-shek found both men accepting anti-Christian as well as anti-foreign agitation within the Nationalist Revolution. Yet in 1925-26 two remarkable Scripture movements coincided: An American Bible evangelist, George T. B. Davis, launched a Million-Testaments-in-China Campaign, and the colorful Christian "warlord" in Manchuria, General Chang Chih-kiang, ordered 6,500 Bibles and 12,000 Testaments for his soldiers and for government officials. Beyond those special drives circulation figures kept climbing, with only a minor recession during the Kuomintang Revolution of 1927, as the following statistics show: 1925--3,733,538; 1926--3,821,393; 1927--3,109,692; 1928--4,674,123; 1929--5,325,293. Thanks to contributions from the Maryland Bible Society, which had previously donated the Canal Zone headquarters, the Peiping (Peking) Bible House opened in 1928 as the first building erected by the ABS outside of American territory.

By 1932 some critics felt that the China Agency was moving too fast in "devolution," the appointment of Chinese, rather than Western, provincial secretaries and the active involvement of Chinese pastors in the work. On the other hand, new executives in London (both former China missionaries) recognized the importance of agreement on general policies. Thus in July, at the invitation of the BFBS, representatives of the British, Scottish, and American Societies gathered in London--

...to deal with the immediate practical relationships in China, South America, Levant and other points where contact of the Societies sometimes leads to friction, but not restricted to these items in opening the way to a full consideration of how the cooperation of the Societies can most further the Kingdom of God.

World-wide implications of this consultation will be discussed more fully in Chapter XV. In regard to the China situation, the Conference recommended closer cooperation among the three Agencies, "with a view to encouraging the formation of a China Bible Society which, having the same basic principles as the cooperating Societies, shall share with them in the world-wide work of the distribution of the Scriptures." Specifically, it urged the immediate formation of an Advisory Council in Shanghai, one-third to be appointed by each Society, its functions being "to consider and advise as to any questions of policy, method, or procedure."

Although, as ABS General Secretary Eric M. North observed much later, "it took much time and struggle to produce the practical results," these agreements represented "a major turning-point." The National Advisory Council was formed by the three Societies in 1933, the same year in which the ABS China Agency observed its centennial. Several Sub-Agencies were combined under single Secretaries, and the South China Bible Society appointed its first General Secretary. The British reiterated their invitation to share their headquarters in Shanghai, but the ABS and NBSS insisted on retaining a salesroom and East China office in the more strategically located Missions Building, in addition to pointing out that merging of stock--a great potential advantage-- would create chaos unless the three Societies could agree on a common title page. Should an organization selling 1,000 copies have its name (presumably in equal type!) on the title page with those who sell 15,000 or 20,000 copies of the same edition? That, wrote the American, "is a finicky quibble, that ought not to hold us up." Joint proof-reading and other editorial functions did finally gain approval.

As in Japan at a much earlier date, the rights and functions and powers of the Advisory Council came under dispute, even with the New York office, when it suggested that some annotations might be mutually acceptable. The Agency Secretary, in response to a mild rebuke, questioned the decision--

[To create a Council] and entrust to it certain duties and responsibilities, and then as soon as they show some tendency to act upon those instructions in a way that may become embarrassing to the Home Boards, or to offer a recommendation that goes contrary to your Home Board's wishes or principles, to raise an alarm cry and try to get the matter taken out of their hands.....The fact that you fear that the Council's recommendations might support the Glasgow point of view rather than the New York point of view is...not a sportsman's right to object to their making such recommentation....That was a risk that had to be taken.

When it came to indigenization instead of annotation, however, New York and Glasgow were in accord as opposed to London. In the light of the 1932 London agreements, the NBSS Agency Secretary declared, the "Parent Societies" "...must give the Chinese Bible Society perfect freedom to develop in its own way, even though it may eventually launch out on lines which the older societies cannot financially support; in which case we could make our contribution to the China Society in the form of scripture grants." On this principle, through a series of conferences and endless exchange of correspondence, a Draft Constitution of the Bible Society in China finally emerged. The officers in Scotland decided that "the church in China was not

ready for a Bible Society of the sort that was being proposed."
Because the British still insisted that a Chinese Secretary
should be assigned to limited cultivation and relations with the
Chinese community, rather than to share equally in administration,
the final document referred only to two "co-secretaries" (ABS and
BFBS). With numerous revisions the plan of merger to form a
China Bible House was approved by the Board of Managers in New
York in November, 1937. By then the wider implications were
largely academic, for China was engulfed in full-scale war.

Japan's seizure of Manchuria in 1931 had cut off that large,
prosperous, industrial section of China, and her attack on
Shanghai in early 1932 destroyed many Bible Society plates and
stocks. Throughout the 'thirties circulation went steadily
downward, due in part to the American depression as well as
Chinese turbulence, for the Agency continually reported demand
greater than the available supply of Scriptures. A successful
Colporteur Training Institute in 1935 emphasized actual selling
in both rural and urban settings, followed by critical discussion
of techniques. Improved transportation facilities throughout
the country made travel and book shipments much easier. In 1937,
the year when major fighting broke out in North China and quickly
spread, the Peiping Bible House sold more copies of Scriptures
than in any other year in its history. And a Chinese in
Manchuria wrote to ask for a copy of the Bible in English "if
it had yet been translated into that language."

The protracted war (1937-45) dislocated life on both sides of
the battle lines and caused irreparable damage to the economy,
to society, and to morale, as well as to physical and political
institutions. Those who remained in occupied areas faced
increasing shortages, of food and money, of paper and printing
facilities. Sensing impending emergency, but little anticipating
its extent, the Secretaries deposited duplicate plates in Manila
and Rangoon. The staff continued to function under grave difficulties until 1942, when all Westerners in Occupied China were
interned.

Conditions in Free China proved, in some respects, even more
desperate. The Chungking Bible House, dedicated in 1939, was
badly damaged by successive bombing raids a year later. Urgent
appeals for Scriptures brought twelve tons through the lines
from occupied cities, five tons by truck over the Burma Road from
India, at least one ton by air into an isolated region. For
awhile it was possible to print the entire Bible in Free China
despite shortages and inflation.

Exigencies of war (in Europe as well as Asia) forced progress
toward unification which had been impossible previously. In
1942 the "hold-out" Scottish Bible Society proposed, as a

working arrangement not a constitutional commitment, a union of the three Bible Societies on the following basis: BFBS forty-five per cent, ABS thirty-five per cent, NBSS twenty per cent. With an Advisory Council in Free China the three Societies achieved the most far-reaching practical merger to date, embracing stock, accounts, letterheads, etc. When the war was over, the NBSS approved an extension of the 1942 agreement, to unite with the China Bible House and to look forward to the creation of a China Bible Society. But post-war inflation, corruption and devastation combined with the Communist advance to nullify those plans. The two Advisory Councils (from previously Occupied and Free China) were merged; offices were opened or reopened in two dozen cities, including Manchuria and Taiwan; the China Bible House became one of the United Bible Societies.

Then came the third Revolution. The People's Democratic Republic embraced the entire mainland of China during 1949. For a time there seemed to be hope of relative religious freedom, divorced from any "imperialistic" ties. Some Christians were forced to burn their Bibles, but others (including the present writer) distributed large shipments of Scriptures to students, pastors, even occasional Communist soldiers, without interference. A villager from Shansi in the northwest carried two successive loads of Bibles, over a hundred pounds each, from the Bible House in Peiping to his home because the village was suffering from "a terrible dearth of Scriptures."

But the new nationalism demanded what Agency Secretary Lacy had pleaded for twenty-five years earlier, the appointment of a Chinese General Secretary. The China Bible House requested complete severance from its "Parent Societies" in 1951. Foreign-owned property was donated to the China Bible House, which would (or could?) accept it only as custodian. The last Western Bible Society representative, Ralph Mortensen, remained in Shanghai under virtual house arrest until 1953, and the following year his Chinese successor was arrested as a "counter-revolutionary."

Scripture circulation dropped by nearly one-half in 1952, to 65,466, due not only to political and propaganda pressures but also to administration reorganization, travel restrictions on colporteurs, the loss of schools and hospitals as institutional outlets, the destitution of churches and church members, and of course elimination of all foreign funds. The China Bible House undertook some printing and, in one comparatively lax period, demanded the right to export books for overseas Chinese instead of having them published in Hongkong. By 1958 Christians had to register their intention even to buy a Bible, and many, many copies were known to have been burned or torn up by the Red Guards during the Cultural Revolution after 1966.

Meanwhile the "Emergency Office" in Hongkong gradually sorted continuing China efforts into three areas: Hongkong, Taiwan, and Southeast Asia. The Hongkong Bible House (later the Bible Societies of Hongkong and Taiwan), under successive Scottish and British Secretaries, carried on translation and revision, not only in various Chinese dialects but for Vietnam, Mongolia, and Formosan tribes. In 1954 the Bible Book and Tract Depot relinquished its previous monopoly on Scripture distribution in Hongkong. In 1966 the old BFBS Auxiliary was converted into an Advisory Council with a three-fold task: to counsel the Secretary, to channel understanding and support from the churches for the Bible cause, and to prepare for future or further emergencies.

Across the straits in Formosa the influx of mainland refugees and missionaries outran the mission depots in Taipei and Tainan. In the early 1950's Madame Chiang Kai-shek, wife of the long-time President, ordered 160,000 Testaments for Nationalist soldiers, and the Gospel Crusade requested 1,750,000 copies of John's Gospel. The Bible Societies of Taiwan, under ABS supervision, separated from Hongkong in 1965. For nearly a decade, however, the Taiwan office had conducted its own active program, including special concern for lepers, the blind, seminarians, other students. It sponsored a Colporteur's Conference, a Bible Van, daily Scripture reading over the radio, a full-time secretary for women's work. In 1966, for its tenth anniversary--and the ABS' sesquicentennial--the Taiwan Agency announced an increase of forty-three per cent in distribution and forty-seven per cent in contributions over 1965.

Whatever the fluctuating political circumstances, no one working in Asia can be unmindful of the millions of Chinese people living in other nations to the south and east. The problem has been how best to minister to them. When Secretary Mortensen finally was allowed to leave Communist China, the American Bible Society assigned him as advisor for work among Chinese in Southeast Asia. A series of conferences in Cambodia, Vietnam, Thailand, Singapore, Malaysia, two in the Philippines, and seven in Taiwan examined methods and resources and personnel and programs which the Bible Society might use to provide Scriptures to these people, who speak many different dialects and are often caught between their own ethnic-linguistic traditions and the nationalistic pressures of their adopted lands. For the present, as the period of this history ends, Hongkong continues to serve as the center for work among Chinese, but Chinese Associates in other Agencies and Societies help to assure attention to the needs of this influential diaspora.

*   *   *   *   *

We are not trying to make Western-style Christians out of the Japanese. That's religious imperialism. We want to put the Word in the hands and minds of the people and let God speak to them through it. Perhaps it will lead the Japanese in ways Westerners will not understand.

The wise words of a Fraternal Secretary in 1961 have applied many times in the past, as they no doubt will apply in the future. For Bible efforts, like other Western relations with Japan, have alternately flourished and floundered as a proud, aggressive people have wrestled with their own inner tensions between rigid traditionalism and imitative adaptability. The Sino-Japanese War of 1895 opened doors, unprecedented in non-Christian countries, for Scripture distribution among Army and Navy personnel, in military hospitals and prisons--and circulation dropped by more than half the following year. The achievement of fifty-five per cent literacy at the turn of the century, from only twenty-five per cent literacy at the turn of the century, from only twenty-five per cent in 1860, coincided with a complete though temporary ban on any religious teaching in schools. The Russo-Japanese War of 1905 revealed Japan as a world power--and as a colonial empire. Eagerness for Western learning, science, and philosophy, produced alternate waves of enthusiasm and revulsion. Count Okuma, the Prime Minister who contributed to the ABS centennial volume on *The Influence of the Bible on the Civilized World*, was--almost at the same moment--attempting to exploit and dominate China through the infamous Twenty-One Demands, a virtual ultimatum calling for major Japanese influence in Chinese political and economic affairs. And the Bible became Japan's best-seller, in that centennial year of 1916, amid widespread agnosticism, militarism, and secularism.

Similar paradoxes afflicted Bible circulation. Because salesmen ranked low in Japan's social scale, few Christians were willing to "lose face" by selling books. In 1901 two foreign missionaries sold over half of the total distribution, although fifty Japanese were engaged in the effort part-time. Yet decades later, after World War II, when colportage had disappeared in many places or been relegated to remote regions, Japanese teams, systematically organized and directed and assigned, in both rural and urban areas, provided most of the domestic income for the Japan Bible Society. The Christian community, eager to possess the Scriptures for prestige or scholarship or even personal salvation, seldom grasped the evangelistic purpose or the essential interaction between Bible Societies and churches.

Relations among the Societies were also unusual. Compressed by geography and history into an early, contentious "togetherness" (see Chapter IX), the joint staffs and the Bible Committee for Japan had finally achieved a remarkable harmony of operation by the end of the nineteenth century. The chief disagreement seemed

to be whether colporteurs should be given salaries or only
commissions. But circulation sagged in the midst of soaring
opportunities, and the officers proposed a precise territorial
division of the main Japanese islands. Agreeing to continue
joint publication and common prices and discounts, haggling only
briefly over a few border prefectures, they assigned the north-
east (with Yokohama headquarters) to the Americans and the
southwest (with Kobe offices) to the British and Scottish,
working in this instance in apparently full accord. Separate
Advisory Councils replaced the Bible Societies Committee, but
they were to include British missionary representatives in the
north and Americans in the south. At the end of a three-year
trial period (1904-07) the ABS Agent reported: "There has been
no trouble in regard to the division of the territory and only
the pleasantest relations between the two agencies."

In the disastrous earthquake of 1923 the American Bible
Society suffered the greatest single loss in its history. The
Bible House, moved to the capital only four years earlier,
survived the seismic shock but succumbed to fires which raged for
hours and days. A Japanese clerk, years later to become the
first Japanese Secretary of the Society, saved the ledger, cash
box, and most vital records, carrying them on his back into the
suburbs and returning after the holocaust to leave a note at the
ruins: "To Mr. Aurell. Staff safe. Tanaka." Yokohama, where
headquarters had stood until 1919, was levelled to the ground,
and in that city, where most of the Agency's printing presses
were located, 15,000 Scripture plates literally melted away,
including many belonging to China, Siam, and the Philippines.

The Bible Society office in the south promptly shipped $500
worth of books and loaned three sets of plates for the printing
of new supplies in Kobe. In its first called meeting in twenty
years the ABS Board of Managers authorized immediate printing
in New York of half a million Japanese Gospels. These books,
plus 8,000 Bibles and Testaments, reached Japan within three
months of the tragedy, although chaos in landing, storage, and
handling delayed their delivery another three months. A special
campaign, focussing on Bible Sunday that year, raised over
$200,000 to meet the losses. This sum from the United States,
added to millions of dollars for other earthquake relief, helped
in some degree to counteract anti-American feeling generated the
following year by the U.S. "Oriental Exclusion" Immigration Bill.

Amid after-tremors, psychological as well as physical,
Scripture distribution continued to climb. The American Bible
Society marked its fiftieth anniversary in Japan by record
sales of 925,148, bringing the total in five decades to seven
million books. Colportage was stepped up, including a bicycle
brigade of nine men, three of whom over fifty years of age had

never ridden before. Circulation of Portions jumped from 491,364 in the four years before the quake to 2,858,948 in the quadrennium after it. Japanese became the second language, after English, in which the whole Bible was published in Braille. Sharing equally with the Gideons, the Society placed 300 English and 300 Japanese Bibles in the Imperial Hotel in Tokyo.

Meanwhile nationalistic pressures began to appear in subtle ways. The "merger plan" of 1890 had expressed the hope "that the Japanese Christians at no distant date will themselves under-take the work, or a large portion of it now carried on by the Foreign Bible Societies." When the New York office suggested to the Acting Agent in Tokyo that half the members of the new Advisory Committee might well be Japanese, he replied that that "would not add to the efficiency of the committee" and that two or three would be enough. In later years, however, the Society endeavored earnestly to encourage participation and support from the Christian community, with minimal success; then suddenly that foreign control became an excuse for Japanese indifference.

In 1930 the National Christian Council instructed its executive committee "to confer with the ABS and BFBS with a view to indigenizing the work of these organizations so that the Japanese Bible would no longer be handicapped by being labelled as a book published by foreign organizations." The Board of Managers in New York moved promptly to recommend an Advisory Committee "of whom a majority shall be Japanese," but the General Secretary hastened to assert, "Let no one think that this action was taken as a consequence of the action of the National Christian Council," and the committee actually appointed, on recommendation from its predecessor, consisted of two Japanese, two Americans, and one Britisher.

From the early 'thirties on, the juggernaut of nationalism and militarism rolled over every aspect of Japanese life. The year 1931 brought the invasion of Manchuria--and the largest Scripture circulation to date: over a million Portions plus 69,292 Bibles and Testaments. In a three-year mass movement Toyohiko Kagawa, a member of the first Bible Society Board of Directors, tried valiantly but vainly to steer his country toward the Kingdom of God instead of imperial conquest abroad.

The American Bible Society faced a dilemma. Genuine concern for indigenous leadership and local responsibility paralled the political necessity of the Japanese situation. The London Conference of 1932 had affirmed both nationalistic and supra-nationalistic aims: the establishment of national Bible Societies within a world federation. Yet the strong and vital-- if not large--Christian movement in Japan had shown meager

involvement in the task of Scripture distribution. In sharp
contrast to "the spontaneous interest of many Chinese," General
Secretary Eric North pointed out, "the Japanese Christians know,
as one pastor remarked, that the Bible came to them from God and
they have not been very conscious of intermediate processes."

Nevertheless autonomy was "coming, ready or not." In 1937,
just as war blazed furiously in China, the three "Parent Societies"
from their divided spheres formed a united Advisory Committee of
the Bible Societies in Japan, which led a year later to the
organization of a Japan Bible Society. Wrote one missionary
member: "In the present situation it will mean everything to the
cause of Bible distribution to have it known that a responsible
Japanese Bible Society has actually been formed and is at work...
altogether one of the most heartening events it has been my
fortune to have a part in since coming to Japan." Sixteen
Japanese, half of them laymen, and eight missionaries composed
the Board of Directors. The Constitution, designed "to encourage
the wider circulation of the Holy Scriptures...without note or
comment," made no reference to NBSS annotations.

For the moment the "Co-operating Societies" retained a large
measure of control by continuing their representatives as
Executive Secretaries of the JBS, by each appointing one
ex-officio member of the Board, and by apportioning indispensable
funds. "The work still to be done," Secretary North reminded his
constituency, "is beyond the capacities of all combined ." In
confirmation a colporteur described one of the growing army of
disabled soldiers who had returned from the China front:
Purchasing the four Gospels and Proverbs, the young veteran spoke
for countless Japanese over the next few years, "When I lost my
leg, I also seemed to lose heart in everything. I need to regain
my strength of mind through religion, and I am so glad you have
brought me the Christian books. I will read them and hope to
find comfort in their pages."

By 1940, allied with the Axis powers, Japan moved into an
"intractable position of extremism and militarism." Churches
were advised, urged, and then forced to renounce all foreign
control and support and to move simultaneously toward autonomy
and consolidation. The Diet (National Assembly) passed a bill
squeezing Buddhist, Shinto, and Christian religions into a
governmental mold--although *The New York Times* correspondent may
have presumed too much in reporting that "the Department of
Education henceforth would tell missionaries what to believe and
preach."

The Bible Society found itself almost the sole Christian
organization without a Japanese chief executive, yet ordered to
get rid of all foreign influence immediately. The "Parent

Societies" moved fast to transfer stocks and plates and buildings
to the Japanese, although the JBS did not acquire legal status
until 1949. No remittances from abroad could be received after
mid-1941. The faithful chief clerk became Secretary of the Japan
Bible Society. For awhile the organization was granted top
priority for rationed paper, but other materials for printing
were desperately short. Consequently, before long, colportage
and publishing ceased entirely; operating the Bible House and
continuing revision of the Old Testament remained the Japan Bible
Society's sole war-time functions.

V-J Day found the Bible House in Tokyo miraculously intact
except for some fire damage on two floors, but eighty per cent of
Japan's publishing facilities had been destroyed. An estimated
one-fifth of 1943 paper supplies, fifteen per cent of binding
materials, practically no glue or twine remained; in fact, one
of the early post-war shipments from the ABS included pencils,
letterheads, wrapping paper, and office equipment. In a massive
project which required more paper than any other edition of
Scriptures in history, the War Emergency Fund provided 150,000
Japanese Bibles and 1,100,000 Testaments in 1946-47. When the
Allied Occupation turned over a naval printing press to the
Japan Bible Society, the ABS sent 105 tons of paper, in addition
to 240 tons produced locally, for the resumption of Scripture
publication. As it turned out, however, the press was not
suitably equipped to print Bibles. By 1948 the Bible ranked
ninth among "best-sellers" in Japan; the Society manufactured
3,900 Braille volumes; at the end of that year total post-war
circulation (over forty months) had surpassed 3,500,000 copies,
compared to an annual distribution of 100,000 before the war.

That was just a beginning. The Tanaka Plan, launched by the
JBS General Secretary, called for publishing and circulating ten
million Scriptures in the next three years, 1949-1950-1951.
Informed of the goal, General Douglas MacArthur, the Supreme
Commander, exulted: "That is magnificent, magnificent. The
Bible is the essential Book in helping towards the moral and
spiritual recovery of Japan."

In each prefecture (or county) a colporteur-in-chief gathered
a team of volunteers, advised by a local committee of laymen and
pastors. Among paid employees roughly one-third were pastors
needing to supplement their microscopic salaries; one-third were
repatriates from Manchuria, China, and Korea; one-third were
dedicated laymen and laywomen from the churches. Although
Portions naturally accounted for preponderant sales, circulation
for 1950 (66,530 above the goal of three million) included more
New Testaments (671,009) than the number of known Christians in
Japan. For the entire period the campaign fell sixteen per cent
short of its target (approximately 8,358,000 volumes, but it was

indeed a "magnificent" undertaking whose far-flung impact on Japan can never be measured.

Dreadful though the bombing devastation had been, defeat left deeper, more slowly healing scars on the minds and souls of the Japanese people. Perhaps it was not surprising, then, that the Bible Society recovered physically and financially, with foreign aid, while basic internal problems remained. One of these concerned relations and attitudes toward the "Parent Societies." General MacArthur cabled to the ABS in 1948: "American resident representative needed in Japan and fervently desired by local Society for aid in permanent promotional program so that message will reach every village and hamlet in the land."

During the "reconstruction" period such a Fraternal Secretary --and membership in the United Bible Societies--were welcomed, if not quite "fervently desired." But when the Occupation ended, the "growing pains" of independence became more obvious. Budgets were irresponsibly overdrawn; the Bible House, which should provide lucrative rent, was mismanaged. Certain staff members regarded the Fraternal Secretary as a "watch-dog" sent to spy on them. A newly established Foreign Department set out to culti- vate direct donations from abroad, in defiance of the UBS pledge not to compete with Societies in other countries.

The second problem concerned relationships to the churches and to the missionary cause of the Bible. After a decade of euphoria it became clear that Japan was not turning en masse to Christianity, that phenomenal Scripture circulation was not reflected in church membership, that the Christian community was more involved in factional disputes and structural reorganization than in evangelism. Still more distressing, the Bible Society seemed to share this unconcern for active outreach. Occasional inquiries about methods of promotion and distribution elsewhere produced little innovation. A thorough study of Scripture Demand and Strategy in Japan, carried out in 1960 by an exceptional team of Japanese and missionaries at the request of the United Bible Societies, confirmed observations made by ABS officers for years: that the Japan Bible Society still made inadequate use of mass media, of the student market, of church support. The goal of a Bible for every church, a New Testament for every inquirer, appeared more than adequate to many of the staff, though it fell far short of the world-wide Bible Society purpose. Prices were kept high to cover expenses instead of low to reach the masses. Of cultivation in local congregations the General Secretary remarked: "Gathering money is an action just like a beggar." Even the translation and revision team, which had labored faith- fully throughout the war, showed more interest in its scholarly reputation than in improving the *kana* (phonetic script) and *Kogotai* (colloquial) versions for popular, modern use.

All this posed for the American Bible Society, now representing the U BS in fraternal supervision, some acute dilemmas,
dilemmas which emerged all over the post-war world but in
particularly delicate form among the proud, sensitive Japanese.
How does any international organization walk the precarious
tightrope between responsible stewardship of resources and
paternalistic interference with partners or brothers? Secretary
North in discussing the withdrawal of a Fraternal Secretary
pointed out that the ABS sought no intervention in Japanese
affairs but did covet a continuation of international fellowship.

Jealously-guarded independence is understandable; two other
circumstances proved more perplexing: first, financial
ineptitude and administrative conservatism in a land so noted
for progressive and aggressive science and industry; second, a
seeming reluctance to accept the wider missionary, or evangelistic, purpose of Bible distribution. Whatever the reasons, by
1964 conservative evangelical groups, largely ignored by the
Japan Bible Society, were threatening to form a separate
organization, which would be a calamitous backward step in the
world-wide task of sharing the Good News. In contrast to most
other fields, the ABS approached its sesquicentennial acknowledging that "the present situation in the Bible Society is crucial"
and that "the future program of our work in Japan may be problem-
atical." Yet it reaffirmed, in spirit and in faith, the
quotation at the beginning of this section.

*   *   *   *   *

"In no mission field, ancient or modern, has the Bible had a
more early, constant, powerful and fruitful influence than in
Korea," declared *The Bible Society Record* of November, 1916.
Although the ABS sent Scriptures into the Hermit Kingdom before
the first Protestant missionaries, and subsidized their earliest
translation efforts, it elected to administer the work from the
Japan Agency through missionary representatives. This indirect
supervision and support caused much of subsequent misunderstanding and criticism. By 1900 the BFBS and the NBSS had moved in
in greater force, directing all colportage in the country.
British and American missionaries, concerned primarily for their
own Board of Translators, set up a Permanent Executive Bible
Committee (which the American Society rejected), then asked the
Societies to assume responsibility for publication and distribu-
tion--but not translation. For four years (1904-08) a so-called
joint agency attempted to operate under three agents, three
policies, three fiscal calendars, plus missionary advisers.
When the BFBS and the local Committee urged the Societies to
work through one Secretary, the Americans decided to carry on
independently, while the Scots withdrew from the field, leaving
all the colporteurs and Bible women and bookstores under British
control.

There were other points of friction besides the administrative structure. The ABS supplied books to American missionaries in Manchuria and discussed opening direct work among Japanese there, though the British regarded that as exclusive territory. The ABS started a competitive bookstore in Pyongyang. The ABS believed that paying colporteurs a regular salary regardless of sales encouraged laziness, waste, and even fraud. The ABS too generously subsidized an independent Baptist missionary and his colporteurs, who ignored the long-standing Methodist-Presbyterian comity agreements. The ABS, supervised from Japan, appeared to many missionaries to be less responsive to Korean needs and desires than the British representatives.

Amid growing dissatisfaction, the options seemed to be four: to continue increasingly abrasive competition, to divide the territory, to withdraw entirely, or to contribute on a pro-rated basis to a joint program under a single Agent. Significantly, most American missionaries as well as others favored the fourth procedure, but the New York office--which later accepted such reciprocal arrangements in many parts of the world--would not consent. Twice, in 1912 and 1917, the ABS offered to exchange exclusive rights in Korea for exclusive rights in the Philippines, though the former was larger and more receptive to evangelical missions. Twice the British refused, once offering Colombia instead of the Philippines, and then abruptly in 1919 it was done. Each Society donated its printing plates to the other; stocks were appraised and purchased--except that worn or damaged books were to be given free for distribution to prisoners! A news release of January 30, 1919, hailed the transfer as "an interesting illustration of the mutual good feeling existing between Great Britain and America in the religious and missionary world."

Korea itself, as a political entity, shared this confusion of jurisdiction. Japanese influence in schools, railways, financial investments, and even government departments grew steadily. The Russo-Japanese War of 1904-05, mediated by President Theodore Roosevelt at Portsmouth, New Hampshire, tipped the scales not only against Russian domination but against effective rule by the Korean monarchy. The formal annexation of Chosen (renamed) as a colony of Japan in 1910 seemed to expand the people's thirst for moral and spiritual sustenance. Officials welcomed colporteurs who carried Scriptures--but woe to spies and other false agents who could not pass the test of reading their books or of singing Christian hymns. During these years of transition the Korean New Testament was published in 1900 and the full Bible in 1911; ABS circulation in not quite two decades of this century totalled 2,652,133 volumes. For twenty-seven years under BFBS administration Korea dropped out of American Bible Society reports, but by the time the Korean Bible Society was formed in

1940, it had become fifth among nations where the Bible was a "best seller."

Although V-J Day brought hope of independence to the Korean people, that dream was not to be realized; instead of an international trusteeship, military occupation divided the country geographically and ideologically. Bible activity had been completely suspended for nearly four years, and the British were in no position to undertake reconstruction around the world. Recognizing a moral obligation to assist any struggling national Bible societies, the ABS delivered 50,000 Korean New Testaments through U.S. Army chaplains. The Bible Committee reconvened in 1946, composed of eight missionaries, eight delegates from churches or religious organizations, and eight representatives of Bible supporters. Pre-war stocks were still intact--for the Japanese had hesitated to commit Holy Scriptures to waste paper supplies as originally planned--but they were totally inadequate to meet demands. Most of Korea's printing presses were located in the industrial north under Communist control, but the KBS managed to publish 10,000 Testaments and 25,000 Portions, plus an edition of Braille Scriptures on the stiff paper of old ledgers. Meanwhile they sent a plea to America for 250,000 Bibles, 200,000 Testaments, 50,000 English Testaments and 15,000 Russian Testaments. One missionary raised half the cost of supplying a Gospel to every home in the port city of Pusan; the Korean Bible Society provided the balance.

Then came war again! The burning of the Bible House in Seoul in 1950 destroyed the Secretary's residence, tons of paper, half a million volumes of Scripture, and several valuable manuscripts. The Hankul Bible (in new phonetic script) was being printed at the time. Four hundred pages were lost in the press and had to be rewritten. The rest of the manuscript, guarded by the Korean General Secretary more lovingly than his own belongings, hidden for a time in pickle crocks, finally reached the refugee enclave at Pusan. Eventually he carried them to Japan for the manufacture of plates, back to Pusan for the actual printing (with a total of eight proofreadings), and publication in October, 1952. Meanwhile chaplains brought in truckloads of Bibles and Testaments, some of them shared with Christian brethren in the north during the brief weeks of United Nations liberation there. Amidst incredible confusion, devastation, and suffering, Koreans distributed over 1,000,000 Scriptures in 1951, double those for the previous year.

The Armistice, which settled little politically, gave respite which was eagerly seized by the Bible Society as well as other South Koreans. Most of the staff returned to Seoul and partially rebuilt the Bible House, although new headquarters were not completed until 1970. Rural Christians, virtually without cash,

paid for their Scriptures with rice and soybeans and eggs and--
on one trip--six brooms and 455 feet of rice-straw rope. Conferences were held for colporteurs, school chaplains, seminary
presidents, leaders of any group that might effectively dispense
the Good News. Office workers labored so ultra-faithfully that
they had to be threatened with fines for working overtime, and
for years the General Secretary could not be persuaded to share
responsibility--or trust--for the challenging task confronting
the Society. Bible Sunday offerings climbed.

By 1960, when student demonstrations overthrew President
Syngman Rhee with political repercussions in staff and Executive
Committee, Scripture circulation once more passed a million, the
only publication in Korean history to do so. When the Advisory
Committee asked permission to publish the Apocrypha, the BFBS
refused, but ABS General Secretary Laton E. Holmgren replied
that the Korean Bible Society was a sovereign, independent
Society with the right to make its own decisions: "If [it] is
needed to enable you the better to fulfill your task in Korea,
we think you should proceed to publish it."

All this initiative and energy contrasted sharply with Bible
work across the Yellow Sea. In a four-year drive to get 3,000
Life Members, the Korean Bible Society enrolled 3,800; ten years
earlier Japanese Supporting Members numbered only 300. With
more than three and a half times as large a population, circulation figures in Japan for 1960 were only eighty per cent higher
than Korea's. More recently, to be sure, the Korean Bible
Society has been caught in denominational schisms and conservative trends. Invidious comparisons are often unprofitable and
unfair, and contributing factors are complex and immeasurable.
Yet the contrast in vitality, in enthusiasm, in commitment to
the missionary purpose of the Bible Society, between Korea and
its neighbor and erstwhile ruler is worthy pointing out, if only
to prove that success in Scripture distribution is not determined
simply by environment, political or economic or cultural.

*   *   *   *   *

Although the final decision in 1918 to swap Korea for the
Philippines appeared to be sudden, the matter had been raised
intermittently for almost two decades. The British and Foreign
Bible Society had tried to penetrate the Philippine archipelago
during Spanish rule; a representative was expelled from there in
1889. Americans had occasionally smuggled shipments of Spanish
Scriptures through a tight Roman Catholic wall. In 1898 the
Spanish-American War dropped the islands into U.S. hands so
abruptly that President William McKinley admitted that he had
to look up their location on the globe because he "could not
have told where those darned islands were within 2,000 miles."(1)

The ABS moved cautiously in sending China Agent John Hykes to investigate the situation and the prospects. Thus, by the time an American Agent, in response to Hykes' favorable recommendation, arrived in Manila via London, Suez, and Shanghai, a British Agent had been on the scene for three months. The initial appointment in New York stressed "the hope that arrangements will be made to guard against competition, and competitive methods of procedure," but that was not to be. The two representatives agreed on a tentative division based, unlike any other situation, on languages and translation projects rather than geography or missionary affiliation. But the British monopolized certain presses, salesmen inevitably traversed the same districts, derogatory reports spread wildly. At least as early as 1902 the New York officers informed London of their readiness to assume responsibility for the entire field. On the basis of government and of missionary personnel, the Manila Agent wrote indignantly, "there is no more reason for their [BFBS] being here...than for being in New York." Suggestions of exchanging North Africa or Egypt, where English interests were clearly dominant, fell on deaf British ears.

Despite protestations to the contrary, differences continued: in discount rates, in sales policies, in personal relationships. After a very cordial conference in 1911 with the British Agent in China (who oversaw the Sub-Agency in Manila), the American representative in the Philippines put the problem in broader perspective:

I wish we could unite. Union is in the air here. The Missions must soon meet it. If the Missionaries cannot get together the Filipinos will go ahead of them and unite. And if that movement is coming surely we Bible Societies ought to be in the forefront and not tagging behind. So we plan to work in harmony as much as possible, not only harmony of spirit but harmony of plans as well.

Five months later the ABS learned that the BFBS planned to erect a Bible House in Manila, and promptly registered strong official protest, that such "a permanent establishment" in "a part of the United States" would violate "mutual relations which have hitherto been carefully observed" and prove that "comity has apparently failed." In 1913 the British emphatically rejected a proposal for Joint Agencies, in Seoul under the BFBS, in Manila under the ABS. Claiming that American missionaries in the Philippines wanted them to stay, and that "delimitation of territory cannot always be determined on national lines," the British criticized the American Society for not using colporteurs and for selling Selections "as tickets of admission to a cinematograph exhibition." In October, 1917, the BFBS General Committee "came to the unanimous conclusion that it was not in the interests of God's Kingdom that the British and Foreign Bible Society should leave the Philippines." Yet thirteen months later, apparently at British initiative, the exchange was ratified, so unexpectedly that the American Agent was on furlough in the United States.

There had indeed been divergent policies and practices, some of them frankly experimental. The ABS did abandon for a long period the use of native colporteurs, as one Temporary Agent believed that the Filipino "for three centuries [had been] trained in deceit till he is a past master in graft and crooked deals of every sort" and regards it as "a game," as his "legitimate prerogative," to "beat the Society." The same Temporary Agent did allow Filipinos under missionary supervision to sell books along with teaching and preaching responsibilities, aware that "this is not orthodox with the Society, but it seems to meet the conditions here, which are certainly peculiar." However the first Philippines Agent, apparently in advance of other fields, proposed that the Society appoint a linguistics expert to superintend several translations, using native helpers rather than relying on missionaries who lacked technical training for such work.

Another Agent did hold picture shows--of Bible story films-- and require the purchase of a Portion (NOT, he insisted, just Selections!) as the price of admission. His exultant "Say, but it is exciting!" might have applied to public response--or to his vigorous methods of excluding any "free" audience: When some fellows climbed a scaffolding to peek, "I gave several ones some good stiff blows...with a good bamboo stick....At another place I had to pick up a chap and souse him in the mud outside to teach him a lesson. It succeeded." "Such stringent measures," while not ordinary, did "add zest to things;" his missionary companion, he reported, was "wildly enthusiastic over the results of the trip," and they sold fifty per cent more books than the BFBS Sub-Agent had sold in the same region two years before!

Despite that one lurid account, that particular Agent was basically committed to systematic coverage of an area rather than "indiscriminate sales," and the traveling picture-lecture method remained in popular demand for two or three decades; to it he attributed a four hundred per cent increase in distribution for 1914. By that time, also, the entire Bible had been translated into two Filipino languages, the New Testament into three others, and Portions into an additional two. Unfortunately *all* printing for the Islands was being done in Japan. Thus the earthquake of 1923 destroyed thousands of Bibles, plates or molds for seven different Bibles and two Testaments, and much paper belonging to the Philippine Agency. In terms of replaceability the New York office estimated the $70,000 loss as greater than that of the

Japan Agency itself. Without books, colportage and grants had to
be discontinued, circulation in 1924-25 combined fell short of
1923, and work from Manila was only "approaching normal" by the
end of 1925.

A travelling library with amplified phonograph music drew
large crowds. An American colporteur bravely navigated an
eighteen-foot sailboat through typhoons along the coast of
Mindanao--and ironically died years later in an automobile
accident. Scripture displays drew attention at colorful fiestas
--in spite of recurrent opposition from Roman Catholic priests.
As late as 1939 children in Zamboanga were encouraged to bring
Protestant literature, including the Bible, to school for a
public bonfire. As in Korea and elsewhere, rural purchasers
bartered rice, beans, rope, sardines, coconut husks for fuel,
in return for the precious Word.

Back in 1923 the ABS Agent voiced his conviction that "someday
--maybe twenty or forty years from now, or sooner, we must
organize a Philippine Bible Society that will be largely self-
supporting, with its own membership, officers, etc. We will never
make much headway in getting support here until we do that." But
his preliminary proposal for a local committee found little
support. Ten years later the New York office initiated a similar
inquiry, and the Agent suggested that a Cooperating Committee
might be representative of language areas rather than denominations or missions.

The problem of active church support loomed large. In 1933
only 69 out of nearly 200 missionaries bought any Scriptures, and
only 61 out of 600 pastors. By 1941 circulation reached a new
high--and so did preparation for impending war. When invasion
did come, Secretary W. H. Fonger was interned apart from his
family; his "fortitude and courage" as a camp leader earned a
"ribbon" from General Douglas MacArthur, but his teen-age son
died of malaria in camp. With similar irony, much of the damage
to the Bible House probably came from American bombing, and many
of the printing plates which survived the war were stolen
shortly thereafter.

In the immediate post-war years the Philippines received
their Independence (1946), the Bible House was rebuilt (1947),
the United Church of Christ in the Philippines got under way
(1948), the Agency observed its Fiftieth Jubilee (1949). (The
merger of Presbyterian, Congregationalist, Independent,
Philippine, Methodist, Disciples of Christ, Evangelical United
Brethren, and several indigenous churches to form the United
Church of Christ in the Philippines produced the largest Protestant body in the islands and an influential "model" of church
union in Asia.) A conscientious Advisory Committee,

reconstituted in 1952 to coordinate Bible work, reported the publication of a Roman Catholic New Testament in Tagalog, recommended original promotional materials and participation in the coming International Fair, requested an automatic film-strip machine for displays, and pointed out certain inaccuracies in current translations. Nine years later, with an initiative lacking in many other fields, the Advisory Committee announced its readiness "to assume responsibility for the administration of a National Bible Society if and when an opportunity is offered by the ABS," and proposed in the meantime to establish regional chapters or auxiliaries which would encourage and "intensify" the work and program of the Bible House in remote places.

In 1956 the Society appointed a Filipino Associate Secretary, who became Agency Secretary the following year. Serving with him was an American business manager (later called Fraternal Secretary) to handle some of the complex problems of taxation, import licenses, duty, etc. The Fraternal Secretary withdrew in 1964, and in the sesquicentennial year of 1966 a completely indigenous Philippine Bible Society became a full member of the United Bible Societies.

In sponsoring an annual Asia Bible Study Week, in organizing a department for Women's Work, in reaching out with evangelistic concern to leper colonies, prisons, orphanages, hospitals, and schools, in urging local churches to enlist volunteers or to sponsor paid colporteurs, the Philippine Bible Society has demonstrated its coming-of-age. For few countries in the world is it more surprising to report that since 1966 Roman Catholics have not only joined the Board of Directors, but participated actively in translation, revision, *and distribution* programs. For the three years which terminate this report, 1965-67, total distribution in the Philippines passed the million mark, even though in those last five years Selections (which represent the preponderant circulation in many areas) ran far below Portions, not much above the combined figure for Bibles and Testaments. This is itself is indicative of vitality and commitment, rather than merely an exuberant scattering of the Seed.

NOTES

1.   Thomas A. Bailey, *A Diplomatic History of the American People*. (New York: 1940) p. 517.

14

"Now In Common Use"

A missionary translator in the past quarter century, when told that an African pastor could not understand a New Testament passage which he had translated, declared that the African undoubtedly "lacked spiritual understanding." Perhaps so, for what Christian brings perfect insight to the "wonderful words of Life"? But Eugene A. Nida, ABS Executive Secretary for Translations, maintains: "If a rendering is consistently misunderstood by the majority of persons for whom a translation has been prepared, then it obviously is not a faithful equivalent, regardless of how much it may formally resemble the original" (*The Bible Society Record*, March, 1971, p. 49).

The American Bible Society has labored for 150 years to provide the Scriptures for men and women and children in their own languages. It rejoiced when the Bible became literally "the Book of a thousand tongues." In recent years, with courage and vision born of its central purpose, it has not only revised its Constitution to offer different versions of the Scriptures, but it has sought fresh idioms and the latest linguistic science to proclaim Good News for modern man.

This has not always been so. As earlier chapters have indicated, there were those who maintained that only the English language could adequately express theological concepts, or that "national" languages (in China, Burma, Thailand, and elsewhere) should supersede tribal tongues. More numerous and more vocal have been those who believed that the King James Version alone represents the authentic inspired Word of God, and for nearly a century the policy of the Society acceded to this point of view.

Successive Boards of Managers and officers and committees have
wrestled with such vital questions as how to get new, accurate,
meaningful texts accepted by strongly partisan traditionalists,
or how to maintain a creative balance between classical styles
or vocabularies and modern, colloquial, "living" speech. Nor do
these questions any longer pertain exclusively either to English
or to foreign versions; both share the need for sacred expression
in popular language.

At the outset of Scripture publication all "editors"--be they
hired proof-readers, ministerial examiners, or textual scholars--
based their judgments of accuracy not only on the Authorized
(King James) Version, but on BFBS editions. Translations from
the highly respected Vulgate Bible were discontinued after 1842
as being too Roman Catholic; in fact, one Methodist missionary
among the American Indians wrote in 1828 of "the chains of papist
superstition" as being "far worse" than paganism. Yet that same
translator was appealing for the Society to take a chance on
publishing preliminary, unverified manuscripts in Indian tongues
rather than to wait for some authoritative text. As late as
1889, in response to requests from Agents Isaac Bliss in the
Levant and Hugh Tucker in Brazil, the Versions Committee
authorized its representatives "to purchase and circulate any
of the versions published by the BFBS where they are deemed more
acceptable than our own."

Gradually, however, even the most conservative scholars came
to recognize that the King James Version contained some errors
or inconsistencies, in translation as well as typography, that
certain spellings had become obsolete, and that no absolute
uniformity existed even as a standard. Therefore in 1847 the
ABS Board of Managers instructed the Versions Committee to undertake a new collation of various editions "in common use" in order
to eliminate discrepancies. Articles, plurals, capitals, hyphens,
italics, these could be handled fairly simply--and usually with
appeal to one acceptable authority or another.

The acute problem arose in regard to "accessories" to the
text. The very first ABS edition, following the Philadelphia
Bible Society precedent, included chapter headings found in the
Authorized Version. Soon afterwards came requests for fuller
summaries of the text, regarded as especially useful for
families without a concordance. A Unitarian clergyman protested
that any such addition was a violation of the "fundamental
article" on which diverse groups supported the Bible Society.
Many other widely divergent denominations and sects acknowledged
that summaries did represent theological interpretations,
whether or not one agreed with the particular doctrine implied,
and that such "accessories" might well be regarded as erroneous
or defective, theologically or textually.

Two conspicuous examples were references to the Church and to Christ in titles for pages in the Song of Solomon, and a 1611 heading for Psalm 49, which read: "An earnest persuasion to build the faith in resurrection, not on worldly power." Obviously both of these represented New Testament interpolations on the Old Testament, interpolations which could not be unequivocally supported from the text. In these particular instances, the Versions Committee substituted "spouse" and "bride" for "Christ" and "Church" and identified Psalm 49 as follows: "The Psalmist calleth upon all men to hear. He sheweth the vanity of trusting in wealth." Thus the amended language as well as the interpretation corresponded more closely to the original version.

In actual fact, the Versions Committee made very few such changes, apart from minuscule corrections. In 1851 the Board approved the committee's recommendations and in 1854 voted to make this revision the ABS Standard edition. Despite advance notice of these minor editorial alterations, it was five years after the first copies appeared before vehement protests erupted. Scattered complaints objected, quite naturally, to individual changes, but the major attacks centered on the presumption of the American Bible Society to tamper in *any* way with the Word of God. Even many loyal supporters said, to quote only one: "Who authorized you to do any such thing? Grant there are errors of translation, obsolete words, and objectionable phrases, was not your Society organized with express purpose to publish and circulate *that Book* as it now is?"

On motion of the Versions Committee itself, the chairman of the Board appointed a select Committee of Nine, distinguished scholars and churchmen, to review the entire matter. With one dissenting vote, that Committee of Nine recommended that no alterations should be made in either text or accessories which could not be directly authorized by previous editions; in other words, that no revision whatever should be made without earlier precedent. The lone minority voice was that of the Rev. Richard S. Storrs, pastor of the (Congregational) Church of the Pilgrim in Brooklyn for over fifty years, editor of *The Independent* from 1848 to 1861, president of the American Board of Commissioners for Foreign Missions from 1888 to 1897. "Sound in judgment, responsible in speech, orthodox in belief, he was one of the most trusted men of his day."[1] Courageously and independently, Storrs advocated such textual changes as might win the *"unanimous consent of Christian scholars affirming their intrinsic correctness"* and the alteration of headings and chapter contents "with a view to make them at once full and concise, more strictly and manifestly biblical in tone, and more thoroughly pervaded by the antique but perennial spirit of the version."

Hurt by the apparent repudiation of their years of labor, all the members of the Versions Committee resigned except the

chairman, Gardiner Spring, one of the "Founding Fathers" of the
Society. Their successors in a new committee adopted the uncon-
tested textual corrections, restored the original chapter headings, and affirmed the Society's responsibility--one step
behind the Constitution itself--to publish the Authorized
Version only "as it has been and is in common use." Public
sentiment divided sharply over the issue, probably leaning
toward the side of tradition. The Maryland Bible Society
expressed its approval of the "revised" ABS Standard Bible of
1861 (approved in 1859 to replace the version of 1854) by
donating $1,000. At least one contributor "on the other side"
defiantly sent $500 for copies of the "original" Standard
Version, but the money was returned as unacceptable for a
project then deemed inconsistent with Society policy.

For over seventy years, until 1932, no further efforts were
made to modify the Authorized Version. In reply to a correspondent, Assistant Secretary James H. McNeill expressed his
conviction in 1858 that "our Board never did a wiser thing"
than when it rescinded its previous endorsement. "That action,"
he continued, "has relieved the public mind, restored confidence,
and greatly strengthened the hold which the Soc'y has ever had
upon the affections of the Christians of this land." But in a
somewhat wistful final paragraph, he added:

> The time may come when a revision will be practicable and
> necessary; and when that time shall have come, then will be
> found a way in which the work can be done without trouble
> or danger--Meantime we have enough to do in supplying the
> vast destitutions even of our own land, which are neglected
> while we quarrel over versions!

It was unfortunate that relatively minor revisions should
founder over the issue of the Society's role and responsibility.
It was particularly ironic that the precipitating article of
protest frankly claimed the Protestant Episcopal Church as the
official guardian of the King James Bible, while scorning the
conceit of the ABS in assuming a role as "divine keeper and
witness of Holy Writ." As early as 1835 the president of the
Society at that time, John Cotton Smith, a former Governor of
Connecticut, had taken a diametrically opposite position, arguing
that the Bible Society *should* be the natural and logical agency
for correlating and editing Scriptural texts, not simply for
publishing and distributing them. "It is most devoutly to be
wished," he wrote, "that Christians of all denominations would
unite in encouraging and aiding the exclusive issues...from a
single establishment.....Will any one deny that the American
Bible Society is precisely such an establishment?"

After the controversy of the 1850's, Bible revisers on both
sides of the Atlantic moved cautiously. A committee of American

scholars in communication with their British counterparts met in the Bible House at Astor Place, New York, and availed themselves of the Society's library resources in examining revisions under consideration in Great Britain. Yet both before and after the publication of the English Revised Version in 1881, the ABS Board of Managers announced that it had "no authority to publish it nor is it expedient to take steps to amend the ABS constitution" to make such an American edition possible. Ostensibly the hesitation arose from doubts about the quality of revision, as well as the constitutional restriction to the Authorized Version. Yet the very next year the ABS notified translators that they were permitted to adopt any deviations "sanctioned or suggested" by either the English or American Revision Committees of 1881.

Still more important, the English Revised Version of the New Testament achieved an incredible sale of 800,000 copies in New York alone on the first day of publication, a record which could not be ignored by the American Society. Increasingly, liberal church groups in the United States urged the ABS either to issue the English Revision or to produce a comparable American version. From Turkey an American Board missionary demanded:

Is it not the privilege of the Bible Society to step to the front in this matter, and get up a movement which shall result in the appointment of a small Committee of capable men, who shall go over the whole ground, utilize the best results of revision labor, and of all the criticism on it, and secure a version which shall be an acceptable standard for another 300 years? I know that this involves a radical change of base for the society, but is not this an absolute necessity? and if it is not done will not the Soc. be ultimately superseded by another?

Still the ABS followed a "wait and see" policy, pointing out that neither in England nor in the United States did the Revised Version have official sponsorship from the Bible Societies. When the American Standard Version (a modest revision of the English Revised Version) finally appeared in 1901, it was printed by Thomas Nelson and Sons and distributed as a commercial venture. Within three years, however, pressure for the Bible Society to issue and circulate this new edition proved irresistible. Contrary to the experience of fifty years earlier, certain church groups and even some newspapers denounced the Society for being too cautious in its policy, for alleged antagonism to the new text. Extensive consultations were held with legal advisers and denominational leaders. Even those who did not approve of the new translation seemed reluctant to prohibit it to others, although no one at that time favored total removal of restrictions on acceptable versions. By constitutional amendment adopted on April 5, 1904, Article I was altered to read as follows:

...The only copies in the English language, to be circulated by the Society, shall be [instead of "of the version
now in common use"] of the version set forth in 1611 and
commonly known as the King James Version, whether in its
original form as published in the aforesaid year or as
revised, the New Testament in 1881 and the Old Testament
in 1885, and published in these years under the supervision
of the Committee of Revision, or as further revised and
edited by the American Committee of Revision and printed
under its supervision in 1901.

Only one serious dispute developed over this particular
version. John 9:38 includes the sentence: "And he worshipped
him." The footnote to the verb read: "The Greek word denotes
an act of reverence whether paid to a creature (as here) or to
the Creator (see ch. 4.20)." Two tiny parenthetical words contained a hornets' nest of Christological controversy: Was Jesus
here to be designated as a creature in contradistinction to the
Creator?

The practical issue, however, was not doctrinal, for the Bible
Society could have avoided sectarian interpretations by simply
deleting the parenthetical phrase, leaving the footnote as a
purely linguistic explanation. The problem was whether those two
words, "(as here)," *could* be omitted from the American Standard
Version without violating the Constitution of the Society, which
bound itself to the text as given. Permission of the printers
and the copyright holders to delete the phrase did not relieve
the Society of its constitutional dilemma. Although it voted in
1924 to omit the parenthetical phrase, the words continued to
appear in subsequent editions until the entire footnote was
dropped in editorial revisions of 1932.

Similar decisions confronted the Society in relation to the
Revised Standard Version, also printed by Thomas Nelson and Sons
and copyrighted by the (present) Division of Christian Education
of the National Council of the Churches of Christ in the United
States of America. New Testament sales of 800,000 copies in the
first year, with the first printing sold out on publication day
(February 11, 1946), hardly competed with the record of the English
Revised Version sixty-five years before. Yet the significance
of such widespread, popular acceptance could not fail to affect
ABS policy. In 1951, just prior to the publication of the RSV
Old Testament, the American Bible Society amended Article I of
its Constitution to add: "...and the New Testament of the
Revised Standard Version first issued in 1946."

Although this "crack in the door" was opened only after full
consultation with the representative Advisory Council and was
passed with only one dissenting vote, it provoked thousands of

letters of protest, some in ignorance, some in anger, some in opposition to the source of the new text rather than the language itself. The ABS assured its constituents that it continued to publish the King James Version (2,000,000 Bibles, 3,000,000 Testaments, 25,000,000 Gospels in five years, 1948-52), and that gifts could be restrictively designated for one version or another.

In 1952 the American Bible Society issued the Gospels and Acts in RSV Portions, and the following year Matthew, Mark, and John in illustrated copies, partly at the urging of the armed forces. Publication of the complete RSV Bible in 1952, coupled with the announcement that Thomas Nelson and Sons would not retain exclusive rights after ten years, opened new opportunity and new obligation for the Bible Society.

Therefore a further constitutional amendment in 1959 abandoned any effort to specify approved versions, stating simply instead: "No version of the Holy Scriptures or any part thereof, whether in English or any other language, shall be published by the Society unless publication of such version has first been approved by the Board of Managers." Two years later the ABS issued 50,000 copies of the Revised Standard Bible. Although the Translation Committee proposed some "modifications" in the text, this appeared to be too involved an undertaking, legally and editorially, for the present.

If, over the years, the Board of Managers was reluctant to endorse any English text of the Scriptures except the King James Version, it was almost as hesitant to approve editions containing only part of the Bible. In their very first year of operation the Managers of the ABS decided that "it is inexpedient for this Board, at present to print the New Testament, in English, separate from the Old." Although some members may have held scruples against such division of the Scriptures, practical considerations entered into the vote: for example, Auxiliaries were placing more orders for full Bibles than could be filled immediately, while commercial printers were beginning to issue Testaments. Less than a year after passing a similar motion in regard to French and Spanish Scriptures--"inexpedient at present"--the Board approved the publication of a Spanish Testament and granted $500 to Frederic Leo for an unexamined New Testament in Paris (see Chapter VI).

Before long requests came in for the printing of Portions, or single books of the Bible. The Society said "no" to a separate printing of the Psalms in 1825; ten years later it advised the Young Men's Bible Society of New York that Testaments would serve the needs of immigrants better than separate Gospels. On the ground that the entire Bible could be purchased so cheaply, the Committee on Distribution decided again in 1852 that "it is inexpedient" to print Psalms and/or Proverbs with the New Testament.

Two exceptions to this general rule had already been made. Where Scriptures were being translated into any language for the first time, the ABS approved--and often subsidized--publication of single books, especially Psalms or the Gospels, as soon as they were ready. In a few other instances, for evangelizing American Indians or for schools in Latin America, the printing of Portions had been permitted. In December, 1860, the Board authorized individual publication of Psalms, Proverbs, and the Gospel of John. Their popularity, especially among servicemen during the Civil War, led to inquiries regarding the other Gospels, Acts, and certain Epistles, although it is not clear just when these were first supplied.

Even though Portions were issued in vast numbers abroad as evangelistic introductions to the Bible, basic ABS policy opposed any further division of the Scriptures until after World War II. Specific requests for the "Words of Christ" (1920), an "abridged Bible" (1920), and "The Sermon on the Mount" (1921) were refused. Only for the blind, whose full New Testament in Braille was bulky to handle, were Selected Portions approved in 1922. Whereas the Society had insisted that evangelistic purposes did not warrant publication of excerpts less than a single book, the claims of literacy finally prevailed. In 1946 sample sheets of Scripture were issued for the use of new literates, especially in Latin America--to compete, as some missionaries urged, with the flood of non-Christian or even anti-Christian reading matter available.

At the same time, having long believed that "The Sermon on the Mount" should be available to a larger reading public, Treasurer Gilbert Darlington raised special funds to produce such an edition outside of the regular ABS budget. Only after several years of such private support proved that there was no serious objection from the wider constituency did the Society feel free to assume direct responsibility for pamphlets containing less than a "book" of the Bible. Even then the Board of Managers did not approve the production of Selections in general; in fact, a request from Argentina in 1953 was declined on the ground that such a project would be contrary to the Society's principles.

The breakthrough came the very next year. Agencies in Latin America produced "The Christmas Story" from Matthew and Luke in Spanish, followed in 1955 by "The Easter Story." Similar Selections appeared in Liberia and the Philippines, attracting an enthusiastic response far beyond anticipation. Not until

1959 did the Board give general approval to this program of Selections in English as well as foreign languages. By 1964 the "Chrispels" and "Easpels" (as they were flippantly called in one report) and "The Sermon on the Mount" were joined by "Lost and Found" (the parables of Luke 15), "The Last Discourse," and "The Pentecost Story."

Meanwhile, however, other vital lessons were being learned from the "younger churches" and the foreign field. Missionaries and native translators began to discover that similar words do not always convey similar meanings. As dedicated as their predecessors to presenting the meaning or intent of the original Scriptures, these faithful men and women found that literal, formal translation into another tongue often caused misunderstanding and confusion. Not only do languages differ greatly in sounds, in grammatical structure, in complexity, but cultural differences, social customs and thought patterns, may seriously distort communication.

In the article quoted at the first of this chapter, Translations Secretary Eugene Nida illustrated these problems convincingly. A language which does not include certain "abstract" nouns comparable to those in English may have to translate Ephesians 1:17 ("God...may give you a spirit of wisdom and of revelation in the knowledge of him."--RSV) as "...to give you the Spirit, who will make you wise and reveal God to you, so that you will know him." Or, the phrase which speaks of the king as "him that holds the scepter" (Amos 1:5, RSV) may be entirely misleading in parts of Africa where the scepter is always held by a servant, while the king is symbolized as sitting on a special stool or owning a royal fan. To "smite the breast" may have been a sign of penitence among the Jews, but in many cultures--including modern America--it is more often a way of congratulating oneself.

Thus it became increasingly obvious that strict adherence to an original text tended to produce an overly literal translation, wooden in style and lacking in idiom, if it did not actually falsify the original meaning. Nida and his associates recognized scientifically what many Bible readers have felt subconsciously about older versions of the Scriptures, even in English. To borrow another of his striking examples, take the first verse of the first Psalm: "Blessed is the man that walketh not in the counsel of the ungodly, nor standeth in the way of sinners, nor sitteth in the seat of the scornful" (KJV). What this means, as Nida pointed out, is that a righteous man "refuses the advice of evil men," should not "follow the example of sinners," or associate with "those who make fun of God."

In short, if the Scriptures are to speak to modern man in vital tones and meaning, "formal correspondence" to ancient

versions or to original languages must give way to "dynamic
equivalence." Put in other terms, "the priority of meaning over
form...takes seriously the specific words of the divinely
inspired text and seeks to interpret them with integrity.....
Thus faithfulness in Bible translation means first a rejection
of literal word-for-word renderings which do violence to the
meaning of the text by failing to communicate the message."

This realization, expressed so frequently and persuasively
by Executive Secretary Nida, came into the forefront of Bible
Society thinking (along with scientific techniques and tools to
be mentioned below) at about the same time that the Board of
Managers opened the way for new versions of the Scriptures.
Largely in the last decade of its first 150 years the Society
applied to America lessons already learned abroad; namely, that
the Word of God is needed at various levels of thought as well
as of literacy, from the classical to the colloquial.

The first venture under the new constitutional provision
consisted of Selections from the New English Bible in Braille.
With unanimous approval from the Translations Committee the
Society prepared "The Sermon on the Mount," "Lost and Found,"
Christmas and Easter passages for the blind in 1962, adding
"Pentecost" the following year. Similarly the Gospel of John
in J. B. Phillips' translation was issued in 1963 as "One Way
for Modern Man," and the first edition, with photographs of
contemporary American life, sold 300,000 copies, 450,000 the
following year. By 1966 Luke, John, Acts, and Romans were
added, these five Portions constituting the first time that an
individual "interpretation" of the Scriptures had been published
in English by the Society.

Meanwhile research continued into other "popular versions,"
research which culminated in the widely hailed *Good News for
Modern Man*. Miss Annie Cressman, a missionary of the Canadian
Pentecostal Assemblies in Liberia, prepared the Epistle to the
Romans in Simple English for the Tchien people. For her translation of Mark's Gospel she requested and received technical
assistance from the ABS, although her own mission handled the
printing, which ran to 13,000 copies in five years. Encouraged
by this favorable response--and the minor, technical nature of
any criticism--the Bible Society agreed to publish Miss
Cressman's version of the Gospel of John (in 1962) under the
title, "He Gave His Only Son," (25,000 copies in four years)
and to sponsor the Mark translation as "The True Servant" (1963).

The popularity of this experiment, not only among Africans
but for evangelistic purposes in Canada and among conservative
missions which had heretofore zealously guarded the Authorized
text, emboldened the Society to attempt a translation in

"popular English" for a wider constituency. Following guidelines adopted for common language translations, Dr. Robert G. Bratcher of the ABS staff prepared a tentative translation of Mark. Several simplified versions were submitted to members of the Advisory Council. To the surprise of some and the relief of others, a large majority of that diverse and representative body favored some kind of popular version, and the Bratcher transla- tion was generally preferred.

This was completed and approved in 1965 as Today's English Version of the New Testament "on a provisional basis, subject to revision based on comments from scholars and suggestions from those who use it on the field." To this was added a Word List (or glossary) to explain technical terms like *Sabbath* and *Sadducees*, unfamiliar words like *nard* and *eunuch*, names of persons and places like *Agrippa* and *Gomorrah*. The original edition carried striking line drawings by Annie Valloton.

The effectiveness of such "popular versions," first inspired by needs abroad, found further confirmation in numerous foreign language editions. In 1964 simple, contemporary translations appeared in Brazilian Portuguese and in popular Thai. Today's English Version encouraged similar efforts in Chinese, Swahili, German, and other tongues. In addition to the initial 150,000 copies published by the American Bible Society--plus Overseas, Australian, and Canadian editions--the Macmillan Company issued a hardcover volume of the TEV New Testament without illustra- tions. After 150 years the Society could at last supply a wide range of needs: authorized standard versions, both King James and Revised, for the traditionally oriented; the New English Bible and the Phillips translation for more sophisticated modern readers; and Today's English Version for popular, idiomatic understanding in the United States and abroad.

Even the controversy over the Apocrypha, which plagued the Bible Societies in their early years (see Chapter VI), had faded with time. Despite the clear resolution of 1828 "excluding the circulation" as well as the publication of the Apocrypha, some exceptions occurred in Eastern Orthodox areas. Exactly a century later, after the Versions Committee had deferred requests from Episcopalians in the United States, an influential officer of the Board bypassed that committee and arranged for the Publication Committee "to purchase one or two thousand copies of the Bible with Apocrypha for any persons who desire them." Comparatively few were ordered at that time. But for distribution in post-war Europe, for greater collaboration with Eastern Orthodox Churches, even for Lutheran and Episcopal constituencies, the Society had more recently to review its official policy. Thus in 1964 the Versions Committee proposed to the Board of Managers "that translations of the Old

Testament Apocrypha which meet the translational standards of
the Society be recommended for publication."

The long, slow, gradual process of expanding policy applied
to many other "accessories" to the text, as successive Boards of
Managers in changing decades sought to remain faithful to both
constitutional requirements: "to encourage a wider circulation
of the Holy Scriptures," yet to do this "without note or comment"
in "the version now in common use."

A phonetic New Testament with a forty-letter alphabet for
illiterates was firmly rejected in 1850, but later privately
printed. The Society declined to issue Scriptures with the words
of Jesus in red type, despite financial offers for that express
purpose. A glossary was declined in 1887, although one was
included in the Armenian-Turkish edition of 1892 and a separate
word list provided for the Muskogee (Indian) Testament in 1900.
The Society decided in 1894 that "Helps" to understanding the
Bible were bound to be more controversial than helpful, no
matter how carefully they might be prepared. Even a strictly
textual concordance was not approved until 1918, published with
the Bible in 1921.

As the art of translation grew more sophisticated, with
greater appreciation of cultural variations, the need for
explanatory footnotes in many foreign languages became more
apparent. In the article previously cited (*The Bible Society
Record*, March, 1971) Secretary Nida illustrates this type of
dilemma. In contrast to Jesus' triumphal entry into Jerusalem
on Palm Sunday, he points out, in many parts of Africa the road
in front of a distinguished visitor should be swept clean, and
deliberately strewing branches or clothes in his way would be
regarded as a definite insult. Similarly many societies, if
they practice circumcision at all, withhold the ritual until
maturity, so that the circumcision of Jesus on the eighth day
might be considered cruel, meaningless, and quite unnecessary.

The important point made by Nida is that translators may,
for the sake of "dynamic equivalence," modify certain linguistic
forms or symbolic, cultural language, but they are never
"justified in altering any historical facts, regardless of how
awkward and difficult they may be for the receptors to understand." For this reason, it may be necessary to insert marginal
notes explaining that strewing palm branches was a gesture of
honor, or that the circumcision of a Jewish infant had distinctive religious significance. Thus another once-rigid policy of
the Society gave way to the primary purpose of making the
Scriptures meaningful and alive, comprehensible and acceptable,
to people unfamiliar with the Biblical setting.

To take another example, the inclusion of Bible Land maps had been requested as early as 1847 and 1854--in vain. Even to appeals from Agents in China and Japan, where Palestinian geography was strange and confusing, the Versions Committee replied in 1876 that "it was not the province of the Society to furnish such helps to the understanding of the Scriptures." Just three years later that decision was reversed, permitting not only maps of the ancient world for English and foreign editions, but also tables of weights and measures.

Since some critics did raise constitutional objections, it is interesting to note the legal justification provided by the Society's counsel:

If a Bible furnished with maps and tables as aids to its study is more in demand than one without them I think the Managers may safely satisfy this demand upon the principle that corporations may do such subordinate and connected acts as are subservient of the main purpose of their organization.

In other words, if the inclusion of maps increased the circulation of Scriptures, that purpose took precedence over anxieties about versions or notes or comments. However another advisor added, as further assurance, that the British and Foreign Bible Society had included maps in some of its editions since 1875 and encountered no serious objection.

A similar position developed gradually in relation to pictures. As in the case of maps, the most urgent appeals came from Asian countries, where little opportunity existed to visualize the Holy Land--although in point of fact the Palestinian terrain, many social customs, modes of dress, etc. would be more akin to Indian or Chinese settings than to American or European life. After much debate and many delays the Board of Managers voted approval in principle to the use of *scenic* pictures, but retained the right to pass on each illustration selected. In over a year only four pictures had been cleared for inclusion in ABS publications. More were sought and submitted, and in January, 1925, the Board authorized the Secretary and Treasurer "to proceed with preparation of pictures approved by the Versions Committee for use in such books as may be deemed desirable by the Committee on Publication." Representation of any Biblical character was still strictly forbidden, and not until 1944 could any "recognizable individual" be shown in such pictures.

At that time a drastic revision of previous rules came about in conjunction with the BFBS, which had been using pictures since 1908, but only as cover or frontispiece, only of "scenes,

objects, manners or customs," only if they "involve no interpretation," and only from the eight pictures which had been
approved over a span of twenty-three years. The new BFBS policy
adopted in 1944 meant in effect that the "Parent Society" had
"now abandoned all the restrictions on the use of pictures
previously in force" except for the avoidance of implicit "note
or comment." Even the ban on pictures of Jesus or other
historical figures disappeared. Since the major motive was
clarification for people in other cultures, the principal question now became what would be acceptable and meaningful for
intended readers, or how far should the Societies go in
utilizing indigenous art?

Despite the lifting of specific restrictions on the type of
pictures to be used, the New York officers deferred formal
action for a full decade. Meanwhile intermittent consultation
with London elicited the opinion that simple drawings might
prove more useful in Africa and among new literates than complex
photographs. Questions of captions and explanatory materials
were referred to archaeologists and Biblical experts. In 1961
the ABS issued a New Testament in the Authorized Version and
two years later in the Revised Standard Version, both copiously
illustrated with photographs of scenes in Bible lands, selected
by Treasurer Gilbert Darlington in consultation with the distinguished Bible scholar, William F. Albright. Agents and staff
members searched in various parts of the world for attractive,
appropriate photographs and/or indigenous art to use for covers,
dust jackets, Selections. Annie Valloton's original art work
was praised as an integral part of the *Good News for Modern Man*,
and subsequent popular Selections have featured all sorts of
colorful illustrations, from scenic photographs of American states
to psychedelic proclamations of Love. What has been excitingly
demonstrated by fresh idiomatic versions and experimental formats is the Society's willingness to revise traditional concepts,
even constitutional restrictions, in its determination "to
encourage a wider circulation of the Holy Scriptures."

Such changes, both cautious and courageous, did not come
about accidentally. In recent years scientific methods have
been applied to the process of translation, as well as to the
text and format of modern editions. By necessity the Bible
Societies were always less restrictive abroad than at home,
more dependent on untried translators and unproved versions.
In the texts sanctioned for publication and distribution and in
the earlier sources on which translations were based, the
criterion of catholicity often meant simply "wide acceptability"
by scholars and missionaries at work in a given language area.
There were no authorized versions, no infallible texts.

Yet the number of translations available to readers around
the world escalated rapidly in the twentieth century. Total

languages represented by at least one book of the Bible followed a steeply rising curve: 770 in 1924, 906 in 1930, 1,017 in 1937, 1,092 in 1956, and 1,280 by the sesquicentennial year of 1966. By 1931 the American Bible Society alone had published one or more books of the Bible in 123 languages (as compared with 86 up to 1900), distributed Scriptures from other sources in 71 languages, and subsidized publication by others in 22 more tongues, making a total of 216 under ABS auspices.

This acceleration reflected a gradual but conscientious effort to systematize the process of translation and to provide scientific tools and techniques. In 1903, in a speech before the Foreign Missions Conference of North America on "The Bible Society and the Translation of the Bible," ABS Secretary William I. Haven suggested an order of priority for translators working on the Bible in a new language: one or more Gospels (usually John, but occasionally Mark first), Acts, the New Testament as a whole, and finally the Old Testament. As early as 1915 the British and Foreign Bible Society offered to their American colleagues full use of their rules and guidelines for translators, but this assistance was not accepted until a decade later. In 1932 the ABS developed for the first time its own *Rules for Translators*, concentrating on suggestions as to the most dependable original sources to be used. Many years later, after waiting five years for the United Bible Societies to agree on a common manual, the ABS issued its own *Guide for Translators and Revisers* in 1961.

The challenges of this expanding task called for new organizational structures as well as new methods. From the outset of his long tenure as General Secretary (1928-56) Eric M. North gave devoted and meticulous attention to problems of translation, often examining and revising manuscripts in languages he did not know, but drawing on his knowledge of linguistics and texts. After fifteen years as an ABS Agent in the Middle East, Dr. J. Oscar Boyd came to New York in 1937 as the first Secretary for Translations (or Versions). At his retirement the Society hired a Baptist minister, Eugene A. Nida, who continued to share his time with the large and effective Wycliffe Bible Translators, to devise a comprehensive program of training and coordination.

The principle of "dynamic equivalence" and the systematic science of linguistics revealed that many earlier translations were inadequate to convey the essential meaning of the Scriptures. Surveys brought to light many tribes and societies which had no portion of the Bible in their native tongue. Missionaries were often working on new languages with no awareness of duplicate efforts, or of research aids available to them. Promptly Nida introduced consultations in various fields to locate the greatest needs and the greatest difficulties, and then to develop

principles for the guidance of translators. Following an international meeting in Holland in 1947, at the invitation of the
Netherlands Bible Society, regional conferences were set up in
many parts of the world: Guatemala, Taiwan, Ecuador, the
Philippines, Africa, and elsewhere.

One of the purposes was to enlist and train more nationals
for translation work with their own native languages. Brief
workshops and consultations proved so valuable that some were
expanded into Translation Institutes lasting perhaps a month;
a dozen of these were held in the early 1960's for nationals and
missionaries. Another aim was the sharing of participation in
this world-wide undertaking. A conference report in 1960 urged
that "translation should not remain a monopoly of the larger
societies which have historically carried on that work." But
emphasis on collaboration requires also clearly defined areas
of responsibility, among missionaries, national churches, and
Bible societies.

These conferences and workshops and Translation Institutes
(comparable to the Penzotti Institutes for training in distribution) seek to develop not only technical tools to deal with
particular problems, but also broader understanding of linguistic
and anthropoligical insights, a deeper sensitivity to cultural
interpretations of the Scriptures. Expert consultants circle
the globe to bring specific advice on manuscripts and methods.
The Bible Translator, first proposed at the Netherlands meeting
in 1947, has appeared as a quarterly guide, encouragement, and
fraternal tie under the sponsorship of the United Bible Societies
since 1950. Sometimes the specialists provide general guidelines
for those engaged in textual revisions; for example, the
Translators' Handbook on Mark, a verse-by-verse analysis covering
the actual text, alternative interpretations, possibilities and
pitfalls of translation. The Greek New Testament Project--
sponsored by five Bible societies but initiated by Secretary
Nida and largely financed by the ABS--has produced an authoritative base for all kinds of translations.

As the American Bible Society ended its first 150 years, a
new and gratifying door was opened for collaboration with Roman
Catholic scholars. In May, 1966, conferees agreed on a number
of areas of possible joint activity: theoretical definitions
and practical recruitment for competence in linguistics and
anthropology, especially among nationals; common procedures for
processing manuscripts in new or updated languages; the formula-
tion of specific aids for translators and editors and readers;
a new, realistic "missionary thrust" through the use of fresh
"common language" translations.

Even--or perhaps especially--in lands which have had a
classical Bible translation for generations, emphasis today is

on the production of a popular or "common language" edition corresponding to Today's English Version. Aware of the importance of anthropological as well as linguistic insights into a particular culture, scholars seek to identify multiple levels in a given language, "social dialects" as well as geographical variations. These cultural phenomena may require different versions of the Scriptures, even within one language; sometimes diglots of two parallel texts teach linguistic as well as exegetical lessons. Increasingly the responsibility for this approach falls on national leaders instead of missionaries; increasingly Protestant scholars are working with Roman Catholic specialists in linguistics and communication. By the time of the 1966 sesquicentennial of the ABS the Translations Department of the United Bible Societies was engaged in providing assistance and guidance to translators working with more than five hundred different languages or dialects.

One of the aids provided is a lending library for Bible translators. Located in the New York Bible House, that office claims that it "probably circulates books in more countries than any other similar type of library in the world." In addition to this utilitarian service, with its aids to translators around the world, the American Bible Society at its new Lincoln Center headquarters possesses one of the most comprehensive and fascinating collections of Scriptural material to be found anywhere.

More than 20,000 volumes of Bibles and Biblical portions trace the history of the Word of God in a thousand tongues, and the history of the Society itself. Thanks to reciprocal donations from other Bible Societies, practically every translation over the past century is included here, and the Master Index lists all known editions of the Bible, whether copies are owned by the ABS or not. Valuable individual items range from a single page of the original Gutenberg Bible, through the Chuana Old Testament translated by Robert Moffat and inscribed by his son-in-law David Livingstone, to the 12-volume set of Braille Scriptures used by Helen Keller.

Library holdings also include extensive reference materials: grammars, dictionaries, translation aids, guides to linguistic methods. In 1931 the Society, for these technical purposes, subscribed to thirty-three periodicals; by 1966, in collaboration with the United Bible Societies, these subscriptions had multiplied exactly ten-fold. A third category of material covers historical archives. Here lie not only the Minutes and correspondence and Annual Reports of the ABS and its numerous committees, but of many Auxiliaries, Agencies, and other Societies. For example, the New Jersey Bible Society, sharing with the ABS the devoted leadership of Elias Boudinot, donated

its Minutes for 1809-39, and the American Revision Committee
under Philip Schaff contributed its papers and worksheets.

Over recent decades the Library staff has produced several
books about Bible translation and circulation. Margaret T.
Hills, who joined the staff in 1929 as an assistant (for Versions)
to the General Secretary, served as librarian from 1938 to 1962,
and retired in 1966 as Secretary for Historical Research, became
one of the world's authorities on Scriptural publication. She
provided much of the research material for *The Book of A Thousand
Tongues, Scriptures of the World*, film strips and sound movies
to present the thrilling story. She edited the definitive
bibliography, *The English Bible in America*, and wrote many of
the essays from which this history was drawn. These resources,
numerous articles, the historic displays of maps and charts and
visual aids in the Bible House library, all help visitors to
comprehend--in small part--the enormous task of the American
Bible Society.

The earliest Bible House on Nassau Street, just a block from
the New York City Hall, contained no library; it housed instead
paper storage, printing presses, binderies, book depositories,
as well as offices. No wonder that even after adjacent buildings
were added to the premises, the Board of Managers complained
about the noise of presses overhead. In the next home at Astor
Place, where the Society moved in 1853, "a large and convenient
apartment was provided immediately under the Managers' Hall...
fire-proof, well warmed, lighted and ventilated, and being back
from the street, free from noise." Little did the designers
anticipate the growth of New York--or Astor Place--or the
library collection. When the American Baptist Historical
Society lost a valuable collection of books and manuscripts by
fire, the ABS Versions Committee suggested to the Board of
Managers "the desirableness of securing more ample accomodations
for the library within fire-proof walls." Since additional construction was impossible at that time, arrangements were made
for storing more than 4,000 volumes with the New York Public
Library.

There they remained until 1936, when the Society moved
uptown to 450 Park Avenue, at the corner of East 57th Street.
By this time annual accessions, mainly new editions of Scriptures,
averaged more than five hundred volumes, and the library at Park
Avenue was allotted 1,400 feet of shelf space, plus supplementary
storage. Within a year this was referred to as "limited space;"
in a decade it became "a very serious problem;" by 1954 the
situation was acute, despite elimination of duplicates and
storage of bulky collections (such as Braille volumes) seldom
needed.

The spacious and gracious library in the Bible House at
Lincoln Center belongs to the new century. To it are coming,
as they did to Astor Place and Park Avenue, world rulers,
distinguished personages, church leaders--and thousands of
humble Christians from every race and nation and tongue, eager
to learn the remarkable story of world-wide Bible circulation
and to pay tribute to it.

But as the Word of Life cannot be contained, so its historic
relics and mementoes cannot be confined in one place. Increasingly the Society has recognized the importance of exhibiting
to wider audiences the priceless treasures from its library
collection: at Fifth Avenue Presbyterian Church for the meeting
of the United Bible Societies in 1949, at the Interchurch Center
on Riverside Drive in New York in 1961, at the sesquicentennial
of Princeton Theological Seminary in 1963, at the New York World's
Fair in 1964, at the Washington Cathedral for six months in 1966
to honor the 150th anniversary of the American Bible Society
itself.

NOTES

1. Albert Peel, *The Congregational Two Hundred* (London: 1948),
    p. 197.

15

Independent and United

We have endeavoured to visualize a position...when the
Churches on the Mission Field shall have been called to
a fuller participation in our common task; and it seems
clear to us that the time is drawing near for the formation of national Bible Societies on the same basic
principles as our own. Such a development leads us in
thought to the vision of a world-federation of Bible
Societies, which shall not only facilitate the inter-
relations between such national Societies, but shall
bear a united witness to the place of the Scriptures in
the life of the world and in the growth of God's Kingdom.

This memorandum from the ABS-BFBS Staff Conference held in
London in August, 1932, drew together two vital streams in the
life of the Bible Societies. As the so-called Younger Churches
"came of age" in the twentieth century, with capable leaders
and established congregations and increasing national pride,
the need for indigenous organization--and responsibility--grew
more and more obvious. At the same time expanding opportunities
for Scripture distribution, coupled with dwindling barriers to
transportation and communication, made cooperation essential and
competition intolerable.

In the aftermath of World War I Vice-President Churchill H.
Cutting, just a month before his election as fifteenth President
of the ABS, proposed a committee to consider "some form of union
for world-wide cooperation of all the Bible Societies in the
world." Some correspondence among the major Societies followed.
Some references hint at a series of consultations about 1926

concerning a "world fellowship." Some records mention a draft constitution--based on history, size, and prestige--calling for an executive council of four representatives from the BFBS, three from the ABS, two from the National Bible Society of Scotland, one each from any additional participants. But no definite plans materialized.

Meanwhile, however, certain rivalries and points of friction became more pronounced. Tensions referred to in previous geographic chapters appeared more acute in a technologically shrinking world. The American Bible Society maintained that it had a duty to follow American missionaries wherever they served, whereas the British regarded this as an invasion of clearly established territories. In certain instances these conflicts had been at least partially resolved: by division of territory within a country (Bulgaria, 1867; Egypt, 1902; Brazil, 1903; Japan, 1903); or by withdrawal or exchange of responsibility (ABS from Persia and Korea, BFBS from Mexico, Central America, and the Philippines).

In China especially, where devolution of Church leadership and responsibility into the hands of national Christians had progressed further than in most other mission fields, divergent Bible Society policies created fresh problems. As noted in Chapter XIII, the ABS Agency Secretary for China, Carleton Lacy, favored the appointment of a co-equal Chinese Secretary in Shanghai, of Chinese provincial secretaries in regional offices, and of Chinese pastors and other workers to handle distribution instead of relying exclusively on missionaries and hired colporteurs. Other differences over discount rates, pricing policies, annotations, and the like continued to agitate both central headquarters and Agencies in various parts of the world.

Changing personnel in London and New York opened the way for a new era of understanding and personal fellowship between the two major Societies. From the new BFBS Secretary, Arthur H. Wilkinson, a former Anglican missionary in China, to his counterpart in America, General Secretary Eric M. North, came a gracious expression of goodwill and prayerful concern for the American Bible Society. North's immediate offer to go to London for consultations elicited a further invitation to address the 1931 Annual Meeting of the BFBS. Warm personal conversations between the two men at that time touched on many administrative issues and geographical areas. They also discussed a proposal from Wilkinson for a "conference of Bible Societies" and "the bearing of a united witness to the community and the world."

Out of these talks grew a proposal for representatives of the American Bible Society, the National Bible Society of Scotland, and the British and Foreign Bible Society to meet in London in July of 1932. The announced purpose of the conference was--

...to deal with the immediate practical relationships in China, South America, Levant and other points where contact of the Societies sometimes leads to friction, but not restricted to these items in opening the way to a full consideration of how the cooperation of the Societies can most further the Kingdom of God.

The American delegation included Daniel Burke, a long-time member of the Board of Managers who was to serve as President of the Society from 1944 to 1962; General Secretary North; Treasurer Gilbert Darlington; Agency Secretaries J. Oscar Boyd and C. S. Bell from the Levant and Carleton Lacy from China. By fortuitous chance Arthur Wilkinson's newly-elected co-secretary for the British Society was another former China missionary, John R. Temple, familiar with the field and its problems.

Participants in this first tri-partite conference later described it in a letter to their "fellow-workers" around the world as "not only unique in the annals of the three Societies, but also rich in significance for our future history." The agreements reached in regard to the principal topic of China have already been sketched (in Chapter XIII). These included "encouraging the formation of a China Bible Society" (at some unspecified future date), the immediate creation of an Advisory Council, and coordination--wherever possible--in policies regarding publication, prices, local auxiliaries, free distributions, etc. Only on the matter of a paid Chinese General Secretary did the National Bible Society of Scotland insist that "the time is not yet ripe for the consideration of such a step."

However the three Societies did pledge themselves to much closer consultation and exchange of information, not only on these practical matters discussed, but also on the final agenda question: "What can the Bible Societies do within the limits of their constitution to stimulate the actual use of the Bible in individual and family life?"

Even more important, the London Conference--by extension from particular situations--erected new guideposts toward autonomous societies, on the one hand, and a world-wide federation, on the other. Secretary North challenged the delegates to recognize, understand, and adapt to "The New Situation"--including the growth of indigenous churches. In response, Secretary Wilkinson appealed "that the Bible Societies be not the last to make use of the new leadership arising on the mission fields." A Scottish spokesman "pointed to the analogy of apostolic missions as a warning to Christian missions today not to delay needlessly the devolution of responsibility upon those who have been won by them to Christ's service." Encouraged by such forward-looking vision, North voiced "the readiness of the ABS to make even long-cherished principles subservient to the present necessity for cooperation."

Following this harmonious three-way exchange of views, unprecedented in Bible Society history, representatives of the ABS and the BFBS continued a series of fruitful Staff Conferences for another week. In the original consultation the British and Scottish delegations consisted largely of Board members concerned with general policies. Although the General Secretary of the National Bible Society of Scotland was unable to participate, the presence of top officials from New York made possible extensive conversations between ABS and BFBS Secretaries regarding practical procedures for implementing long-range principles. On questions directly related to China or the Middle East the Agency Secretaries took part; otherwise the chief consultants were Temple and Wilkinson for the BFBS, North and Darlington for the ABS. It is important to note that here, as on countless other occasions during his long tenure as treasurer of the American Bible Society (1920-57), Gilbert Darlington's broad knowledge, vision, imagination, and dedication cast him in the role of co-secretary in wide areas of Bible work, not merely as a financial officer.

Executives of the two Societies needed to face up to their immediate relationships in various parts of the world. At that stage there were twenty-two areas where a single Society had exclusive organization and recognition: Korea, Persia, Northeastern Europe, Central Europe, Mexico, Central America, Colombia-Ecuador, Iraq, Algeria, Tunisia, Morocco, West Africa, East Indies, Siam, Indo-China, Sudan, Puerto Rico, Haiti, British West Indies, Madagascar, Santo Domingo, Virgin Islands. In five countries a territorial division of Scripture distribution had been effected: Bulgaria, Greece, Japan, Brazil, and Egypt. In at least eight regions more than one Society was at work: Turkey, Syria, China, Arabia, Holy Land, Transjordania, Syria, and South America generally. Elsewhere Bible activities were often limited and unorganized.

To deal with this situation Secretary Wilkinson proposed a series of factors (which were not fully discussed) governing the entry of any Society into a particular field: (a) the need; (b) each Society alone responsible in dominions under its own flag; (c) the ABS principle of relationship to missionaries of the same nationality, especially where they predominate; (d) the desirability of maintaining traditional ties and appeals to the home-base; (e) Christian stewardship and administrative economy in the total enterprise; (f) the possible bearing of political affinities.

The Staff Conference proposed that, pending the achievement of autonomous national societies, measures of co-ordination or

even unification should be pressed forward. In some instances
this might involve sole administrative responsibility under one
headquarters, with the other contributor assured of full information and consultation. In some instances it might involve
"joint occupation" with two Agency Secretaries collaborating on
common editions, imprints, staff, pricing policies, distribution,
etc. In still other cases, the greatest effectiveness might call
for territorial division of a country, with common editions,
prices, and policies as far as possible. The Joint Agency in
particular proved to be "the great forward step in eliminating
competition and friction on the field."

In fact, by the time the United Bible Societies came into
existence in 1946 the policy had moved so far that General
Secretary Eric North could assert in retrospect: "At no point
in the field of work were the two Societies (ABS and BFBS) in
competition with each other." At this stage the American Bible
Society retained very few agencies in which the BFBS did not
share, whereas the British still had a number, especially in
Africa and Southeast Asia, without ABS participation. By the
1960's, however, practically all of the foreign field had
become a joint operation.

Back in 1932, however, the officers of the two Societies
were seeking for practical ways to eliminate duplication and to
increase effectiveness. They called for joint planning or mutual
consultation "wherever possible" in the training and assignment
of colporteurs; in determining discount rates to missionaries,
pastors, and bookstores; in all questions of translation or
revision; in sharing experiences with a view to increased development of the work. In many of these areas the consultants
hammered out more specific agreements which in turn became guidelines for policy and practice in remote parts of the globe.

Even then these top executives were looking beyond the need
for closer collaboration to the establishment of independent
partners in the total task. Although it was recognized that
each local situation would have to develop along the lines of
its own historical, economic, and structural conditions, the
Staff Conference recommended "a policy of the formation and
encouragement of National Bible Societies which shall be--"

1. Founded on the common basic principles of our Societies;

2. Indigenous, with their roots deep in the life of Church
    and Nation;

3. Self-governing and responsible for the work within
    their own borders;

4.   Responsible for such measure of financial support as
     each is able to provide;

5.   Participants in the world-wide Bible work.

The "common basic principles" were never officially defined,
but they presumably implied non-profit organizations whose
central purpose was missionary distribution through low-cost
sales; non-sectarian bodies seeking always to produce versions
of Scriptures both accurate and acceptable to the widest variety
of Christian groups; drawing support and cooperation from the
entire Christian community.

In the long run, as Secretary Wilkinson of the BFBS affirmed
in a statesmanlike "position paper," "the vision to be kept in
mind is a World Federation of autonomous but not necessarily
financially independent Bible societies." Part of the incentive
appeared to be an acknowledgement of national pride and responsibility, the thrust for independence; part of it, equally
clearly, represented a strengthening of the world-wide distribution of Scriptures through interdependence. The officers asked
themselves very candidly: "Are these principles applicable
anywhere immediately? Can a programme of progress to this end
be devised" (or must it develop gradually, spontaneously, under
the guidance of the Holy Spirit)? In conclusion the conferees
affirmed "the ultimate creation of a World Federation of Bible
Societies as the probable form of organization the Societies
will need if the maximum of cooperation is to be attained."

Looking back on those summer days of 1932 in London, General
Secretary Eric North (now Emeritus) summed up their importance
in words that deserve to be quoted in full:

These two conferences taken together may be said to form
the greatest single advance in 150 years of Bible Society
work, for out of them proceeded the gradual consolidation
of the field work of the British and American and ultimately other Societies upon which many national Societies
were founded--and founded in a relationship which had its
natural expression in the United Bible Societies of the
world. In spite of halting steps, inter-society suspicion,
inadequate administrations, and the effects of two world
wars, the spirit, the vision and the friendships of these
conferences set goals of practical cooperation before the
whole Bible Society cause which were made effective in the
elimination of overlapping and competition, in drawing the
"younger churches" into the common cause, in putting the
talents of any one society into the service of all and
best of all greatly increasing the distribution of the
Scriptures to the multitudes of mankind.

During the next few years the Societies moved forward with "halting steps" in various parts of the world. Sketchy geographical surveys in earlier chapters do not indicate the genesis of many steps toward unity. Often participants themselves did not realize that Joint Agencies (e.g. Chile 1936, Paraguay-Uruguay the same year) or territorial divisions (e.g. Bible Lands, North and South, in 1938) or independent societies (e.g. China and Japan in 1938) owed their incentive if not their inception to the London Conferences.

Seven years later another consultation offered even greater scope and greater promise—until the Second World War cut off its immediate fulfillment. To Woudschoten, Holland, came representatives not only from the ABS, the BFBS, and the NBSS, but also from the Bible Societies of Belgium, France, and the Netherlands. In addition to reviewing "Bible distribution throughout the world...methods of work...and policies concerning translation," the agenda called for consideration of a federation of Bible societies.

Clearly such a proposal had integral if not organic relation to the world-wide missionary movement. This fact was highlighted by the presence, in the American delegation, of John R. Mott, world mission statesman and a Vice-President of the ABS, and A. L. Warnshuis, Secretary of the International Missionary Council. Said Mott to the delegates assembled: "Your work is the most fully multiplying there is. It is also the most strategic, as it is the basis for all else. It moves me with awe when I think of what God can do as he breaks through the pages of the gospel which you circulate." And at the opening session Hendrik Kraemer, Dutch mission theologian, urged the Bible Societies to take active steps to awaken mission authorities and national churches overseas to the necessity of a fuller use of the Bible (see *The Bible Society Record*, October, 1939).

On the very eve of World War II—in fact, two years after the onset of the Sino-Japanese conflict—the Woudschoten Conference declared:

The steady increase of population, the more rapid growth of literacy, the manifest evidence of the hunger of vast multitudes for spiritual guidance, the peril that powerful opposition to the gospel may shut off large populations from the opportunity to receive the gospel, confront the Societies with very great issues.

In this sober mood delegates acknowledged that very little had been done to promote Bible-reading or to cooperate with other Societies. At the same time they reaffirmed the 1932 goal of forming national groups which would "encourage the younger churches to share with them the world-wide work of distributing the Scriptures."

Considerable attention centered around the formation of a "council" of Bible Societies, which would "serve primarily as a center for the discussion of common problems and as a clearing house for appraising and acting upon various emergency conditions..." Some delegates also felt it highly desirable to have "an ecumenical body which could represent the Bible Societies and the Bible Cause in the world councils of the churches and of the missionary enterprise."

To that end the Woudschoten Conference recommended to its constituent bodies the establishment of such a Council of Bible Societies, to facilitate exchange of information and services, to represent the Bible enterprise in related movements, to encourage common agreement on policies and on "plans for meeting the challenge of fields unoccupied, closed, or inadequately served." Membership was to be open to Bible Societies which held, as their *principal or sole* function, "the wider circulation of the Holy Scriptures without note or comment of a doctrinal nature." The outbreak of war in Europe less than six weeks later prevented full implementation of the plan, but with remarkable faith and courage the Societies concerned announced their approval of such a Council.

Within the first few days of the European conflict the ABS Board of Managers voted its readiness "to render any assistance possible" to sister Societies across the Atlantic, to maintain the supply of Scriptures within their national boundaries or for their work abroad. Reference has already been made to the War Emergency Fund (Chapter X). The first urgent need for inter-society aid was to supply books and paper to the Dutch Indies, East and West. French Scriptures were provided for occupied areas of France and Belgium through a variety of channels. In October, 1940--after a year of bombing and blockade--the "Mother Society" in London authorized the ABS to take over its work in any country where the BFBS was unable to operate. Specifically these areas included Madagascar, Europe, Latin America, Africa, and Canada, most of which had been heretofore "exclusive" BFBS territory. At home the London office received from New York, in 1942, a folding and binding machine in partial replacement of more than $80,000 worth of machinery destroyed by enemy bombs.

This emergency assistance--translation in one locale, printing in another, shipping for still another--laid deep foundations for subsequent cooperation. In 1944, with an armistice hopefully in sight, BFBS General Secretary John Temple

journeyed to New York to discuss post-war problems and programs
of Scripture distribution. Specifically the British Society
invited the active participation of the ABS "in all European
areas on a cooperative basis," stressing that the financial
partnership was "secondary" to the "importance of the joint
witness." A year earlier the ABS Advisory Council, representing
thirty-seven denominations, had adopted a manifesto which could
stand--for the Bible enterprise--alongside of the Atlantic
Charter:

> We are agreed that all postwar plans will be made of
> sand unless they are cemented together by the spiritual
> and moral principles found in the Word of God. We there-
> fore heartily approve of the Society's postwar program
> (1) to place (in consultation with the British and other
> Societies) a minimum initial supply of Scriptures in every
> reopened country; (2) to provide sums of money to encourage
> the early undertaking of Bible production in all reopened
> countries where that is practicable; (3) to establish
> national Bible Societies in other lands, soundly based on
> the Christian churches and committed to participation both
> in the national and the world cause; and (4) to instigate
> a general use of the Scriptures in the reconstruction
> period of the postwar world.

In informal conversations and informal presentations to a
called meeting of the Board of Managers, Secretary Temple and
Secretary North explored the implications of these goals. In
the following months, with the war not quite over, the British
Society adopted twenty-six proposals for post-war reorganization;
these in turn were boiled down in New York to thirteen recommendations, eight of which the ABS Board of Managers accepted in May,
1945. They included provisions for joint administration or
mutual assistance in Europe, the Philippines, Korea, Japan, the
West Indies, and Brazil.

During his visit to New York, Temple raised, among other
"general matters...the subject of a Council of Bible Societies
on a world scale, the basis of cooperative work, circulation
statements, and imprints." Especially in Europe, where Bible
Societies abounded although seriously devastated by years of war,
the need for integrated planning could not be denied, and a
central office on the continent was recommended. In their joint
memorandum the two Secretaries suggested that such headquarters
for Bible distribution might well be associated with the office
of the World Council of Churches (in process of formation), but
responsible to the Bible Societies for budget and services,
not a department of the World Council.

With the end of World War II and the gradual reconstruction
of programs as well as material facilities, the Bible Societies

moved toward an historic conference. To "Elfinsward," the
diocesan center of Chichester in Sussex, England, the BFBS
invited representatives from a dozen countries of Europe and
from the United States. The sixty-three delegates who gathered
there in May, 1946, included not only Bible Society executives,
but leading churchmen, such as Bishop Hans Lilje of Germany,
W. A. Visser t'Hooft of the World Council of Churches, Bishop
Eivind Berggrav of Norway, who was elected chairman of the Bible
Society conference. Nearly one-fifth of these men had spent
time in prison or in concentration camp during the war. Common
concern for sharing the Scriptures made possible this assemblage
of Christians from diverse political and military backgrounds,
more rapidly and harmoniously than most post-war conferences.
The American delegation consisted of Secretary and Mrs. Eric
North, Secretary and Mrs. Rome Betts, Associate Secretary Eugene
Nida, and Treasurer Gilbert Darlington.

The preliminary agenda emphasized "the problems of Bible
Society work in Europe, particularly as it affected the formation
of National Societies, their inter-cooperation, and the service
of a general staff through a central council, possibly ultimately
to become a world conference." But in the second session the
purpose was made more explicit: "to get information about the
needs of the various countries in and beyond Europe; to pool
our knowledge; to think and take counsel together, believing
that in union is strength; to set up some Central Office, some
clearing house, for the coordination of our plans." In addition
to the needs of Europe, themes for discussion included the
principles and operation of the Bible Societies, methods of
securing support, and the organizing of the Societies for
cooperation.

The delegates at "Elfinsward," "moved by the need of the
world for the Word of God and by the Christian fellowship of those
who work together for its spread," resolved to recommend to their
constituent Societies the establishment of a joint organization,
to be known as United Bible Societies (a title the ABS Board of
Managers had already moved to incorporate, perhaps with the
United Nations designation in mind). The original provision
called for a Council composed of ten members from each Society,
but within a year participants acknowledged that smaller
Societies could not afford that many representatives. Indeed,
the reduction of the Council to one delegate from each Society,
with an Executive Committee of seven, proved far more manageable
as the number of national bodies multiplied rapidly.

Headquarters of the UBS were located in London, with provision
for other branch offices. The conference elected Bishop Berggrav
as first President, John R. Temple of the BFBS as General
Secretary; a year later Oliver Beguin, war-time Secretary for

Chaplaincy Aid to Prisoners of War under the embryonic World
Council of Churches, became Geneva Secretary for the UBS. The
constitution called for incorporation as soon as six bodies
eligible for membership had approved the plan, but by the time
the Executive Committee held its first meeting thirteen months
later, sixteen Societies were represented.

The draft constitution also contained two specific "limitations" designed to protect the autonomy and freedom of member
Societies. One asserted that no action by the UBS Council,
Executive Committee, or staff would be binding on any of the
component members without their "express concurrence." The
other pledged that the United Bible Societies would not compete
with individual members in the solicitation of funds or infringe
on their freedom of work within their respective countries.

Positively, however, the Societies acknowledged many areas of
interdependence. The exchange of information regarding translation, publication, and distribution of Scriptures implied a
readiness to coordinate these tasks to avoid duplication.
Instead of stopping with joint efforts to "secure data" on
world-wide Bible needs, the document went further to suggest a
cooperative allocation of funds and other resources. More
specifically than ever before the delegates at "Elfinsward"
included two still broader aims. One was to--

  interpret the values and importance of Bible Society work
  in areas where it is not carried on and of united service
  in areas where the work is not united, to the end that
  National Bible Societies or Committees rooted in the life
  of the peoples and churches concerned may be formed and
  participate in the world-wide work.

The other provision was to safeguard freedom for the circulation
and use of the Holy Scriptures. In the post-war world, where
secularism and political repression both threatened religious
liberty, these goals may be difficult to achieve, but they
represent an eternal moral affirmation for the United Bible
Societies.

At the June (1946) meeting of the ABS Board of Managers
Secretary Eric North, who had been praised by the "Elfinsward"
conference for "his skill and patience in introducing the United
Bible Societies," assured his associates in New York that the
UBS would not compete or interfere with the direction of ABS
work. The American Bible Society thereupon became the first to
signify its approval of and membership in the new organization,
followed by Societies in Denmark, Scotland, the Netherlands,
Norway, Great Britain, and the French committee. A year later,
when the Executive Committee met near Amsterdam, these nations

had been joined by Australia, Belgium, Canada, Czechoslovakia, Finland, India, Japan, New Zealand, and Sweden. Thus in 1947, the same year when the World Council of Churches came into full operation, the United Bible Societies officially and legally took its place among the international organizations of Christian forces in the world.

During the next two decades a number of national Bible Societies--like a score of "new" nations in Asia and Africa-- achieved independence and promptly reached out for autonomy, for responsibility, for mature and mutual interdependence. By 1970 there were thirty-two full members and eighteen associate members of the United Bible Societies. Many of the obvious practical goals had been achieved to a greater extent than even the most optimistic advocates had anticipated: global coordination in many aspects of translation, publication, and financing. The old but freshly articulated aim of publicizing the Bible and its values had made significant progress. New developments in the world and in the life of the Christian Church had unexpected impact on the circulation of Scriptures.

One of these proved to be the Second Vatican Council, which convened at Rome in four sessions between 1962 and 1965. From it emerged new attitudes toward other Christians (see *Unitatis Redintegratio*, "On Ecumenism"), toward missions (see *Ad Gentes*, "On the Church's Missionary Activity"), and toward the Bible. In *Dei Verbum* ("On Divine Revelation") the Council declared: "Easy access to sacred Scripture should be provided for all the Christian faithful." Protestants who have read of Roman Catholic opposition to Bible distribution in the past, especially in Latin America, might well be surprised. Still more startling and heartening, a footnote to the most widely used edition(1) admits: "This is perhaps the most novel section of the Constitution [on Revelation]. Not since the early centuries of the Church has an official document urged the availability of the Scriptures for all."

This affirmation has transformed the climate of Scripture circulation in many parts of the globe, especially in predomi- nantly Roman Catholic lands. It has enabled priests and laymen to participate in advisory councils and boards, to cooperate in publicity and sales campaigns, even to serve on Bible Society staffs. Furthermore, the Roman Catholic Church has indicated its willingness to work with Protestants not only on linguistics and the mechanics of translation, but on the Scriptural product as well. The paragraph cited above closes with these two sentences:

Since the word of God should be available at all times, the Church with maternal concern sees to it that suitable

and correct translations are made into different languages,
especially from the original texts of the sacred books.
And if, given the opportunity and the approval of Church
authority, these translations are produced in cooperation
with the separated brethren as well, all Christians will
be able to use them.

*   *   *   *   *

As cooperation expanded between the ABS and denominational
bodies (see Chapter X), as well as with national Bible Societies
and ecumenical agencies, the remaining Auxiliaries--which had
provided the original support--continued to decline. In recognition of a vastly altered administrative pattern, the Committee
on Auxiliaries and Home Agencies changed its name in 1938 to the
Committee on National Distribution. By 1946, when the American
Bible Society passed its 130th birthday, central headquarters
listed ten state Auxiliaries or cooperating groups (without
mentioning New York and Virginia, two of the oldest) and ninety-
three county or local societies. But twenty-one of these were
marked as "inactive," two as "passed or passing out of existence,"
and 21 others not so designated showed neither donations nor books
distributed during that calendar year.

Those Auxiliaries which remained active served two basic
functions: to raise money for the national Society and to
distribute Scriptures. Financial support from all of them
combined totalled $10,248.64 in 1946; circulation was more diffi-
cult to estimate because some societies handled commercial stock
as well as ABS books. By 1960, when the ABS shifted to regional
organization, the active list was pruned still further, on the
basis of three criteria: "Where investigations revealed the
non-existence of a former organization or of its bank or book
account, the auxiliary relationship was regarded by ABS as
dissolved."

On the other hand, the national Society continued to encourage
those local groups still carrying on effective support:

Those that remain have continued to serve their chartered
purpose with zeal and with great effectiveness.....They
have an important ministry of giving the Scriptures to
Bibleless people in their respective fields "without cost
and without price."....[They] have continued to support the
worldwide work of the American Bible Society, thus aiding
and serving the Bible cause at home and abroad far more
effectively than would otherwise be possible without their
help. (Annual Reports, 1952 and 1953)

In some instances (as with the historic Pennsylvania Bible
Society in 1959) the ties with national headquarters have been

spelled out in more formal agreements than existed previously. While the ABS assumed specific staff and budgetary commitments, the local or regional society sought "to secure increased contributions on the part of Churches and individuals for the work of the American Bible Society in this District and throughout the United States and for the work of the Society in all lands." With books and money supplied from the New York office, the "Auxiliary" would undertake "to conduct the missionary circulation of the Scriptures by colportage and such other methods as may be devised."

By 1966 the number of such affiliates had dropped to thirty-three. Most of the nine state organizations, which included all of New England, retained administrative independence. A few, like Pennsylvania and California along with Chicago and Washington City, had their own boards but depended on the ABS for executive personnel. Still others, the remnant of the original Auxiliary system, served primarily as a source of funds for the "Parent Society."

For Christians in each country, as for the delegates at "Elfinsward" in 1946, the challenge remains the same:

> Being led to a fuller vision of the world need, and realizing that the privilege of the Open Book brings with it the responsibility of sharing it with others, they pledge themselves to stimulate the work of the Bible Societies in their respective countries and undertake to explore all possible means of increasing the interest of the Christian Churches in their own constituencies, inviting them to join in prayer and service.

NOTES

1. Walter M. Abbott, ed., *The Documents of Vatican II*. (New York: American Press, 1966) pp. 125-126.

16

150 Years of the Bible

"He shall reign forever and ever, King of Kings and Lord of Lords, Hallelujah!" With the stirring notes of Handel's *Messiah*, performed on November 15, 1966, by the New York Philharmonic Orchestra and the chorus of Westminster Choir College, the official observance of "The Year of the Bible" came to an end. It was appropriate to celebrate 150 years of American Bible Society activity around the world, an anniversary proclaimed by President Lyndon B. Johnson and all fifty state governors.

The "special events" began on January 19 with a Bible presentation to President Johnson, symbolic of the 750th millionth copy circulated by the American Bible Society. In March a Pittsburgh, Pennsylvania, audience first viewed a color film, "Faith for Every Frontier," which traced the story of Bible distribution from Samuel J. Mills (see Chapter I) to the present day. An exhibit entitled "Dynamic Encounter" employed not only "op art" and modern printing styles, but also indigenous illustration: for example, the herdsman as an African, a Latin American gaucho, or a Western cowboy, in the Selection on "The Lost Sheep." On Palm Sunday the Society dedicated its new Bible House at 1865 Broadway in New York City, adjacent to the Lincoln Center for the Performing Arts. On May 11 an anniversary service was held in City Hall, commemorating that historic assemblage of May 8-11, 1816.

Then on May 12, 1966, three thousand guests, including seventy visitors from twenty-eight foreign countries, gathered in Philharmonic Hall at Lincoln Center to mark the sesquicentennial. The Rev. Porter Routh, Executive Secretary of the

Southern Baptist Convention, delivered the invocation--and those
who knew their Bible Society history (Chapter VI) rejoiced that
ancient wounds had long-since been healed. Ralph Bunche, Under-
Secretary of the United Nations, read the Scripture lesson from
Isaiah 55. Billy Graham, noted evangelist who was also a Vice-
President of the United Bible Societies, spoke on the relevance
of the Bible to the problems of the world. Dr. F. Donald Coggan,
Archbishop of Canterbury and President of the United Bible
Societies, pronounced the benediction. ABS President Everett
Smith and Vice-President Charles Parlin, one of the Presidents
of the World Council of Churches, shared in conducting the meeting. It was a stirring occasion, culminating in a procession
two blocks down Broadway to the new Bible House, dedicated less
than six weeks earlier.

But the sesquicentennial "Year of the Bible" looked to the
future, not to the past. The stated objectives were those of a
pilgrim people, simply pausing at one stage of a long, continuous
march:

to dramatize the influence of the Bible on national, state,
and civic levels;

to emphasize the importance of the Bible in America's past,
present, and future;

to create special events capable of attracting nationwide
attention to the Bible and the work of the ABS;

to stress the influence of the Bible on literature, art,
music, politics, social action, and secular education;

to attract the support of secular, as well as religious,
organizations for the Bible cause;

to encourage reading of the Bible by producing Scriptures
in attractive new formats and up-to-date language;

to obtain all possible publicity in order to make the
American people more aware of the Bible and its relevance
in day-to-day living;

to make 1966--THE YEAR OF THE BIBLE.

The "new formats and up-to-date language" included the publication of "Good News for Modern Man," the New Testament in
Today's English Version (see Chapter XIV), as well as the
translation by J. B. Phillips, printed with thirty-eight
contemporary photographs as "The Inside Story." Other editions
appearing in 1966 were a New Testament in popular Spanish and a

Greek New Testament designed for translators. The Society also
celebrated "The Year of the Bible" with a record circulation of
38,981,620 copies of Scriptures in the United States and
48,417,341 in 149 countries abroad. As one evidence of the
year's impact, the first two months of 1967 brought 20,000
orders, contrasted with 6,000 during January and February of
1966, an increase of 233 per cent.

The 150th anniversary of the American Bible Society marked
also the twentieth birthday of the United Bible Societies (see
Chapter XV). In the development of national Bible societies
and of full collaboration--for translation, publication, and
distribution--throughout most of the globe, the previous two
decades had witnessed miraculous changes. In one sense "The
Year of the Bible" simply dramatized a "new look" in methods
and processed of Scripture circulation which had been under way
for some time. The 1966 Annual Report of the ABS affirmed:

> 'God's Word for a New Age' [a publicity campaign launched
> in 1964] is being increasingly recognized as the current
> label under which the traditional work of the Bible
> Societies is being conducted, intensified, and orientated.
> Not only has it helped to provide a new image of the
> Bible Societies as dynamic, forward-looking agencies of
> the Church of Jesus Christ in a rapidly changing world,
> but it has forced the Societies to take greater pains to
> adjust to current trends of thought, without, however,
> giving up the traditional approach. In particular, it
> has led the Bible Societies toward a new expression of
> their relationship with the churches.

As earlier chapters have shown, the Society from its origin
had been consciously--even self-consciously--a non-sectarian
institution. The earliest Agents and Auxiliaries sought
support in and through every denomination and congregation which
would give them a hearing. More than that, the Society had been
an organization of individual Christians committed to the Bible
cause. Its Founding Fathers belonged to eight different denominations, but only the Quakers came as official representatives.
Its first officers came from eight churches; its twenty presidents have been members of at least nine denominations--"at
least" because not all the records even mention religious
affiliation.

Over the past century and a half practically all of the
Boards of Managers have consisted of laymen, but probably a
majority of senior staff officers have been clergymen. Whereas
William Jay originally proposed excluding all ministers from
office in the Society, Elias Boudinot warned that such discrimination would needlessly arouse "a formidable Phalanx against

us," especially if--as he surmised--few of the clergy were
likely to attend meetings anyway. Whereas the provision "without note or comment" was adopted directly from the British and
Foreign Bible Society (and prior local societies in the United
States), the non-sectarian emphasis reflected the freedom and
pluralism of America--in contrast to the BFBS, one half of
whose Managers had to be Anglicans. As far back as 1778
Boudinot had expressed to his daughter not only his view of
denominationalism, but his faith in the Bible to transcend such
differences:

> As you advance in life, you will find the Christian World,
> unhappily split into a Multitude of Denominations,
> Professions and Names. Each will tell you, that his,
> is the only right Way, as those mentioned in Scripture,
> who tell you, lo! here is Christ, or there is Christ,
> but believe them not. *The true Catholicism of the*
> *Scriptures* will teach you to take them all into the Arms
> of your Love & Charity, and look upon all as the Servants
> of the same Master, as far as they follow his Example,
> remembering that he that is not against us, is for us.(1)

Achieving this "true Catholicism of the Scriptures" often
required deliberate effort, as well as "Love & Charity." The
very first Annual Report pledged that "in conducting the
business of the Board, the most scrupulous attention is paid
to the diversity of denomination which exists among Christians."
In the first full year of operation, two successive committees,
created to deal with this thorny issue, recommended that annual
replacements on the Board of Managers "be of the same religious
denomination respectively with those persons whose places they
are appointed to supply." The Board, however, considered that
clause too restrictive and substituted the following policy:
"...to make such a selection from the several denominations
that may belong to the Society as will ensure to each of them
a just and equitable representation in this Board."

In his first Annual Address Elias Boudinot, still too ill to
journey to New York to deliver it in person, urged his
colleagues to disregard sectarian controversies:

> Let it become a common proverb, 'See how these members
> of the American Bible Society love one another, though
> consisting of every denomination of Christians among
> us.' Let a motto be written in letters of gold on the
> most prominent part of your hall of deliberation--*'By*
> *this shall all men know ye are my Disciples if ye love*
> *one another.'*

So seriously and literally did the Board of Managers take that
admonition that two months later it instructed the Standing

Committee to prepare a marble slab with gilded letters for
erection in their meeting room, as a reminder of those appropriate words from Scripture. Whether this was done, or what
became of the inscribed stone, history fails to recall. William
Jay, at the same first Annual Meeting in 1817, responded to
certain criticisms from the Baltimore Bible Society with an
exhortation: "The Society must engage in no controversy--She
must know no enemy--her sphere is one of love & harmony.....It
ought not to appear from her Reports, that a single individual
on earth viewed her with jealousy and dissatisfaction."

Throughout its history the Society has manifested acute concern, admonished during its very first year, for *"preserving
with all care the religious* and political balance necessary to
prevent every suspicion of Sectarian influence." In 1838,
fearful lest even the employed staff might appear partisan, the
Board authorized the appointment of Honorary Secretaries "to
embrace the several different denominations represented in the
Board."

Still more cautiously, this company of goodly and Godly men
abstained from prayer at Board meetings until 1858, lest any
devotional statement other than reading from the Scriptures "in
common use" might raise sectarian specters. In fact, the
original By-Laws cautioned the Society to "avoid all interference
with the various opinions of its Members respecting the forms of
religious worship." On the other hand, certain Auxiliaries found
the omission of prayer a shameful embarrassment and repeatedly
pleaded with the "Parent Society" for this much acknowledgement
of divine sanction. One vitriolic critic of the ABS Standard
Bible of 1854, the Rev. Arthur Cleveland, took the occasion to
condemn the heathenish character of this Society which
"celebrated its great anniversary festivals, in the presence of
hundreds of professed ministers of CHRIST, without a prayer for
his blessing, or an ascription to the glory of the Holy Trinity."

The point of emphasis here is that the American Bible Society
and its Auxiliaries were inaugurated and supported at the outset
by individuals, Christians, churchmen, acting *outside* of their
denominational structures. True, the proclamation of the new
Society was read from a number of New York pulpits on Sunday,
May 12, 1816. By October of that first year appeals for support,
together with copies of the Constitution and the Address to the
Public, were mailed to every ordained minister in the United
States. Local congregations were offered Bible shipments
equivalent in value to one half of any donations made to the
Society. To be sure, Traveling Agents did most of their speaking
and preaching in churches of various denominations and occasion-
ally received congregational offerings.

Actually the proceeds from this type of solicitation amounted
to very little. After fifteen years, during which Auxiliaries
were extremely active, congregational contributions in 1831 came
to only $268. These gifts increased as Auxiliaries declined,
and by 1856 local churches donated $17,970, although this dropped
back to $13,416 four years later. But these were local efforts,
not national or denominational as such. Most collections for
the Bible Society went through local Auxiliaries. Even the
Society's grants of books or funds for Sunday Schools and
missions were ordinarily sent to individuals rather than to
institutional headquarters.

Not until the end of the nineteenth century, when Auxiliaries
and Agents both failed to meet the needs of a changing order,
did the ABS turn for support directly to denominations. On one
hand, earlier patterns of Scripture distribution and fund-
raising had proved inadequate. If Auxiliaries raised money at
all, they used it for local projects and remitted little to New
York. On the other hand, denominations were developing central
treasuries and boards of their own and demanding systematic
support for them.

The Bible Society, therefore, had to represent itself as what
it had always been: an independent agency doing one of the
essential missionary tasks of the Church--circulating the
Scriptures. Denominations and local congregations had to learn,
in their turn, that the Society could not carry on this vital
function without ecclesiastical backing. Churches and individual
Christians might respond generously to emergency appeals in war
and other disasters, but the daily, monthly, yearly needs for
Bible distribution, the endless job of translation and revision
of Scriptures in foreign languages, required regular, dependable
financing.

When seven Field Secretaries replaced the Society's District
Superintendents in 1898, they undertook as their principal
assignment the cultivation of church groups, local and national.
In pulpits and budget committees, in denominational assemblies
and executive offices, representatives of the ABS interpreted
"a wider circulation of the Holy Scriptures without note or
comment" as a joint responsibility--or, to put it another way,
as a missionary obligation of all Christians, in which the
Society was set up to act as the instrument or agency for the
churches.

The inauguration of an Advisory Council in 1919 provided
opportunity for understanding and consultation on the part of
ecclesiastical leaders. From seven churches in 1919 this
liaison group expanded to include twenty-nine by the end of its
first decade, seventy by 1965 on the eve of the sesquicentennial.

If certain denominations too often appointed already over-
burdened and sometimes indifferent bishops or executive secretaries, the educational function was nonetheless worthwhile, and
more recently lay and clerical delegates to the Advisory Council
have manifested conscientious, informed commitment to the Bible
cause. From the first commendation by the Presbyterian General
Assembly in 1816, denominational bodies have been encouraged--
sometimes by the Society, sometimes by their own members--to
adopt resolutions of support for the ABS. Within the first
seventy-five years twenty churches had voted formal endorsement
to the Society, and nine of these recommended annual collections
in its behalf.

Such church relations were not always smooth, yet even the
harshest criticisms came generally from local rather than
national units, from individuals rather than denominations. When
Bishop John Henry Hobart in 1816 opposed *any* inter-church
cooperation (see Chapter II), other Episcopalians not only
accepted office in the new Society, but publicly refuted his
position. Even in the deplorable *Baptizo* controversy, the most
serious denominational dispute in ABS history, a few Baptists
remained as active supporters of the organization, whatever their
position on the crucial issue may have been. In the 1860's some
Congregationalists in New England, a Presbyterian Synod and a
Methodist Conference in New York, questioned the financial
procedures of the Society and even implied "mismanagement of
funds," focussing complaints on the seemingly disproportionate
and unproductive costs of the Agency system. In that instance
attacks were abated by sensitivity and flexibility on the part
of ABS officers, a willingness to correct an immediate regional
situation and at the same time to make long-range modifications
in administrative procedures.

On the other hand, accusations of the Society's inordinate
wealth were quickly shown to be founded on distortions of fact
or on misunderstandings about the use and limitations of endow-
ment funds. Occasionally an individual charged that staff
appointments showed denominational bias. Where such a preponderance did occur, it was usually temporary and local, accounted
for in perfectly natural ways: a large constituency of a certain
denomination, unintended imbalance when jobs were filled on the
basis of qualifications without regard to church affiliation, the
unwillingness of some churches to release their capable men for
non-denominational work, even acute shortage of applicants for
the strenuous tasks of frontier Agent or traveling colporteur.

Intermittent friction also arose, or threatened to arise,
with denominational publishers and bookstores. As churches
increasingly prepared and sold their own literature--and a wide
assortment of other religious publications and accessories--some

competition proved inevitable. Bookstores blamed the ABS for
"cut-rate" discounts on Scriptures, most of which could be
traced to local Auxiliaries over which the "Parent Society" had
no control. Far from subsidizing such competitive sales, as
complainants charged, the ABS hoped and expected to receive contributions from the Auxiliaries. Those state, county, regional,
and local Bible Societies which continued to operate independently of the ABS have in most instances contributed generously
to the national organization, but their local pricing policies
are their own.

Church bookstores also objected to direct promotion of sales
among local churches, especially of "luxury trade" editions. The
Protestant Church-Owned Publishers' Association, formed in the
early 1940's, appointed a liaison committee in 1959 to keep in
touch with ABS policies, practices, prices, and publicity. In
response to specific complaints, the Society granted to all
bookstores as well as ministers a ten per cent discount. Pointing out that leather-bound editions accounted for less than three
per cent of ABS sales of English Bibles, and that many cheaper
books were attractively bound to look more costly, the Society
nevertheless agreed to omit "so-called expensive editions" from
its catalogues, as well as games, books about the Bible, and
other accessories which might compete with denominational stores.
It also offered to restrict general cultivation to direct mailings
from New York, and to avoid "cutting in" on denominational programs
like Promotion Day. In short, the Bible Society found itself,
for comity and consistency, reaffirming its original missionary
purpose, concentrating on needy groups and institutions, rather
than on the general public which could afford to buy from
commercial outlets.

Thus in many ways the Society endeavored to strengthen
cooperation and goodwill with the churches. Thirteen denominational representatives composed a Co-operating Committee to plan
the Centennial celebration in 1916. That same year the Board
adopted a new administrative structure in which the Co-Secretaries,
who had previously shared similar responsibilities, divided their
functions between Finance (including Ways and Means) and
Translation-Distribution. In the former post Secretary Frank H.
Mann launched a promotional campaign which included a system of
regular letters of appeal to individuals, advertising in church
journals, and staff attendance at denominational conferences,
assemblies, conventions, and synods.

Also, in the midst of the First World War, Universal Bible
Sunday became a national institution. Proposed in 1900,
observed in 1903 and 1904 in honor of the British and Foreign
Bible Society Centenary, it was revived in 1915 to inaugurate
the Centennial of the ABS. For a nation under the spiritual as

well as physical burden of war, President Woodrow Wilson proclaimed Universal Bible Week, culminating on December 9, 1917,
and the observance of Bible Sunday has been continued ever since.
From 1919 to 1923 the date set aside was the last Sunday in
November; then it was changed to the third Sunday before
Christmas. Designation of an entire week has enabled churches
to observe the Sunday at either end, whether they followed
primarily the calendar year (second Sunday in December) or the
Christian year (second Sunday in Advent), when the two do not
always coincide.

After fifteen years it was estimated that 10,000 congregations
from fifty denominations celebrated Universal Bible Sunday,
nearly half of them requesting Bible Society materials for the
occasion. Although a large proportion of churches took--and
still take--special offerings for the ABS on that date, staff
officers emphatically deny that this is a fund-raising "gimmick."
Secretary George W. Brown voiced the purpose beautifully in 1930
when he called the observance "not an offering, but a hearing,
not a collection, but a presentation."

Directly or indirectly, Bible Society services to the
churches will continue as long as the Scriptures are central to
the Christian faith. As long as denominations recognize their
essential missionary purpose to be the proclamation of "God's
Word for a New Age" they will encourage and support the Bible
Society. It is to be hoped that history will never say of the
churches--as it did of Agents and Auxiliaries--that their
usefulness in Scripture distribution is at an end, that they
are failing in that vital task. Yet the extent of dependence
seems to be declining.

In a General Report of 1965 John H. McCombe, Jr., Executive
Secretary in the Church Relations Department, declared
optimistically that "the ABS reasonably and prayerfully anti-
cipates that in the foreseeable future 50 per cent of its income
will come from the churches." Statistics seem to contradict
that hope. To be sure, the actual amounts contributed by
churches have risen substantially. Between 1901 and 1930
direct receipts totalled $4,006,343.74, from 1931 to 1965
$18,047,355.11, not counting emergency appeals. Yet denomina-
tional potential appeared almost limitless. In 1946 (to take
but one example) among forty-three denominations, thirteen gave
less than one cent per member to the Bible Society, only seven
contributed over five cents per member.

On the other hand, percentages showed a downward trend
throughout the 1960's, even before the 1970 financial crisis in
the churches. Although nineteenth-century figures do not indicate how much of Auxiliary contributions came from local churches,

during only one period (1840-59) did the *direct* church
proportion of ABS income surpass ten per cent. Other, more
effective channels were then in use. Since 1900, however, the
average percentage by decades reflected first the emphasis on
church giving--and then its recent decline:

1900-09	15.73%	1960	23.5%
1910-19	25.09%	1961	23 %
1920-29	40.62%	1962	23 %
1930-39	21.26%	1963	22 %
1940-49	29.94%	1964	22 %
1950-59	27.78%	1965	20.5%
		1966	20 %

If one asks what other source seemed to be "taking up the
slack," in addition to sales, bequests, and investments, the
answer appears to be individual gifts. Statistical conclusions
are often dangerous, but another table may provoke further
speculation about financial trends:

	Direct Income from Churches	Income from Individuals
1861-70	$ 165,000	$ 319,000
1871-80	130,700	211,000
1881-90	124,000	205,000
1891-00	239,200	191,000
1901-10	509,000	335,000
1911-20	1,108,000	399,000
1921-30	2,341,000	1,389,000
1931-40	1,125,000	1,101,000
1941-50	3,784,000	4,178,000
1951-60	8,447,000	11,883,000
1961-66	7,369,000	12,109,000

For fifty years, 1890-1940, concentration on the churches as
principal sources of income (after the Auxiliaries declined)
produced a positive effect. Since then individual donations
have leaped far ahead. The decade of 1950-60 showed a steady
increase, not only in the total amount of individual gifts, but
in the number as well: from 191,066 to 766,699. In a definitive report on fund-raising, prepared in 1961, General Secretary
Robert Taylor made two complementary affirmations:

1. Church relations must receive first consideration. The
Society must maintain and strengthen the links with the
churches.

2. The churches have never provided sufficient support for
the work of the Society and there is no present indication

that they will. Cultivation of individual gifts must be
continued and expanded.

These twin "facts of life" were reflected in promotional
programs and materials many years earlier. Somewhere in the fog
of the Great Depression (1929-34) or under the shadow of impending
World War II, the Bible Society caught a fresh glimpse of an
eternal truth: that "an unread Bible is useless." In 1935 the
400th anniversary of the first printed English Bible provided an
occasion for focussing public attention on the Scriptures. One
of the earliest national radio broadcasts featured an address by
Secretary of State Cordell Hull and talks by distinguished laymen
from three different cities. In addition to countless local
celebrations and pageants, the Society distributed millions of
leaflets to encourage Scripture reading.

Although an organized Nationwide Bible Reading campaign was
first considered in 1940, its success gained impetus from the
loneliness and anxieties of war. A young marine on Guadalcanal
asked his family to join with him in reading the same daily
verses of the Bible. Captivated by the possibilities, the ABS
polled thousands of Protestant chaplains and other clergymen to
select thirty-three passages for the days between Thanksgiving
and Christmas, 1944. Endorsed by Joint Resolution of Congress,
by President Franklin D. Roosevelt's Thanksgiving Proclamation,
and by denominational assemblies, publicized by the secular as
well as religious press and by national advertising, the
campaign drew instant and enthusiastic response. Fourteen
million bookmarks listing the selections were distributed that
year, twenty million in 1945 when it became Worldwide Bible
Reading in nineteen countries. By 1946 the Society established
a separate Promotion of Use Department, to encourage systematically what had always been assumed as a vital dimension of
the Bible cause, along with translation, publication, distribution, and financing.

Like the Nationwide Bible Reading campaign, the use of
promotional seals had the dual purpose of wide national publicity
and supplementary fund-raising, appealing to individuals rather
than to church groups. ABS Secretary Frank Mann had worked with
the Red Cross when Jacob Riis, well-known writer and social
worker, brought back from Europe the idea of promotional seals,
which became the hallmark of the anti-tuberculosis drive then
conducted by the Red Cross. It was Secretary Rome A. Betts,
however, who--during the Lenten season of 1939--mailed out
"general purpose" seals with the slogan: "Read the Bible." The
initial experiment included an offer that any church group
disposing of fifty sheets of seals at $1 each might designate
a Life Membership in the Society. Proceeds the first year,
devoted largely to the War Emergency Fund, reached a modest
$19,757 for an expenditure of only $4,190.

The 1940 seals were designed by Rockwell Kent, noted illustrator, and by 1941 Bible seals had become a "major operation," since at that time only the Tuberculosis Association was employing this type of cultivation. In 1952 the popular movie and television stars, Roy Rogers and Dale Evans, sponsored the sale of "general purpose" seals just before Christmas, and the success of the venture (104,362 sheets) led to specially designed Christmas seals the following year. Distribution figures for both the general and seasonal designs revealed a rapid growth in popularity and acceptance: in 1953, 309,525 sheets; 1956, 986,849 sheets; 1961, 6,654,000 sheets; and 1966 7,601,470. A trial of Easter seals in 1959 was not repeated because it proved "insufficiently productive," but the Bible cause has been widely advertised across the nation by these colorful and profitable reminders at Christmas time. In 1958 Secretary Robert Taylor declared: "The Seal Campaign is thus far the only successful method of enlisting new contributors."

Some other promotional projects fared less successfully. Vest-pocket calendar cards were issued for about a dozen years after World War I; wall calendars foundered on competition and on disagreement over the most desirable format; Christmas cards in 1941-42 and Easter cards in 1952 failed to "catch on"--but have been reintroduced more recently. Since 1962, however, the Bible-a-Month program has captured the attention and support of many "middle-level" donors. To the tune of $25 annually and the words of "You don't *get*--you *give*--a Bible a month!" hundreds of thousands of books have been sent to dozens of countries. Here again the shifting ratio of church and individual support showed clearly in statistics: In 1962 churches contributed $47,025 to the Bible-a-Month plan, individuals $82,501; in 1965 the respective figures were $38,212 from churches and $194,688 from individuals.

Since the original announcement of the formation of the American Bible Society in 1816, direct mailings have constituted a major--sometimes *the* major--channel of information as well as solicitation. In July, 1818, the Managers authorized the circulation of "Extracts from the Correspondence of the ABS." First quarterly, then monthly or bimonthly, often irregular, this publication fluctuated from a 5"x8" pamphlet to newspaper size. It became *The Bible Society Record* in 1843 but did not initiate serial numbers as a regular periodical until 1856. When the new name of the magazine was adopted, the Annual Report for 1844 promised:

> To the love of novelty and the spirit of sect it can
> minister nothing. Yet those who delight in the word of
> the Lord, and desire above all things to see this word
> prevail, will find much now to interest, and more as the
> operations of the Society extend.

"Subscription" figures are difficult to evaluate because they have varied in scope and purpose over the years, up to the present policy of mailing the *Record* to every contributor of two dollars or more per year. Before 1875 printing ran to some 35,000 copies annually; by 1930 this had grown to 370,000. Admittedly a "house organ" to keep its constituency informed, the magazine experienced a "circulation explosion" at the beginning of its second century. Between 1940 and 1947, pre-dominantly war years, *The Bible Society Record* achieved the greatest expansion of any Christian journal in the United States, a five hundred per cent jump from a *monthly* average of 40,000 copies to 210,000. By 1964 circulation, for ten issues per year, totalled 9,164,000 copies, with some monthly printings running as high as 973,000. Since the sesquicentennial this figure has passed the million mark.

Other direct mailings carry appeals to prospective donors. The Society has utilized lists from many sources, while promising that it, in turn, will not release its list of donors for other organizations to use--unless there has been no contribution and no communication for three to five years. When the Managers in 1921 authorized the purchase of mailing lists for direct appeals, the first recipients included Negro Business Men, Sunday School Superintendents, and the Social Registers of selected cities. Since then prospective donors approached have ranged from purchasers of Chinese art (presumably interested in China) and Republican Party Fund contributors in New York, to the National Wildlife Federation and Lions Club presidents.

In more traditional methods of cultivation the Bible Society has reached out to specialized groups directly, rather than working only through denominational channels. As early as 1930 staff officers paid systematic visits to seminaries and devised mailings to seniors at seventy-three theological schools, introducing them to *The Bible Society Record* and other informa-tion and resources. By 1963 the National Campus Ministry warranted a separate desk and full time Secretary in the Department of National Distribution.

Just a year earlier the ABS hired its first Secretary for Women's Work. A hundred and fifty years ago various Female Auxiliaries gave devoted support to the General Supplies and to missionary appeals, as well as to regular distribution and finance. In the "middle years" of the Society "liberal and pious females" often contributed to make their pastors Life Members, as a gesture of respect, as a means of pecuniary aid for the Bible cause, and as a way of educating ministers and congregations about the work.

But women have not played a major role in ABS administration--except at the giving end. No woman has ever been elected

President; of the long list of more than three hundred Vice-Presidents, no woman was included until two were chosen in 1919; only three others have been elected since that time. Among 118 Headquarters Officers listed by the Society during its century and a half, only eight were women, every one of them serving in "modern times" into the 1960's (though one began as early as 1919). Their particular roles were as follows: two in Women's Work, two in Library and Research, one each in Legacies and Estates, Ways and Means, Work for the Blind, and the Latin American Office. But the modern equivalent of Female Auxiliaries is an active "Circle of the Concerned," and the modern involvement for "liberal and pious females" is through a nation-wide Women's Speakers' Bureau.

Another major portion of Bible Society income, dependent entirely on individuals, came through gifts and legacies and bequests. Elias Boudinot, the first President, set two noteworthy examples. When the Society was established in 1816, he transferred to it 100 shares of Bank of America stock worth $10,000 and yielding dividends of $350 per year. Others followed suit with direct donations of several hundred dollars each as well as Life Memberships. Richard Varick, the Treasurer, made his contribution of $750 in the form of Life Memberships for five relatives, presumably grandchildren, all five namesakes of his.

In addition to his initial gift of stock, however, Elias Boudinot willed to the Society 4,589 acres of land, "Particularly for sending the Gospel without note or comment among the Heathen that they may be brought to the knowledge of Jesus Christ and the scheme of salvation thro' his all atoning blood." Each Annual Report during the first decade of ABS operations printed on its first page, as a not-so-subtle reminder, a "Form of Bequest to the Society." With somewhat misdirected zeal the Managers resolved in 1821 "that every acting executor, who shall pay over a legacy of three hundred dollars, or upwards, shall be thereby constituted a Member for Life of the American Bible Society." Before 1962 legacies never reached an annual total of $400,000; five years later receipts in this single category amounted to $1,503,978.61.

As the Annual Report for 1851 admitted, this was "a very fluctuating source of revenue." In 1849, for example, bequests had brought $30,000 to the Society, the following year only $13,000. Even earlier, however, in 1843, a layman in Massachusetts offered to donate $500 to the ABS on condition that he would receive interest on the sum as long as he lived. The Committee on Publication and Finance accepted the proposal, offered six per cent interest per annum, and thus inaugurated what has been called "both the world's first and largest gift investment program." Not until 1919 did Secretary Frank H. Mann develop a full-fledged Annuity Agreement Program, which the Society has advertised widely ever since. It is worth noting that the individual value of these annuities has been small, averaging less than $1,000. But while the average *amount* in 1966 ($1,385) was only $86 more than the average amount in 1921, the *number* of such annuity agreements had grown from 207 to 1,499, thus netting a total in 1966 of $2,076,772.

Because of their essential inter-relationship, the twin tasks of fund-raising and publicity have long gone hand-in-hand, within the organization as well as in reaching the public. Both of these functions were assigned, appropriately, to the Ways and Means Committee in the administrative restructuring of 1916. Both proliferated so enormously in the next five decades that they had to be divided, sub-divided, and further sub-divided. Although Francis Carr Stifler began in 1936 a long, creative tenure as Editorial Secretary (later Secretary for Public Relations), it was not until 1945 that the Board created a separate Committee on Education and Publicity (renamed the Committee on Education and Information in 1959).

That was the period—so difficult to remember or even imagine today—when radio was only beginning to "come of age" as an influential, nationwide medium, and television was still totally unknown. The first commercial radio broadcasts were put on the air in 1920. Two years later the Pacific Agency of the American Bible Society experimented with some local programs —although the Board of Managers in New York did not give its official approval until October, 1923. As already indicated, the 400th anniversary of the first printed English Bible provided the occasion for one of the very earliest national hook-ups, in 1935. On December 7, 1941 ("Pearl Harbor Day") Secretary Stifler inaugurated a program entitled "The Living Bible." Gradually this developed into a Bible Quiz program, sometimes featuring contestants from various New York churches and Sunday schools. It won a wide listening audience and conveyed a vast amount of unfamiliar information about the Bible and the work of the American Bible Society. With the advent of omnipresent television, this became the "Know Your Bible" TV quiz in July of 1952.

Hard as it is to realize, in this day of rapid technological change, it was only in the late 1940's that filmstrips fully and permanently replaced stereopticon slides as the common visual aid in schools and churches. Moving promptly on this effective, if elementary, level, the Bible Society produced between 1946 and 1966 some thirty-four different filmstrips dealing with its own world-wide work or with the content of the Bible. The great expense of production and projection delayed extensive use of

religious moving pictures, though some mission films were prepared as early as 1925. The American Bible Society produced one
outstanding movie in 1943, "The Book for the World of Tomorrow,"
but by 1955 it had issued or sponsored seven sound films. Most
impressive of these was the 1954 documentary, "Our Bible--How it
Came to Us." Although it cost the Society nearly $260,000,
that expenditure was repaid from rentals within just over ten
years. With these and many other products the Department of
Visual Materials, established in 1945, carried the message of
the Bible Society to thousands who had never heard--or seen--it
before.

The hand of history has swung full circle. The Society which
relied at its inception on the commitment and generosity of
individual Christians, which developed elaborate networks of
Auxiliaries and Agencies and Regions and denominational appropriations, turns once again--or still--to the people who cherish
their own Bibles so deeply that they want to share the Good News
with all mankind. For every church member who hears about the
American Bible Society once a year on Universal Bible Sunday--
and makes a meager contribution--there are scores who purchase
Christmas seals by mail, who join the Bible-a-Month Club, who
leave to the Society a modest annuity or a magnanimous bequest.

This is only right, for the Bible is an intensely personal
Book. It was never intended to displace the fellowship of the
Church, to substitute for social action, to be an alternative to
responsible living in a secular world. On the contrary, the
Holy Scriptures--rightly understood--should enhance and vitalize
the individual's participation in Christian community. But the
Bible itself--as an object of meditation and inspiration and
insight--is a very private treasure, a direct channel of power
and grace. For many, Protestants especially, cut off from the
ministry of church or pastor or missionary teacher, it has been
the only intermediary to God: for the pioneer woman on the
American frontier, for the lonely schoolboy in an Indian village,
for the sailor at sea or the prisoner in jail, for the colporteur
rebuffed in a Muslim town, for a widow old and blind, for a
Chinese pastor tormented by the Red Guard.

And the American Bible Society is not just a great corporation,
spewing forth its products by the modern millions. The
technological marvels of computerized orders and assembly-line
shipments at the Wayne, New Jersey, depository find meaning only
when a precious Book reaches eager hearts. The American Bible
Society is not an imposing office building, or a Board of
Managers, or a fiscal report, or a network of cablegrams, or a
sesquicentennial history--any more than the Bible is a piece of
embossed leather or a scrap of paper in the Ganges mud. Rather,
it is an earthen vessel which may, in faithful hands, carry
"God's Word for a New Age."

It is a Negro woman in New York in 1822: "This is the first book ever given to me. I love the Bible, and may the Lord reward you with a thousand books."

It is a cavalryman in the Spanish-American War, scribbling on the flyleaf of his torn Testament: "Trenches before San Juan, after night attack. This book has been a great comfort to me."

It is a prisoner in Brazil in 1944: "I am fulfilling my sentence in this prison, and, reading a Bible belonging to a friend who is a fellow prisoner, I have come to know the true way.....If it is possible for you to send me this messenger of Peace I shall be very grateful. I desire very much to follow its teachings."

It is a "pagan" King of Siam, seeking amid ancient values and modern ideas: "When you shall have attained a refuge, a religious faith, that is beautiful and good and suitable, hold to it with great joy, and follow its teachings, and it will be a cause of prosperity to each one of you."

It is a young Scandinavian immigrant in 1876: "The testament you gave me has been the means, by reading it, to open my spiritual eyes. I saw my ruined condition, and resolved to seek the Lord with all my heart, and, thank God, I found peace and salvation in the Lord Jesus."

It is a blind girl forty years earlier, groping over pages of "line letters" before the invention of Braille: "When I think of the pleasure of being able to read the Word of God myself, a pleasure which I never expected would be mine, my heart is filled with joy for this unexpected blessing. A new day has opened for me, far brighter than I ever hoped to realize."

It is a dock worker in Venezuela after the First World War: "In this book is the truth of Christianity to be found? Well, give me one; I want to know the truth."

It is a Liberian chieftain, who had learned Arabic in order to read the Koran, but came across the Gospel according to St. John: "Hallelujah! I have found that for which I have so long sought, for which I hungered and thirsted, and now I am satisfied."

It is a prominent writer of Latin America: "It is wonderful to observe what occurs with regard to this great book. Until now the Bible only had a historic significance for many people, like a great many curious and rare books. But the work of the Bible Societies is revealing to the world what the Bible is worth and what truth it contains--'the salvation of the people'."

It is a president of the University of North Carolina in 1833: "Amidst the uncertainty of the future, with which the Lord in his gracious providence surrounds us, we are sure in general that the animating promises of his word will never be fully accomplished until the Bible shall be a common possession to all the nations of the earth."

It is two brothers through whom the Gospel transformed a village on Okinawa. In the late months of World War II an American army chaplain and an interpreter heard this amazing narrative, as they toured a town remarkably clean and prosperous and happy by comparative standards. Thirty years before, an American missionary on his way to Japan had stopped in the village for a few days, just long enough to convert two young brothers and leave them a Bible. Reading those pages changed their lives, and the pair resolved to build their community on the principles they found there. One became the village headmaster, applying the Gospel to administration and justice in a local Christian "democracy." The other became the school teacher, imparting the Scriptures daily to successive generations of pupils. As they concluded their story, the brothers bowed apologetically and said: "We're sorry if we seem a backward people. We have, honored sirs, tried our best to follow the Bible and live like Jesus. Perhaps if you will show us how....." (*Bible Society Record*, April, 1950, p. 58)

Days later a tough army sergeant, still incredulous, remarked to his Christian companion: "I can't figure it, fellow--this kind of people coming out of only a Bible and a couple [of] old guys who wanted to live like Jesus." Then, thoughtfully and insightfully: "Maybe we've been using the wrong kind of weapons to make the world over!"

Maybe we have. "Not by might, nor by power, but by my Spirit, says the Lord of hosts." (Zechariah 4:6) Maybe the history of the next 150 years, certainly for the American Bible Society, will be written by a few individuals--or a couple of million men and women and children--who want to live like Jesus, and who know that one essential way is to share, with the multitudes who have never heard, the Good News for modern man.

NOTES

1. G. A. Boyd, *Elias Boudinot: Patriot and Statesman* (Princeton: Princeton University Press, 1952), p. 45.

Index of Names

Index of Places

Index of Subjects

About the Author

Creighton Lacy was born and raised in China by missionary parents. His father, Carleton Lacy, was Agency Secretary for the American Bible Society in China from 1921 to 1941, and Bishop of the Foochow Area in the Methodist Church from 1941 to 1951.

After serving pastorates in Vermont and Connecticut, Creighton Lacy himself became a missionary of the Methodist Church in China from 1947 to 1951, serving at the University of Nanking and the Anglo-Chinese College and Fukien Union Theological Seminary in Foochow.

He received the A.B. degree in political science from Swarthmore College in 1941, the B.D. in missions from Yale Divinity School in 1944, and the Ph.D. in social ethics from Yale University in 1953. Since then he has done further study at Yale Institute of Far Eastern Studies, the College of Chinese Studies in Peking, China, and the University of Delhi in India. He has been on the faculty of Duke University Divinity School since 1953 as Professor of World Christianity, and has written several publications on Asian cultures. He is also the author of *Frank Mason North*, a biography of Eric North's father, a well-known mission executive.